D1599123

JOSEPH STURGE

and the Moral Radical Party
in Early Victorian Britain

JOSEPH STURGE

and the Moral Radical Party in Early Victorian Britain

ALEX TYRRELL

CHRISTOPHER HELM

London

© 1987 Alex Tyrrell
Christopher Helm (Publishers) Ltd, Imperial House,
21-25 North Street, Bromley, Kent BR1 1SD

British Library Cataloguing in Publication Data

Tyrrell, Alex
    Joseph Sturge and the "moral Radical party"
    in early Victorian Britain.
    1. Sturge, Joseph   2. Philanthropists —
    Great Britain — Biography   3. Politicians
    — Great Britain — Biography
    I. Title
    322.4'4'0924   HV28.S8
    ISBN 0-7470-3200-9

Printed and bound in Great Britain by Biddles Ltd, Guildford and Kings Lynn

Contents

Acknowledgements

All books are collective enterprises, and my warmest thanks are due to the many people who have made this one possible. I have been fortunate in my university: La Trobe has generously provided me with the time and facilities for research and writing; colleagues in the History Department have been supportive and helpful; Ms Shirley Horton, Mrs Merelyn Dowling and Mrs Kim Reynolds have transformed my crude versions into an elegant typescript; and the Library staff have provided me with an efficient and painstaking service.

Like nearly everyone else in Australia who writes on modern British History, I have been indebted over the years to Dr F.B. Smith of the Australian National University. He has patiently commented on each chapter of this book. I am also indebted to Dr Bill Murray who read the first draft and offered helpful comments. I have received advice and help with sources from Professor John Clive, Mr and Mrs James Cropper, Mr Richard Dupuis, Dr Tom Dunning, Miss Barbara Hubbard, Mr John Hunter, Mr Bruce Knox, Mr and Mrs Cecil Langford, Professor Norman McCord, Mr Frank Manders, Dr Stephen Newton, Mr Paul Pickering, Professor Keith Robbins and Dr Bertram Wyatt-Brown. Librarians and archivists too numerous to name have given me the benefit of their expertise; their labours on my behalf will be seen in the notes for every page. I owe thanks too, to Bevan Leviston for his technical advice.

I wish to thank the editors of the Historical Journal, the Bulletin of the John Rylands University Library of Manchester, the Journal of Religious History and the English Historical Review for giving me permission to use material that appeared in articles I have published in their journals.

This is the biography of a Quaker, and I have received invaluable help from many Friends: not only from the official Quaker libraries in London, Dublin and Woodbrooke College but from Mr Roger Clark; Mrs Olive Phipps of the Bull St Meeting House, Birmingham; Mrs Joyce Roper; Mrs Kathleen Wormleighton; and Friends of the Bewdley Meeting. I owe a special debt of gratitude to members of the Sturge family: Miss Monica Sturge, Mrs Sylvia Lewin, the late Mrs Maud Sturge, Mr P.A.J. Sturge, Mr Peter Sturge and Mr Wilson Sturge. When Stephen Hobhouse looked back on the reception that his biography of

Joseph Sturge had received from an earlier generation of the Sturge family he remembered their distress because he had occasionally assumed a critical tone towards their famous forebear. I trust that my own freedom of judgement will give no disappointment to the members of a family from whom I have received so much help.

At every stage I have been assisted by my wife: she has been research-assistant, scrutineer of style and proof-reader. I dedicate the book to her.

Introduction

Businessman, provincial, Dissenter: Joseph Sturge was one of the 'new men' who forced their way into British public life as reformers during the early Victorian era. Born at the close of the eighteenth century when the leisured gentleman was still the social ideal and power belonged to the landowners, he acquired his wealth and came before the public during the forty years of peace after 1815 when men of his status aspired to carry through a 'moral revolution' which would reshape the values of the nation and establish their ascendancy over it.(1) They were 'gentlemen of station and character', Sturge and a deputation of his friends told Lord Aberdeen, the prime minister, in 1853; as chief magistrates of large towns, ministers of religion, merchants, manufacturers and professional men they were 'inferior to no class in this country for their intelligence and moral and religious worth'. Speaking for 'many of their fellow citizens', they had a right to wield an influence on matters of state.(2)

This confrontation, which arose from a conference of the peace movement in Manchester, exhibited several characteristics of Sturge's reform movements. Conscious of their numbers, wealth and influence in the society that was being created by the Industrial Revolution, he and his associates used the new language of class to express their resentment at finding themselves still on the periphery of the political world. With more than their fair share of the prevalent suspicion of central government they saw London as the bastion of the aristocratic, Anglican Establishment, unlike the new centres of population in the provinces where the society of the future seemed to be rising. Many of them were Dissenters, no longer prepared to play the part of second-class citizens in a confessional state. Influenced by the evangelical revival of the early nineteenth century, they saw themselves going forth to convert Britain and the world to their version of vital religion. They analysed political issues in moral terms, and from an earlier and more conservative generation of moral and humanitarian reformers they took over the pressure group as their political instrument, transforming it into 'the pressure from without' as a mass mobilisation of public opinion through which they could force their ideas on Parliament. The term 'moral Radical party' was used to describe them by one of their newspapers, and they made a

1

disproportionate contribution to the reform movements of the era; for it is a mistake to typify the nineteenth-century British middle class as 'conservative', 'wary of the large idealist causes' and 'narrowly self-interested'.(3) L.J. Saunders' reference to Edinburgh applies to many other early Victorian cities and towns where middle class reformers were active: they were 'humming with good causes and transcendental schemes of human progress and perfection'.(4) This is not to suggest that Sturge and the 'moral Radical party' spoke for the whole middle class or even for all middle class radicals; they formed an important part of what D.A. Hamer has called a 'political sub-culture' during the Victorian era, 'a world which is very different from the political world in which we live today and yet one which was in some respects more democratic, more open to popular participation and influence'.(5)

In his lifetime it was often said that Sturge's prominence in this form of public life would assure him a 'bright page in England's future history',(6) but reputations are like wines; they sometimes fail the test of time. Herbert Spencer who knew Sturge in the 1840s regretted to see that his name was 'scarcely known to the present generation' fifty years later,(7) and even in Birmingham, Sturge's adopted town where his statue had stood in public since 1862, newspaper articles appeared bearing titles such as 'Who was Joseph Sturge?'. Nowadays he is remembered, if at all, as one who played a troublesome subaltern role in reform movements associated with the names of William Wilberforce, Sir Thomas Fowell Buxton, Richard Cobden and John Bright. His attempt to set up the National Complete Suffrage Union as a third force in popular politics alongside the Chartist movement and the Anti-Corn Law League is probably his best-known exploit.

The Buxton Monument which stands almost in the shadow of the Houses of Parliament suggests one of the reasons for this decline into obscurity. It was erected by Charles Buxton 'in commemoration of the emancipation of slaves 1834 and in memory of his father, Sir T. Fowell Buxton and those associated with him, Wilberforce, Clarkson, Macaulay, Brougham, Dr Lushington and others'.(8) T.F. Buxton and Sturge had been rivals in the anti-slavery movement, and by listing the leaders in this way Charles Buxton was making his contribution to one of those brawls in which the Victorians engaged so frequently on behalf of the reputations of their relations and friends. In the process he was also confirming a tendency to write the history of the British anti-slavery movement around the activities of a few parliamentary leaders and their associates. An earlier anti-slavery memorial erected by Sturge's missionary friend, William Knibb, had told a different if no less selective story. Above an inscription hailing the abolition of slavery in 1838 Knibb placed the bas relief profiles of three British emancipationists: William Wilberforce, Granville Sharp and, in the central position, Joseph Sturge. Knibb knew more than most people about the movement for emancipation on both sides of the Atlantic during the 1830s, and his choice of heroes merited attention, but his monument stood forgotten in the Baptist chapel at Falmouth, Jamaica.

Sturge's reputation also suffered because the best-known early history of British anti-slavery was written by Sir George Stephen, a participant in the events he related who did little to conceal his distaste for the 'new people' in the movement. In Stephen's account Sturge appears as 'head-strong' and 'eccentric' - a remarkable criticism from a man who had such a tetchy notion of his own esteem that he once threatened to call out Buxton and the Quaker members of the Anti-Slavery Committee to fight a series of duels.(9) Esther Copley's History of Slavery and its Abolition which was extended in its second edition (1839) to take in the years of Sturge's anti-apprenticeship campaign received little attention. And so it has remained to the present. Subsequent histories of the anti-slavery movement have stopped short in 1834 or passed briskly over later events when Sturge ousted Buxton from the leadership.(10)

As an unashamed capitalist Sturge also suffered from the economic and social class interpretations that have influenced twentieth-century history writing. By 1919 even Stephen Hobhouse, his sympathetic biographer, could find Sturge guilty 'in the eyes of the Socialist critic' of 'endeavouring to reconcile two things which are quite incompatible, namely, the dictates of the Gospel of co-operative Love and the competitive strife of the profit-making system'. Hobhouse found excuses for Sturge: 'The stars of the Socialist and co-operative movements were then only glimmering feebly above the national horizon'.(11) Others were less merciful. Eric Williams's influential study of the British anti-slavery movement rested on an important proposition which was intended to knock the abolitionists off their pedestals: 'Politics and morals in the abstract make no sense'. The stricture was an appropriate one at a time (1944) when sentimentality coloured many writings about British humanitarianism, but Williams exposed himself to the counter-charge that he had created a one-dimensional man - homo economicus. 'The decisive forces in the period of history we have discussed are the developing economic forces', he concluded, and he presented Sturge as the spokesman for Birmingham ironmasters whose 'vested interest' was served by the abolition of slavery and the downfall of the old colonial system.(12) Similarly, Sturge's Complete Suffrage experiment has been seen as a proof of the axiom that the only significant component in the model of social relationships during the early 1840s was the polar opposition of middle and working-class consciousness. He has been taken to represent 'the smug ideals of the respectable middle-class Radical' who was 'tactless and supercilious', 'extremely foolish' and 'curiously insensitive' towards working-class Radicals. G.D.H. Cole's excellent corrective of this interpretation (1941) has received less attention than it deserves.(13)

But, above all, Sturge suffered the fate of those who were judged to be faddists during the Victorian era: many of the causes he supported - teetotalism and hydropathy, for example - became unfashionable or simply failed, leaving little or no legacy to make them immediately relevant in the modern world. His favourite instrument of reform, the voluntary society, lost many of its practical functions during the late nineteenth and twentieth centuries when central and local governments increasingly intervened to provide educational and other services staffed by professionals. It seemed an oddity that a private individual could ever have conducted a juvenile reformatory with minimal state involvement. The title which was most often applied to Sturge, 'the Christian Philanthropist', acquired a dated and even a discredited appearance because of its association with rich men who were atoning for the sins that had made their fortunes by setting themselves up as benevolent busybodies in the lives of the less fortunate. All in all, Sturge's career seemed to be a succession of dead ends and a reminder of some of the least attractive features of the Victorian era.

This biography is written from the point of view of recent historians who have emphasised the need to understand the Victorian reformer within the context of his own values. Quoting L.P. Hartley's dictum that 'the past is a foreign country: they do things differently there', Brian Harrison has commented that the historian who is interested only in seeking out 'ancestors' of what he finds in his own day runs the risk of contracting the range of possibilities at both ends of his time scale by ignoring or downgrading the unsuccessful reform movements. Harrison's call for historians to explore the world of the losers as well as the winners in history as 'a sort of passport into the past which makes it easier... to re-create lost situations and relationships' is appropriate to the writing of Joseph Sturge's biography.(14)

Thus, although it would not have been difficult to depict Sturge as one of the dotty reformers satirised in T.L. Peacock's Crotchet Castle (1831), he is offered here as a man whose world view commanded respect in his day. Strongly influenced by the overlapping ideas of evangelical Dissent and laissez-faire economic theory, he saw the inner-directed, self-improving Christian as the social ideal and the voluntary society as the most congenial form of collective action for social and political purposes. He was an adherent of what has been called 'the doctrine of the free choice', the belief that men must take their own decisions as the true test of their moral stature,(15) but he went further than most by interpreting this as a call to crusade against arbitrary power and vested interests, not only in the plantations where they were easily identified in the form of negro slavery, but in Britain itself where he spoke of a class of 'white slaves'. Disappointed by the 1832 Reform Act, he and his circle acted as a self-appointed public interest group for promoting reforms on behalf of 'the people' against a traditional 'Establishment' which had no place for democracy and the mass political party. Sturge's values were shared by many working men, and his attempts to promote their interests made a contribution to the emergence of Britain as a 'peaceable kingdom' in which a cohesive culture triumphed over the divisive influences attending the emergence of a class society.(16) No one worked harder to promote the . mellow form of middle-class Liberalism that constituted so important a part of the mid-nineteenth century social and political consensus.(17)

This is not to deny the existence of continuities between Sturge's activities and developments in our own day; his career formed part of a tradition in English religious and political life that spans the last three hundred years. From his reading of seventeenth-century history Sturge obtained a source of inspiration for the reforms he proposed during the

1830s and 1840s, and through his influence on the next generation he helped to transmit this tradition of Dissent into the twentieth century where it is still associated with aims and attitudes that he would immediately recognise. His cheerful admission that he only felt comfortable in public life when he was in a minority calls to mind the recent suggestion that middle-class radicals of the 1960s were driven forward by a 'propensity to endorse minority or deviant standpoints on a broad range of public issues'. Their 'expressive politics' in which action was prompted by the satisfaction of adhering to principle rather than by the prospects of success bore a remarkable similarity to his ideas and practices. Likewise, the arguments offered by church leaders against those of their co-religionists who politicized Christianity through the Campaign for Nuclear Disarmament were couched and answered in almost identical terms to those exchanged between early Victorian denominational leaders and members of Sturge's circle of 'moral radicals'.(18) The tradition stretches down to the present in many parts of the English-speaking world, intruding a morally charged radicalism into the agenda of government and raising the claims of underprivileged sections of society. As I write (August 1985) the first nuclear disarmament Senator, a Quakeress, has taken her seat in the Australian Parliament, brought there by a commitment to values shaped, not only by her opposition to nuclear power, but also by her observation of race relations in Australia and the United States as well as by her experiences of the English social class system that made her 'well and truly ready for a fight'.(19)

Finally, something should be said about the strategy followed in the writing of this biography. The task has proved more difficult than it might seem to those who share Brian Harrison's belief that biography is 'procedurally the easiest of the historian's activities'.(20) Admittedly, the life span of the subject provides a ready-made structure, but this still leaves major problems for the biographer of a man who took on so many concurrent commitments that, as Richard Cobden commented, he acted as if he were several people. To take the easy way out, as to a great extent two previous biographers did, by discussing Sturge's reforms seriatim in separate chapters is to run the risk of obscuring influences which imparted a unity to his career. It is as if Sturge's biographer needs some equivalent of the musician's counterpoint to offer several themes simultaneously and yet display an overall harmony.

Part 1 complies with the basic requirement that the biographer's duty is to 'understand how it was that a person came to act and behave in the way he did, hold the opinions he did - in short, how he came to be the man he was'.(21) This has not been taken as an invitation to exaggerate early influences and ignore the emphasis placed by recent psychologists on development as a lifelong process.(22) The first two chapters separately analyse two important influences that went into the making of Sturge as a 'Christian Philanthropist' (his family experience and his evangelical Quakerism), a process of personal development that stretched over his first thirty years and included several major changes of outlook and lifestyle. A third influence, his career as a businessman, is followed throughout his adult life to bring out the sources of his wealth and trace the evolution of his concept of stewardship. This strategy of describing the parts of Sturge's life thematically is abandoned after the early 1830s are reached. By then he had been set free from business pressures to participate in public life on what was almost a full-time basis, and his commitments had rapidly multiplied. Within a limited chronology each subsequent chapter allows his reform movements and other activities to come foward and jostle each other for attention much as they did at the time. The element of jerkiness which is imparted to the discussion will be offset, I hope, by a more true-to-life picture of Sturge's career and of his wide-ranging perception of reform. His public and private lives overlapped so much that no attempt is made after Part 1 to keep them separate in the chapter structure. Part 5 calls for special comment. In 'The World of the Christian Philanthropist' the chronological sequence is interrupted at the peak of Sturge's career to show how philanthropy had become a way of life for him and how his reforms had come together as a personal crusade for the transformation of the world into a place of peace, progress and well-being.

I offer the outcome as a contribution to the task of showing how reform movements of this era were related to each other, for, although we now have many scholarly studies, the movements remain self-contained entities. The feeling of so many reformers that they had embarked on an exhilarating quest for the perfection of mankind has been lost. Until this feeling is retrieved the individual reform movements will not be fully understood, and some of them - water cures and phonetics are obvious examples - will be dismissed as amusing fads. It is here that the justification of this biography is to be found. One man's career could not encapsulate the full range of reforming aspirations during that era, but by studying the life of an individual who 'came close to being the Compleat Reformer' Sturge's biographer can begin the task of re-creating the scattered mosaic of early Victorian middle-class radicalism. Its completion must await a second book.(23)

NOTES

1. H. Perkin, The Origins of Modern English Society 1780-1880, London 1969, Chapters II and VIII.
2. Herald of Peace, April 1853.
3. E.P. Thompson, The Making of the English Working Class, London 1965, p. 820.
4. L.J. Saunders, Scottish Democracy 1815-1840, Edinburgh 1950, p. 93.
5. D.A. Hamer, The Politics of Electoral Pressure. A Study in the History of Victorian Reform Agitations, Hassocks 1977, p. viii.
6. Public Good, 1850, pp. 272-76.
7. H. Spencer, An Autobiography, London 1904, vol. I, pp. 251-52.
8. The monument stands in Victoria Tower Gardens.
9. Sir George Stephen, Anti-Slavery Recollections: In A Series of Letters, Addressed To Mrs Beecher Stowe, London 1854, pp. 210-13; Papers of Sir Thomas Fowell Buxton, 1st Baronet, 1786-1845, vol. 15, Sir

T.F. Buxton to Sarah Buxton, 14 December 1836.

10. A. Tyrrell, 'The Moral Radical Party and the Anglo-Jamaican campaign for the abolition of the Negro apprenticeship system', English Historical Review, XCIX, July 1984, pp. 481-82.

11. S. Hobhouse, Joseph Sturge. His Life and Work, London 1919, p. 25.

12. E. Williams, Capitalism and Slavery, New York 1966, pp. 158, 210-11.

13. J.T. Ward, Chartism, London 1973, pp. 165-66; A. Wilson, 'The Suffrage Movement' in P. Hollis, ed., Pressure from Without in Early Victorian England, London 1974, pp. 89-90.

14. B. Harrison, Separate Spheres. The Opposition to Women's Suffrage in Britain, London 1978, chap. 1.

15. G. Best, Mid-Victorian Britain 1851-1875, London 1971, p. 258.

16. B. Harrison, Peaceable Kingdom. Stability and Change in Modern Britain, Oxford 1982, p. 5.

17. T.R. Tholfsen, Working Class Radicalism in Mid-Victorian England, London 1976, chap. 4.

18. F. Parkin, Middle Class Radicalism. The Social Bases of the British Campaign for Nuclear Disarmament, Melbourne 1968, pp. 3, 29, 36, 72.

19. National Times (Sydney), 23-29 August 1985. The sociologist Alain Touraine has commented on the comparative weakness of this tradition in France, Guardian Weekly, 15 September 1985.

20. Harrison, Peaceable Kingdom, p. 323.

21. R. Skidelsky, Oswald Mosley, London 1975, p. 23.

22. P.B. Baltes, H.W. Reese and L.P. Lipsitt, 'Life-Span Developmental Psychology', Annual Review of Psychology, 1980, pp. 66-101. I am indebted for this reference to my late colleague, Professor R.B. Joyce. See also S. Chess and A. Thomas, 'Infant Bonding: Mystique and Reality' American Journal of Orthopsychiatry, 52, April 1982, pp. 213-21. I am indebted for this reference to Peter Rendell.

23. The quotation is taken from H. Temperley, British Antislavery, London 1972, p. 72.

PART 1

THE MAKING OF A CHRISTIAN PHILANTHROPIST

1 The Family Man
(1793-1822)

Joseph Sturge was born on 2 August 1793 in the parish of Elberton near the village of Olveston about nine miles from Bristol. He was the second of six sons and the fourth of twelve children, eleven of whom would reach adulthood.(1) To judge from their choices of residence the Sturges had lived in dignified comfort during the previous two hundred years, and in 1793 they were tenant occupiers of an impressively gabled manor house from which the family's grazing business was carried on. Sturge's father, another Joseph Sturge and the fifth of the name to farm in the area since the late sixteenth century, described himself as a yeoman or grazier specialising in the buying of sheep and black cattle from Dorset and Merionethshire for fattening and re-sale.(2) A kind and affable man, he was also remembered as a stickler for the observance of his Quaker faith, but he seems to have influenced his children in little else. None of his sons, with the temporary and reluctant exception of Joseph, followed him on the land, and as grown men of radical opinions they looked back with wonderment on his strongly conservative ideas.(3)

The mother, Mary née Marshall, also came from a line of farmers. As steward for the Warwickshire lands of the Marquis of Hertford her father, Thomas Marshall, had advanced to a position of substance and standing. Although family memoirs refer to Mary as the 'stay' of the household and the one who had most influence on the mental development of her children, her few surviving letters have none of the liveliness and intelligence attributed to her as a young woman; they show only that the bearing and upbringing of twelve children were taking a heavy toll, reducing her to a state of melancholia during her later pregnancies.(4) To make matters worse her eyesight began to fail at the turn of the century, a condition for which her doctors administered a painfully ineffective course of treatment. Believing, like so many of their contemporaries, that electricity was 'a considerable article in the materia medica', they electrified her eyes four times every other day. Suffering in vain, by 1803 she was praying for death to save her from the total loss of her sight.(5) There is no suggestion that the children suffered from neglect, but they spent their days roaming the countryside in each other's company, becoming, so Henry Richard was told, 'rather wild'. A sense of closeness between Sturge and his brothers and sisters was forged during these years, and it was then, as early as the age of eight, that Sophia's 'great love' of Joseph was first commented on by their parents.(6)

Possibly it was with the intention of reducing Mary's burdens that the children were sent on long visits to Kingley, Thomas Marshall's farm near Alcester in Warwickshire. The old man held an important place in the family circle (the eldest son was named in his honour) and he seems to have taken a significant part in the upbringing of the grandchildren. Joseph spent the years between 1800 and 1803 at Kingley where he became the protégé of his grandfather. It was an unquestioned assumption that he would become a farmer; the only uncertainty was whether he would follow his grandfather as an arable farmer in preference to joining his father as a grazier.(7)

Both sides of the family had been Quakers (members of the Society of Friends) since the mid-seventeenth century, and there was a heritage of 'plainness' that could have cast a shadow over Sturge's early years. One of his relatives never forgot the jeering torment that was heaped on those who ventured on to the streets of Bristol 'dressed as little Quaker scarecrows, with collarless jackets and broad-brimmed white beaver hats'.(8) But Sturge's rural childhood was happy enough. The first description we have of him reveals a boy who was sharing the farm chores at Kingley but for the rest was usually left free to wander as he pleased, indulging a passion for bird nesting or hunting and fishing with his grandfather. Similarities with William Cobbett's descriptions of country life spring readily to mind; for, strongly though he detested Quakers, Cobbett would have found much to praise in the Marshall household where the old man lived in traditional style, dining with his family and servants at the kitchen table and reading or yarning with them around the winter fire-place.(9) With the exception of four years at school this was the pattern of Joseph's life until the age of twenty-one - daily life on the Sturge and Marshall farms interspersed with ample opportunities for hunting, swimming and riding. Although there are some references in family letters to childhood illnesses (at the age of three he was thin, pale and of poor appetite), he grew up to be a man of above-average strength. Brown haired and blue eyed, with a ruddy complexion, powerful forehead and squarely-built figure of middle height, until late in life he was the image of a strong and healthy farmer.(10) By the age of seven he had already earned a reputation as a person prepared to 'kill himself at work'.(11)

When Henry Richard described Sturge's country upbringing in a Quaker family, he remembered two lines from Gray's Elegy:(12)

Along the cool sequester'd vale of life
they kept the noiseless tenor of their way.

Reality was less idyllic but more interesting; the characteristic quietism of eighteenth-century Quakers was already giving way to the public concerns of their nineteenth-century successors. As the 1796 Yearly Meeting Epistle admitted, the frequency with which Friends had been warned against political discussion was an indication of their incorrigible weakness for it, and later observers were to note that Quakers of Sturge's generation grew up as Whig and even radical reformers. Runs of periodicals (the Gentleman's Magazine, the Universal and the Monthly) which were disposed of when the parental home was broken up in 1819 suggest that Joseph's father, conservative though he was, kept abreast of current affairs during the years that followed the French Revolution.(13) For their part, the Marshalls had not forgotten an earlier revolution; they preserved the memory of an ancestor who had been one of the officers in attendance at Charles I's execution in 1649. Thomas Marshall sometimes recounted political anecdotes for his fireside circle while Joseph lived at Kingley, and it is likely that they were coloured by the antagonism between 'Country' opposition and 'Court' politicians that was so powerful during the eighteenth century. The single recorded example of Joseph's mother's reading tastes suggests the sort of ideas that found favour on this side of the family - The Letters of Junius, a notoriously vituperative attack on George III and his early ministers.(14)

Formal education played little part in Sturge's life. In one of her letters Mary Sturge took a very strong line against 'altogether useless' subjects and rejected Sophia's request for drawing and French lessons at a time when the needs of a large family imposed restraints on household expenditure.(15) Joseph fared no better. Only after he returned from his grandfather's farm at the age of ten was he sent for one year to a school in Thornbury (three miles from Olveston), followed by three years as a boarder at a Quaker school at Sidcot in Somerset. The Sidcot prospectus emphasised behaviour and morals, but the curriculum offered by the master, John Benwell, was substantial enough for those who could take advantage of it - reading, writing, English grammar, arithmetic, merchant's accounting, the Classical languages and 'the useful Parts of mathematics'. The Sturges cut this down to a 'plain English education' for their son, and even this seems to have been rather defective. With good reason Sturge would always feel diffident about committing his thoughts to the printing press; later in life four years as President of the National Complete Suffrage Union did not suffice to teach him that 'sufferage' was a mis-spelling.(16) At a time when many of his generation and social status received no more than a rudimentary education, none of this would have seemed important. 'Self-culture' in the typically early nineteenth-century style - time snatched after work for individual study and 'mutual improvement' - would have to satisfy any yearning for knowledge. It was in this spirit that Sturge went on to join the Bristol Endeavour Society, a group of young Quakers who met regularly to discuss science, literature and the fine arts. He delivered papers on astronomy, optics and meteorology.

Sturge took the Endeavour Society seriously. In his own words, it opened up the prospect of science as the best pursuit for 'an intellectual being'.(17) It may even have undermined his willingness to be a farmer, but there was no escaping the consequences of the training he had received: though lectures and scientific experiments attracted an enthusiastic following in the early nineteenth century, they could do little to enhance a young man's career prospects. In 1811 at the age of nineteen Sturge decided to follow his grandfather's example and establish himself on the Midlands corn belt, a sensible choice at a time when British corn farmers were prospering from high prices during the war with France. Wheat sales rose to famine prices in 1812. Understandably therefore he was disappointed when he failed to obtain the tenancy for which he had hoped, but in fact he had been lucky, and within a few years he was congratulating himself on a narrow escape. Over the two years beginning in September 1813 the average price of grain fell nearly 50 per cent compared with the 1812 average. Until the mid-nineteenth century corn farmers were to lament their declining fortunes.(18) In an attempt to keep him on the land Sturge's father installed him on a small grazing farm at Aust, a village on the Severn within easy ride of home, but the venture was not successful, and in 1814 he accepted the offer of a partnership in a corn factor's business. Family letters refer to his decision as a 'considerable tryal' for the father; they leave no doubt that it was a liberation for the son.(19)

For the first time in two hundred years there would be no Joseph Sturge farming in Gloucestershire, a break with tradition that is less surprising that it might seem. Already one of Sturge's uncles had settled in London where he founded a whaling company - Sturge Island in Antarctica was named after the son who made this a flourishing venture - and Sturge's brothers all went into trade: Thomas as a wool stapler, Charles as a corn factor, John and Edmund as industrial chemists, and Henry as a carpet manufacturer. Soon their cousins, James and Cyrus Clark, would also abandon farming and set up the shoe-making business which still bears their name.(20) The disappearance of the yeomanry was one of the laments of the age, and it was very noticeable amongst Quakers. Nine years before Sturge's birth the Yearly Meeting had deplored the tendency of young Friends 'to quit their quiet habitations in country places, to crowd to cities and great towns': by 1806 Thomas Clarkson was confidently prophesying that soon there would be few Quakers left on the land.(21)

Sturge's decision to become a corn factor took him away from home as well as farming. On 13 July 1814, just short of his twenty-first birthday, he arrived in Bewdley, the Severn port where the partnership was to be based, and for the next thirteen months he resided with the family of his partner, Henry Cotterel, at the Summer House, their home on the heights above the river. With two changes of address he would remain in Bewdley until 1822. He was treated kindly, but his earliest surviving letter, written three weeks after his arrival, refers to 'an agony of grief' on leaving 'the bosom of an affectionate family'. A year later he was still describing 'so lonely a situation'. The Cotterels were the only Quakers in the town; the meeting house had been closed; and in an effort to avoid unsuitable company he had been keeping himself to himself. His comments reveal the prudishness of one who had little experience of life outside his family and the Society of Friends: 'there is scarcely a single person in this neighbourhood in whom I feel inclined to place my confidence', he told his brother.(22)

The austerity of the young man's outlook was evident again, when he moved across the river in 1815 to the accommodation he had rented at the rear of the Black Boy tavern near the partnership's warehouse. In comparison with the Summer House, 'one of the most beautiful situations in the kingdom', it was a 'dull habitation' - 'a little barn of a house' in which he lived a 'hermit-like existence'. He saw only one redeeming feature: he could satisfy his preference for 'independence with a bit of bread and cheese to its opposite with all the luxuries that art can invent'. Joseph Sturge was always a firm advocate of the values which would later be summarised as 'the Protestant Ethic'. Better still, the 'barn' made it possible for him to bring Sophia to Bewdley as his housekeeper, and by March 1816 they were describing themselves as well settled.(23) With two short breaks they would live together until her death in 1845.

It was not that Sturge was a bachelor by conviction while he lived in Bewdley; if anything, he seems to have been too eager for matrimony. His nephew was told many years later that he was engaged (probably in 1821) but abandoned all thoughts of marriage in tragi-comic circumstances when a cousin intervened and claimed that he had a prior engagement to her. The setback brought brother and sister closer to each other. Writing to Sophia in 1822 Sturge would not totally discount the possibility that he would find a wife, but he dismissed his recent 'visions of bliss' as 'the fervour of youth'. Setting aside his sister for a wife, he added, would probably be tantamount to losing 'a greater for a less treasure'.(24) For her part Sophia never envisaged marriage. Severely ill from early childhood, by the age of twenty-five she was describing herself as 'debilitated by disease and medicine'.(25) She was no sick room recluse, however; she was one of the many Victorian spinsters who have been described as 'surrogate wives to bachelor brothers', a status that attracted less prurient comment then than it would now.(26) Until she died, she struggled against ill health to act as her brother's housekeeper, commercial book-keeper, secretary and confidante. Although Sturge would marry twice in middle age, Sophia was certainly the most important woman in his life. Her life affords an insight into the important supportive roles often taken on by women of character and ability during an era when they had few opportunities to create a life of their own.

Increasingly over the next few years the family life of the Sturges revolved around Joseph and Sophia. On 14 June 1817 their father died, leaving a distraught widow and seven dependent children. During the previous ten years Mary Sturge's sight had failed almost entirely; in 1808 Anna, her one year old daughter, had died; and the death of her father in 1810 had been a blow from which she prophesied that she would never fully recover. Now, suddenly bereft of her husband, she saw life as a 'howling wilderness'.(27) By this time several of her children were establishing themselves independently, and others were at an age when they could be sent to boarding school. Charles, the third son, moved to Bewdley and joined Joseph in the corn business. Two sisters, Priscilla and Rebecca, remained with their mother until 25 May 1819 when death provided her with the release she had long desired. The eldest brother, Thomas Marshall Sturge, could do little to help - he was struggling to maintain his own young family at a time when his business as a wool-stapler was sharing the declining fortunes of the textile industry in the West Country. Fortunately Joseph, Sophia and Charles had moved into a larger house. Delightfully situated on the Severn, Netherton (the name was taken from the ancestral farm of the Marshalls) became the home of the dependent children and the focal point of the family circle.

Prior to 1814 the lives of Sturge and other members of his family can be glimpsed only fleetingly. After that year several of the brothers and sisters corresponded frequently when they were separated, and it is possible to see, not only some of the individual personalities, but also the characteristics of the family circle in Bewdley. Some of Sturge's letters show the care he took to help his family at a time when the parental home was breaking up. For example, a great deal of his planning went into an unsuccessful carpet manufacturing enterprise which was to be conducted by one brother, Henry, with dyeing expertise from John, a brother who had been apprenticed to a London pharmacist. Frequently too the letters provide vignettes of one or other of the family. Charles, displaying characteristics which were always to worry Joseph in their joint business ventures, is coarse-grained and impetuous. John, the principal contributor to the correspondence, is always the scholarly-minded commentator on the events of the world, inspiring and informing the rest of the family from his vantage point in London. Very much the privately well-read woman, Priscilla comes before the reader as one who gives every morning to study, writes poetry, sketches, and learns Hebrew. With other members of the family she goes boating, botanising, gardening and conducting a Sunday school. Her vivacity and questing intellect (whether galloping 'like a heroine' through the countryside or discussing Byron's latest poem) still delight the reader of the fading, criss-crossed lines in her letters.(28)

Their correspondence reveals the Sturges as a circle of enthusiastic auto-didacts. Although literature was expensive and libraries were few, John's residence in London made it easier for them to purchase books and subscribe to newspapers. Some of them also joined reading societies - co-operative ventures in buying books for lending and subsequent sale to the members. The result was a surprisingly rich choice of reading material. They read Johnson's Lives of the Poets, Hume's History of England, Mackenzie's Man of Feeling, Locke's works, Gibbon's Decline (less deistical than they had expected), Paley's Philosophy (they found it 'amusing'), the Life of Cowper, Addison's Spectator, works by Mme de Stael, Boswell's Johnson and writings by Southey. They read the Edinburgh Review, then reaching the height of its reputation, and they received Sir Walter Scott's novels with discriminating enthusiasm. Byron was another of their favourites, although his private life and some of the cantos of Don Juan caused them some unease. The variety of this reading and the types of imaginative literature which it included are the more surprising when they are compared with the experiences of contemporary Quakers such as Mary Howitt who had to indulge similar tastes in secret because they were 'almost out of the pale of permitted Quaker pleasures'.(29)

But so was 'party zeal' if we may judge from Yearly Meeting Epistles, yet this correspondence contains excited references to the political events of the day. Already their father's conservatism was beginning to look antiquated. In one of his earliest letters to Joseph, John described the previous thirty years as 'more replete with wonderful events than any era in history' and welcomed Bonaparte's escape from Elba as the augury of further reforms in France.(30) For a time 'the Queen's Case' (George IV's controversial attempt to divorce Queen Caroline in 1820) prompted the Sturges to purchase London newspapers and keep up to date with the dispute between the King's Tory ministers and the Queen's Whig and radical supporters. In an interesting exchange of letters John, their arbiter of London opinion, was asked to define the word 'radical' for the benefit of his provincial family; like many of their contemporaries they had only just heard of it. In his answer John took the point of view of one who saw himself as a constructive critic of the Government:(31)

> The term Radical, I believe was first introduced by the most violent class of reformers, the advocates of annual parliaments and universal Suffrage, who by applying it to their own principles, which were almost republican and required a new modelled constitution, sought to distinguish themselves from all the more moderate and respectable friends of freedom. In short this epithet from its constant use among them soon became the watchword of Hunt and his party. When it had once become appropriated thus, it was directly laid hold of by the enemies of freedom and the interested advocates of abuse and, like puritan of old applied indiscriminately as a term of reproach to all who, in the spirit of patriotism, lamented the corruptions of their government and endeavoured to remove them. It was meant by those who applied it thus, to identifiy this most respectable class with the lowest and most contemptible demagogues. Those who use it generally flee to its aid and shelter themselves behind it, when pressed by arguments which they cannot answer. It is probably the more useful, because it now means nothing in the mouths of nine out of ten of those who most frequently employ it. It is an answer to every argument, a defence for every abuse, and is itself unanswerable.

Typically, seventeen year old Charles went further than this by referring to himself as 'a Jacobin if not a radical'. Priscilla intervened as their 'high party', receiving support from Sophia, a moderate reformer, who reminded them that the cry of liberty could lead on to misdeeds and despotism.(32) The discussion was conducted with good humour, but its value as a political education should not be underestimated. This family was sharing in the heightened political consciousness that historians have often remarked on as one of the characteristics of these years.

It is surprising therefore, in view of his later reputation, to find that Sturge took little part in the political and intellectual exchanges between his brothers and sisters. He did not disapprove; according to Sophia he simply had too little leisure in 1816 to share her literary pursuits. Writing in March 1821, he described the business difficulties of the previous two years as so pressing that he had had to give them his almost undivided attention. He did what he could. He joined a reading society; he started to learn Hebrew; he and Sophia studied the 1817 Poor Law Committee Report; and his letters referred favourably to Smith's Wealth of Nations and Johnson's Lives of the Poets.(33) Before leaving his parents' home he had begun his lifelong involvement in the work of the Bible Society; now he and Priscilla joined the Peace Society, which had been founded in 1816 by a committee consisting of Quakers and evangelicals. She offered some suggestions for articles to be published in the Herald of Peace ('a very second rate concern' in her opinion); he established an auxiliary Peace Association in nearby Worcester.(34) Thus, even at this stage when business absorbed most of Sturge's energies, there was no doubt that his was a household of earnest pursuits and a sense of civic responsibility.

Family loyalties of exceptional strength were created during these years in Bewdley. In 1822, still under the pressure of business, Sturge would remove to Birmingham, but he soon drew several of his brothers and sisters after him again, providing them with a temporary home and encouraging them to marry and settle near him at Edgbaston.

NOTES

1. Gloucestershire County Record Office, D1340 A1/R1, Quarterly Meeting of Gloucestershire and Wiltshire Births. The same source records the births of Sturge's brothers and sisters as follows: Rebecca 12/3/88; Mary 21/8/89; Thomas Marshall 30/7/91; Sophia 17/8/95; Priscilla 12/8/97; John 4/10/99; Charles 5/7/1801; Henry 6/10/1802; Lucretia 19/8/1806; Anna 31/7/1807; Edmund 8/12/1808.

2. Elizabeth Sturge, Reminiscences of My Life And Some Account of the Children of William and Charlotte Sturge and of the Sturge Family of Bristol, Private Printing 1928, p. 155; Sturge Papers (Lewin) C.D. Sturge, The Sturge Family, MS, p. 38.

3. Annual Monitor, 1818; H. Richard, Memoirs of Joseph Sturge, London 1864, p. 269.

4. Sturge Papers (Lewin), Mary Darby Sturge, Record of Family Faculties [1884]; Sturge Letters (Marshall), Mary Sturge to Rebecca Collins, 16 September 1807 and Rebecca Collins to Mary Sturge, 21 September 1808.

5. Sturge Letters (Marshall), Mary Sturge to Rebecca Collins, 13 June, 23 November 1803; Joseph Priestley, The History And Present State of Electricity, With Original Experiments, 3rd ed. 1775, vol. I, p. 472; W.J. Turrell, 'Three Electrotherapists Of The Eighteenth Century: John Wesley, Jean Paul Marat and James Graham', Annals of Medical History, 3, 1921, pp. 361-67.

6. Richard, Sturge, p. 6; Sturge Letters (Marshall), Mary Sturge to Thomas Marshall, 8 December 1803.

7. Richard, Sturge, pp. 7-10.

8. Sturge Papers (P.A.J. Sturge), William Sturge, Some Family And Personal Records, p. 16.

9. Richard, Sturge, pp. 7-10; W. Reitzel, ed., The Autobiography of William Cobbett, London 1977, pp. 197-99.

10. Sturge Letters (Marshall), Mary Sturge to Thomas Marshall, 28 January, 24 March 1794, 2 September 1796; Sturge Papers (Lewin), Record of Family Faculties.

11. Sturge Letters (Marshall), Mary Sturge to Thomas Marshall, 1 October 1800.

12. Richard, Sturge, p. 6. I have corrected his mis-quotation.

13. Epistles From The Yearly Meeting Of Friends Held in London, To the Quarterly And Monthly Meetings in Great Britain, Ireland, and Elsewhere, London 1858, vol. II, p. 97; Sturge Letters (Marshall), Priscilla Sturge to John Sturge, 1819.

14. A.W. Brown, Evesham Friends In The Olden Time, London 1005, pp. 224-25; Richard, Sturge, p. 8; Sturge Papers (Lewin), Record of Family Faculties.

15. Sturge Letters (Marshall), Mary Sturge to Sophia Sturge, 16 August 1809.

16. F.A. Knight, A History of Sidcot School. A Hundred Years Of West Country Quaker Education 1809-1908, London 1908, pp. 17-19; Manchester Public Library, Wilson Papers, Joseph Sturge to George Wilson, 20 April 1857.

17. Richard, Sturge, p. 21.

18. Richard, Sturge, pp. 19-20; L.P. Adams, Agricultural Depression And Farm Relief in England 1813-1852, London 1932, pp. 148-49; Sturge Letters (Marshall), Joseph Sturge to Rebecca Collins, March 1816.

19. Sturge Letters (Marshall), Mary Sturge to Rebecca Collins, 1 September 1814 and Joseph Sturge to John Sturge, 2 July 1815.

20. Elizabeth Sturge, Reminiscences, p. 166; G. Murray, The Antarctic Manual For the Use Of The Expedition of 1901, London 1901, pp. 336-41; G.B. Sutton, A History Of Shoe Making in Street, Somerset, C. and J. Clark 1833-1903, York 1979, chap. 1.

21. Epistles From The Yearly Meeting of Friends, vol. II, p. 58; T. Clarkson, A Portraiture Of The Christian Profession And Practice Of The Society Of Friends, Glasgow 1869, pp. 121-22.

22. Sturge Letters (Marshall), Joseph Sturge to John Sturge, 6 August 1814, 2 July 1815, 22 August 1815.

23. Sturge Letters (Marshall), Joseph Sturge to John Sturge, 22 August 1815 and Joseph Sturge to Rebecca Collins, March 1816.

24. Sturge Papers (Lewin), The Sturge Family, p. 244; Sturge Papers (M. Sturge), Joseph Sturge to Sophia Sturge, 15 August 1822.

25. Sturge Papers (M. Sturge), Sophia Sturge to John Sturge, 20 February 1820.

26. The term is used by P. Jalland, 'Victorian Spinsters: Dutiful Daughters, Desperate Rebels and The Transition To The New Woman', paper delivered at the Australasian Modern British History Association Second Conference 23-25 August 1982.

27. Sturge Letters (Marshall), Mary Sturge to Rebecca Collins, 16 January 1810, 11 November 1817.

28. This paragraph draws on several letters in the Sturge Letters (Marshall) collection, especially Priscilla Sturge to John Sturge, 8 November 1818.

29. These literary tastes are described in a series of letters in the

Sturge Papers (M. Sturge), c 1820. For Mary Howitt's words see S.J. Hale, <u>Woman's Record,</u> New York 1855, p. 699.

30. <u>Epistles From The Yearly Meeting Of Friends,</u> vol. II, p. 191; Sturge Papers (Lewin), John Sturge to Joseph Sturge, 12 March 1815 and John Sturge to his sisters, 11 April 1815.

31. Sturge Papers (M. Sturge), John Sturge to Charles Sturge, 13 October 1820.

32. Sturge Papers (M. Sturge), Charles Sturge to John Sturge, 1820, and Sophia Sturge to John Sturge, 5 November 1820.

33. Sturge Letters (Marshall), Sophia Sturge to John Sturge, 10 November 1816; Sturge Papers (M. Sturge), Joseph Sturge to John Sturge, 10 March 1821.

34. Sturge Papers (M. Sturge), Priscilla Sturge to John Sturge, n.d; H. Cossham, <u>Lecture On The Life, Labours, And Character Of The Late Joseph Sturge, Of Birmingham,</u> Bristol 1860, p. 8.

2 Quaker and Evangelical (1793-1822)

The correspondence between members of the Sturge family during the first quarter of the nineteenth century contains few references to their religious convictions; for Sophia was expressing the attitude of her generation of Quakers to religion when she wrote that 'we speak least of what we deeply feel'.(1) Her restraint would have surprised the Sturges who had adopted Quakerism in the mid-seventeenth century when 'the first publishers of truth' preached against formality in religion and offered membership in a Society free from priesthoods, creeds and liturgies. In the person of Elizabeth Stirredge (an earlier version of the name) the Sturges had even produced one of the messianic figures who turned the world upside down during these turbulent years - 'a troublesome woman', according to a harassed magistrate, who had done more harm to the Church of England in her area than 'all the [rest of the] Quakers ever did'.(2)

Elizabeth Stirredge's journal reached its fourth edition in 1795, one of many indications that the example of the early Friends was still venerated in Sturge's lifetime. Quakers continued the practice of sitting in silence awaiting the 'inner light' of divine inspiration which alone entitled them to speak at meetings for worship, and as late as the 1830s an observer noted the existence of 'a school of prophetesses possessing great fluency, power and gift of language'.(3) Amongst them could be found some of the staunchest upholders of what were called the 'peculiarities' of the Friends - their 'plain clothing'; their 'plain speech' with its 'thee', 'thou' and disuse of titles; their refusal to designate the months and days by names derived from pagan deities; and their opposition to oaths, music, public holidays and other parts of normal English life. Early nineteenth-century Quaker preaching still offered the assurance that these testimonies would eventually triumph throughout the world.

Nothing in the recent history of Quakerism justified this optimism. The ecstatic sect that George Fox had organised for the conversion of the world had long since settled down as a small, inward-looking, rule-bound denomination. George Crabbe's famous description of the Baptists could more appropriately have been applied to the Quakers:(4)

> This I perceive, that when a sect grows old,
> Converts are few, and the converted cold:
> First comes the hotbed heat, and while it glows,
> The plants spring up, and each with vigour grows:
> Then comes the cooler day, and though awhile
> The verdure prospers and the blossoms smile,
> Yet poor the fruit, and form'd by long delay,
> Nor will the profits for the culture pay;
> The skilful gard'ner then no longer stops,
> But turns to other beds for bearing crops.

In her old age Fox's widow had warned the Quakers that they were returning to the 'Jewism' of formal religion; later in the eighteenth century John Wesley saw them as 'dead, formal men'.(5) The institution of 'birthright membership', the relentless disownment of those who 'married out' and a difficult procedure for admission by 'conviction' worked together to produce the endogamous community that was nicknamed 'the Quaker cousinhood': in 1837 the Yearly Meeting was told that Christ himself would have been excluded by the rules.(6) Long before Sturge was born the pentecostal experiences of seventeenth-century Quakerism were replaced by a set form of worship in which the silence could be broken only by 'ministers' whose preaching had been found acceptable by their Monthly Meeting. Sitting in special galleries facing the congregation, they were sometimes referred to as a Quaker priesthood. There were not enough of them: according to statistics published in 1839, only 121 out of 419 meetings had ministers.(7) Both at Olveston and Bewdley where he had the old meeting house re-opened after his brothers and sisters joined him, Sturge worshipped for years on end in a silence occasionally broken by ministers visiting 'with a concern'. Even in meetings where there was a ministry, as in Birmingham's Bull Street Meeting House which Sturge attended after 1822, prayer and preaching were accompanied by rituals which received adverse criticism both from outsiders and from Friends themselves. A sing-song voice indicated that words were being spoken under divine inspiration, and a liturgical language of specialised expressions was used which Quakers found difficulty in explaining. Listening to the prophetic outpourings of Sarah Lynes Grubb, one of the best known ministers of this era, a hostile critic was reminded of the sect of Irvingites whose members spoke in tongues known only to themselves. Joseph and Sophia Sturge always claimed that they derived more spiritual satisfaction from their silent meetings in Bewdley than from the ministry they were offered in Birmingham.(8)

In Sturge's lifetime Quakerism moved rapidly to a point of crisis. Numbers were falling - every observer agreed about this(9) - and an important minority of 'gay Friends' was adopting the ways of the world in such matters as dress and speech. But it was not easy to bring in reforms of worship and discipline after the testimonies of the first generation of Quakers had hardened into a canon. Although more people actively participated in the business meetings of the Society than at meetings for worship, decisions were reached by consensus, not by voting, and the conservatism of a small number of Friends, variously nicknamed the 'weighty Friends', the 'princes', the 'ruling Friends' and the 'Upper House' exercised a disproportionate influence far into the nineteenth century. Referring to years of discussion by his Monthly Meeting about the banning of upright gravestones, William Lucas (1804-61), whose diary is an important source for the Quakerism of this era, despaired to see 'the so-called free, shackled by rules and forms'. Implicitly the Society found a solution by accepting what were virtually separate categories of membership. For example, Lucas was told in 1839 that he would never be eligible to hold office as long as he persisted in his 'unfaithfulness in those minor concerns such as dating a letter "February"'.(10)

This was Quakerism as Sturge knew it during his boyhood and youth: mystical but formal and hierarchical; strict in enforcing its regulations in some matters, but haphazard in applying them to others. At a time when the Gloucestershire and Wiltshire Monthly Meeting freely admitted to a 'degree of drowsiness' no one seems to have cared that he and his brothers and sisters were acquiring tastes for country sports, literature and politics that had no place in Quakerism as defined by the Yearly Meeting Epistles and such contemporary writings as Thomas Clarkson's Portraiture of Friends.(11) It was enough that their father had strictly insisted on family worship in the Olveston meeting house; that their mother had instilled adherence to the 'plain' testimonies; and that the family had year by year endured the distraint of grain and livestock for refusing to pay church rates and tithes.(12) These lessons were well learned. To the end of his days Sturge's speech, clothing and many of his fundamental attitudes identified him with the traditions of Quakerism. He never offered himself in the ministry, but he did take a share in the offices of elder, supervisor and representative which contributed to the administration of the Society of Friends,(13) and for forty years he was an assiduous attender at the London Yearly Meeting, the parliament of British Quakerism. Even as a hard-pressed young businessman in Bewdley he regulated his time according to the Society's calendar. Many years later, in a tribute to Sturge's religious dedication and his remarkable physical stamina, one of his friends called to mind four days beginning with a Preparative Meeting at Worcester on the Sunday and ending with a Quarterly Meeting at Ross in Herefordshire on the Wednesday. Sturge attended both, relying on overnight coaches to transact business during the intervening days at Mark Lane in London and at the Bristol market.(14)

An event which occurred while he was farming at Aust - the first of many occasions when he publicly defied the law of the land - shows the importance of traditional Quakerism in forming Sturge's attitudes. When he was drawn for the militia he refused either to serve or to pay the £10 fine imposed for his default. As a consequence on 16 April 1813 two ewes and six lambs were confiscated from his farm by legal distraint. Britain was then at war with the United States as well as with Bonaparte's France, and the militia was expected to ease the strain on the regular army during the crisis. It was a time when Lord Castlereagh (admittedly not the most sensitive barometer of public opinion) could claim that the country supported the Government's defence measures, but his words would not have meant much to Sturge: for a Quaker the testimony of the Society of Friends constituted a higher law than any parliamentary statute.(15) Similarly Sturge and his business partnership went on experiencing distraints of goods (2 silver spoons valued at £1-13-0 in 1823; 4 chairs valued at 15/6 in 1824; and so on) rather than pay the dues required for the support of those who had been described by George Fox as 'the hireling priesthood' of the Church of England.(16) Some of the public agitations he supported - peace and anti-slavery, for example - were long-established Quaker good causes, and he pursued them with that uncompromising dedication which Clarkson and other observers regarded as a Quaker trait. It could never have been said of Sturge as it was of John Bright that he was 'more Englishman than Quaker, more citizen than sectarian'.(17)

Nonetheless, it would be a mistake simply to refer to 'Joseph Sturge the Quaker'; those who knew him in his prime saw him as one who had transcended the religion of his boyhood. J.A. James, a prominent Birmingham Congregational minister who shared many of his interests for thirty years, saw Sturge as 'a truly devout and holy man, upon sound evangelical principles': 'His piety was not the vague spiritualism of some of the more early "Friends"; but was enlightened by the positive doctrinal teaching of the New Testament, as set forth in the writings of that eminent and saintly man, Joseph John Gurney.'(18) James's words point to an important part of the crisis which engulfed early nineteenth century Quakerism. During the late eighteenth century, the time when the pattern of Quaker philanthropy was being established, the Society was becoming less inward looking as members participated in interdenominational associations where they shared platforms with clergymen and laymen from the Established and Dissenting churches. For this was the era of the evangelical revival, and the good causes which attracted Quaker support (very notably the anti-slavery movement and the Bible Society) were often favoured by evangelicals of other churches. Unsettling currents of religious thought poured over the walls of Quaker exclusiveness, giving rise to the belief that the early Friends had subordinated the Scriptures to 'man made testimonies' and mystical inspiration. Birth-right membership and the 'peculiarities' were sometimes described as 'formal religion' and compared unfavourably with the 'new birth' of conversion to 'vital Christianity'. The new influences were set forth most powerfully by J.J. Gurney (1788-1847), the banker turned theologian whose writings offered 'consistent Quakerism on an evangelical foundation' as the 'perfection of religion'. There were reports of crowded meetings listening to his addresses on the Scriptures, silent worship and the New Birth.(19)

Although there was no single moment of conversion when Sturge was won for evangelicalism, the turning point of his religious life occurred in 1813 when he was twenty. In that year he first heard the preaching of William Forster, a young Quaker minister who was then touring Gloucestershire and the surrounding counties. Deeply moved, Sturge interrupted his farming and spent some time travelling with him.(20) It was an experience he revered for the rest of his life. Like

Gurney, Forster combined the traditional Quaker belief in the 'inner light' with a high regard for evangelical spirituality, and his preaching dwelt powerfully on the great themes of evangelicalism - the primary of Scripture, man's fallen nature, Christ's atonement and the doctrine of justification by faith. This was not a tolerant creed. Within the Society of Friends Forster was the firm opponent of those who would have made Quakerism into 'a sort of spiritualized deism'; outside it he feared the growth of Unitarianism and religious infidelity. According to his own testimony, the religious opinions of Richard Carlile, the radical publisher, made him 'almost ill'.(21) Sturge's admiration for Forster and other evangelicals does much to explain why his career as a reformer philanthropist subsequently aroused animosities as well as admiration. Sturge's evangelical friends might see his life as 'a continuous illustration of the practical character of vital Christianity', but others recoiled from him as 'an intensely bigoted quaker of the Gurneyite school'.(22)

It was under evangelical inspiration that Sturge took his first steps into public life. In the same year that he came under Forster's influence he attended a meeting of the British and Foreign Bible Society in Bristol and became secretary of the Thornbury branch. This was a seminal experience, because, although the Bible Society had existed only since 1804, it was already well on the way to becoming the largest of the evangelical foundations in this 'the age of great societies'. Sturge was introduced there to the ways of the voluntary associations and pressure groups which would henceforward absorb so much of his life, and it was there too that he met evangelicals of other denominations whose visions of a regenerated social order went far beyond anything that could be achieved by the old-fashioned Quakerism of his boyhood. There 'is scarcely any species of misery', he wrote in his journal, 'but there is some charity open to relieve it; and may these charities continue to increase until misery and want are driven from our happy shores!'.(23)

His optimism should be placed in the context of the sermons which were delivered at evangelical meetings - sermons such as the one that was preached in 1812 to the Bristol branch of the British and Foreign Bible Society. Assuring his listeners that their efforts were hastening the day when Christ's 'sceptre of righteousness and love' would hold sway over 'a happy and an enlightened world', the preacher encouraged the Society's members to study scripture so that they could

> lift up the veil of futurity, and exhibit to view an auspicious day, when the knowledge of the glory of the Lord shall fill the whole earth - Its doctrines are adapted to relieve human misery in every form; and to heal all the diseases of the moral world. Its precepts impose a restraint upon the sensual, and the malevolent passions - inculcate universal benevolence - and extending their empire over the barriers which divide political states, tend to unite all mankind, as one happy family, in bonds of brotherly love.(24)

Both then and later this type of reform was sometimes seen as a mawkish substitute for secular radicalism - there was a shared

25

language of fraternity and social regeneration - but for people who took their Bible seriously it was an attractive ideology in its own right. Combining the ideals of self-help and Christian fellowship, it was carried forward on a surge of energy provided by post-millennial theology, the fashionable belief that the millennium of peace and prosperity foretold in the Bible would commence, not at some distant date with the Second Coming of Christ, but soon because of the labours of religious and benevolent societies.(25)

It was evangelicalism therefore, to a greater extent than the formal Quakerism imbibed in childhood, that imparted a sense of social purpose to the young man who settled at Bewdley between 1814 and 1822. In the few leisure hours left to him by his business and family responsibilities, Sturge no longer obtained a sense of achievement from hunting and country sports - compassion for animals was one of the evangelical virtues - he could be fulfilled only if he contributed to the triumph of Christian charity both at home and overseas. For his was never a version of the 'telescopic philanthropy' that Charles Dickens satirised in the person of Mrs Jellyby who always seemed to 'see nothing nearer than Africa'.(26) Shortly before Sophia joined him he drew up a paper entitled 'A proposed plan of life which I hope to pursue when I become a housekeeper on my own account'. There he carefully divided his time and income between commercial, family, religious and charitable commitments. Household expenses for the whole of the first four years were not to go beyond £1000, and after the needs of the business had been satisfied, any income was to be used for good causes rather than luxuries. He envisaged giving time to charity schools and money to the relief of the distressed. Although the plan broke down in the face of business failures at Bewdley, Sturge persisted with the general strategy, cutting his domestic expenditure to £100 p.a. for several years and even depriving himself of the occasional meal so that he could meet claims on his benevolence.(27) He was certainly speaking from experience when, towards the end of his life, he told the Friends' Yearly Meeting that early manhood was the time to catch 'the habit of charity'.(28)

NOTES

1. Sturge Papers (M. Sturge), Sophia Sturge to John Sturge, 5 November 1820.

2. E. Stirredge, Strength in Weakness, London 1795, p. 53.

3. W. Sturge, Some Recollections of a Long Life, Bristol 1893, p. 42.

4. 'The Borough' in The Poetical Works of George Crabbe, London 1858, p. 114.

5. A. Neave Brayshaw, The Quakers. Their Story and Message, London 1938, p. 180; Matilda Sturge, Types of Quaker Womanhood, London n.d., p. 8.

6. E. Isichei, Victorian Quakers, Oxford 1970, p. 66; Christian Advocate, 5 June 1837.

7. Inquirer, February 1839.

8. Christian Advocate, 23 May 1836; Thomas Pumphrey, 'Joseph

Sturge, The Christian Citizen. A Biographical Sketch', The Old Banner Essays, no. 6, n.d.

9. The statistics show a fall in membership from 18,040 in 1821 to 13,755 in 1864. See R. Currie, A. Gilbert & L. Horsley, Churches And Churchgoers. Patterns Of Church Growth In The British Isles Since 1700, Oxford 1977, p. 156.

10. G.E. Bryant, ed., A Quaker Journal Being the Diary and Reminiscences of William Lucas of Hitchin (1804-61). A Member of the Society of Friends, London 1934, vol. I, p. 185 and vol. II, p. 494.

11. Gloucestershire County Record Office, D 1340 A1/M3, A Record Of the Minutes and Transactions of the United Quarterly Meeting of Gloucester & Wilts. See, for example, the entries for 24 September 1793, 31 March 1807.

12. Sturge Letters (Marshall), Mary Sturge to Charles Sturge, 23 June 1817; Gloucestershire County Record Office, D 1340 A1/M4, An Account Of The Sufferings Of Friends Of The Quarterly Meeting of Glocester [sic] & Wilts (1793-1827).

13. As shown by Preparative, Monthly and Quarterly Meeting Minutes for 1823-59 held in the Bull Street Meeting House, Birmingham.

14. Pumphrey, 'Joseph Sturge'.

15. An Account of the Sufferings Of Friends of the Quarterly Meeting of Glocester & Wilts, entry for 16 April 1813; Annual Register, 1813, p. 202.

16. Bull Street Meeting House, An Account of the Sufferings Of Friends Of The North Monthly Meeting Of Warwickshire (1793-1872), entries between 1823 and 1858.

17. Birmingham Journal, 19 August 1857.

18. J.A. James, Christian Philanthropy: As Exemplified In The Life and Character of the Late Joseph Sturge, Esq. A Sermon Delivered in Carr's Lane Chapel on Sunday Morning, May 22, 1859, London 1859, p. 20.

19. B. Seebohm, ed., Memoirs of William Forster, London 1865, vol. II, p. 80; Christian Advocate, 16 April 1832.

20. Richard, Sturge, pp. 22-23.

21. Seebohm, Forster, vol. I, pp. 150, 184, 234-42, 381; A Tribute To The Memory Of The Late William Forster By One Who Honoured And Loved Him, London 1857, pp. 10-11.

22. Annual Monitor, 1860, p. 172; C. Taylor, British and American Abolitionists. An Episode In Transatlantic Understanding, Edinburgh 1974, p. 272, R.D. Webb to Maria Chapman, 16 July 1846.

23. Richard, Sturge, p. 21.

24. Proceedings Of The Public Meeting Held At the Guildhall, In The City Of Bristol, On Thursday, Feb. 13, 1812, Being The Second Anniversary Meeting Of The Bristol Auxiliary Bible Society, Bristol 1812, pp. 13-14.

25. G. Shepperson, 'The Comparative Study of Millenarian Movements' in S.L. Thrupp, ed., Millennial Dreams in Action. Studies in Revolutionary Religious Movements, New York 1970, p. 44.

26. Charles Dickens, Bleak House, London 1963, pp. 34-36.

27. Richard, Sturge, pp. 29-30; Pumphrey, 'Joseph Sturge'.

28. Friends House Library, London, MS Vol. S127, Joseph Rowntree's Yearly Meeting Notes and Diary, 1857.

3 The Businessman (1814-59)

Catching 'the habit of charity' in itself would have given Sturge no claim to fame; the national network of religious and benevolent societies was full of such people in his lifetime. His reputation was based on his wealth. 'Have you a California of your own', Richard Cobden asked him in 1857, 'or is the miracle of the widows cruise [sic] performed for you in sovereigns instead of oil, or how do you continue to give away five times more than other people, and still keep up your credit in Mark Lane?'.(1) California in this case was a commercial empire built around one of the largest corn importing businesses in mid-nineteenth Britain. It was new wealth, the product of a success story that could have found a place in Samuel Smiles's eulogies of the self-made man. Smiles never described Sturge's career, but a like-minded contemporary did not neglect the opportunity of teaching young men the lessons to be learned from this 'architect of his own fortune and renown' who had set out from a 'humble starting post' and triumphed over adversity by an 'industrious and persevering way of life'.(2)

Wisely the writer did not suggest that Sturge's choice of business showed an innovative spirit; for Quakers were so disproportionately represented in the corn trade that they had to defend themselves against charges of setting up a monopoly of scandalous proportions. 'The corn market in Mark -lane' wrote Robert Huish,

> without an abundance of broad-brimmed hats, unlappelled coats, buckled shoes, and the demure, sanctified, and hypocritical countenance of the quaker, would be as rare a sight, as the immediate purlieus of Westminster Hall during term time, without the cauliflower wigs, worsted gowns, red bags and blue bags of the hateful tribe of lawyers....the quakers have for a length of time had the controul of the corn market, and they can regulate its prices accordingly, as they have succeeded in producing a scarcity in the market by the power of their insatiable monopolising spirit.(3)

The commercial advantages of being a member of the Quaker 'cousinhood' were undeniable; all the same they offered no royal highway to success in the corn trade. Sturge's partnership with Henry Cotterel collapsed in 1817, and by 1822 he was facing bankruptcy.

Bewdley turned out to be an unsuitable base; formerly the bustling Severn port for the Midlands, it declined after the building of the Staffordshire and Worcestershire Canal.(4) The corn trade itself was such a fluctuating one that Sturge diversified into other commodities, notably coal, timber and provisions. In an attempt to exploit the differences between price levels in various corn markets he spent much of his time travelling by coach and on horseback to Shrewsbury, Gloucester, Bristol and further afield - to Chester, Liverpool, Manchester and London. But there was no escaping the vagaries of harvests and defaults by customers. In 1815-16 the partnership badly misjudged the state of the market; in 1816-17 depreciation of stock and bad debts ate into profits; and, although by 1820 prospects had improved to such an extent that Sturge could congratulate himself on increasing his property, 'having sailed as it were against wind & tide' for several years, this was only a respite. After a disastrous speculation at a time of low prices, he lost most of his capital in 1821. Seeing only one way out of his difficulties (this was also the time of his ill-fated engagement), he left the remnants of the business to Charles and moved to Birmingham for a fresh start in 1822. His losses had been so severe that for a time he had to take lodgings instead of maintaining an independent household.(5)

Sturge's first reaction to his new home was the conventional one: Birmingham was 'a smooky [sic] and dirty place', he told Sophia, but it had 'the credit of being a healthy one'.(6) His reasons for settling there must have seemed too obvious to mention; for the town was a rapidly expanding urban frontier where attitudes to business and money-making prompted contemporaries to think of America and (later) Australia. Its inhabitants, Alexis de Tocqueville wrote in 1835, 'work as if they must get rich by the evening and die the next day. They are generally very intelligent people, but intelligent in the American way'.(7) The smoke and dirt were created by the town's prospering hardware industries, but Birmingham was also a major agricultural entrepot with well-established markets including one for selling corn by sample, and it enjoyed the advantages of good communications by canal with other economic regions of England. Beginning with a wharf warehouse and a one room office, within eight years Sturge had turned these advantages to good account by creating a company with a capital of £22,000.(8) The family gathered around him again in these favourable circumstances. Sophia rejoined him at the house he took in Monument Lane and later accompanied him to the fashionable suburb of Edgbaston. She spent one morning a week book-keeping at the office. Soon John and another brother, Edmund, set up a chemical company in Birmingham, and after living for some time with Joseph and Sophia they settled as neighbours in Edgbaston. In 1831 Charles was brought to Birmingham as Joseph's partner, and their elder brother, Thomas Marshall Sturge, who had been bankrupted as a wool-stapler, was employed to manage a branch which was opened at Gloucester in 1829.(9)

It was a homely commercial enterprise in many ways, and during

the 1820s when Sturge was buying and selling at country markets it was
an unremarkable one, but with the opening of the Gloucester branch
and the conversion of the business into one where corn was imported on
commission the company rapidly expanded into an empire of impressive
scale, range and modernity. It is certainly a mistake to see Sturge as
one who held fast to old-fashioned rural values; his career supports the
proposition that 'childhood experiences...may limit, but they do not
determine. Freedom, imagination, will and chance are all at play
through life'.(10) Sturge never regretted leaving the land, and he took
to commerce with relish: 'I am perhaps too fond of it', he confessed in
1820.(11) By 1836 when he was interviewed by a House of Commons
Select Committee on Agriculture six-sevenths of the firm's
consignments came from Ireland. Subsequently he and Charles
imported extensively from the Baltic, from the Western Mediterranean
and from the Black Sea provinces of the Russian and Turkish Empires.
The height of the firm's prosperity seems to have been in 1850 when its
capital amounted to £47,564 and its name, according to an employee,
was well known in the great markets of 'Odessa, Paganrog [sic],
Marianople, Constantinople, Galatz and Ibrail'.(12) Sturge's Corn
Circular, a survey of marketing conditions which was usually compiled
under Joseph's personal supervision, became a work of reference in the
trade.
    The brothers always called themselves 'commission merchants'
thereby misleading historians who take this modest self-description at
face value;(13) for the management of their corn importing company
and much of the capital in it were inseparable from other major
economic enterprises. J. & C. Sturge pushed forward the development
of Gloucester, a significant inland port in their day thanks to the
Gloucester and Berkeley Canal which had cut the cost of goods in
transit to and from the Midlands by providing a connection with the
Bristol Channel for vessels of up to 700-800 tons. As early as 1829
Joseph built the first of his warehouses there. Soon he and Charles
bought substantial shareholdings in the Severn Navigation Company and
the Gloucester and Berkeley Canal Company. An article in Sturge's
Corn Circular shows their interlocking directorships at work, reducing
canal dues on corn shipments by 30% and building a railway siding on to
the Gloucester quayside for the direct transfer of cargoes. No wonder
it could be said that mid-nineteenth century Gloucester's prosperity
was dependent on J. & C. Sturge. An old corn porter would later
remember how he had 'once walked across ships from one side of the
dock to the other. The whole dock was wedged with shipping, and the
greater part of them were for J. & C. Sturge'.(14)
    The Sturges were prompt to see the importance of the new
railways as investments in their own right as well as for the rapid
transit of corn. Joseph and Charles put money into the Liverpool and
Manchester Railway, the first of the major lines, out of which they
were believed to have made a profit of £1000. At various times they,
together with John and Edmund, became directors of the Birmingham
and Gloucester Railway, the Birmingham and Bristol Railway, the
Midlands Railway, and the London and Birmingham Railway. A
statement by Charles that he and his 'personal connections' owned more

than one tenth of the Birmingham and Gloucester Company's shares in 1842 suggests that the family had learned the advantages of combining its investment strategy.(15) These were not sleeping partnerships. The Sturges were energetic capital raisers and managers, none more so than Charles who even won an honourable mention in a nineteenth-century tribute to business enterprise by travelling with his engineers during the trials of experimental railway engines on the troublesome inclines of the Bromsgrove section of the Gloucester line.(16)

It comes as a surprise therefore to find references in Sturge's letters to a sense of uneasiness about his life as a businessman. The 'temptations to wider business & speculation in the Corn Trade are very great', he told Charles in 1856, 'and the results generally disasterous [sic] and the moral effects when pecuniarily successful of greatly fluctuating incomes mostly bad'.(17) In an earlier letter he had even despaired of making 'reparation to Society and those still connected with us by exhibiting an example of true moderation in Trade (not living to trade but trading to live) and conducting the business on the principle of strict Xtian equity and uprightness'.(18) His misgivings probably owed something to the traditional unpopularity of middle men who came between the farmer and the consumer. Feelings ran high against corn merchants during Sturge's lifetime, and there were attempts to discredit him as a public man by denouncing him as a speculator who had battened on the needs of an immiserated people.(19) Reasonably enough, Sturge defended his trade as an essential service to the nation - even in one of his most self-critical letters he could write that 'there are few businesses more legitimate or perhaps useful'(20) - but there is no doubt that he was associated with dubious practices. George Griffith, one of his employees, described an attempt in 1832 by 'a coalition of the corn merchants in various English ports' to raise the price of English wheat by buying up supplies which were then very cheap. In accordance with the Corn Law sliding scale this would have had the effect of increasing prices and lowering the duty on foreign wheat, making it possible for the engrossers at one and the same time to make an easy profit and expand their business as importers. Like similar manoeuvres that may be assumed to have occurred, this one would probably have gone unrecorded if the £1000 which Sturge had sent to the Croppers of Liverpool as his share of the risk capital had not been embezzled by a clerk.(21)

Sturge's sense of guilt was increased by the strict standards that the Society of Friends imposed on its members, and he had reason for knowing the consequences of violating them. In 1807, when he was thirteen, one of his uncles had been stripped of his eldership after what seems to have been a most un-Quakerly series of disputes, judgements and appeals culminating in a decision by the Yearly Meeting that his speculations had gone beyond his means and were therefore improper.(22) In 1825 the Society issued an unmistakable warning to men of his sort:(23)

if any, whether of the more affluent, or of those who cannot be ranked in this class, are deviating from safe and regular methods of business, if they are carried away by uncertain and hazardous,

31

though plausible schemes for getting rich, if they yield to a desire rapidly to enlarge their possessions - such are in imminent danger.

This contrast between 'safe and regular methods of business' and 'hazardous though plausible schemes for getting rich' implicitly pointed the finger of accusation at Sturge himself; for the two principal sources of his wealth were among the most speculative in the business world. Varying harvests, political convulsions in the countries of supply and the tariff sliding scale made the corn trade a by-word for quick profits and catastrophic failures. As for railways, their appeal to the early Victorian imagination no less than to the profit motive gave rise to investment fluctuations of manic intensity. Sturge's search for a standard of business morality took him beyond his company's affairs. He came to believe that a legitimate business was one where the temptation to speculate was reined in and where private enterprise served the general good. Called before the Select Committee on Agriculture in 1836 he blamed the sliding scale for contributing to the fluctuations that drove prudent men away from the corn factor's trade and injured the interests of all sections of the community; free trade on the other hand would have 'a tendency to keep things more steady'. Years later, when the corn laws had been repealed, he was described as rejoicing in the freedom to deal in 'a regular article of consignment ... like other mechandise' instead of seeing his company used by 'a wild set of Corn Gamblers'.(24) The same moral objection brought him to his feet in railway board rooms to protest against fellow directors when their share dealings made a mockery of his own belief that the railway companies should act as 'trustees of great public interests'. At a meeting of the Birmingham and Gloucester Railway Company in 1845 it was reported that:(25)

He (Mr Sturge) had been very much grieved to see the gambling turn which the share market had taken and which could not fail eventually to fall heavy upon some parties. He believed if there was one man who ought to be more careful than another in selling shares, it was the director of a public company, and he wished to take that opportunity of impressing it upon directors, that if in their situation they gained information which others could not have access to, they ought not to use it to their own gain and the injury of others. Such conduct could not be considered the act of an honourable and honest man.

But first and foremost Sturge salved his conscience by setting down a code of regulations for his own behaviour as a businessman. The housekeeping plan which he drew up after his arrival in Bewdley was the earliest version, and others survive from the 1840s and 1850s. Essentially the later ones were summaries and adaptations of the Christian Advices issued by the Friends' Yearly Meeting: 'trading to live, not living to trade'; managing a mercantile concern with usefulness rather than pecuniary gain as the principal object; never encouraging others to take risks by renewing bills or giving loans that exceeded their resources; avoiding speculations that put others' property at risk; never allowing business to crowd out the higher duties of life; neither hoarding wealth nor using it for selfish gratification; leading a 'plain life'; and avoiding extravagant hospitality. The code made much of philanthropy as the businessman's defence against mammon. Wealth would corrupt its creators and destroy the next generation: Christians should therefore regard themselves as stewards of their wealth, withdrawing from business as soon as possible and dedicating themselves to religion and benevolence.(26)

Sturge was fortunate therefore that his brother was willing to assume responsibility for day-to-day management of the partnership in 1831. The division of responsibilities between the two was never complete; Charles entered public life in his own right, most notably as a Birmingham town councillor, and Joseph retained an important financial and personal connection with the firm's management. But it was understood that Joseph's priorities would be religious and philanthropic. The arrangement brought its own problems; for Joseph's letters show that he worried about the effects of mammon on Charles and on Charles's sons after they joined the business. A swashbuckling capitalist if ever one existed (his seal bore the appropriate motto 'Acta Non Verba') Charles preferred grand speculative gestures to the painstaking chores of administration, and with good reason Joseph was often appalled by his partner's 'almost entire ignorance of the state of many heavy accounts'. Between 1831 and 1851 £150,000 were lost in bad debts.(27) Joseph's letters (he felt so strongly that he could not speak to Charles on several occasions) show him setting down rules and threatening to break off the partnership.(28) But though Charles might be briefly restrained, he could not be reformed. In 1847 only a loan raised from a consortium of Quaker businessmen saved J. & C. Sturge from bankruptcy, and according to Charles's son, bad management was responsible for the decline after Joseph's death that led to the firm's collapse in 1886.(29)

One of the most serious disputes between the brothers points to the growing importance of moral considerations in Sturge's business philosophy. Joseph became a teetotaler and he refused to supply grain distilleries, sell malt or rent his warehouses to wine and spirit merchants. Finally, in 1844, as a result of his ever-deepening convictions, he refused to be associated with any further sales of malting barley. Charles was a teetotaler too, but the drink trade was an important customer for corn merchants, and he disagreed with Joseph so heatedly that he believed they had dissolved the partnership. Eventually, with some persuasion from his wife, Charles gave way, and the Mark Lane dealers were informed of the decision.(30) Conduct such as this weakens the claim that commercial vested interests were the real driving forces in Sturge's public life: no vested interest could have placed much reliance on a man with such an inconvenient conscience.(31) Conversely it shows that Sturge's vision of himself as a 'Christian Philanthropist' must be taken seriously; for this was only one of several instances where his good causes acquired a momentum that took him against the conventional business practices of the day.

Doing 'all to the Glory of God and making it [business] subservient not to any selfish purpose but to the moral and religious improvement as well as the temporal comfort of all connected with it':(32) Sturge's prescription for labour relations was another example of his search for business legitimacy. His attitude seems to have mellowed over the years; for at first he was a strenuous task master. One of the firm's clerks (c. 1830) was surprised to find that 'the hours were both early and late: six o'clock in the morning until eight at night with two hours and a half allowed for breakfast, dinner and tea times. The master himself was as punctual as clock-work at these hours and sometimes stayed later at night to write his letters'.(33) Years later in a speech to the Birmingham Association for the Abridgement of the Hours of Labour (a movement which tried to persuade shopkeepers and other businessmen to close voluntarily at an earlier hour) Sturge confessed that he had not always agreed with their principles but had seen the error of his ways: now he honoured 'the maxim that property had its duties as well as its rights' and rejoiced that it 'was being more and more recognised, better understood, and more generally acted upon'.(34) In his case the maxim produced an interesting blend of paternalism and the self-help temperance ethic. On the one hand, he took a great deal of trouble to establish a face-to-face relationship with the eighty men whom he employed at Gloucester, even visiting them at home on occasions of illness and bereavement: on the other, he tried to employ only teetotalers. He even devised a teetotal version of the annual feasts which Victorian employers commonly offered their employees. On these occasions Sturge and specially invited speakers addressed the workers and their families on temperance and related themes such as 'economy' and 'keeping out of debt'; employees were presented with bookcases, and over the years they were given books to build up a library.(35)

There is no saying how far these attitudes were reciprocated by the employees. J.C. Stone, a member of the office staff, wrote that Sturge was 'among my Dearest and best Friends'; Herbert Spencer who was briefly employed in the Sturge business empire during the mid-1840s always remembered him as a kind and considerate man; and when Sturge died his employees drew up a public testimonial.(36) But other evidence suggests that the appearance of appreciative deference sometimes concealed less acceptable truths. Posters had to be put up threatening the firm's Gloucester workers with dismissal if they were found asking for money or drink; in 1841 Thomas Marshall Sturge was shocked to discover that one of their steadiest men was keeping a beer shop and dismissed him; and two years later another of their longest serving workers confessed that he had been keeping a cider shop to raise extra money after his wife and children had suffered serious illnesses. He was dismissed too, a decision that influenced Sturge to stop his own dealing in malting barley.(37) It is all very inconclusive. The discipline was severe and the paternalism which tempered it was intrusive, but Victorian expectations were different from our own. Historians have even referred to the widespread belief in these rights and duties as a contribution to the social harmony which characterised many cities in mid-nineteenth century Britain.(38)

NOTES

1. British Lib. Add MSS. 43722, ff. 243-4, Richard Cobden to Joseph Sturge, 20 May 1857.
2. Pumphrey, 'Joseph Sturge'.
3. R. Huish, The History of the Private and Political Life of Henry Hunt Esq. MP for Preston, his times and contemporaries, London 1835, vol. I, pp. 100-101.
4. C.W.F. Garrett, 'Bewdley And The Stinking Ditch. An Exposition' in L.S. Snell ed., Essays Towards A History Of Bewdley, np.nd., p. 11. George Griffith's memoir, Going To Markets And Grammar Schools, London 1971, pp. 12-13, suggests that the decline has been exaggerated. Griffith was one of Sturge's clerks.
5. This account of Sturge's business activities in Bewdley has been constructed from the series of letters in Sturge Letters (Marshall) and Sturge Papers (M. Sturge) between 1814 and 1822. See also C.D. Sturge's MS. account, Joseph & Charles Sturge in Sturge Papers (Lewin). C.D. Sturge was Joseph's nephew and a partner in the business for many years.
6. Sturge Papers (M. Sturge), Joseph to Sophia Sturge, 27 October 1822.
7. Alexis de Tocqueville, Journeys To England And Ireland, New York 1968, p. 82.
8. C.D. Sturge, Joseph & Charles Sturge.
9. The Sturge Family records many of the activities of Sturge's brothers and sisters at this time.
10. B. Crick, George Orwell: A Life, Harmondsworth 1980, p. 32, and Introduction footnote 22.
11. Sturge Papers (M. Sturge), Joseph Sturge to John Sturge, 11 October 1820.
12. Second Report From The Select Committee [Of The House of Commons] Appointed To Inquire Into The State Of Agriculture; With The Minutes of Evidence, and Appendix, 1836, p. 161; C.D. Sturge, Joseph & Charles Sturge; Sturge papers (M. Sturge), Joseph Lamb to the editor of the Morning News (newscutting), 11 September 1875. Lamb was employed by J. & C. Sturge for 47 years.
13. For example, E. Sager, 'The Social Origins of Victorian Pacifism', Victorian Studies, Winter 1980, pp. 216-17, who refers to Sturge as 'conditioned by the experience of life in a small-town nonindustrial social order', because he spent part of his childhood on a farm.
14. C.D. Sturge, Joseph & Charles Sturge; J & C Sturge's Corn Circular, 12 February 1845; Sturge Papers (M. Sturge), Birmingham Gazette, 20 January 1887 (news cutting).
15. Sturge Papers (M. Sturge), Joseph Sturge to John Acton, 6 December 1824 and later note to this letter, and letter from Charles Sturge to an unnamed newspaper (news cutting), 2 February 1842. References to the Sturge directorships are scattered through the Birmingham press.
16. F.S. Williams, The Midland Railway: Its Rise and Progress. A Narrative of Modern Enterprise, London 1877, p. 77.

17. Sturge Papers (M. Sturge), Joseph Sturge to Charles Sturge, 1856.

18. Sturge Papers (M. Sturge), Joseph Sturge to Charles Sturge, 2 October 1851.

19. See, for example, Leeds Mercury, 12 June 1847.

20. Sturge Papers (M. Sturge), Joseph Sturge to Charles Sturge, 19 May 1849.

21. Griffith, Going to Markets, pp. 61-62; Sturge Papers (M. Sturge), Thomas Marshall Sturge to Charles Sturge, 3 September 1832; Henry E. Huntingdon Library, The Macaulay Papers, Margaret Cropper to Hannah Macaulay, 18 February, 13 March, 18 March, 20 March 1834.

22. Pen Pictures of London Yearly Meeting 1789-1833 Being The Notes of Richard Cockin, supplemented by those of James Jenkins and others, London 1929, pp 107-109.

23. Epistles From The Yearly Meeting of Friends, vol. II, p. 212.

24. Second Report From the Select Committee etc., 1836, pp. 162, 163, 166, 170, 172; Sturge Papers (M. Sturge), Thomas Marshall Sturge to Charles Sturge, 27 May 1848.

25. Birmingham Journal, 8 March 1845.

26. The code was set out in a series of letters from Sturge to his brother Charles and to his nephews C.D. Sturge and Wilson Sturge: Sturge Papers (M. Sturge), Memorandum from Joseph Sturge to Charles Sturge [1830s]; Joseph Sturge to Charles Sturge, 2 August 1844; Joseph Sturge to Charles Sturge, 6 March 1847; Joseph Sturge to Charles Sturge, 19 May 1849; Joseph Sturge to Charles Sturge, 2 October 1851; Memorandum from Joseph Sturge to Charles Sturge [1856]. See also Sturge Papers (Lewin), Joseph Sturge to Charles Dickinson Sturge [1850s] and Sturge Papers (P.A.J. Sturge), Joseph Sturge to Wilson Sturge, 13 May 1859.

27. Sturge Papers (M. Sturge), Joseph Sturge to Charles Sturge, 19 May 1849, and Joseph Sturge to Charles Sturge, 2 October 1851.

28. Letters cited in footnote 26.

29. C.D. Sturge, Joseph & Charles Sturge.

30. Sturge Papers (M. Sturge), Joseph Sturge to Robert Nevins, 5 November 1844 (news cutting); Mary Darby Sturge to Charles Sturge, three letters, n.d.

31. cf. Williams, Capitalism and Slavery, pp. 158, 210-11.

32. Sturge Papers (M. Sturge), Joseph Sturge to Charles Sturge, 2 August 1844.

33. Griffith, Going to Markets, p. 12.

34. Birmingham Journal, 8 May 1847.

35. Pumphrey, 'Joseph Sturge'; Sturge Papers (M. Sturge), Birmingham Gazette, 20 January 1887 (news cutting).

36. Sturge Papers (M. Sturge) J.C. Stone to Joseph Sturge, 27 July 1835; Spencer, Autobiography, vol. I, pp. 251-52; Richard, Sturge, p. 607.

37. Sturge Papers (M. Sturge), Thomas Marshall Sturge to Charles Sturge, 13 January 1840, Thomas Marshall Sturge to Charles Sturge, 5 October 1843 and Joseph Sturge to Charles Sturge, 2 October 1851.

38. Tholfsen, Working Class Radicalism, chap. 7.

PART 2

BREAKING THROUGH

4 Citizen of Birmingham (1822-30)

Birmingham provided Sturge with a wider field for his religious and civic interests as well as his business ambitions. In comparison with Bewdley where he had found a disused meeting house, he now attended one of the largest Quaker meetings in the country, and the records for his district show that he was soon holding offices in the Society of Friends as a member of various committees and a representative of his Monthly Meeting.(1) They also make it clear that he was not impressed by the quality of religious life amongst the Birmingham Quakers, who had long ago settled into a comfortable routine as befitted one of the wealthiest groups in the town. According to a story told much later, Sturge quickly reached the same conclusion as the passer-by whom he once observed mockingly counting the number of carriages and pairs lined up outside the Bull Street meeting house awaiting 'the self denying Quakers'. He was so incensed on learning that wealthy Friends were paying tithes and church rates rather than suffer distraints of their goods that within a year of reaching Birmingham he became the driving force in a committee which interviewed the deviants and secured their disownment.(2)

The transactions of the reading circle which he joined in April 1823 reveal some of his interests during these years. The Birmingham Friends Book Society was a group of twenty-five men and women who subscribed to a fund for buying books and periodicals with each member having the right to nominate titles for purchase. Unlike Sturge's brothers and sisters at Bewdley, they complied strictly with the official warnings against unsuitable literature, and there was a pervasive earnestness which was neatly summarised by the title of one of the books suggested by Sturge - The Art of Improving Time. Most of Sturge's recommendations were travellers' descriptions of distant parts of the world, and he nominated several memoirs, works on religion and collections of poetry (Specimens of American Poets and Poetic Vigils). His choices also included a scattering of titles ranging from A History or Description of Active and Extinct Volcanoes to Death Bed Scenes. His evangelicalism was shown by his nomination of J.J. Gurney's Letter on Christianity and his humanitarianism by titles such as Suttee's Cry to Britain.(3)

One of the books Sturge recommended, Samuel Wilderspin's Infant

Schools, bore testimony to his rapidly acquired interest in the social problems of Birmingham. The town had long suffered from an unenviable reputation: it was the devil's 'nursery-garden and hothouse', Robert Southey had written in 1807, a place of 'infernal noises' and 'infernal fires' where filth had become 'a living principle of mischief' and the population had been 'poisoned soul and body'.(4) But the bleakest aspects of industrial and urban change were only becoming apparent when Sturge settled there in 1822. At the turn of the century Birmingham still had some of the characteristics of a country town, and its inhabitants preserved many values and behaviour patterns from the rural culture of the past. S.J Pratt, a writer who took an interest in the manufacturing population, was one of the few early nineteenth-century visitors to see this. From a vantage point overlooking the town centre he watched the inhabitants of the surrounding villages streaming in on market day and concluded that it was here that town and country found a harmonious 'balance'. Within easy walking distance he was delighted to find a large expanse of allotments ('guinea gardens') girdling the town with 'a zone of vegetable beauty' where artisans raised flowers and vegetables amidst 'a Chinese view' of summer houses. Less enthusiastically, he also noted the robust pastimes of a district notorious for bull-baiting and other blood sports.(5)

All this was changing swiftly while Sturge lived in Birmingham. Between 1801 and 1831 the population doubled; it doubled again between 1841 and 1871. Workshops and working-class housing absorbed available building sites and sprawled far over the boundaries of the parish. In 1828 a popular song entitled 'I Can't Find Brummagem' described the puzzlement of a Birmingham man on returning home after an absence of twenty years:(6)

> But every place is altered so,
> There's hardly a single place I know.

It was a sign of the times when a public meeting was called in 1834 to encourage cricket, racket and other games because the 'guinea gardens' had been built over and there was no place in the town for 'manly exercises'. Soon contemporaries were lamenting the rise of gin palaces and beer shops, seemingly at every corner, as evidence of a deterioration of the popular culture.(7) Meanwhile the wealthier inhabitants were moving out to 'spruce and snug villas' in nearby Edgbaston, the fashionable suburb that had been protected by legal covenant against commercial development and low cost housing. It was there, as soon as his business fortunes allowed, that Sturge built Southfield in Wheeley's Road for Sophia and any brothers and sisters who chose to follow them. Although he did not live ostentatiously, the days of bread and cheese in a 'barn' were over; visitors to his home referred with pleasure to the carefully cultivated 'wilderness' of his extensive garden and to the sitting rooms that gave on to a conservatory 'brilliant with pink and yellow azalias, golden calceolarias, and a profusion of other beauties'.(8)

But Birmingham was never abandoned to its own devices by a middle class of the type that Friedrich Engels would soon claim to have seen in Manchester, commuting from the desirable suburbs to 'their places of business, without ever seeing that they are in the midst of the grimy misery that lurks to the right and the left'(9) The town had shared the spirit of urban improvement during the eighteenth century, and it experienced a surge of the civic pride that was characteristic of the nineteenth. Writers of guide books told the truth, if not the whole truth, when they pointed to its cultural life, its wide array of religious, philanthropic and educational institutions, and the improvements in its architecture and thoroughfares.(10) The poor were not forgotten; at a time when the regulation of social problems by government was often inhibited by laissez-faire theories and fears of 'Old Corruption', Birmingham was full of voluntary societies and schemes for creating a new social order. 'The March of Mind' was one of the catchcries of the 1820s, and there was a strong enthusiasm for popular education on the part of progressives and radicals. Sturge was soon attracted to two of the most typical experiments of the decade. In September 1825, with his brother John, he was elected to a committee that was planning an infant school for the children of working mothers; during the same month he joined a provisional committee that was set up to provide Birmingham with a Mechanics' Institute where working men could enrol for lectures relevant to their trades and enjoy access to a reading room with facilities for scientific demonstrations.

Sturge brought Wilderspin's <u>Infant Schools</u> to the attention of the Birmingham Friends Book Society at this time, and it was the author's school at Spitalfields in London that the committee members of the Birmingham Infant School Society took as their model. For Wilderspin seemed to have found the remedy for a problem that was causing considerable anxiety at this time - the collapse, as it was described, of the working-class family in large towns where mothers had gone out to work, leaving their children to run wild in the streets or otherwise grow up under inadequate supervision. Under his guidance the Birmingham committee proposed to set up a large airy apartment and playground where suitable teachers could take charge of children between the ages of two and six years of age during parental working hours. Although their first plans allowed for an enrolment of only 150 to 200 children, the committee also spoke of building a Lancasterian girls' school on the same site and using the combined facilities for an extensive programme of Sunday school education. Ambitiously, they even looked forward to the time when the venture would develop into a model school where teachers would be trained for other infant schools in the district.(11) The same spirit could be seen in reports projecting the Birmingham Mechanics' Institute as a means of complementing this elementary education and providing the poor with a ladder of opportunity stretching all the way from nursery school to night classes for the vocational training of adults.(12)

The two ventures exhibited a mixture of motives that was typical of the 1820s: an alloy of high-mindedness and the baser metal of social control. Wilderspin was exerting a beneficial influence on contemporary educational philosophy and practice by calling much-needed attention to the physical health and mental well-being of young children. The playground was one of the most important features of his school, and he has been described as the founder of 'a network of several hundred infant schools which were, at their best, the most advanced and sophisticated educational institutions in England'. Like him, the committee of the Birmingham Infant School presented themselves first and foremost as a group of enlightened realists who understood the harsh economic facts that drove so many mothers into the labour force, and they pointedly refused to join in the chorus of condemnation that was often directed against working-class parents. Their school, it was emphasised, was to be no place of 'confinement' for the children of the poor.(13) As for the Mechanics' Institutes, they were exactly the form of worker education to be expected from men such as Sturge who had flocked to lectures and joined associations such as the Bristol Endeavour Society in the belief that science was the most fitting pursuit for 'an intellectual being'.

    None of this absolves Sturge and his associates from the charge that they were social engineers frankly intent on making over society in accordance with their own values. The mechanical metaphor used by the Infant School Committee says it all: schools must be 'engines of intellectual and moral culture', where teachers would preside over 'a scene ... of activity and amusement, of intellectual improvement and moral discipline'. From there, as if by an extension of the monitorial sytem that was often used in the schools of that day, the children would carry home to their unenlightened parents the lessons of 'cleanliness and decorum, of cheerful and ready subordination, of courtesy, kindness and forbearance and of abstinence from everything impure or profane'.(14) Likewise, members of the Mechanics Institute Committee were not content with offering science lectures. They wanted to destroy 'idle and sensuous habits', develop skills and inventiveness, and inform working men of 'the mutual rights and interests of themselves and their employers'. In other words, Sturge and his associates were teaching the ideal of self-improvement within the competitive market economy of the emergent capitalist system.(15)

    By the late 1820s it was a measure of Sturge's involvement in the affairs of his adopted town that he was invited to join the Commissioners of the Street Act, the most important instrument of local government in Birmingham. It was also a measure of his growing wealth; for Commissioners had to be assessed to the poor's rate at £15 p.a. and possess property valued at 1000.(16) Like other towns which had developed during the previous two centuries, Birmingham had no town council - its eighteenth-century historian had rejoiced to be free from the Corporations that acted elsewhere as a 'shackle' on new men and new ideas(17) - but under a series of Acts of Parliament dating from 1769 the Street Commissioners were empowered to collect rates and provide a variety of services such as street lighting and the regulation of the markets. Although the members were co-opted, not elected, they were described as a good cross-section of religious and political opinion in the town, and Sturge was serving with them in 1828 when a new Act gave them the authority to levy a rate for their most ambitious project so far, the building of a Town Hall.(18) The conjuncture was unfortunate for him. At the very moment when he seemed to be entering the urban elite, the terms of the Act provoked him into launching a moral crusade that set him against the civic pride of Birmingham and earned him a reputation as a fanatic.

Sturge took his stand, not against the building of a public hall with ratepayers' money, but against the section of the Act designating the Town Hall as the venue for the music festivals that were held triennially in Birmingham. The damage he was inflicting on his reputation can be appreciated only when it is realised how important a contribution these festivals had made to Birmingham life since they began in 1784. By the 1820s, not only did they constitute the largest single source of funds for one of the town's principal charities, the General Hospital, but they were also major cultural events in their own right. They brought eminent musicians to Birmingham; they were presided over by noblemen; bishops preached opening sermons; and in 1826 George IV himself headed the official list of patrons. In short, they provided townsmen with an effective answer to anyone who echoed Southey's gibe they were all 'train-oil and emery'. Now, thanks to the 1828 Act, the festivals were to be set free from the cramped facilities provided by St. Philip's Church and provided with an architectural setting worthy of the town's cultural aspirations. Modelled on the Temple of Jupiter Stator in Rome, the Town Hall was to be one of the largest and finest public halls in Europe, where the choral works beloved by contemporaries would receive the backing of an organ that had no equal anywhere. The 1834 festival, the first to take place there, was nothing short of a triumph, according to reports which referred to a remarkable outburst of emotion during the performance of Handel's Messiah, the traditional climax of the programme:[19]

> The audience rose as one mass, silent, breathless, and expectant, awaiting the first grand burst of this imperishable monument of greatness. All that knowledge, power and precision could do was done - the shout of hundreds, the blast of trumpets, the deep-toned diapason of the organ, the thunder of the drums, conspired to fill the mind with such overwhelming and indescribable sensations, that most trembled, while many wept as children, so uncontrollable were their feelings.

Obviously, Sturge was setting himself against a powerful current of opinion in 1829 when he condemned the Hospital Music Committee's rights to use the Town Hall and persisted with his opposition in 1834 and 1837. His defence that he was subordinating self-interest to moral principle did not rest on the Quaker teaching that music was 'unfavourable to the health of the soul'.[20] Sturge came forward to lead an interdenominational evangelical pressure group consisting of a few Quakers and some prominent local clergymen including the Rev Thomas Moseley (Anglican), the Revs Thomas Swan and Thomas Morgan (Baptist) and the Rev J.A. James (Congregationalist). Bibliolatrists to a man, they condemned the singing of Scriptural words for recreation as a 'profanation': using tracts, the newspaper press and petitions, they waged a vigorous campaign to discredit the idea that any Christian could approve of oratorios or sanction a rate-supported 'musical hall' where actors and actresses ('sometimes of exceptionable character') could turn God's word into an entertainment. 'The excitement of the Festival is over', Sturge informed his fellow-townsmen in 1834:

> retire now to your closets, and with that sacred volume before you, from which the most momentous truths have been extracted, to be sung for your amusement, by actors and actresses, and to be mixed up in the same entertainment with the fancy ball, and the songs and glees of the stage, ask yourselves the question, whether while believing your eternal happiness to depend upon your personal interest in the death and sufferings of your Redeemer, you can stand guiltless in the sight of God, for the sanction and encouragement you have given to the prostitution of this infinitely solemn subject.

It was in vain that he tried to raise a voluntary subscription for the Hospital and that he asked his fellow Street Commissioners to seek the repeal only of those sections of the Act referring to the festivals; his motion was not even seconded. In 1830 he resigned to endure distraint of his goods rather than pay the rate. During the bitter exchanges that took place at this time Sturge confessed that large sections of the middle and upper classes were opposed to him and that he had been badly shaken by the reprimands he had received from people he respected.(21) Evangelical opinion was divided on the subject of oratorios, and, if William Wilberforce could allow his son to attend one, it is not difficult to understand why a journalist could conclude that the agitation against the Birmingham festivals was conducted by 'fanatics ... [with] bad heads or bad hearts'.(22)

The controversy foreshadowed some of the most important features of Sturge's involvement in public life during the next three decades. He would never be comfortable in any role where he was accountable to a diverse constituency of opinion; he could be a pressure group leader (a 'faddist' to use the Victorian term) - not a politician, public office-bearer or credible spokesman for a class. The satisfaction he derived from public life would often have to come, not from the successful implementation of specific proposals, but from the consistency with which he upheld his moral values.

NOTES

1. Bull Street Meeting House, Preparative Meeting Book, 1807-26, vol. 3; Monthly Meeting Minutes, North Division, 1822-27, vol. 15; Quarterly Meeting Minutes, 1819-36, vol. 7.

2. Bull Street Meeting House, C.D. Sturge's Notebook & Scrapbook, vol. 1, p. 247 and vol. 2, p. 3.

3. Friends Book Society, Birmingham, Minutes 1822-30.

4. Robert Southey, Letters from England, London 1951, p. 197.

5. S.J. Pratt, Harvest-Home: consisting of supplementary gleanings, original dramas and poems, contributions of literary friends, etc., London 1805, vol. 1, pp. 255-58, 276-77; S.J. Pratt, Local and Literary Account Of Leamington, Warwick, Stratford, Coventry,

Kenilworth, Hagley, the Lesowes, Birmingham, And The Surrounding Country, Birmingham 1814, p. 163.

6. R. Palmer, ed., A Touch On The Times, Harmondsworth 1974, pp. 78-79.

7. J.A. Langford, A Century Of Birmingham Life, Birmingham 1868, vol. 2, p. 611; Birmingham Journal, 25 July 1835; Reformer, 7 January, 3 March 1836.

8. The Picture of Birmingham, Birmingham 1831, p. 13; H.B. Stowe, Sunny Memories of Foreign Lands, London 1854, pp. 141, 185; Grace Greenwood, Haps and Mishaps Of A Tour in Europe, Boston 1854, p. 10.

9. F. Engels, The Condition of the Working-Class in England From Personal Observation and Authentic Sources, Moscow 1973, p. 78.

10. For example, An Historical And Descriptive Sketch Of Birmingham; With Some Account Of Its Environs, etc., Birmingham, 1830.

11. Birmingham Public Library, Birmingham Scrap Book, vol. III, 'Birmingham Infant School, Report of First Anniversary Meeting, 10 October 1826', and 'Rules of the Birmingham Infant School 1826'. By 1831 three other schools had been formed, and six teachers were in training for infant schools in the district. See Sixth Annual Report Of The Birmingham Infant School Society, Birmingham 1831. The Minutes of the Society show that Sturge was actively involved in the affairs of the Infant School until March 1858.

12. Aris's Birmingham Gazette, 3 October 1825.

13. P. McCann & F.A. Young, Samuel Wilderspin and the Infant School Movement, London 1982, Introd. & pp. 21-26, 164; Aris's Birmingham Gazette, 12 September, 26 September 1825.

14. Aris's Birmingham Gazette, 12 September 1825.

15. Ibid., 3 October 1825.

16. Ibid., 14 March 1825.

17. W. Hutton, A History Of Birmingham, Wakefield 1976, p. 328.

18. Langford, A Century Of Birmingham Life, vol. 2, pp. 445-46.

19. The Birmingham General Hospital and Triennial Musical Festivals, Birmingham n.d.; Southey, p. 197; The Stranger's Guide To Modern Birmingham, With An Account Of Its Public Buildings and Institutions, Its Show Rooms And Manufactories, Birmingham n.d., p. 84.

20. A Selection From The Christian Advices Issued By The Yearly Meeting Of The Society Of Friends, Held In London, London 1851, p. 279.

21. Sturge's involvement in the anti-oratorio campaign is described in the following: Langford, vol. 2, pp. 481-82; Newscuttings Relating to Birmingham, vol. 2, 'Joseph Sturge, To The Commissioners of the Birmingham Street Act', 28 April 1830; ibid., 'Birmingham Oratorio', n.d.; ibid., Joseph Sturge, 'Birmingham Musical Festival', 20 October 1834; Birmingham Journal, 1 May, 8 May 1830, 27 September, 4 October 1834; Birmingham Public Library, Extracts From Minutes Of Street Commissioners Relating To The Building Of The Birmingham Town Hall, typescript 1934; Philanthropist, 21 September 1837.

22. A.M. Wilberforce, ed., Private Papers of William Wilberforce, New York n.d., p. 184; True Sun, 20 September 1837.

5 The Rise of the Abolitionist Storming Party (1823-33)

Joseph Sturge was always a man of many good causes, but if there was one that sometimes looked as if it might crowd out the others during the 1820s it was anti-slavery. There was nothing to suggest that this would happen when he arrived in Birmingham in 1822. Apart from a letter in which his brother John had welcomed Bonaparte's decision to suppress the French slave trade in 1814, his family's correspondence during the Bewdley years had made no reference to the subject.(1) Slave holding had long provided grounds for disownment in the Society of Friends, so that in a general sense the Sturges would have taken their anti-slavery sympathies for granted, and they had grown up at a time when there was little opportunity to participate in an abolitionist movement. In 1791 and 1792 William Wilberforce and other anti-slavery leaders had appealed with some success for public support, but after the French wars broke out in 1793 they concentrated on winning votes in parliament, a strategy that was rewarded by the banning of the British slave trade in 1807. Although the status of those who were already slaves was not altered by this legislation, public interest subsided for fifteen years.(2) It was not until 1823 that the situation was transformed by the founding of the Anti-Slavery Society (its full title was 'The Society for the Mitigation and Gradual Abolition of Slavery throughout the British Dominions') and the commencement of the campaign that led up to the Act of Emancipation in 1833.

Many years later in the course of a speech to the British and Foreign Anti-Slavery Society, Edmund Sturge looked back to this time:(3)

> My early interest in the Anti-Slavery cause was due to my residing in the family of my brother, the late JOSEPH STURGE when, as early as 1824, the agitation was commenced for the extinction of British Colonial Slavery. Most fearful were, humanly speaking, the odds against it, and very fanatical it seemed. The West India body were dominant in Parliament, and controlled every Ministry .... [Wilberforce and the anti-slavery leaders] confined themselves to the ameliorating of the Slave's condition, and discouraged the advocacy of a present emancipation.

The statement bears testimony to Joseph's influence within his family circle: its implication that he was pressing for a 'present emancipation' in 1824 is less credible. The reality was that for several years after 1823 'emancipation' had no commonly agreed meaning and that terms such as 'present' or 'immediate' did not carry their face value when they were used by abolitionists.(4) Sturge did not escape the resultant confusion. Before he finally declared for immediate emancipation by Act of Parliament he supported three anti-slavery strategies (sometimes concurrently) during the 1820s: the amelioration of slavery and its gradual abolition; repeal of the tariffs that protected sugar produced in the British Caribbean colonies; and a boycott of slave-produced sugar. Only the third was spoken of as a policy of 'immediate emancipation', and inevitably its effectiveness was a matter of surmise.

The first strategy revealed the limitations of the anti-slavery movement at this stage of its evolution as a pressure group. On 19 March 1823 William Wilberforce addressed the House of Commons in support of a petition he had concerted with the Society of Friends. The petition, which called for 'the gradual termination of Slavery within the British dominions', modestly declined to 'presume to suggest to Parliament, the way in which this desirable object may be accomplished'.(5) As a further demonstration of the movement's moderation Thomas Fowell Buxton, the philanthropist and Member of Parliament whom Wilberforce had chosen to succeed him as leader of the movement, gave Cabinet ministers advance notice of several legislative proposals he wished to have debated, the most important of which would have set free all children born in the colonies 'after a certain day'. Buxton was well supported by petitions when the debate took place on 15 May, but he did not press the Commons to a division after George Canning replied to his speech by moving several amendments expressing the Government's sympathy for an undefined policy of gradual emancipation and promising that a set of regulations would be issued to improve the conditions of the slaves.(6) The operation seemed to have been successful: in the provinces the rank and file had done their duty by petitioning, and in Westminster the anti-slavery leaders had committed the Government to take action. The local anti-slavery societies which started to come into existence at this time were left with little to do other than to remain ready for similar manoeuvres in case the Government failed to honour its word.

These were soberly realistic tactics at a time when the values of the eighteenth-century hierarchy were still so powerful that there was a strong feeling against thrusting policies on Parliament from outside: influence could do more than pressure. With its list of patrons selected from the civil, military and ecclesiastical establishment and its London-based 'select party' of leaders who could summon up the energies of provincial 'auxiliaries', the anti-slavery movement seemed to be the very model of a pressure group during the 1820s. According to Sir George Stephen, it was commonly believed that 'Wilberforce, Buxton, Brougham, Lushington, or Macaulay, or any others of their social status, could work with a thousand times more effect than all the Antislavery societies then existing could have done together'. 'I have not even a morsel of Radicalism about me', Buxton admitted many years later, and he never felt comfortable in any agitation that was disrespectful towards established authority.(7)

For several years Sturge often took an appropriate place in this model. At the Friends' Yearly Meeting in 1823 he heard an appeal for assistance on behalf of the Anti-Slavery Society, and in the following March he helped to arrange a public meeting in Birmingham at which Canning's proposals were welcomed and a petition was endorsed recommending their application throughout the Empire. In November 1826 he became one of the secretaries of the newly-established Birmingham Anti-Slavery Society where he found himself in the company of other evangelicals - Anglicans and Nonconformists as well as Quakers. Their first resolution called for the united efforts of British Christians; the second envisaged a long-term strategy of educating public opinion, petitioning Parliament and otherwise assisting the London leaders. They were not 'advocates of any rash or intemperate proceedings'.(8)

From its beginnings, however, the Birmingham Society adopted a concurrent strategy which offered the provincial auxiliary societies more room for initiative: it campaigned against the benefits that the West Indian slave owners were receiving from the imperial system of commercial tariffs and bounties. The theory underlying this form of anti-slavery action came from James Cropper, a wealthy Quaker businessman and philanthropist who travelled round Britain during the 1820s delivering speeches in which religious ethics were inextricably interwoven with the teachings of Adam Smith. Laws had been 'fixed in the nature of things', Cropper believed, through which God regulated free market economies for the general well-being. Taking up Smith's famous reference to the inefficiency of slavery in comparison with wage labour, he argued that the West Indian slave owners would be driven by the logic of their cash ledgers to see the merits of emancipation if the British Government could be persuaded to allow East Indian free labour sugar equal access to the British market.(9)

Sturge was in the audience when Cropper explained his theories to the Friends' Yearly Meeting in 1824, and during the next two years he made the arrangements for a campaign of speaking tours which brought Cropper to Birmingham and the surrounding counties.(10) They became firm friends, confiding to each other for many years not only their opinions on anti-slavery matters but also their anxieties about the spiritual life of the Society of Friends. Sturge assumed a deferential tone to the older man who must have seemed the personification of a Quaker philanthropist. Cropper was dedicating his later years and much of his wealth to a variety of philanthropic ventures, and his blending of current economic theory with the older ideal of the Christian stewardship of wealth could hardly have failed to interest a prospering young businessman in search of a code of ethics. It is a measure of the closeness between the two men that during January 1825 Sturge interrupted his business commitments to travel with Cropper from town to town attending seven anti-slavery meetings in the space of nine days.(11) Cropper's influence could also be seen in the Short Review Of The Slave Trade And Slavery, With Considerations

On The Benefit Which Would Arise From Cultivating Tropical Productions By Free Labour which Sturge's brother John wrote in 1827.(12)

Unlike Buxton, Cropper envisaged a self-sustaining form of pressure group activity for the rank and file of the movement. During the long drawn out process of persuading Parliament to repeal the sugar tariffs and bounties, he believed that private individuals could go over the heads of the parliamentarians and exert pressure directly on the slave owners. To this end he set up a Tropical Free Produce Company in 1825 which was to raise a capital of £4,000,000 for the production of sugar and cotton within the Empire by free labour. Cropper was sometimes criticised for reducing anti-slavery to a set of commercial propositions, and his investments in free produce ventures exposed him to accusations that he practised a mercenary form of philanthropy, but his proposals were inspired by a high-minded theory of imperial commerce. By promoting the cultivation of free labour tropical products in Britain's Asian, African and Caribbean colonies he believed that he could not only destroy slavery but also cure the ills of Ireland, because some of the cotton would have been processed in the factories which he tried to set up to stimulate the Irish economy. In short, if Cropper had had his way, the anti-slavery movement would have been transformed into a vocation for philanthropic businessmen.(13)

Although the Tropical Free Produce Company had to be abandoned when the House of Lords rejected a Bill that would have given it legal status, there was another attempt to use abolitionist purchasing power which did make some headway, a boycott ('abstinence' was the contemporary word) of slave produced sugar. Precedents for this, the third strategy that Sturge took up during the 1820s, went back to the 1790s when the 'anti-saccharites', as they were known, had 'resolved never to use sugar...derived...through the medium of the Slave Trade', but between 1824 and 1829 this ineffectual gesture was spectacularly recast when it was linked to the cry of 'immediate emancipation' and taken to the nation's doorsteps by women abolitionists who had been trained in the ways of the evangelical district-visiting societies.(14)

Nearly thirty years later during a conversation with Harriet Beecher Stowe Sturge gave the credit for this more militant form of abolitionism to Elizabeth Heyrick, a Leicester Quakeress whose anonymous pamphlet, Immediate Not Gradual Abolition, went through at least three editions in 1824. Heyrick had no faith in public opinion that merely expressed itself 'in exclamations, in petitions and remonstrances'; she wanted the British people to 'compel the planter to set his slaves at liberty' without conditions or delays. But, although she spoke of succeeding in a few months if one tenth of the British population would agree to stop buying West Indian sugar, Heyrick revealed more about the 'expressive politics' that were gaining ground amongst the provincial rank and file of the movement. Her version of immediate abolition had a moral rather than a strictly temporal meaning, and she envisaged a boycott which would demonstrate the strength of the nation's commitment to Christianity. The British public would be brought to a heightened consciousness of slavery as a national sin; individuals would undergo 'sacrifices' and 'tests' to make amends; and principle rather than expediency would be injected into public affairs. Heyrick shared Cropper's admiration for the 'providential arrangements' that connected duty with self-interest, but she did not regard these as sufficient to spur decisive action against slavery. That would have to come from Christians who listened to the voice of conscience and acted on 'simple and direct' distinctions between 'right and wrong, virtue and vice'. Even if the boycott failed, she promised that its supporters would enjoy an 'abundant reward' when they thought of their 'clean hands'. Cautiously she introduced a few words of respect for Clarkson, Wilberforce and Buxton, but her conclusions were unmistakable: parliamentary manoeuvres for gradual emancipation were 'the very master-piece of satanic policy'. Only 'strong excitement, and intense feeling' could overthrow slavery. Putting action to words, she carried out a door-to-door canvass of much of Leicester, pledging householders not to purchase slave produced sugar.(15)

Heyrick's attempt to transfer the struggle from Parliament to the nation's households and shop-counters would virtually have turned the anti-slavery movement into a 'mission' for women, and some of the more conservative leaders including Wilberforce were appalled by the prospect.(16) The Sturges, on the other hand, energetically took up the new tactics, especially Sophia who was one of the founder-members of 'The Female Society for Birmingham, Westbromwich, Wednesbury, Walsall and their Respective Neighbourhoods for the Relief of British Negro Slaves'. This was the earliest of the women's anti-slavery societies, and for a time in the 1820s it was the centre of a nation-wide network of affiliated individuals and groups. As a member of the sub-committee which canvassed the whole of Birmingham on behalf of the sugar boycott Sophia personally visited 3000 households between 1826 and 1829. Women in several other towns followed this example, and in 1830 there was an attempt to compile a National Register of those who had taken the pledge to support the boycott.(17)

It was an unrewarding task - so unrewarding that at one stage the Birmingham women had to console themselves with the hope that their efforts were 'not wholly useless'.(18) But even at the time it was evident that the anti-slavery movement was entering an important new phase as a result of actions such as these. All over the country a groundswell of anti-slavery feeling was spilling beyond the restraining influence of the London leaders and driving planter spokesmen into defeatist attitudes. As early as 1824 a Jamaican clergyman referred to the hawking of anti-slavery handbills, petitions, placards, pamphlets and pictures 'through every village in Great Britain'. In 1828 the West India Committee which looked after planter interests in Britain was warned that hundreds of publications depicting the sufferings of slaves were being distributed at the Wiltshire markets and that 'anti-slavery clubs, and anti-slavery needle-parties, and anti-slavery tea-parties' were flourishing in that county. It was a watershed in the development of the British political nation. Using the pressure group as their vehicle, sections of society (businessmen, Dissenters, provincials and women) which had previously been told to be content with 'virtual representation' were assuming a right to influence national policy-making directly.(19)

Between 1827 and 1833 the rapidly changing context of British politics gave the militants all the opportunities they needed to produce the 'strong excitement and intense feeling' that Heyrick had called for. In 1827 the death of Lord Liverpool, Prime Minister since 1812, deprived the Tories of the one leader acceptable to their bitterly divided factions, and suddenly it was as if all the demands for change that had been denied or delayed since the 1790s fell with irresistible force on Parliament. In 1828 and 1829 under public pressure, the Tories repealed the Test and Corporation Acts which discriminated against Dissenters and conceded Catholic Emancipation; in 1830 the Whigs, the party of 'Reform', attained power after nearly a quarter of a century in the wilderness. It was one of the eras of high optimism in British history, a time when the possibilities of progress seemed to be limitless.

Sturge was one of the abolitionists who lost patience with the London leaders during these years. What was needed, he told the Secretary of the London Anti-Slavery Society in March 1828, was a wave of public meetings and petitions on the model of the movement against the Test and Corporation Acts in which whole congregations of Dissenting denominations had taken part. 'There never was a time', he added, 'when the government were less able (even if they were disposed) to withstand the voice of the country'; public opinion would carry 'almost any reasonable measure in favour of this Great Cause'.(20) The specific reforms he called for at this stage were still very moderate: he helped to organise a public meeting in Birmingham during April 1828 at which a petition was endorsed asking Parliament to confer freedom on the children of slaves, to facilitate the manumission of adults and to remove the sugar duties.(21) But his attitude soon hardened, and in 1830 he came out in support of immediate emancipation by Act of Parliament. By this stage even an appeal from Cropper that he should concentrate his efforts on the repeal of the sugar duties could not hold him back.(22) Like Heyrick six years previously, he would now take his stand only on high religious principle. In May 1830 he announced his conversion at the Friends' Yearly Meeting and successfully called on his fellow Quakers to insist on total and immediate emancipation:

> When the Christian is convinced that the principle upon which he acts is correct, I believe it does not become him to examine too closely his probability of success, but rather to act in the assurance that if he faithfully does his part, as much success will attend his efforts as is consistent with the will of that Divine leader under whose banner he is enlisted.

This was the philosophy that had taken him into conflict with the Birmingham Street Commissioners in 1829, and once again it separated him from those whose opinions he valued. Respectfully but firmly he made it clear that he was challenging the judgement of some of the

51

Friends whose pronouncements carried 'so much weight with many of us, that we took for granted their opinions must be correct'.(23) The gesture of independence was unavoidable given the close relationship between Buxton and some of the 'weighty Friends'. Buxton's mother was a Quaker, and his wife was one of the Gurneys; in the small world of early nineteenth-century Quakerism these were facts that swayed opinions.

As Sturge must have known, his impatience was shared by the anti-slavery rank and file all over the country. At its annual meeting on 8 April 1830 the Birmingham women's society passed a resolution refusing to send further payments to the London leaders until they were 'willing to give up the word gradual in their title' and withdraw their endorsement of Canning's resolutions. A month later the annual meeting of the London Anti-Slavery Society was thrown into turmoil when one of the younger members moved an immediatist amendment from the floor expressing dissatisfaction with the leadership of the movement. Later that year in Edinburgh an anti-slavery meeting broke up in farcical disorder when the Lord Provost scuttled from the platform after a speaker used the aphorism 'fiat justitia, ruat coelum' to support a motion demanding immediate, not gradual, emancipation.(24) A form of religiously inspired radicalism was in the air, and even the cautious Conference of Wesleyan Methodists gave a standing ovation to a resolution calling for 'the entire abolition of slavery throughout the British dominions'. Addressing an anti-slavery meeting soon afterwards, one of their ministers spelled out the implications of the decision: henceforward the Wesleyans 'as a body' would 'agitate the subject by petitions and every other lawful means'.(25)

It was in this context that the anti-slavery militants carried through their most important experiment in rousing public opinion. In July 1831 they set up an Agency Committee with an independent fund and sent a team of paid lecturers ('agents') round the country to win over the unconverted and co-ordinate activities in support of immediate abolition. Little is known about the origins of this venture, and all subsequent accounts (including Henry Richard's Memoirs of Joseph Sturge) have relied heavily on the reminiscences of Sir George Stephen, one of the participants. Stephen described himself as the leader of a group called 'the young England abolitionists' who devised the Agency Committee with advice from Daniel O'Connell and used it to carry though 'a complete revolution in tactics' which hastened the successful outcome of the abolitionist struggle by a generation. Sturge and Cropper appear in his account, but only as two of several Quakers whom he persuaded to contribute generously to the Agency funds.(26) Stephen was a writer of some note in his day, and his account is full of vivid vignettes and episodes, but it must be read with some reservations. He wrote as a man who was convinced that his own merits had never been properly recognised: he said nothing about the groundswell of anti-slavery militancy that had been gathering outside London since 1824.(27)

In fact, the Agency scheme can be traced back to the most active and militant abolitionists of the 1820s, the women's anti-slavery societies with which Sturge and Cropper had strong connections through their female relatives. The earliest reference to anti-slavery stipendiary agents seems to date from April 1830 when the Birmingham women passed their resolution refusing to send money to the national Society as long as it had the word 'gradual' in its title. A second resolution went on to vote funds for the support of 'travelling Agents' who would go through the British Isles protesting against Canning's resolutions, urging people to boycott slave produce, calling for the 'utter extirpation of slavery', and setting up more women's societies. A few months later when the Hibernian Negro's Friend Society sent a representative over to England on a fund-raising tour the Birmingham women paid him *50 as part of an agreement by which he was to incorporate a statement of their policies in his lectures.(28) Stephen seems to have seen the importance of public lectures at this time too, and with the help of Cropper and Sturge he offered a more extensive version of the agency scheme to the London Anti-Slavery Society in May 1831. Sturge was present as a member of a Birmingham deputation when the proposal was accepted and a few days later the Society placed the following advertisment in the press acknowledging the venture as one that had been brought to London from the provinces:(29)

> The Anti-Slavery Society having been informed by its Subscribers in the country, that much advantage has been derived from the system of Agency, partially adopted last summer, has resolved to carry it into operation on a more extensive and systematic principle, and to employ Agents to deliver Lectures explanatory of the nature and effects of Colonial Slavery in all the principal towns throughout the United Kingdom.

The experiment was a triumphant success. Within twelve months all the 'principal towns' south of the Trent had been visited and one of the agents was reporting that he had been received with 'an ardour equal to political enthusiasm' - a telling comparison at a time when parliamentary elections could throw whole towns into frenzied excitement for days on end. Another agent, George Thompson, quickly acquired a reputation as one of the leading orators of the age by addressing public meetings where he evoked such heated demonstrations and counter demonstrations that the police had to stand by in readiness for violence.(30) Planter spokesmen replied as best they could, but events conspired against them when a slave rising broke out in Jamaica at Christmas 1831. If the Jamaican whites had not over-reacted, the episode could have damaged the anti-slavery movement by reviving the old fears of negro bloodlust. As it was, they restored their authority with great brutality. Even more rashly, considering the strength of evangelical Christianity in Britain, they harassed the Baptist and Methodist missionaries on the island and allowed Colonial Church Union mobs to destroy Dissenting chapels. Sensational reports of planter cruelty reached Britain, especially after William Knibb, one of the Baptist missionaries, came home to shock public meetings with his tale of suffering.(31) By August 1832 the Jamaican Colonial Agent in London was so anxious that he informed the island's Committee of Correspondence that they must henceforward reckon on 'the fiercest hostility against Jamaica. The demolition of the Chapels, and the resolutions of the Church Union Societies have been made the pretext for this infamous persecution which is raised against us - I am afraid it will operate most fatally for us at the general election'.(32)

Only once were operations suspended - in May 1832 after the House of Lords had rejected the Whig Government's Bill for reforming Parliament.(33) For a week the nation faced the most serious possiblity of revolution since 1688. In few cities was the Lords' action more resented than Birmingham, where muffled bells tolled after the news reached the town and excited mass meetings took place on Newhall Hill. At this juncture a minor sensation was created when twenty Quakers, including Joseph, John and Charles Sturge, joined the Birmingham Political Union, the largest and best known parliamentary reform society in the country. It was not difficult for local conservatives to taunt the twenty by referring to quietist statements in Yearly Meeting Epistles, but the Sturges were even less inclined to be excluded from politics than they had been when they lived in Bewdley, and they offered a spirited defence.(34) Prominent Whigs had been sympathetic to the anti-slavery movement in Opposition, and there were high hopes that they would emancipate the slaves after they reformed Parliament. The Christian Advocate, a newspaper closely associated with the Agency Committee, was even looking to the Reform Bill as the means of placing Parliament under the control of a purer constituency and bringing 'into active influence and exertion the Christianity of the country'.(35)

When the crisis subsided after the Lords allowed the Bill to pass, Sturge resigned from the Political Union in August to resume the anti-slavery struggle. Hitherto the Agency Committee had worked in concert with the Anti-Slavery Society (their memberships overlapped and they shared the same premises), but the new body was more militant than the old, and in mid-1832 members of the Society were so alarmed by the vehemence of Stephen's appeals to public opinion that they denied the Committee the use of the shared facilities. On 4 July 1832 the Agency Committee defiantly re-constituted itself as the Agency Society. The Christian Advocate saw the division as a source of strength: 'new men and new measures' could now take the place of those who saw themselves as 'the chief ornaments of the Society'.(36)

The newspaper went on to praise Birmingham as a centre of the 'new measures': it could have mentioned Sturge as one of the 'new men'. In 1831, after his brother Charles joined him in the business, Sturge was set free to give long spells of time to his religious and philanthropic pursuits. He co-ordinated Agency work in the Midlands and he began to make protracted visits to London.(37) In a letter from there in November 1832 he described himself as being up to his neck in the work of arranging the Agency Society's strategy for the first general election to be held under the terms of the Reform Act. The reference was to a scheme for administering a pledge in favour of immediate emancipation to all parliamentary candidates and publishing the results for the guidance of voters, a precedent that has been followed by many British pressure groups down to our own day. On 5 November Sturge temporarily settled in London so that he could join the Committee of Correspondence which was to co-ordinate the administration of these pledges all over the country and draw up three schedules to give voters a choice between pledged, unpledged and doubtful candidates. It would be a mistake to rely on the goodwill of the Whigs, he wrote at this time; the only way to obtain a satisfactory Emancipation Bill was to make it clear to everyone that the Agency Society would direct its supporters to vote according to the schedules.(38) It was an attitude that Stephen would later summarise well: they had transformed themselves into a 'storming party'.(39)

In the aftermath of the election the Agency abolitionists did not reach the same conclusion as recent historians who have emphasised the similarities between the first Reformed Parliament and its predecessors: there did seem to be grounds for the belief that religious and moral considerations could influence constituency politics as never before. Writing from Coalbrookdale, Sturge's sister-in-law revelled in the astonishment of the local Tories when they saw 'the energy and industry of the Quakers' as anti-slavery election organisers.(40) Similar reports were received from other parts of the country, and it was calculated that 104 pledged M.P.s had been elected. The sense of victory was enhanced by the weakened state of the West India interest in the House of Commons; not only had some of its seats been abolished by the Reform Bill but the election had halved its representation in the House.(41)

By the beginning of 1833 therefore it was certain that some sort of emancipation scheme would emerge. In January a Colonial Office memorandum admitted that public opinion was such that if the Government did not act someone else would. Sturge would have left the Whig Government with no choice at all: a letter dated 10 January 1833 shows Buxton cautiously setting aside his suggestion that the anti-slavery M.P.s should seize the initiative by introducing 'a simple motion' in favour of total and immediate emancipation.(42) Initially the Whigs considered the possiblity of bringing in a scheme based on this principle, but the West India Committee convinced them that a fatal shock would be administered to the deteriorating economies of the Caribbean colonies if this extreme course of action was adopted.(43) The resultant contrast between the inescapable pragmatism of a Government, even a reforming one, and the high principle of a pressure group was evident in every line of the speech delivered by Edward Stanley, the Colonial Secretary, when the Government eventually presented its Emancipation Bill to the Commons on 14 May:(44)

> The Government was placed between two conflicting parties - one having a deep pecuniary interest in the question, intimately acquainted with the subject, connected with the colonies by social ties, and at present labouring under embarrassments which rendered it doubly jealous of any measure which might affect their interests. On the other hand, a universal and extended expression of feeling pervaded the country, and there never was a time when

the determination of the people was more absolutely or more irresistibly expressed, because it was founded on that deep religious feeling, on that solemn conviction of principle, which admitted of no palliative or compromise, and which pronounced itself in a voice to which no Minister could be deaf.

The indecisiveness of the Whigs and rumours about their intentions had meanwhile brought about a resurgence of anti-slavery agitation. On 28 March one of Sturge's correspondents spurred him to action with the news that the Whigs were in full retreat from emancipation:(45) 'Sin will be at our door if we do not agitate, agitate, agitate. We must all become Radicals and Unionists, for if we sit down quietly with our hands before us Government will laugh at us. The people must emancipate the slaves.' The crisis brought the Anti-Slavery and Agency Societies into alliance, and 'the pressure from without' was again brought to bear on Parliament. M.P.s were reminded of their pledges, and Parliament was inundated with petitions. Buxton needed the help of three men to carry an unprecedented petition from the women of Britain into the House of Commons.(46) Bolder still, in a radical gesture which created something like an anti-parliament, 339 delegates, most of them elected at public meetings, were brought to London to declare the will of the nation on emancipation. The <u>Christian Advocate</u> saw this assembly as the beginning of a new era in politics: for the first time the whole nation had come together on an issue and chosen 'representatives from its men of intelligence and of religion'. Many of them were Dissenting ministers, and when they were granted an interview by the Government they signalled the new departure in British political life by processing through the streets of London in a long column of black-coated figures.(47) Their Memorial to the Prime Minister took a high tone:(48)

we feel bound, publicly and emphatically to declare that while slavery obtains under any form, however modified, or however sanctioned, we will never relax from our efforts, nor swerve from our purpose, to exert that influence which we may collectively or individually possess, to effect by all legitimate means its immediate and entire abolition.

Together with Cropper, Sturge had been given the task of ensuring that the West and North of England produced their quota of delegates, and he took part in the assembly as a representative for Warwickshire.(49) The idea of an assembly of 'men of intelligence and of religion' was one to which he would often recur during the next twenty years as a means of solving national and international problems.

Stanley's Bill was carefully designed to disperse this 'pressure from without'. Although the slaves would continue to serve their masters as unpaid 'apprentices' for 40 $\frac{1}{2}$ hours a week for a further twelve years, there was a sense in which the Bill could be described as ending slavery with effect from 1 August 1834. The status of slave was abolished; the apprentices were given important legal rights; the Government was to appoint special magistrates for the administration of plantation discipline; and all children less than six years of age were to have unconditional freedom, in itself an advance on the policy that Sturge had supported as recently as 1828. £20,000,000 were voted to compensate the planters. It was a skilful political exercise, and immediately the new-found unity of the anti-slavery movement collapsed. Buxton accepted the Bill in principle with the understanding that he would propose amendments during the Committee stage, but the Agency Society saw his action as a sacrifice of conscience to party political considerations.(50) 'The truth is', the <u>Christian Advocate</u> told its readers, 'that Whiggery runs wild in Aldermanbury [the Anti-Slavery Society's headquarters]; and your true Whig will sell his own father, if Whig ministers require it'. Sturge and other Agency leaders now commonly used the term 'Radical' to distinguish themselves from those who had accepted Stanley's compromise.(51) It was a line that cut across even the most ardently abolitionist families. Thomas Marshall Sturge, for example, lost patience with his militant younger brothers: 'As regards the Negro, (or course excepting the apprenticing provisions) he is placed at once upon an equal footing with other British subjects, and is this no <u>benefit</u> or <u>advantage</u>?'.(52)

Sturge spent much of July in London attempting to alter the Bill. He took part in a second conference of delegates and went on a deputation to Stanley when he enjoyed the satisfaction of condemning the apprenticeship scheme to its author's face and hearing other delegates threaten to call on their parliamentary supporters to throw the Bill out. They were unmoved by the warning that these tactics would deny the slaves any prospect of freedom.(53) As always during the crises of his public life, Sturge relied on Sophia for support. Few of her letters have survived, but fortunately on this occasion her advice is known. It was imbued with the strict religious principles that the women abolitionists had upheld since 1824:(54)

> It is very certainly not <u>your</u> wish to embarrass Ministers but you must not for the sake of avoiding that appearance of evil desert your high vantage ground of uncompromising justice, you must not even for the sake of the slave consent to evil that good may come to him.

There must be no compromise 'even for the sake of the slave': her words vividly reveal the mentality that Sturge brought to his good causes - the well-being of the slave was less important than the moral principles of the abolitionist. On this occasion, although the Agency Society had done so much to place emancipation on the political agenda, these 'expressive politics' confined Sturge to the role of 'barking' (his own term) while the Government's Bill passed into law.(55) He was not consoled by Buxton's success as an 'instrumental' politician. Parliament cut the unpaid apprenticeship from twelve years to six in the case of predials (agricultural workers) and four in the case of non-predials, but as far as Sturge was concerned this was still slavery under another name.

NOTES

1. Sturge Papers (Lewin), John Sturge to his sisters, 11 April 1815.
2. There were occasional references to slavery in the Epistles From The Yearly Meeting Of Friends between 1807 and 1823.
3. Sturge Papers (M. Sturge), Anti-Slavery Reporter, July and August 1893 (newscutting reprinting a letter from Edmund Sturge, 6 August 1891).
4. D.B., Davis, 'The Emergence of Immediatism in British and American Anti-slavery Thought', Mississippi Valley Historical Review, XLIX, September 1962, pp. 209-30.
5. Annual Monitor, no. 12, 1824; R.I. & S. Wilberforce, The Life of William Wilberforce, London 1838, vol. 5, p. 170.
6. Charles Buxton, Memoirs of Sir Thomas Fowell Buxton, London 1849, pp. 111-17.
7. Wilberforce, Life of William Wilberforce, vol. 5, p. 166; Stephen, Anti-Slavery Recollections, p. 115; Papers of Sir T. Fowell Buxton, vol. 17, Buxton to Sir George Grey, 23 February 1838.
8. Richard, Sturge, p. 80; Aris's Birmingham Gazette, 29 March, 5 April 7 June 1824, 4 December 1826; Birmingham Public Library, Birmingham Anti-Slavery Society, Minute Book, vol. 1, 1826-37, 29 November 1826.
9. Aris's Birmingham Gazette, 3 October, 4 December 1826; Brit. Lib., Add. MS. 41267A, ff. 104-6, James Cropper to Zachary Macaulay, 10 May 1822; K. Charlton, 'James Cropper And Liverpool's Contribution To The Anti-Slavery Movement', Transactions of the Historical Society of Lancashire and Cheshire, CXIII 1972, pp. 57-76.
10. Richard, Sturge, pp. 80-85; Extracts From Letters of the Late James Cropper, lithograph n.d., James Cropper to Joseph Sturge, 14 October, 30 November 1825.
11. Series of letters from Cropper to Sturge during the 1820s and 1830s in Extracts From Letters and the Cropper Papers. See also F.A. Conybeare, Dingle Bank. The Home of the Croppers, Cambridge 1925.
12. [John Sturge], A Short Review Of The Slave Trade And Slavery, With Considerations On The Benefit Which Would Arise From Cultivating Tropical Productions By Free Labour, Birmingham 1827. Authorship was attributed to John Sturge in Proceedings Of The General Anti-Slavery Convention Called By The Committee Of The British and Foreign Anti-Slavery Society, London 1841, p. 356.
13. Cropper Papers, Slavery Scraps (newscuttings), New Times, 26 March 1825 and Bath and Cheltenham Chronicle, 26 April 1825; ibid., Letter Book (James Cropper), Tropical Free Labour Company Report of the Provisional Committee, 9 October 1826; Sturge, A Short Review, pp. 118-19; K. Charlton, 'The State of Ireland In The 1820s: James. Cropper's Plan', Irish Historical Studies, XVII, March 1971, pp. 320-39.
14. J. Leifchild, Memoir Of The Late Rev. Joseph Hughes, A.M. One Of The Secretaries Of The British and Foreign Bible Society, London 1835, pp. 129-30; Considerations addressed to Professors of Christianity of every Denomination, on the Impropriety of Consuming West-India Sugar & Rum, As Produced by the Oppressive Labour of Slaves, n.p. 1792.

15. Immediate Not Gradual Abolition; Or, An Inquiry Into The Shortest, Safest, And Most Effectual Means Of Getting Rid Of West Indian Slavery, London 1824. See also Mrs Elizabeth Heyrick, Leicester n.d. The distinction between the temporal and moral definitions of immediatism is made by A.C. Loveland, 'Evangelicalism and "Immediate Emancipation" in American Antislavery Thought' Journal of Southern History, XXXII May 1966, p. 173.

16. Wilberforce, The Correspondence of William Wilberforce, vol. 2, pp. 494, 501.

17. The activities of the Birmingham women are described in Birmingham Public Library, Minute Book Of The Ladies Society For The Relief Of Negro Slaves, entries from 8 April 1825 - 8 April 1830; Birmingham Journal, 7 May 1853; Friends Monthly Magazine, April 1830.

18. Minute Book Of The Ladies Society etc., 30 October 1827.

19. D. Hall, A Brief History Of The West India Committee, St. Lawrence 1971, p. 8; G.R. Mellor, British Imperial Trusteeship, 1783-1850, London 1951, p. 97; G.W. Bridges, Dreams of Dulocracy, London 1824, pp. 1-2.

20. Rhodes House, Mss. Brit. Emp. S18, C1/60, Joseph Sturge to Thomas Pringle, 20 March 1828.

21. Aris's Birmingham Gazette, 21 April 1828.

22. Ibid., 1 Nov. 1830; Extracts From Letters Of The Late James Cropper, James Cropper to Joseph Sturge, 30 March, 10 May, 22 June 1830.

23. Richard, Sturge, p. 90.

24. Minute Book of the Ladies Society etc., 8 April 1830; Viscountess Knutsford, Life and Letters of Zachary Macaulay, London 1900, p. 452; H. Cockburn, Memorials Of His Time, Edinburgh 1872, pp. 405-6.

25. Christian Advocate, 5 August, 9 September 1830.

26. Stephen, Anti-Slavery Recollections, pp. 127-58.

27. L. Stephen, The Life of Sir James Fitzjames Stephen Bart., KCSI, A Judge Of The High Court Of Justice, London 1895, pp. 27-28; Sir George Stephen, A Memoir Of The Late James Stephen, One of the Masters In The High Court Of Chancery, In Relation To Slave Emancipation, Brighton, Victoria 1875, pp. 35-73.

28. Minute Book Of The Ladies Society etc., 8 April 1830, 12 April 1831; Christian Advocate, 16 May 1831; Library of the American Antiquarian Society, Worcester, Mass., Anne Knight to Abby Kelly, 17 August 1841.

29. Christian Advocate, 13 June 1831, 1 July 1833; Rhodes House, Mss. Brit. Emp. S18, E2/3, [London] Anti-Slavery Society Minutes, 25 May 1831.

30. Report Of The Agency Committee Of The Anti-Slavery Society, London 1832, p. 11; Christian Advocate, 23 July 1832. Sturge Papers (Maud Sturge), Rebecca Waterhouse to Eliza Cropper, August 1832.

31. J.H. Hinton, Memoir of William Knibb, London 1849, chap. X; Cropper Papers, Edward Cropper to James Cropper, 25 July 1832.

32. Jamaica Archives, 1B/5/14/6, Committee of Correspondence, Out-Letter Book of Agent in England, William Burge, 1832-1834,

William Burge to the Committee, 15 August 1832.

33. Birmingham Anti-Slavery Society, Minute Book, 14 May 1832; Richard, Sturge, p. 99.

34. Birmingham Journal, 12 May, 19 May 1832; Birmingham Political Union, Reports, 1830-1838, 'Report of the Proceedings Of the Public Meeting Of The Inhabitants of Birmingham, Held At Newhall-Hill, May 10, 1832', pp. 4-7.

35. Christian Advocate, 10 September 1832.

36. The Tourist; Or, Sketch Book of the Times, 26 November 1832; [London] Anti-Slavery Society Minutes, 4 July 1832; Christian Advocate, 23 July, 13 August, 20 August 1832, 17 June 1833.

37. Christian Advocate, 19 November 1832; Richard, Sturge, p. 96.

38. Sturge Papers (M. Sturge), Joseph Sturge to Charles Sturge, 28 November 1832; [London] Anti-Slavery Society Minutes, 5 December 1832.

39. Stephen, Anti-Slavery Recollections, p. 245.

40. Sturge Papers (M. Sturge), Mary Darby Sturge to Charles Sturge, 7 November 1832.

41. I. Gross, 'The Abolition of Negro Slavery And British Parliamentary Politics 1832-3', Historical Journal, 23, (1980), p. 65; B.W. Higman, 'The West India Interest in Parliament, 1807-1833', Historical Studies, XIII, October 1967, p. 4.

42. Brit. Lib., Add. MSS. 51820, ff. 91-97, Colonial Office paper, 7 January 1833, and Add. MSS. 43845, f.1, T.F. Buxton to Joseph Sturge, 10 January 1833.

43. Institute of Jamaica, Sligo Papers, MS 275 f.18, Lord Howick to Lord Sligo, 2 April 1838.

44. Christian Advocate, 20 May 1833. The Hansard report differs slightly in phrasing but not in substance.

45. Sturge, Richard, pp. 101-102.

46. Christian Advocate, 20 May 1833.

47. Ibid., 22 April 1833.

48. Memorial To The Right Honourable The Earl Grey, KG, From Anti-Slavery delegates of the United Kingdom, 18 April 1833.

49. [London] Anti-Slavery Society Minutes, 3 April 1833.

50. Buxton, Memoirs, p. 273.

51. Christian Advocate, 3 June, 10 June, 17 June 1833; Sturge Papers (M. Sturge), Joseph Sturge to Charles Sturge, 4 July 1833.

52. Sturge Papers (M. Sturge), Thomas Marshall Sturge to Charles Sturge 18 July 1833.

53. [London] Anti-Slavery Society Minutes, entries for 8 July - 22 July 1833; Christian Advocate, 15 July, 29 July 1833; Sturge Papers (M. Sturge), Charles Sturge to Mary Darby Sturge, 16 July 1833.

54. Sturge Papers (M. Sturge), Sophia Sturge to Joseph Sturge, n.d.

55. Ibid., Joseph Sturge to Charles Sturge, 4 July 1833.

6 The Emergence of the Moral Radical Party (1834-36)

With the passing of the 1833 Emancipation Act the pattern of life suddenly altered for Sturge; no longer did he spend weeks on end helping to devise abolitionist strategy in London or campaigning in the provinces. Business also absorbed less of his time now that Charles had assumed responsibility for management. With time to think of his future he decided to marry. He chose well. Eliza Cropper, the daughter of his closest associate in the anti-slavery movement, was 'a stiff damsel' according to Zachary Macaulay, but she was well suited to Sturge; for James Cropper had brought his children up as reformers and philanthropists. Her portrait shows her, pen in hand, very much the public-spirited Quakeress. As her father's secretary she had often accompanied him on his philanthropic journeys, and Sturge had travelled with her to anti-slavery meetings as long ago as 1826. They must have met frequently afterwards in similar circumstances. On her wedding day she was thirty-three; Sturge was forty-one.(1)

John Sturge once ventured the opinion that his family was destined to be disappointed in love;(2) he could have added that they were awkward wooers and cited Joseph's courtship of Eliza as an example. Firstly, there was opposition within the Cropper family; then, according to a later story, Sturge went off precipitately and proposed to someone else only to find that Eliza had overcome her family's objections and was holding him to his word. Obviously he had learned nothing from the fiasco of his previous engagement. Wedding arrangements proceeded until February 1834 when they were threatened by a dispute over the £1000 sent by J. & C. Sturge to the firm of Cropper and Benson in 1832 as a contribution to the cartel which had been set up to manipulate the corn market. The money, it was said, had never arrived, but in 1834 evidence was received which led to the conviction of one of the Cropper and Benson clerks for embezzlement, and angry letters were exchanged between Sturge and Eliza's brothers. Margaret Cropper (Zachary Macaulay's daughter) described Sturge at this time as 'grasping and head-strong', denying himself a 'fine fortune' from his bride for the sake of a smaller claim against her family's business, but the story can be interpreted differently. Suspicion had fallen on all connected with the transaction, aggravating the dubious circumstances of this business arrangement.

61

When Cropper and Benson eventually made payment, J. & C. Sturge handed the money over to charity. It must have been an embarrassing experience for a man who had cut back on his business commitments to create more time for works of benevolence.(3)

Eventually on 29 April 1834 the wedding took place at the Hardshaw West meeting house, where in Quaker style the wedding party sat in silence for half an hour before Joseph made his declaration to Eliza. For Margaret Cropper the whole occasion was thoroughly distasteful: in contrast with his bride who looked 'really lovely' (the compliment was weakened by the reflection that she looked ten years younger than usual) Sturge was 'so clownish, so lumpish, so short, thick, fat, hot, heavy, everything that was bad, unutterably bad', and the plainness of the ceremony was 'really awful'.(4) Dressed in Quaker drab, Sturge's squarely built figure would not have created a graceful impression as he moved around with his distinctive rolling gait, but Margaret Cropper's opinion was too severe; a few years later another observer would comment that he had never seen more 'regular or pleasing features'.(5) And even Margaret Cropper had to admit that Joseph and Eliza were likely to be happy with each other. After a short visit to Wales the couple settled down in Birmingham to a life of shared interests in religion and philanthropy. Eliza's letters at this time refer to her 'perfect happiness' and complete agreement with Joseph. But it was all too brief. Soon Eliza knew that she was pregnant, and a sense of foreboding overshadowed any happy expectations she may have felt; mortality in childbirth was commonplace among women of her age. She started to return the letters that her correspondents had sent her over the years, and she made arrangements for the disposition of her property. On 14 February 1835 she gave birth to a daughter: four days later she and her child were dead. They were buried in the same coffin in the Friends' burial ground in Birmingham. Eliza and Joseph had been married for ten months.(6)

James Cropper, who had travelled to Birmingham to be near his daughter at the time of the birth, bore testimony to the strength of Sturge's religious convictions under this blow:(7)

> After dear Joseph had knelt down at the bedside in prayer for those who were left, I felt my mind engaged to speak of the thankfulness which was due from us to our Heavenly Father, who had heard our prayers, and those of the dear departed object of our love; and had, in boundless mercy, granted what we had sought in the sweet assurance of acceptance which she was permitted to feel. So far we have been enabled to experience it a time of rejoicing, rather than of mourning; except that the feeling of our own great loss cannot always be excluded.

In an age when great importance was attached to a dying person's belief in a future blessed state Eliza's pious death was a source of comfort and religious inspiration.

Sturge was also sustained by Sophia's support. For her, his decision to marry Eliza had been virtually a form of divorce that displaced her from the closest relationship and the only role she had known since 1816. There had been no question of her remaining in Joseph's house. As she explained to Mary Darby Sturge (Charles's wife), she could not even remain in Birmingham.(8)

> Notwithstanding my firm conviction that the step my dearest brother is taking will much increase his happiness, my attachment to him has been so peculiar, so exclusive, the long period we have passed together thro' many trying vicissitudes have [sic] so strengthened these tender bonds that nothing short of entire separation will even with Divine aid enable me to enter into the new relative position in which we shall in future be placed.

Like other middle-class women in her circumstances, she became a governess, but her infirmities made her duties burdensome, and she lingered unhappily over her thoughts of the past. After Eliza's death she easily resumed her accustomed place, and while she lived Sturge seems never again to have considered marriage.

Cropper and Sophia both gave Sturge the same advice: he must accept his bereavement as God's will and turn it to positive ends. In other words, he must dedicate himself to the life of 'the Christian Philanthropist'. Henceforward this was how Sturge saw himself, and increasingly it was how he was depicted in speeches, prose writings, poetry, paintings, and statuary - a man who had withdrawn from a career of self-advancement to enter a form of public life where his talents and wealth were dedicated to God and mankind. The high-sounding sentiments should not be dismissed as an absurdity or a sham: at a time when governments were influenced by laissez-faire principles or, worse still, by the vested interests of minorities with access to political power, philanthropists helped to create a valuable tradition of voluntary public service. Some of them were conservatives offering paternalistic humanitarian schemes to avert political and social upheaval, but others, like Sturge, made an important contribution to the ideas, techniques and institutions of radical reform which were passing through an important phase in their evolution during the second and third quarters of the nineteenth century. Using the pressure group and the voluntary society, they mobilised support for ideas that would otherwise have received scant attention, and they made public opinion a force in national politics.(9)

Sturge's adoption of the role of 'Christian Philanthropist' could be seen in the prayerful reflections on his bereavement which he recorded shortly before mid-night on New Year's Eve 1835.(10)

> 1835. 12/31. Near Midnight. - How eventful have been the occurrences of the past year to me! How has death destroyed my pleasant pictures! O Lord grant that it may be sanctified to me! that if before the close of another year it may please Thee to call me home, I may, through the boundless mercy of a crucified Redeemer, find forgiveness for my sins, though they are, indeed, as the sand of the sea for multitude, and if Thou should'st see meet to continue me as a sojourner upon earth, and take away

more of my pleasant gourds, grant, I beseech Thee, a continuance of that resignation to Thy divine will which I have thankfully to acknowledge Thou hast in the past year so mercifully extended in my times of greatest need. Enable me faithfully and diligently to fulfil Thy divine requirements in any path Thou may'st point out to me. The principal duties, it appears to me, in which I may be called to labour in the ensuing year are:

The cause of the poor African both in our own colonies and in other parts of the globe.

The question of birthright membership in our Society.

The prevention of first-day travelling on the London and Birmingham Railway; and

The promotion of the recognition of the free Gospel ministry.

Each of these New Year's resolutions was under way at the time of writing. Anti-slavery headed the list in every sense; for Sturge never altered his opinion that the unpaid Apprenticeship was 'slavery under another name'. At first he hoped that the system would be unworkable and that the planter-dominated legislatures in the colonies would follow the example of Antigua and Bermuda which had proceeded immediately to confer full freedom on the slaves as they were entitled to do under the terms of the Emancipation Act.(11) But this did not happen, and a trickle of reports from missionaries and others on the spot testified to the persistence of a degree of brutality that seemed to require prompt action by the British abolitionists.(12) In the months that followed Eliza's death Sturge and George Stephen tried to revive the anti-slavery movement, but almost immediately divisions appeared again, and it soon became evident that Sturge could not count on full co-operation from the leaders of either of the two national societies. Buxton preferred to work through official Government channels to correct abuses, and the London leaders of the former Agency Society made it clear that, although they saw the need for an agitation against the Apprenticeship, they had no intention of allowing it to fall into the hands of an unmanageable provincial activist like Sturge. As their organ, the Abolitionist, explained, the lead in any future movement would be taken by 'men of rank ... public leaders and parliamentary advocates': Quakers and others of 'status more obscure' were fit only to bear the heat of the day.(13) In practice this meant that much of 1835 and 1836 was given over to manoeuvres in the House of Commons where Buxton attempted to secure the appointment of a Select Committee on the working of the Apprenticeship. In a regression to the strategy of the mid-1820s the rank and file were confined to a subdued petitioning role.

Sturge's dissatisfaction was strengthened in June 1835 when the London leaders accepted the Government's assurance that all was well in the West Indies. Cropper had to dissuade him from summoning a national meeting of anti-slavery delegates to remind them that they had taken a pledge never to relax 'while slavery obtains under any form, however modified'. Instead, Sturge had to content himself during the second half of 1835 with building up Birmingham as the base for a future agitation. In July he reorganised the Birmingham Anti-Slavery

Society, and on 14 October he arranged a 'Great Anti-Slavery Meeting' in the Birmingham Town Hall where it was resolved that Parliament should be petitioned to meet promptly and suppress the Apprenticeship.(14)

Meanwhile relations between Sturge and Buxton steadily deteriorated. The minutes of the London Anti-Slavery Society show that, although Sturge occasionally attended the Society's meetings, the two men were irreconcilable by the end of 1835. Their most heated quarrel occurred when Sturge resigned from the Anti-Slavery Society rather than condone the payment of compensation to slaveowners in Mauritius, but there were deeper reasons for disagreement. Buxton wanted the British Government to regulate colonial labour relations under the terms of the Emancipation Act rather than leave the former slaves to the mercies of the colonial legislatures and magistracies. His own letters retained a tone of studied moderation, but feelings ran high in Buxton's family circle against 'that obstinate good little Dog Jos. Sturge' who was hindering this strategy. For his part, Sturge spoke of the clash as one between a compromising parliamentarian and a man who would 'not sacrifice principle to worldly expediency'.(15) The harsh judgements were unfair; in their different ways both men were products of the early nineteenth-century world of evangelical religion and philanthropy. As a Whig parliamentarian Buxton tried to influence British colonial policy within the competing pressures of the political system: as a provincial Quaker and businessman Sturge judged policies by a simpler standard of morality, and he had little faith in government as an agent of progress. But until 1837 it was Buxton who led the anti-slavery movement, and in May 1836 he persuaded the Commons to set up a Select Committee to inquire into the workings of the Apprenticeship. Agitation hung fire pending its report.

Sturge's New Year's resolution to do something about the birthright membership rules of Quakerism fared no better in 1836. Birth to Quaker parents was the usual way of being admitted to membership of the Society of Friends, but, like other evangelicals for whom true religion consisted of personal conviction and a life of vital Christianity, Sturge was disturbed by any implication that faith and fellowship could be inherited. On 9 December 1835 he set out his ideas as a proposition for consideration by the Warwickshire North Monthly Meeting: 'To consider whether the Rules with regard to Birthright Membership are consistent with the doctrine of Christ and his Apostles and the practice of primitive Christian Church as set forth in the New Testament.' The matter was discussed, adjourned to the next Monthly Meeting on 13 January 1836 and dropped.(16)

There were good reasons why Sturge did not persist: in 1836 the Society of Friends was riven by schism. The occasion was the publication in 1835 of A Beacon To The Society of Friends, where the author, Isaac Crewdson, described 'the desolating heresy' of Hicksism which had recently divided the Society in the United States. Crewdson associated Hicksism with deism, and he insisted that it was nurtured by the belief that mankind could acquire a knowledge of God 'immediately by the SPIRIT, independently of his revelation through the Scriptures'. This was an unmistakable assault on the traditional 'inner light' theology of Quakerism, and when the debate intensified Crewdson did not conceal his misgivings about silent worship, female preaching and other practices inherited from the early Friends.(17)

Looking to Sturge as a potential supporter, Crewdson sent him a copy of the Beacon and asked him to promote its sale in Birmingham. The book arrived shortly before Eliza's death, and they read it together, but, although they agreed with many of its criticisms, they refused to abandon the foundations of Quaker belief and practice. 'We are neither of us', Eliza wrote at this time, 'prepared to give up a belief in the perceptible influence of the Holy Spirit. We believe persons not only in our Society but in others, have occasionally & do still speak under that immediate guidance although we are ready to admit that we know of very few in the present day whose ministry we should stamp so highly.' Shrewdly, she was also quick to see the threat to female preaching: 'If we give up this principle [the inner light] how can we any longer receive the ministry of women?'(18) During the uncharacteristically bitter factionalism that culminated in Crewdson's secession to set up a short-lived Society of Evangelical Friends Sturge took the same position as Gurney and other Quakers on whose religious opinions he had come to rely: 'consistent Quakerism on an evangelical foundation' was the 'perfection of religion'.(19) Much had been done to redefine Quakerism in this sense by 1836, and the 'Gurneyites', as they were sometimes called, were content to remain in the Society and work for further change. For the moment it was no time to raise difficulties about birthright membership.

Sturge pursued his resolution to end Sunday travelling on the London and Birmingham Railway with more perseverance. As a director of the Company he raised the issue at board and shareholders' meetings between 1836 and 1838, supported by his brother John who summarised their position in a pamphlet entitled Remarks On The Regulation Of Railway Travelling On Sundays, Addressed To The Directors And Proprietors Of The London And Birmingham Railway. Quakers did not regard any one day as holy, and the pamphlet did not advocate sabbatarianism on religious grounds. The argument was pitched towards demonstrating that the Sabbath was an important civil institution 'essential to the welfare and improvement of the working classes', because schools as well as church services were available to large sections of the population on that day alone, and it was almost the only opportunity working people received for rest and family life: if work was required, the moral and physical deterioration of the nation would set in. Rising before the shareholders' meeting in 1838, Sturge supported a petition submitted by the Company's workers and forcefully argued that they could even be driven to insanity by a seven day working week. But the shareholders would vote only for a compromise motion allowing a limited timetable of services on Sundays;(20) for this had been an expensive line to build, and Sturge's proposal made poor business sense.(21) As always, compromise was unacceptable to him, and when the amendment was carried he resigned.

'The promotion of the free Gospel ministry', the fourth of Sturge's resolutions for 1836, is in some ways the most revealing indication of the way his mind was setting in the mid-1830s; it refers to the bitter campaign that he and other Dissenters waged against the Established Churches of England, Scotland and Ireland. This was a very recent development, quite unlike attitudes during the first quarter of the century when Dissenters had customarily yielded precedence to Anglican clergymen. The 'manliness of our Christian character was almost lost', the Eclectic Review complained in 1844:(22)

> and a servility of temper, adapted to engender contempt rather than to conciliate esteem, was induced. Those of us who can look back fifteen or twenty years, must remember some disgusting instances of this. The platforms of public meetings have frequently exhibited the disgraceful spectacle of dissenters pandering to the pride of priestism, magnifying the excellencies of men who condescended to associate with them in supplying the perishing with the bread of life, - dilating in inflated terms on virtues which had no existence, to their own disgrace, and the disgust of all intelligent hearers.

The tone of the writer was itself a product of the more assertive mood that swept across Dissent after 'the constitutional revolution of 1828-32' had raised hopes that the Whigs would reform the Church as well as the State, but it was soon evident that the Dissenters did not speak with one voice. Militant Congregationalists and Baptists in the provinces advocated voluntaryism, a theory that the Birmingham Reformer summarised in two propositions: '1. That there is to be a perfect equality of Christian sects. 2. That no sect of Christians is to be paid or supported by the State.' Leading London Dissenters and some provincials, on the other hand, favoured the piecemeal redress of grievances with respect to marriages, burials, university entrance and ecclesiastical imposts.(23) Although the voluntaryists were sometimes accused of irreligion and jealousy of the Established Church, it is important to recognise that their agitation was grounded on their version of evangelicalism: their spokesmen often referred to a struggle in which the ecclesiastical establishments of Antichrist would be overthrown before Christianity fulfilled its triumphal mission of converting the world. Close links were being forged between the sister churches on both sides of the Atlantic during the 1830s, and there were many references to the precedent set by the United States where Church and State had been separated.(24) Militant Dissenters also took heart from the 'storming party' approach to anti-slavery in which so many of them had participated (a contrasting decline of Anglican support for the movement was often noted), and compared their own unequal status at home with the slavery that had recently been abolished in the colonies.(25) In the words of the Christian Advocate the provincial activists should simply brush aside the 'truckling, or equivocal Dissenters' and set up an equivalent of the Agency Society. The opportune moment seemed to have come in 1834 when a national assembly of Dissenting delegates threw out some moderate proposals devised by the London leaders and voted that Voluntary Church Societies should be set up all over the country to work for the disestablishment of the Church of England.(26)

In December 1833 R.M. Beverley, a Dissenting journalist and polemical pamphleteer, approached Sturge to find out if the Society of Friends would join other Dissenters in a public campaign for disestablishment. As Beverley pointed out, the Quakers had a long history of refusing to recognise the claims of the Established Church, but when Sturge went to London a month later to canvass the opinion of the 'weighty Friends' he knew that he had little hope of success.(27) Richard Cobden's later comment was apt: Quakers had a reputation for 'keeping company with the "great" ' and they had usually looked to the patient cultivation of their influential associates for improvements in their legal situation.(28)

And so it was on this occasion; the Society of Friends would not make common cause with the voluntaryists of other churches. Sympathetic Quakers could only join Baptists and Congregationalists as individual members in the pressure groups which kept up a brisk campaign against the Church Establishment during the 1830s. Together with his brothers Charles and John, Sturge became a leading member of the Birmingham Voluntary Church Society and the Birmingham Church Rate Abolition Society, making the most of the opportunity to provoke some of the most bitter disputes during that exciting era in the town's history. But although Sturge helped to make Birmingham a stronghold of the movement, his actions divided the town's Dissenters; the Unitarians, the Methodists and J.A. James, the Congregational 'bishop of Carr's Lane', would have nothing to do with voluntaryism.(29)

Sturge's strategy was two-fold: at the same time as he attacked any Government offer of reform that fell short of disestablishment he would make the church rate system unworkable at the local level. Speaking from the chair at a Birmingham Voluntary Church Society meeting on 28 December 1835 Sturge gave a 'very appropriate and firm introduction ... on the subject of the Dissenters not resting satisfied with any measure of relief from [Cabinet] ministers less than a separation of the Church from the State'. He 'would rather wait twenty years longer', he told the meeting, 'and get rid of it [the payment of church rates] entirely, than accept any compromise of it now'. He took the same message with him to London a few weeks later when he formed part of a deputation to Lord John Russell, the Home Secretary.(30) In the meanwhile he was putting the complementary part of his strategy into practice. In August 1835 he challenged a church rate ('a legal robbery', he told the magistrates) and insisted that any distrained goods should be sold, not by private contract, but by public auction. This was described at the time as a manoeuvre to give publicity to the issue, but its full implications were not shown until a year later in nearby Aston when some distrained goods were offered for public sale by the church wardens. The voluntaryists sent out a bell man to announce what was happening, and the sale had to be called off in the face of an angry crowd. Here was one corner of England where the question had been 'finally settled', Charles Sturge told the Anti-Church Rate Society.(31)

Rather than compromise, 'they would have nothing': this summary of the Birmingham Voluntary Church Society's address to Lord John Russell in 1836 reveals Sturge's mentality in middle life. His attitude to temperance provides another example of this disposition, and it is rather surprising that his New Year's resolutions for 1836 made no reference to his involvement in the total abstinence movement. Temperance societies had originated in the United States, but like other religious and moral crusades of this era they soon developed a constituency on both sides of the Atlantic, and the Birmingham Temperance Society was founded in 1830. Sturge was one of the first to take its pledge.(32) These early pledges were modest commitments if judged by later standards; they required total abstinence only from spirits. The gentleman could still take wine, and the working man could have his beer, provided that moderate quantities were consumed. In London a British and Foreign Temperance Society came into existence as a national co-ordinating body under the patronage of bishops, peers, admirals and others of high rank: in the provinces local societies sprang into existence during the early 1830s to enrol members from all levels of society. At this stage there was a strong resemblance to the anti-slavery movement before the formation of the Agency Society.(33)

The Birmingham Temperance Society rapidly developed into one of the largest in the country, guided by a committee which included middle-class men who were already involved in the philanthropic activities of the town. Several of them, including Sturge, were members of the Mendicity Society which was founded in the same year to administer a strictly controlled ticket system of charitable gifts to the needy,(34) and from the start they concentrated on winning working-class adherents to the ideal of temperance as a form of social improvement through self-help. These were the years when the last remnants of Birmingham's 'guinea gardens' and other open spaces were covered over by rapid urban expansion, giving rise to concern for the leisure requirements of the poorer inhabitants. The same complaint was made there as in other large towns: the drink trade was expanding so rapidly that it would fill the social vacuum with poverty, crime and madness if working men were left to their own devices.(35) But temperance was more than a bracing regimen administered by middle-class disciplinarians to the working-class victims of 'The Bleak Age'; it was suffused with the millennial optimism that was powerfully influencing contemporary Britons of all classes. In 1834 the British and Foreign Temperance Society described its mission as one of protecting 'commercial intercourse and enterprise'; 'establishing relations of amity among nations as well as individuals'; and 'preparing the way of the gospel of peace'. A year later the Birmingham Temperance Society was assured that with the support of the religious world total abstinence would bring in 'something like the Millenium before that day twelve months'.(36)

The reference to total abstinence was important; for scarcely had the temperance movement got under way before there were complaints that the moderation pledge was not strong enough to prevent working-class beer drinkers from back-sliding into drunkenness. Increasingly the contrast offered by William Hogarth's famous engravings of 'Gin Lane' and 'Beer Street' (beer was described as 'the temperance drink' before the 1830s) fell from favour: both roads seemed to lead to social disaster, particularly when the liberal licensing regulations of the Beer Act (1830) could be blamed for causing drunkenness and debauchery.(37) Harsh comments were also made about the bad example of upper-class members who attended public dinners where the giving of healths encouraged excessive wine drinking. Dissatisfaction welled up in Preston where the famous 'seven' rejected 'moderationism' in 1832 and endowed the language with the word 'teetotal'. From this 'Jerusalem of teetotalism ... the word went forth in every direction', giving rise to grand gestures and frenzied agitation. Sturge's cousin, Cyrus Clark, had already shown the way by smashing his bottles of distilled liquors and incorporating the glass in the building materials of a new house; now his future brother-in-law, James Cadbury, poured a valuable stock of wines down the drain. Temperance meetings increasingly relied on emotional appeals from those whom G.J. Holyoake would later describe as 'drunkard bred teetotalers ... elevated to the platform before the fever of their last debauch has cooled in their veins'.(38) The gentry could not be expected to accept the new restrictions or preside over meetings such as these: in 1836 the teetotalers were warned that the movement in the London area was being destroyed by disputes over the rival pledges, and that, if they persisted with their aggressive proselytism within the British and Foreign Temperance Society, the Anglican clergy and other patrons would abandon the Society rather than be driven beyond the original pledge. It was an empty threat, and increasingly the movement fell under the sway of provincial men of humbler origins.(39)

Between 1834 and 1836 the Birmingham Temperance Society allowed its members to choose between the moderate and total abstinence pledges, but from April 1836 it was 'tee-totalism or nothing'.(40) Sturge was one of the prime movers of the change. In 1827, before there were any temperance societies or pledges in Britain, he had become a total abstainer (on medical advice), and in 1832 or 1833 he started to decline invitations to public dinners. Steadily during these years he cut back on his business dealings with the drink trade. He appears in Joseph Livesey's Reminiscences of Early Teetotalism as one of 'the pioneers of our cause', in the company of men who believed that a 'coup de main ... could destroy the drinking system in a few years, root and branch'.(41) Regularly on the annual licensing day he formed part of the temperance deputation which opposed any expansion of the drink trade in Birmingham, and he gave his support to a team of medalled and beribboned teetotalers who provoked disorders in the town because of their attempts to preach down the allied trades of the publican and pawnbroker.(42)

In Birmingham and other places where teetotalism became a significant force the effect was to deepen the social divisions within the working class at this time. Turning aside from the public houses which played such an important part in contemporary life, teetotalers formed their own temperance hotels, coffee houses, benefit societies and juvenile associations. Women members even took a special pledge to marry teetotalers, and newspaper reports referred to what was evidently a very full social calendar of meetings, tea parties and excursions for all members of the family.(43) Within this distinctive community middle-class Dissenters found a role as patrons. At one large social gathering in 1838 Sturge was described as presiding over 'four to five hundred persons' mostly of the working class who sat down to 'tea and plum-cake' in the Town Hall during the Easter holiday, traditionally a time of heavy drinking in the town. An atmosphere appropriate to an embattled minority is suggested by a description of the decorations on the walls:(44)

> Among the numerous mottoes inscribed upon banners, and hung round the body of the hall, were "It is good neither to eat flesh, nor to drink wine, nor anything whereby thy brother stumbleth, or is offended, or is made weak;" "God is with us;" "The Drunkard shall not inherit the kingdom of God;" "Strong drink is raging;" "Wine is a mocker;" "Domestic comfort;" "Intemperance destroys reason, impairs the health, deprives its victim of present happiness, and the hope of eternal blessedness" etc.

Anti-slavery immediatism, religious voluntaryism and total abstinence - again and again Sturge's reform movements during the 1830s exhibited similar characteristics: an uncompromising emphasis on principle; an upsurge of Dissenting self-confidence; a suspicion of parliamentarians and other bearers of traditional authority; a belief that moral and political virtue would have to be forced on London by plain men from the provinces; and the adoption of the word 'radical' to point up a contrast with others who claimed to be working to the same ends. A distinctive political constellation was emerging that had some of the characteristics of the better known 'Nonconformist Conscience' of the late nineteenth-century. One crucial difference, however, was that there was no question of acting within one of the major parliamentary parties; at this stage the search for reform was pursued most typically through societies which acted as a 'pressure from without' on Parliament. Exponents of this form of radicalism could be found in any district where there were evangelical Dissenters and militant ministers.(45)

Two incidents show what was happening. On 16 April 1835 a new weekly newspaper, the Reformer (later re-named the Philanthropist) was launched in Birmingham financed by capital which Sturge had raised.(46) It was a radical newspaper dedicated to policies derived from 'Christian principle'. It advocated voluntaryism, peace, free trade, the rights of the colonial apprentices, and the reform of manners; its columns gave considerable space to the reporting of temperance meetings; and it called for an extended suffrage supplemented by other organic reforms which would weaken the power of the aristocracy. But the prospectus offered more than a subscription to a political newspaper; it summoned 'sincere and disinterested patriots' to work towards 'that glorious period, when justice shall have established the universal fraternity of amity and peace; but which is to be accelerated by something more than inactive hopes and the quiet speculations of the study.' In short, readers were introduced to a Dissenter's millennium where all institutions 'civil and commercial' would be replaced by 'more pure, beautiful, rational, and

71

benignant institutions, than the world has ever yet dreamt of'. One of the newspaper's correspondents even found a name for those who shared these aspirations: they were 'the moral Radical party'.(47)

A second and closely related incident occurred in December 1836 when the Reformer/Philanthropist group of Dissenters selected Sturge as their candidate in any electoral contest for the Birmingham parliamentary seat currently held by Thomas Attwood, the founder of the Birmingham Political Union. The move was a measure of their dissatisfaction with the Union's Council which had engrossed control of electoral affairs in the town since 1832 and paid insufficient attention to the views of the local Dissenters. Led by Captain C.R. Moorsom, Sturge's associates set up an election committee, reduced his views to a political platform, and offered him to their fellow citizens as 'one of the very best specimens of the moral Radical party'. The move came to nothing when Sturge withdrew his name, but the platform is worth quoting as a statement of his political principles at that time:(48)

> Mr STURGE'S opinions on the political and social questions now publicly agitated, are most comprehensively liberal. Thus he is for the vote by ballot, for short Parliaments of certain duration; for a thorough reform of the House of Lords; for an extension of the elective franchise; for the abolition of church rates and all other ecclesiastical demands; for placing all Religious Denominations not only in Great Britain, but also in Ireland, on an equal footing of entire civil and social equality; for the abolition of the corn laws; for the practical application of the principles of free trade in every branch of industry; for sweeping reductions in the expenditure of every department of the State.

NOTES

1. Henry E. Huntingdon Library, Macaulay Papers, Zachary Macaulay to Selina Macaulay, 24 April 1824; Extracts From Letters of the Late James Cropper; Richard, Sturge, p. 82.

2. Sturge Papers (M.Sturge), John Sturge to Charles Sturge, 30 May 1830.

3. Macaulay Papers, 23 February 1834; Sturge Papers (Lewin), The Sturge Family. Macaulay Papers, Margaret Cropper to Hannah Macaulay, 18 February, 13 March, 18 March, 20 March 1834; Cropper Papers, James Cropper to Eliza Sturge, 10 August 1834.

4. Macaulay Papers, Margaret Cropper to Hannah Macaulay, 30 April 1834.

5. [James Grant], Portraits of Public Characters, London 1841, vol. 2, p. 291.

6. Extracts From Letters of the Late James Cropper, James Cropper to Eliza Sturge, 12 July 1834, and James Cropper to Martha Fletcher 21 February, 22 February 1835; Sturge Papers (Maud Sturge), Rebecca Waterhouse to Eliza Sturge, 26 May 1834 and Eliza Sturge to Rebecca Waterhouse, 28 June 1834 & n.d.

7. Extracts From Letters of the Late James Cropper, James Cropper to Martha Fletcher, 19 February 1835.

8. Sturge Papers (M. Sturge), Sophia Sturge to Mary Darby Sturge, n.d.

9. Hamer, The Politics of Electoral Pressure. A Study in the History of Victorian Reform Agitations, pp. viii, 1-10.

10. Richard, Sturge, pp. 111-12.

11. Sturge Papers (Maud Sturge), Eliza Sturge to Rebecca Waterhouse, 11 September 1834.

12. [T. Middleditch], Youthful Female Missionary: A Memoir of Mary Ann Hutchins, London 1840, pp. 106-35.

13. Abolitionist, August 1834; Christian Advocate, 17 August 1835.

14. [London] Anti-Slavery Society Minutes, 27 May 1835; Buxton, Memoirs, pp 318-19; Cropper Papers, James Cropper to Joseph Sturge, 20 June 1835; Reformer, 30 July 1835; Report Of The Proceedings Of The Great Anti-Slavery Meeting Held At The Town Hall, Birmingham, On Wednesday, October 14 1835.

15. [London] Anti-Slavery Society Minutes, 30 November 1835, Joseph Sturge to T. F. Buxton. See also The Papers of Sir Thomas Fowell Buxton, T. F. Buxton to J. Jeremie, 16 November 1835, Joseph Sturge to T. F. Buxton, 30 November 1835, T. F. Buxton to Joseph Sturge, 4 December 1835, T. F. Buxton to Zachary Macaulay, 4 December 1835, Robert Stokes to T. F. Buxton, 7 December 1835, Priscilla Johnston to Hannah Buxton, 8 December 1835.

16. Bull St., Meeting House, Monthly Meeting Minutes, North Division, 9 December 1835, 13 January 1836.

17. Crewdson, A Beacon To The Society Of Friends, London 1835, pp. 5-7, 9, 153.

18. Sturge Papers (Maud Sturge), Eliza Sturge to Rebecca Waterhouse, two undated letters in 1835.

19. Seebohm, Forster, vol. II, p. 80.

20. [John Sturge], Remarks On The Regulation of Railway Travelling On Sundays, Addressed To The Directors And Proprietors Of The London And Birmingham Railway, London 1836; Birmingham Journal, 3 February, 10 February, 24 February 1838; Philanthropist, 22 February 1838.

21. P. Lecount, The History Of The Railway Connecting London and Birmingham, London 1839, pp. 1, 19-20.

22. Eclectic Review, XVI, July-December 1844, pp. 342-43.

23. Reformer, 16 April 1835; Eclectic Review, VIII, July-December 1832, pp. 526-28.

24. Philanthropist, 19 May, and 15 December 1836, 16 February 1837; F. Thistlethwaite, The Anglo-American Connection in the Early Nineteenth Century, New York 1971, chap. 3.

25. Birmingham Journal, 27 July 1833; E. F. Hurwitz, Politics And The Public Conscience, London 1973, pp. 83-88.

26. Christian Advocate, 23 December 1833, 12 May 1834; Birmingham Journal, 17 May 1834.

27. Sturge Papers (M. Sturge), R. M. Beverley to Joseph Sturge, 13 December 1833, and Charles Sturge to Mary Darby Sturge, 1 January 1834.

28. Brit. Lib. Add. MSS., 43722 f. 8, Richard Cobden to Joseph

Sturge, 3 January 1854; Isichei, Victorian Quakers, pp. 191-93.

29. The Sturge brothers' voluntaryist activities were reported during the mid-1830s in the Birmingham Journal and the Birmingham Reformer/Philanthropist. For the divisions of the Birmingham Dissenters see Birmingham Journal, 15 February, 22 February 1834 and R. W. Dale, ed., The Life And Letters Of John Angell James: Including An Unfinished Autobiography, London 1861, pp. 338-39, 588.

30. Birmingham Journal, 2 January 1836; Christian Advocate, 29 February 1836.

31. Reformer, 27 August 1835; Birmingham Journal, 17 September 1836.

32. J. H. Lear Caton, Gleanings From The Past Seventy Years, Birmingham 1901, pp. 4-11; British and Foreign Temperance Herald, March 1832.

33. Report of the British and Foreign Temperance Society, London 1832.

34. Birmingham Journal, 9 January 1830, 23 May 1857.

35. Ibid., 14 February 1835.

36. British and Foreign Temperance Herald, July 1834; Reformer, 20 August 1835.

37. The 'bad press' received by the Beer Act is discussed by Harrison, Drink and the Victorians, London 1971, pp. 81-86.

38. [J. Livesey], Reminiscences of Early Teetotalism, Preston n.d., pp. 5-10; Street Teetotal Society, 1835-1935, p. 5; Sturge Papers (Lewin), The Sturge Family; G. J. Holyoake, The Social Means of Promoting Temperance With Remarks On Errors In Its Advocacy, n.d., p. 5.

39. Christian Advocate, 24 October 1836; Harrison, Drink And The Victorians, pp. 137-38.

40. Temperance Penny Magazine, April 1836; Preston Temperance Advocate, November 1836.

41. Birmingham Journal, 30 October 1841; Pilot, 20 December 1845; [Livesey], Reminiscences, pp. 29, 36.

42. Birmingham Journal, 9 July, 23 July 1836, 8 September 1838.

43. Philanthropist, 3 March, 10 March, 7 April, 14 April, 5 May 1836.

44. Birmingham Journal, 21 April 1838.

45. The type is described in various Nonconformist biographies and memoirs e.g. J. Guinness Rogers, An Autobiography, London 1903, pp. 4, 23, 41, 53 (describing his father and school); C. M. Birrell, The Life of William Brock, D.D., London 1878; Edwin Paxton Hood, ed., The Earnest Minister: A Record of the Life, and Selections from Posthumous and Other Writings of the Rev. Benjamin Parsons, of Ebley, Gloucestershire, London 1856; William Leask, Struggles For Life: An Autobiography, London n.d.; A. Mursell, James Phillippo Mursell. His Life and Work, London 1866; A. Miall, The Life of Edward Miall, London 1884.

46. Cropper Papers, 29 April 1835; H. R. G. Whates, The Birmingham Post 1857:1957, Birmingham 1957, pp. 31-32.

47. Reformer, 16 April 1835; Philanthropist, 15 December 1836, 29 June 1837.

48. Philanthropist, 15 December, 22 December, 29 December 1836, 12 January 1837. See also Birmingham Journal, 17 December, 31 December 1836. Sturge was in the West Indies at the time, Sturge Papers (M. Sturge), Joseph Sturge to Charles Sturge, 28 December 1836.

7 The Battering Ram of Public Opinion (1836-38)

It was as a 'moral Radical' that Sturge openly defied the authority of the Government and the London leaders of the anti-slavery movement between 1836 and 1838; he was not prepared to defer to men of rank who did not share his vision of the future.   Consequently, when Buxton's Select Committee reported in June 1836 that on the whole the Apprenticeship was working well and that its major provisions should not be disturbed,(1) there was no question of his accepting this as a satisfactory statement: it had to be discredited.   As he would do on several future occasions, he simply by-passed official channels and went directly to the scene of the dispute.   Once again his thoughts for the future were entwined with his meditations on the lessons he should learn from Eliza's death.   On 2 August 1836 (his forty-third birthday), he read a private record of her dying moments and prayed for divine guidance before committing himself to the visit to the West Indies that he had 'long' contemplated.   As if in answer to his prayers, on the same day James Cropper wrote and encouraged him to set out quickly.(2)   Plans soon took shape, and he found three men to accompany him on an unofficial tour of investigation: Thomas Harvey, the Rev. John Scoble and William Lloyd.   Their journey required some bravery, not so much because of the sea journey and the notorious risks to health in the West Indies, but because the 'cantcraft faction' was reviled by a white population which had used violence against the negroes and their champions in the recent past.(3)   The party left England on 17 November 1836, taking twenty-seven days to reach Barbados by sail.   From there Scoble and Lloyd went on to British Guiana, while Sturge and Harvey proceeded to Jamaica by way of Antigua, Montserrat, Dominica and the French island of Martinique.   Sturge was absent from Britain for seven months.

The Sturge mission to the West Indies gave rise to two books: Sturge and Harvey's The West Indies in 1837 (written up by Harvey from Sturge's journal) and Lloyd's Letters from the West Indies.   From these and other sources it is possible to see that the inquiry was not what it claimed to be, a dispassionate investigation by men who had sought the facts from a wide variety of witnesses.(4)   From the beginning Sturge anticipated that conditions in Antigua where the slaves had been set free in 1834 would compare favourably with the situation in the colonies which had instituted the Apprenticeship; he ignored economic and social differences between the islands. He also made it clear that he set little store by the opinions of officials including Sir Lionel Smith, the Governor of Jamaica, who reported to the Colonial Office that Sturge had snubbed him and placed himself in the hands of 'violent, disaffected people of Color, or in those of Partizan Magistrates'. In part this was a misunderstanding by the Governor who had offered the traditional hospitality of a Government House dinner unaware of his visitor's teetotal objections to this form of hospitality, but Sturge's account of his visit to Jamaica (half his time in the West Indies was spent there) shows that he consorted freely with Baptist missionaries who opposed the Apprenticeship.(5) Like other evangelical Quakers, Sturge was sympathetic to the work of the foreign missions, and he had become a member of the Birmingham branch of the Baptist Missionary Society in 1833. The 'intelligent negroes' whom he claimed to have interviewed on seventy to eighty Jamaican estates seem often to have been Baptist converts.(6)

Predictably, Sturge drew the conclusion that the apprentices were being treated with a brutal indifference to the rights they were supposed to have been given by the Act of Emancipation. There had never been any prospect that he would accept the view commonly expressed in official circles that the Apprenticeship, imperfect though it was, offered the planters and the servile population an opportunity of gradually adjusting to the freedom that would prevail after 1840. He looked for abuses, and they were not hard to find: denials of the apprentices' statutory free time and the authorisation by some special magistrates of harsh punishments by flogging and the treadwheel. In these circumstances he had no hesitation in judging the Emancipation Act to be a fraud: 'in every essential particular, it has been violated by the planters, with the connivance and even the active participation of the Executive Government'.(7)

Thus from the time of his return to Britain in May 1837 Sturge directed his efforts to ensuring that the predial majority would enjoy the same rights as the non-predials who were to be released from the Apprenticeship on 1 August 1838. His first action, which assured him of the funds needed to support a renewed public agitation, was to deliver a report on his mission to the Society of Friends, the principal paymaster of the anti-slavery movement in all the past agitations. Then, returning to Birmingham, he opened the campaign on 6 June 1837 at a public breakfast in the Town Hall. Over the years he had often spoken at meetings, but he had been content for the most part to leave this form of leadership to others. Now, as 'the chief apostle of Emancipation', he had to deliver speeches all over the country.(8) Even his friends at the Philanthropist conceded that he was often a disappointing public speaker, but there were occasions when his words and benevolent appearance could move audiences which shared his sentiments. J. A. James referred to his 'truly tender eloquence', and a writer who was present 'on several occasions at meetings of 4000 or 5000 persons' was greatly impressed to see Sturge 'so overpowered by his feelings as to burst into tears and be unable for some time to proceed with his address, when referring to the woes and wretchedness of his fellow-creatures'.(9)   An ability to weep was no disadvantage when evangelicals rallied to their good causes. But increasingly as the campaign gained momentum some of the stridency of the demagogue found its way into Sturge's speeches, until he could even threaten to drive the Whig Government from office for standing in his way. 'We ask your sympathy, your prayers', he told an obviously excited Town's Meeting in Birmingham during April 1838:(10)

> and I appeal to this great assembly, whether, if the minister of the crown again refuse our claim for negro freedom, I say, I ask ought they any longer to wield the destinies of this great nation. (Loud cries of No, no.) I repeat the query, are such men fit to govern a free people? (Cries of No, no) Well, Birmingham has ere this, given the note to a chorus in favour of liberty, which has reached the senate and the throne, and you will not be backward to strike it again, in favour of those who have none to help them.

The Select Committee on the Apprenticeship was re-convened to hear evidence that differed so sharply from its own earlier report, but, although the members spent seven days interviewing Sturge, the procedure was fruitless and ended in acrimony.(11) Discussions with the London anti-slavery leaders also broke down. Buxton would not do anything to justify the accusation that the anti-slavery movement was 'a band of enthusiasts who disdain all caution, and renounce all prudence'. His opinion was endorsed by George Stephen who performed a startling volte-face at this time. Stephen had been so incensed against the committee of the Anti-Slavery Society at the end of 1835 that he had threatened to challenge its members to a duel but he had subsequently changed his attitude and decided, in the interests of his 'seven little ones', to seek a knighthood with Buxton's assistance.(12)

Their opposition did little to hinder Sturge. Exploiting the authority conferred on him by his first-hand knowledge of the West Indies, he quickly called together a national meeting of delegates in November 1837. The meeting took place in London, but the invitations pointedly excluded anyone living within ten miles of the metropolis, and the delegates rejected the previous practice of placing the movement under the leadership of a parliamentarian. The spokesmen who would put their views before Parliament were to be the instruments of the movement, not its leaders; and at all costs, 'Downing St. influence' was to be kept at bay.(13) As a consequence, control remained in the hands of men whose political and social status was decidedly unimpressive by the standards of the day. Admittedly, they set up a London-based Central Negro Emancipation Committee to co-ordinate activities, but this was something of a facade; it was to correspond with the provincial delegates and act for them.(14) Several of the most important leaders of the anti-Apprenticeship movement, including Sturge, were not members. As William Lucas noticed when he attended a second meeting of delegates at Exeter Hall in March 1838, the most active of the zealous philanthropists were:(15) ' "in primis et super omnibus" Joseph Sturge ... Wm Wilson of Nottingham ... Scales of Leeds, S. Bowly, Wm Bunting, G.W. Alexander, J.T. Price,

Burnett, Josiah Forster, Dr Greville, Peter Clare, Geo. Stacey, W.D. Crewdson, Scoble, Boultbie of Birmingham, G. Thompson, Beverley and T.W. Blair of Bath.'

Lucas's list endorses the judgments that were often made at the time about the social composition of the anti-Apprenticeship movement. Four were Nonconformist ministers, and eight were Quakers, but there were no Anglican clergymen: five of them were provincial businessmen, but there were no members of the gentry. It was such a radical departure from the earlier model of the pressure group that the Christian Advocate warned them that they were doomed to failure:(16)

> As a "pressure from without" on Parliament, we predict that it will be wholly inoperative to work a more speedy abolition of the system. The House of Commons, whenever it turns a backward eye on matters out of doors, inquires not only what is said, but by whom it is said! not only what is done, but who are the doers! And should it ask these questions about the Exeter Hall demonstration, the answer will be somewhat less than satisfactory, though what was said was well said.

But the sort of agitation Sturge had in mind was not designed to give parliamentarians much opportunity to indulge their sense of hierarchy; from the beginning he made it clear that he was determined to 'humble the Colonial Office and awaken the nation from its trance'. During the months that followed the November convention of delegates he put his unrivalled knowledge of the anti-slavery movement on both sides of the Atlantic to good use by launching a two-pronged attack on the Apprenticeship. In the words of the British Emancipator (the organ of the movement) 'the battering ram of public opinion' was to smash its way through the British Parliament: simultaneously, William Knibb and other Baptist missionary allies were to put pressure on the planters in Jamaica, the home of half of the apprentices.(17) Secure in the knowledge that he himself would never compromise, Sturge confidently built up a crisis and awaited a failure of nerve in Westminster and Spanish Town.

Seldom have 'expressive politics' enjoyed such a triumph. Sturge got the movement off to a good start by publishing a heartrending pamphlet entitled The Narrative of James Williams which had the desired effect of raising a public outcry. Williams was a young Jamaican apprentice whom Sturge had purchased, manumitted and brought to Britain as a living exhibit of the horrors of plantation life. Ghost-written as a penny pamphlet of twenty-four pages, his was a chillingly simple story of persistent brutalisation by flogging and the treadmill. The agitation was given a fillip when the Colonial Office set up a special commission of inquiry which confirmed the worst of the allegations, and Sturge soon had agents at work all over the British Isles turning the scandal to good advantage by setting up a network of anti-slavery societies. Sympathetic M.P.s, especially Lord Brougham, Sir George Strickland, Sir Eardley Wilmot and Daniel O'Connell gave invaluable assistance at the next stage by initiating debates in

Parliament, and, on the two most important of these occasions in March and May 1838, Sturge summoned national meetings of delegates to London to demand the abolition of the Apprenticeship.(18) In 'every direction', Sophia told one of Sturge's Jamaican correspondents in March 1838,(19)

> instruments appear to have been raised by a special Providence to aid & advocate this holy cause - The Delegates assembled this week have amounted to nearly or quite 466 - several of them have been in town for some weeks, many are from the most distant parts of the United Kingdom, some engaged in extensive business, others of advanced age, many pastors of large and flourishing congregations, & not a few defraying the whole expenses of their journey, residence in London etc. - Men who will do all this must with the blessing of God finally succeed.

When they assembled again in May, the delegates divided into sixty groups which systematically hunted down nearly every member of both Houses of Parliament 'urging every consideration to obtain their influence and vote on behalf of the oppressed'. William Smeal saw what was virtually a waggon-load of petitions presented to the House of Commons on this occasion. Everyone agreed that the movement revolved around Sturge: travelling round the country or co-ordinating tactics from a base in Parliament Yard, he was 'the impersonification of activity and ubiquity'.(20)

It was in vain that W. E. Gladstone and other hostile parliamentarians objected that they were being treated as 'mere machines' for voting according to outside instructions.(21) Sturge and his associates saw themselves as spokesmen for 'the many' and 'the people', a vaguely defined but very wide constituency of both sexes whose wishes they refined and mediated through public meetings, petitions, press comment and the election of delegates. Above all, they spoke as the conscience of a nation cruelly deceived by politicians who had retained slavery in all but name.(22) Reaching what were described as new heights of 'moral grandeur & dignity' in public oratory, George Thompson summarised what they stood for when he offered Gladstone (the son of a plantation owner) and Sturge as contrasting examples of men in public life: 'while he, Gladstone, was wallowing in wealth, arising from the hire of his labourers kept back by fraud - the cry of the labourers meanwhile having entered into the ears of the Lord of Sabaoth - Joseph Sturge had been engaged in a Mission of love - a circumnavigation of charity etc.'(23)

In the meanwhile Sturge and his Baptist missionary allies were setting out to make the predial apprenticeship unworkable in Jamaica by August 1838. It was a dangerous policy which carried an undeniable possibility of disorder, but there was nothing mealy mouthed about the 'moral Radicals'; 'fiat justitia, ruat coelum' was a running refrain throughout this phase of the anti-slavery movement. Brushing aside Buxton's misgivings about the danger of raising the expectations of the negroes, Sturge translated the adage into plain English when he addressed the convention of delegates in November 1837: 'He was fully convinced that if the consequences were what some apprehended, they would, in the sight of God and man, rest upon those who denied justice, and not upon those who asked for it.'(24)

The reports of Sir Lionel Smith show that Sturge had made a start while he was in Jamaica. Not only did he arrive there with a pile of anti-slavery posters (one of which found its way into Smith's hands), but the way he pursued his inquiry had been enough to make the negroes believe that he was 'a great "Buckra" [white man] come to terminate their Apprenticeship'. When William Lloyd reached Jamaica he found some of the apprentices wearing broad-brimmed 'Sturge-hats' as a gesture that must have been seen as defiance of their masters.(25) More importantly, while he was on the island, Sturge persuaded William Knibb to instruct the members of the Baptist churches that they must immediately manumit their apprentices with a fanfare of publicity. This was perfectly legal, but the intention was to create an expectation that the whole population would be set free on 1 August 1838. By September 1837 Knibb could write to Sturge that their strategy had created 'a great deal of excitement' in the colony and that they should persuade Lord Sligo and other sympathetic plantation owners to set their apprentices free and 'blow the system to atoms'. They even encouraged reports that a general strike of predials would take place in August 1838, a form of protest which would have required a remarkable degree of restraint at a time when insurrection and cruel repression were fresh in everyone's memory.(26)

In public Lord Melbourne's Cabinet upheld the belief that the Emancipation Act of 1833 was a compact with the planters which the British Government could not unilaterally dissolve, but the failure of nerve on which Sturge was counting occurred as early as March 1838 when Sir George Strickland brought in a motion for the termination of the predial Apprenticeship on 1 August. Although Strickland was defeated, Lord Holland confided to his diary that the lobbying had intimidated 'members from populous places' and shaken Lord Glenelg, the Colonial Secretary.(27) On 2 April, taking advantage of the temporary lull which followed the debate, Glenelg began the process of backing down by writing confidentially to the Governors of the Caribbean colonies that they should follow up any indication that the local assemblies were prepared to end the Apprenticeship by their own legislation. The two reasons he gave were a tribute to Sturge's effectiveness as an agitator: 'the force of public opinion' in Britain, coupled with the difficulty of maintaining 'tranquility in the colonies'.(28) The Jamaican planters had been following events with close attention, and Sir Lionel Smith seems to have encountered little opposition when he told the Council and Assembly members that in the circumstances they had no choice other than to confer freedom on all the apprentices on 1. August 1838. By then reports were coming in that other colonies were taking similar action. On 16 June the Jamaican Act for abolishing the predial apprenticeship passed into law.(29)

It was well that the Jamaican legislature was prepared to give way, for on the other side of the Atlantic Sturge's campaign was relentlessly reaching its climax. On 22 May Sir Eardley Wilmot, backed by all the lobbying and petitioning resources that Sturge could provide, pushed a resolution in favour of total and immediate emancipation through a thinly attended House of Commons.   The vote had no legislative force, but Wilmot prevaricated when the Government urged him to transform the resolution into a Bill which Parliament could debate (and defeat) before the official packet ships sailed for the West Indies.   Eventually, on 25 May he revealed the abolitionists' course of action.   They were interested only in the effect their triumph would have in the colonies, and already they had independently sent news of the Commons' vote to the West Indies: they would therefore proceed no further in the House.   As several MPs pointed out, this was a ruthless exploitation of parliamentary procedures, a means of creating a mistaken impression that Parliament had abolished the Apprenticeship: when the truth became known there would be a strong likelihood of an outbreak of disorder by the disappointed predials.(30) The possibility of a major disaster in the Caribbean was very narrowly averted in mid-1838.

1 August 1838 was a moment of triumph for Sturge.   All over the British Empire the predial apprentices celebrated the freedom that Parliament would have withheld from them until 1840.   In a letter to Sturge one of the former slaves described what happened in his part of Jamaica.   At daybreak the people assembled in the Moravian mission chapel and 'hailed the free sun ... with beautiful anthems and solemn hymns'.   Later in the day there was a 'universal scene of animation' during a religious service which culminated in an address of praise for the labours of Sturge and other abolitionists.   In five days of celebration there was none of the drunkenness and violence that opponents of emancipation had often prophesied.(31)   The principal celebration in Britain occurred appropriately enough in Birmingham, where the day opened with a Festival attended by 3500 children, mostly from the Baptist Sunday schools, who had marched through the town to the site of the Negro Emancipation School Rooms.   There Sturge laid a foundation stone with an inscription which hailed him as 'the friend of the Negro, the friend of the children, and the friend of man'.   The celebrations were continued at a meeting in the Town Hall that evening, and a public breakfast took place the next day which was attended by Daniel O'Connell and other well known opponents of slavery.   In a final petty gesture the guest lists for these meetings did not include T.F. Buxton.   He would not have felt at ease; for the 'new men' who had rallied to the anti-Apprenticeship movement were intent on celebrating a triumph over all their opponents.   The Rev. Thomas Scales delivered an address contrasting this gathering with the scenes in 1791 when a 'Church and King' mob had attacked the property of Dissenters in the town, and both Sturge and O'Connell spoke ominously of undertaking future tasks now that the 'pressure from without' had demonstrated its effectiveness as an instrument of reform.(32)

NOTES

1.   House of Commons.   Report from the Select Committee on Negro Apprenticeship in the Colonies, 1836, p. viii.

2. Extracts From Letters of the Late James Cropper, 2 August 1836.

3. Richard, Sturge, pp. 130-31.

4. Kingston Chronicle and City Advertiser, 13 June 1837. J. Sturge & T. Harvey, The West Indies in 1837, London 1838, p. vii.

5. Philanthropist, 12 January 1837; Public Record Office, CO 137/222, ff. 135-38, Sir Lionel Smith to Lord Glenelg, 16 July 1837.

6. Philanthropist, 8 June 1837.

7. Sturge & Harvey, p. 371.

8. Christian Advocate, 29 May 1837; Philanthropist, 8 June 1837.

9. Philanthropist, 15 December 1836; Christian Advocate, 8 February 1836; [James Grant], Portraits of Public Characters, vol. 2, p. 89.

10. Birmingham Journal, 21 April 1838.

11. Sturge's evidence to the Committee does not seem to have been preserved, House of Commons, Report from the Select Committee on Negro Apprenticeship in the Colonies (1837). See also Christian Advocate, 20 November 1837.

12. The Papers of Sir Thomas Fowell Buxton, T. F. Buxton to Josiah Forster, 3 November 1837, T. F. Buxton to Sarah Buxton, 14 December 1836; George Stephen to T. F. Buxton, 23 June 1837.

13. Christian Advocate, 20 November 1837; British Emancipator, 17 January 1838; Birmingham Anti-Slavery Society Minute Book, 14 September, 14 October, 25 October 1837.

14. The Papers of Sir Thomas Fowell Buxton, Josiah Forster to T. F. Buxton, 17 November 1837.

15. The members of the Central Negro Emancipation Committee were listed in the British Emancipator, 2 April 1838. See also Bryant & Baker, eds, A Quaker Journal, I, p. 131.

16. Christian Advocate, 19 March 1838.

17. John Rylands University Library of Manchester, Raymond English Collection, George Thompson to Elizabeth Pease, 31 May 1837; British Emancipator, 7 April 1838; Hinton, Knibb, p. 244.

18. Regent's Park College, Oxford, The Fenn Collection, E19.Y., Joseph Sturge to Rev. John Clarke, 23 March 1837; James Williams, A Narrative Of Events, Since The First of August, 1834, London 1837; Public Record Office, CO 137/221, f. 77, Commissioners of Inquiry to Sir Lionel Smith, 23 October 1837. The British Emancipator chronicled the events of this agitation between December 1837 and August 1838.

19. Fenn Collection, E19.Y., Sophia Sturge to John Clark, 31 March 1838.

20. Birmingham Anti-Slavery Society Minute Book, 4 July 1838 & 1 August 1838; British Emancipator, 2 April, 13 June 1838; Friends House Library, Box H2/7, William Smeal, 1793-1877, Memorandums relating to the Yearly Meeting 1838, the Anti-Slavery Cause etc.

21. Hansard, 30 March 1838.

22. See, for example, British Emancipator, 7 April 1838.

23. Smeal, Yearly Meeting 1838.

24. Philanthropist, 23 November 1837. Sturge and his friends refused to allow Buxton to propose a motion calling on the apprentices

to be peaceable and obey the laws until they were set free. See The Papers of Sir Thomas Fowell Buxton, T. F. Buxton to Sir George Stephen, 3 April 1838.

25. Public Record Office, CO 137/220, ff. 32-4, 172, Sir Lionel Smith to Lord Glenelg, 12 June, 16 July 1837; CO 137/222, ff. 135-40, Smith to Glenelg, 16 July 1837; W. Lloyd, Letters From The West Indies, London 1840, pp. 179-80.

26. Hinton, Knibb, pp. 244-48; Rylands English MSS 741 (136), transcribed letter from William Knibb to Joseph Sturge, 12 September 1837; Philanthropist, 4 January 1838; British Emancipator, 2 April 1838.

27. A. D. Kriegel, ed., The Holland House Diaries, 1831-1840, London 1977, p. 385.

28. Lord Glenelg to Colonial Governors, 2 April 1838, in M. Craton, J. Walvin, & D. Wright, Slavery Abolition and Emancipation: Black Slaves and the British Empire, London 1976, p. 342.

29. Public Record Office, CO 137/231 ff. 229-30, Sir Lionel Smith's Speech to the Jamaica legislature, 5 June 1838. See also W. L. Burn, Emancipation and Apprenticeship in the British West Indies, London 1937, p. 359.

30. Christian Advocate, 28 May 1838; Hansard, House of Commons, 24 & 25 May 1838.

31. British Emancipator, 8 August 1838; The Papers of Sir Thomas Fowell Buxton, W. Hamilton of Lennox, Jamaica to Joseph Sturge (newscutting).

32. Birmingham Anti-Slavery Society Minute Book, 1 August 1838 (including booklet presented to children and a specially printed pamphlet); Birmingham Journal, 4 August 1838; The Papers of Sir Thomas Fowell Buxton, T. F. Buxton to Joseph Sturge, 30 July 1838.

PART 3

'WHITE AND BLACK SLAVES'

8 Always Beginning
(1838-40)

'The real doctrine of agitation, and I am a thorough agitator is this - to be always beginning.'(1)   Daniel O'Connell's words on 1 August 1838 could almost be taken as a description of Sturge's activities during the next five years: a life of commitment to an ever-growing number of reform movements and philanthropic ventures at home and overseas. Some idea of the jostling reality of his varied interests at this time was conveyed in a letter he wrote in May 1839 asking Lord Brougham (an important ally within the political world at Westminster) to move in the House of Lords for the official correspondence on the slave trade; offering an opinion on coolie immigration schemes in the colonies; touching on 'the Corn Law affair'; and ending with a postscript, 'Please not to forget Mauritius'.(2)   At the age of 47 in 1840 Sturge was in his prime as a reformer, 'blessed with such a good constitution', he admitted on one occasion, 'that he was too apt to forget' that his associates might not 'be favoured with equal physical strength'.(3)   J.A. James probably spoke for many of them when he good-naturedly protested that, though he felt honoured by the number of times Sturge visited him to discuss philanthropic matters, he had sometimes thought: 'what Mr Sturge here again!'.(4)   As Sturge explained at a public meeting in 1840, his calling was to public life:(5)

> God had been pleased to sever for ever some of those ties which often made the claims of families and domestic duties paramount to those of a public nature - that he was in a position which left him less excuse than many others, not to give his fellow countrymen the benefit of his best exertions, if they considered that he could in any way serve them, or promote the interests of their common country.

The reference was to the death of Eliza and their child.   He was still the centre of an extended family, and he associated them with his reforming ventures, but his commitments often took him away from Birmingham for extended periods of time, so that even Sophia had to admit that she could do little to save him from 'over anxiety & mental pressure & want of sufficient time for quietude & retirement'.(6)
     Anti-slavery matters remained in the forefront of his concerns

for several months after the ending of the Apprenticeship. They were only on 'the threshold of their labours', Sturge told the Birmingham meeting on 1 August; in the Empire the legal rights of the freedmen had yet to be defined, and large numbers of men, women and children remained in bondage in the United States and elsewhere.(7)   In particular, the continuing problem of Jamaica often claimed his attention during the second half of 1838 and much of 1839, for he rightly feared that the local legislature had terminated the Apprenticeship 'in the worst possible spirit'.   There were schemes for importing coolie labourers from Asia that looked suspiciously like a new form of the slave trade, and his missionary friends warned him that the abolitionists must remain ready to oppose vagrancy and police legislation designed to make a travesty of freedom.(8)   More importantly, it now became evident that Buxton and the Colonial Office had been correct to fear that an abrupt termination of the Apprenticeship would entail hardships for some of the black population.   The whips and chains that abolitionists had so often flourished at their meetings had not told the whole story of plantation life; reciprocal rights and expectations had emerged during the previous two hundred years.   J.J. Gurney, who visited the West Indies in 1840, was told that on 'many of the estates' the slaves had been 'well fed and clothed, and were kindly treated in other respects.   Their provision grounds were often ample, the poor and infirm were supported with the rest, medical attendance was given, and many of them found opportunities for saving money.'(9) Reality had often fallen below this happy state, but these were certainly some of the 'indulgences' of slavery, and they had been incorporated in the Apprenticeship system.   Suddenly on 1 August 1838 they had no legal standing.

The abolitionists had been warned that this would happen, but they had either brushed the possibility aside or welcomed it.(10) Sturge had envisaged that the freed population would remain on the plantations for the most part, paying rent for their houses and allotments as well as supporting the aged and infirm out of wages negotiated according to market forces.   Now the Baptist missionaries told him that a 'combination' of masters was imposing unjust wage and rent settlements on pain of eviction.   There were even cases such as the one he forwarded to Lord Holland in which a woman who wished to remain at home with her baby instead of working in the fields was physically ejected from her house while her furniture was destroyed and her pig was shot.   William Knibb feared that there was a real possibility of seeing the negroes reduced to 'the miseries which have so long afflicted Ireland, by an extended pauperism and debasement, the result of absenteeism and a rate of wages which grinds her to the dust'.(11)   But the Irish comparison turned out to be appropriate in other ways too; as was often noted at the time, the events of the 1830s had given the Baptist missionaries such a hold over large sections of the local population that they could be compared with the Catholic clergy in Ireland.   Faced by large numbers of former apprentices seeking their advice about the planters' terms of employment, Knibb and his brethren started holding public meetings at which they set down a minimum wage and initiated strikes. Soon there were hostile reports of a gigantic Baptist 'combination' led by Knibb - the 'Pope', the 'Mahomet' and the 'O'Connell of the blacks'. Collectively the Baptist missionaries acquired a reputation as 'the Joseph Rayner Stephenses of the negroes'. And there is no doubt that several of the missionaries took to the role of trade union leader with relish. It was reported that the Rev. Samuel Oughton, to give only one example, 'tells the people, publicly, that no man has so much power in the Parish as he; and he will make the planters come to him, and come into his measures, or stop the estates'.(12)

If Sturge had any misgivings about this flouting of early Victorian notions of industrial relations, he seems to have dismissed them and allowed himself to be carried along by the momentum of events. Smoothly, almost imperceptibly, as chattel slavery receded into the past he and his missionary friends redefined abolitionism as a movement for the civil rights of the freedmen. He acted as the missionaries' intermediary with the Colonial Office, and he helped to organise a Legal Defence Committee to support them when their activities gave rise to prosecution in the Jamaican courts.(13) Together they set out to turn the island into a model society. During his visit to the Baptist mission stations in 1837 Sturge believed he had seen 'a Christian and civilized people'; a year later he was told that Knibb and his brethren were winning an ascendancy over the majority of the population. Letters and reports from the Baptist missionaries during the early months of freedom exultantly referred to overflowing chapels and to enthusiastic support for the institutions they had founded to promote the virtues of self-help and Christian respectability in the daily work, family life and social activities of the converts: institutions such as schools, temperance societies, savings banks and self-supporting dispensaries. They set up anti-slavery societies to promote the cause of freedom in other lands, and there were plans to send black missionaries to West Africa to exploit their affinities with the local population.(14)

The vision that took shape in Sturge's mind revealed Jamaica as something like a social laboratory for the programme of the 'moral Radical party'. 'I think you have one of the finest opportunities in history for carrying the voluntary principle fully out', he wrote to the Rev. John Clark in October 1838, and he successfully threw his influence against any temptation to accept government grants for Baptist schools. The local population, he insisted, must bear the burden, aided only by gifts from well-wishers. He worked hard to obtain these gifts, becoming the driving force of the Jamaican Education Society which provided money for the opening of schools in neglected parts of the island.(15) An engraving that probably dates from this period shows him with his hand on the shoulder of a grateful West Indian child. Soon, he told an anti-slavery meeting, Jamaica would become a truly self-governing community: 'Let the people have a colonial legislature; let such an extension of the franchise be given as to insure the voice of the people being heard, and there was no doubt but that they would protect themselves.'(16) For several years the 'moral Radical' programme had envisaged a wider franchise for Britain, but it was from this time, in response to events in Jamaica as well as Britain, that the connection between social and political progress became a prominent theme in Sturge's public statements.

Above all, as he wrote in his letter to Clark, the success of their experiments in Jamaica depended on the ability of the freedmen to obtain 'fair & equitable wages'.(17) Consequently, when he heard that the planters were determined to batten down on the wage level, he supported the Baptists in their most ambitious plan so far, a scheme for creating free townships. Sturge had seen free townships in Antigua in 1836, where he had been told that they filled a useful function as 'reservoirs of surplus labour, enabling planters to employ many or few hands, according to their actual wants', and at the time he had cited them as proofs of the abolitionist argument that free labour would be cheaper than slavery.(18) But he moved beyond these crude economic propositions when he set up a West India Land Investment Company to buy up bankrupt plantations for subdivision and resale to members of Baptist congregations who wished to acquire small-holdings. According to the Company's prospectus the object was:

> to transfer the controul of West India property gradually from those who have systematically opposed the advancement of the Negroes in civilization, knowledge and christianity, to such men as would really promote their moral and religious welfare, and also to afford places of refuge to those of the West India Peasantry who may still be harassed by various forms of oppression.

£100,000 were to be raised from the sale of shares at £500 each, and, as was usually the case with British anti-slavery ventures, the scheme depended on Quaker paymasters. With ten shares Sturge made the largest commitment, and other Quakers, including some of his relatives, agreed to make up much of the rest. Although the Company ran into legal difficulties (it violated the law on mortmain) and had to be dissolved, Sturge went ahead and made substantial loans for the purchase of suitable sites. 'MR JOSEPH STURGE advanced the money, and we soon paid it back', Knibb told the Anti-Slavery Convention in 1840.(19)

The free townships were a great success, sufficient to make their historian describe them as having a revolutionary effect on Jamaican society. Between 1838 and 1844, 19,000 freedmen and their families, possibly 100,000 people in all, settled in them. As Knibb noted in a letter to Sturge, freeholds carried votes, and he seems to have envisaged the townships as an electoral base for a Baptist political party, but the bid for political dominance failed after a few years, and they developed into a variant of the community-building that was a common feature of the English-speaking world during the second quarter of the century. Clustered around their chapels and schools, they were like the 'little utopias' in the contemporary United States where social and religious theories were put into practice as models for mankind.(20) In this instance they offered a proof that voluntaryism could be something more than opposition to the Established Church: that it could be a positive creed for originating practical reforms and sustaining a Christian way of life independently of the State. The atmosphere of idyllic Christianity was captured in a letter to Sturge where the people wore described as gathering for 'devotional exercises every morning, before going forth to labour, and in the evening when the toils of the day are over'.(21)

Thus within a year of the ending of the Apprenticeship Sturge could reasonably believe that a prospering nation of freedmen was rising from the ruins of the old slave society in Jamaica. The letters he received from his missionary friends depicted a scene of profound tranquillity in mid-1839 where an industrious population was hard at work: some on the estates; others reclaiming waste land for small holdings; and others setting up new villages. Plans for agricultural improvement were under way; machinery was being introduced; and railways, the symbol of early Victorian progress, were being planned. It seemed to be 'the dawn of a brighter day'.(22) It was also a time when the Baptist missionaries permanently altered the map of the island by scattering the names of their benefactors over the newly established free townships: Clarksonville, Thompson Town, Sligoville, Wilberforce, Buxton and many others. One of the new settlements was named Sturge Town, and Knibb carried the compliment further in 1839 by commissioning a marble memorial for his chapel on which 'The Emancipated Sons of Africa' could acknowledge their debt of gratitude to three men: Granville Sharp, William Wilberforce and Joseph Sturge.(23)

Knibb's memorial rounded off one phase of the history of the anti-slavery movement, the campaign against negro slavery and the Apprenticeship in the British Empire. Another event in the same year marked a new departure: Sturge was instrumental in founding the British and Foreign Anti-Slavery Society, the organisation from which the present British Anti-Slavery Society traces its descent. This was an attempt, not only to keep a watch on events within the British Empire, but also to play a part in opposing slavery anywhere else. It was also an excellent example of what Sturge's ceaseless energy could achieve during months of travelling around England winning support for the idea of abolishing slavery throughout the world.(24)

A phrase in a letter Sturge sent to Lord Brougham in October 1838 shows that he anticipated disagreements over the correct course of action: the use of force, he wrote, was a 'hopeless' method of suppressing the slave trade that was still carried on under foreign flags. This was a reference to the squadron of the Royal Navy which patrolled the African coast to put down the sea-borne trade in slaves. Loopholes would always exist in this blockade, Sturge believed, as long as there were slave-owning countries to offer lucrative 'temptation' to shippers. He was right. An historian has referred to the continuing profitability of the trade during these years.(25) But beyond these pragmatic considerations Sturge was opposed to the African Squadron in principle: it was a violation of the Quaker peace testimony, a denial that the best and only moral way to suppress the slave trade was to destroy slavery itself. On this principle he set out an abolitionist agenda in a letter to the editor of the British Emancipator on 23 January 1839:(26)

The first step to be taken would probably be an efficient organization of a society. For this purpose a meeting of a few of our friends should be held, to discuss the basis on which it should be founded; to be followed in a few weeks by one of a more general character, when the measures proposed might be considered and determined on, and a public meeting might afterwards be held to give them sanction and due notoriety. Such a society would of course vigilantly watch the infant liberties of our negro population, and the removal of the last vestige of slavery in the British Colonies....

Amongst the means which suggest themselves as likely to be effectual in this great cause, are the opening an active correspondence with the abolitionists in America, France, and elsewhere, and aiding and encouraging them by every means in our power; the use of free grown produce in preference to slave-grown, and the promotion of fiscal regulations in favour of the former; the circulation of information on the enormities of the slave-trade and slavery; the urging unequivocally the full recognition of the principle in every part of our dominions, equally with England itself, that the slave, of whatever clime or colour, should be perfectly and forever free on treading on British soil; the opening a correspondence with Hayti and the British West Indies etc.; the circulating information in slave-holding countries, proving not only the safety, but the great advantage of freedom even in a pecuniary point of view; marking abhorrence of the system by avoiding association with all slave-holders who may visit England.

On 27 February he met sixteen well known abolitionists in the Guildhall Coffee House, London, where they accepted this programme and arranged for a further meeting at Exeter Hall on 17 April to which they invited all prominent abolitionists including those who had attended the anti-slavery conventions during the 1830s. The meeting took place; the British and Foreign Anti-Slavery Society was formally constituted; and Sturge was given the status of Honorary Corresponding Member with the right to attend and vote at Committee meetings. It was no sinecure position. Not only did much of the Society's correspondence come through his hands but, thanks to the new railways, he regularly attended and chaired the Committee meetings in London. Particularly in the early years he exerted a decisive influence on policy-making.(27)

Once again Sturge's activities aroused concern amongst Buxton's friends. 'I think he is anxious to forestall Mr Buxton, and if possible to take the lead out of his hands in this question also', one of them wrote on 1 January 1839.(28) For Buxton too had reached the conclusion that the only way to destroy the slave trade was by destroying slavery itself. In 1839-40 he published The African Slave Trade and its Remedy where he argued that Africa must be transformed by the introduction of systems of agriculture and commerce which would offer greater rewards than the slave trade. To this end he proposed that the Royal Navy should maintain its coastal patrol as long as was necessary and, more importantly, that an expedition should be fitted out by private individuals and the Government to carry out a pilot scheme of economic development on the upper reaches of the Niger.(29)

Although some abolitionists gave their support to Buxton as well as Sturge on the grounds that their plans were complementary, this was not Sturge's attitude. 'Our friend Joseph Sturge is somewhat restive about my slave trade views', Buxton told J. J. Gurney on 5 March 1839 and 'won't go along with me'. Sturge would have no part in the African Civilization Society which Buxton set up in June of that year. It was a matter of principle, he told Gurney a year later in a letter expressing surprise to find him sanctioning the Niger Expedition; no Quaker should endorse the use of armed force.

> Now I believe that those views are not only strictly scriptural but constitute one of the most important testimonies of the Society of Friends. We I think justly hold that taking any human life whether in war or by an armed police to be murder and I believe we should both agree that it is better or at least not worse to murder a man ourselves than to encourage or hire another to do it for us.(30)

Gurney sent Sturge's rebuke on to his brother Samuel who explained the problem away in a letter that would have made the proverbial Jesuit blench. It was true, he admitted, that the expedition would be carried on armed vessels, but these were the responsibility of the Government, not the African Civilization Society whose agents would be concerned only with agricultural and commercial matters. He had, he added, written to Sturge expressing displeasure on learning of his opposition to the scheme and reminding him that the Gurney family was currently making an important contribution to the funds of the British and Foreign Anti-Slavery society.(31) Sturge later made excuses for J. J. Gurney, a man 'so anxious at all times to promote love & harmony that I sometimes think he does not allways [sic] sufficiently guard against (at least an apparent) compromise of principle rather than give offence', but there is no doubt that the incident further undermined his reliance on the 'weighty Friends' as influences on his public life.(32)

These disagreements over matters of principle owed something to the social and political differences that had earlier helped to set Sturge apart from Buxton's anti-slavery circle. Samuel Gurney was one of the 'weighty friends ... [with] weighty purses' who earned nineteenth-century Quakers a reputation for 'keeping company with the great', and the African Civilization Society has been described as 'the most aristocratic of all British antislavery bodies'. At its great public meeting in Exeter Hall on 1 June 1840 Prince Albert was in the chair and there was a list of speakers which included bishops, peers, Sir Robert Peel and 'the City King', to give Samuel Gurney the name used by a fellow Quaker.(33) The British and Foreign Anti-Slavery Society on the other hand, did not even have a list of patrons; as Sturge explained to Lord Brougham, its only separate category of membership, the Honorary Corresponding Members, was not suitable for peers. As for bishops and leading Wesleyans, he wrote on another occasion, 'we are I think better without them'.(34)

This scant respect for the 'Establishment' did not save Sturge from criticism by other radicals: he was told that his was a 'telescopic philanthropy' which overlooked problems at home. In 1838 the writer of two letters in the <u>Birmingham Journal</u> regretted that Sturge's 'moral power' had not been 'engaged to alter and repeal the laws that operate against the very existence of the working people' and that he had not become 'the professed and fearless advocate of English freedom'.(35) In one sense this was a just assessment - Sturge had concentrated heavily on the campaigns against slavery and the Apprenticeship during the 1830s. But in another it was unfair, as his association with the programme of 'moral radicalism' should have made clear. If he was to become the 'advocate of English freedom' he would have to change his priorities, not his range of reforms, and signs of such a change began to appear during the year that followed the ending of the Apprenticeship. Writing to the Rev. John Clark in February 1839, about developments in Jamaica, Sturge added that he had taken up the corn law question as 'a vital one to the poor of this country'. Six months later he told Clark that he was preoccupied with the struggle for liberty at home, especially in Birmingham where he blamed the Government for the recent Chartist riots.(36)

Sturge's belief that the Corn Laws should be repealed long preceded the foundation of the Anti-Corn Law League. In 1836 when he was invited to give evidence before the Select Committee on the State of Agriculture he insisted that the Corn Laws were 'injurious to all classes of the community', and as early as 1831 he had published similar statements in his company's <u>Corn Circular.</u> His opinions had been influenced not only by the standard arguments for free trade but by his belief that the sliding scale of corn duties encouraged speculations of the sort that had caused him so much embarrassment in 1834.(37) So important was the matter to him that within a few weeks of the ending of the Apprenticeship he exchanged letters with C. P. Villiers and Lord Brougham (two of the parliamentarians who had given him most assistance) about the possibility of opening a campaign against the corn laws. Villiers had been heartened by Sturge's demonstration of what could be achieved by 'the pressure from without', and he had spoken of transferring the strategy to other reform movements. Brougham was also encouraging: 'I heartily rejoice at your coming into the corn law controversy. I regard you as already a veteran, and a veteran who has gained a great victory; and I hereby constitute and appoint you my lieutenant-general against those equally vile and silly corn-laws.'(38)

These letters suggest that an agitation against the Corn Laws could have taken up where the anti-Apprenticeship campaign left off, with Sturge organising the 'pressure from without' while Villiers and Brougham attended to the parliamentary manoeuvres. As it happened, Sturge spent much of the second half of 1838 preparing the way for the British and Foreign Anti-Slavery Society or otherwise attending to abolitionist business, and the Manchester Anti-Corn Law Association took the lead. Adjusting to a secondary role, Sturge gave his assistance to the moves that led to the setting up of the Anti-Corn Law League in March 1839, and until early 1842 he continued to play a significant although intermittent part in the affairs of the new movement. The writer of an article in the <u>Anti-Bread Tax Circular</u> saw him at this time as the champion of the 'White and Black Slaves'.(39) True to his all or nothing philosophy of agitation, Sturge called for total and immediate repeal; he would have nothing to do with the alternative proposal for a fixed tariff. 'If I say any thing on the subject', he told J. B. Smith, the League's President, 'I think I shall tell the people they must consider those who go for any thing short of total & immediate repeal as greater enemies than those who oppose any alteration at all'. Many years later Richard Cobden told Henry Richard that this was Sturge's 'best service' to the movement.(40)

Soon the Whig Government which had so often borne the brunt of Sturge's intransigence on such matters as church rates and the Apprenticeship met him again on deputations from the League. Two mentalities confronted each other over a gulf of mutual incomprehension: on the one hand, the Whigs - men of 'moderation, stability and compromise' with a strong distaste for 'extremists, fanatics and zealots' - and, on the other, the League, which often presented itself on such occasions as the successor of the heart-warming evangelical crusades of earlier years.(41) The distinction was vividly captured in Archibald Prentice's description of one of these encounters.(42) When one of the Leaguers attempted to describe the sufferings of a working-class family

> his feelings completely overpowered him, convulsive sobs choked his utterance, and he was obliged to pause till he recovered from his deep emotion. The tears rolled down the cheeks of Joseph Sturge; John Benjamin Smith strove in vain to conceal his feelings; there was scarcely a tearless eye in the multitude; and the ministers looked with perfect astonishment at a scene so unusual to statesmen and courtiers....Joseph Sturge made a powerful appeal to the ministers, placing the whole question upon the eternal principles of justice and humanity, which, he said, were shamefully outraged by a tax on the food of the people.

As a 'veteran' agitator and authority on the corn trade Sturge had much to offer the relatively untried Manchester leaders of the new movement. His advice was sought by Cobden; he attended national delegate meetings; he supplied statistical information for League publications; and he was largely responsible for setting up the Birmingham Anti-Corn Law Association on 30 November 1838.(43) It was soon apparent, however, that there was little prospect of turning Birmingham into a League stronghold. As the country slipped into a serious economic recession most of the town's radicals turned by preference to the Political Union which was revived in 1837. Blaming the nation's problems on misgovernment by a Parliament that had been insufficiently reformed in 1832, the Political Union devised the National Petition and helped to launch the Chartist movement's campaign for a six point programme of parliamentary democracy. Dismissing corn law repeal as a distraction, they outvoted Sturge in

November 1838 when he brought the subject forward at a public meeting.(44)

But the division between Sturge and the leaders of the Political Union went deeper still. They had taken up parliamentary reform in 1830, as they now took up universal suffrage, in the hope that a reformed Parliament would introduce a non-convertible paper currency which the Government could regulate to produce a mild inflation, thereby stimulating demand and overcoming the existing crisis of underconsumption and unemployment. They have been accused of holding these beliefs with fanatical intensity.(45) Sturge's 'moral radicalism', an equally fanatical creed, was grounded on his religious opinions, and his closest associates were fellow members of the anti-slavery, temperance, Baptist Missionary and Voluntary Church societies in the town - men such as Captain C. R. Moorsom and the Baptist ministers, Thomas Morgan and Thomas Swan. Although their organ, the Reformer/Philanthropist, had ceased publication in April 1838, they retained a separate identity during the late 1830s and the 1840s.

The dividing line between the two forms of radicalism was blurred by shared attitudes, and the word 'party' should not be given its modern meaning when applied to the 'moral Radicals'; particularly at election times there was usually an over-riding belief in an anti-Tory alliance or 'Liberal Party' which had a claim on the loyalty of all reformers. And so it was in December 1838 when liberals of all shades of opinion, having campaigned successfully for the incorporation of Birmingham, carried the first municipal elections so decisively that they defeated the Tories in every ward. Joseph and Charles Sturge, both of whom had declared for incorporation, were elected to the Town Council, and Joseph became an alderman.(46) The position was less important than might have been expected. Existing local authorities, including the Street Commissioners, were not superseded, and the Council had so few responsibilities that it has been described as little more than a debating society. But for a voluntaryist such as Sturge who had a very limited notion of government it was enough that there was a forum for his 'expressive politics': 'he only valued his seat at that board', he told the Town Council in February 1840, 'for the opportunity it afforded him of giving free and public expression to his sentiments'. In this spirit the Sturge brothers immediately struck a blow for the voluntary principle by refusing to make the usual declaration requiring Town Councillors not to harm the interests of the Established Church. Sturge was also successful in persuading the Councillors to discuss matters of national concern, and he brought forward a petition for the repeal of the Corn Laws.(47)

But these were matters of minor importance in comparison with an episode that did more than anything else to establish Sturge's reputation as a radical in domestic politics: in 1839-40 he led the campaign against the Police Act that was imposed on Birmingham by the Whig Government. It was a local problem with national significance; for the British system of policing was in flux during the 1830s while a change was being carried through from what one historian has called 'an "unpoliced society" - where police functions were carried out (if at all) by citizens or their appointed constables, to a "policed society" in which a paid force operated, relying not only on coercion, but also on the moral assent of most of the population to the role of a police force as enforcer of law and order'.(48) The Municipal Reform Act (1835) had made Town Councils responsible for local policing - it was the only significant task entrusted to the Birmingham Town Council - and the recently formed Metropolitan Police was available as a model, but the relationship between the Home Office and local police forces had still to be defined. Typical of many contemporary radicals who were fearful of a centralised system on the French plan, Sturge warned his fellow Councillors at a Town Council meeting in April 1839 that something like a standing army might be created through which the Government could threaten popular liberties. Suddenly in mid-1839 his worst fears were confirmed by Whig policy towards Birmingham. A contingent of the Metropolitan Police was sent in to break up Chartist meetings, and when serious disorders resulted, a Birmingham Police Act was rushed through to impose a rate on the town for the upkeep of a police force responsible to the Home Secretary.(49)

These measures were a response to the militancy of the Chartists. During the winter of 1838-39 the skies above the factory towns of Lancashire and the West Riding had often glowed 'like the reflection from a large city in a general conflagration' as throngs of excited working men surged through the streets to attend torch-light meetings addressed by J. R. Stephens, Feargus O'Connor and other advocates of the people's right to implement the Charter by force.(50) In May 1839 Birmingham (and its extensive armaments workshops) became the principal source of anxiety when a Convention of Chartist delegates met in the town; for even before the delegates arrived it was obvious that crowd control had passed out of the hands of the Political Union. Having contributed so much to the Chartist movement in 1838, the leaders of the Union had been deserted by their mass following when they resigned their Convention seats in March 1839 as a protest against O'Connor's violent speeches.(51) At a time when Birmingham was still policed in the old style by a small force of street-keepers, night-watchmen, thief-takers and (in emergencies) special constables, the magistrates had subsequently been unable to enforce a ban on the nightly meetings that the Chartists organised in the Bull Ring, the central concourse of the town.

By 4 July the situation had deteriorated so much that the mayor and two magistrates travelled to London and returned immediately with a contingent of the Metropolitan Police. In what has generally been seen as at least a precipitate action - R. C. Gammage, the first historian of Chartism, called it 'a riot of the authorities against the people' - the police marched directly from the railway station to the Bull Ring and attempted to disperse an illegal meeting by force. Overborne by resistance, they had to call on the help of the army. But it was not until the fifteenth of the month that the most serious disorders occurred. By then Parliament had debated and rejected the Chartist National Petition, and in Birmingham the magistrates had committed several Chartists for trial. That night an angry crowd attacked the Public Office, ransacked shops in the Bull Ring and set them ablaze. It took a charge by a troop of dragoons to restore order. Even four days later the Mayor could describe a town that was still patrolled night and day by strong units of special constables, soldiers and the Metropolitan Police.(52) Amidst scenes in Parliament where the Duke of Wellington and other M.P.s presented grossly exaggerated estimates of the destruction, the Government carried through a Bill to raise a police force for Birmingham. Initially, Lord John Russell envisaged entrusting the responsibility to the Town Council, but on the suggestion of Sir Robert Peel he eventually placed control in the hands of a Superintendent responsible to the Home Office.(53)

Throughout the crisis the Town Council had been ignored and inactive, but there was uproar as soon as members learned the terms of the Bill. On 6 August Sturge quickly took the lead. It was reported that he 'did not feel much surprise at the warmth of expression he had heard. He believed it was difficult for the members of the council to restrain their feelings. (Hear, hear). For some days past he could hardly express his own, with anything like temper. (Applause).' He successfully proposed a series of resolutions condemning armed police forces; asking the Government to withdraw the Metropolitan Police contingent and the Birmingham Police Bill; setting up a committee of inquiry into the riots; and petitioning against the carrying out of the death sentences on some of the rioters. Once again he brought the 'pressure from without' to bear on Parliament. To save the condemned Chartists he raised petitions from ward meetings all over the town, from the Society of Friends and from 'The Ladies of Birmingham': to win support for the struggle against the Police Bill he wrote to other city corporations and headed a deputation to London in the hope that 'it may be possible to throw it out in the Lords'.(54)

Although some of his contemporaries believed that Sturge was opposed to professional police forces on principle, in fact, his views were broadly similar to those that have guided British policy until very recent times. He wanted to see elected local governments controlling unarmed professionals who were closely identified with the communities they served. These forces would be small ones, consisting of men of good moral character who were known to the local inhabitants, and in times of emergency they would call on the assistance of the citizens to maintain the peace. The Government police that took up its duties towards the end of 1839 was a very different force: responsible only to the Home Secretary; officered in some instances by men who had learned about law and order while serving as volunteers in the Spanish civil wars; and armed with cutlasses on the outbeats. Sturge protested in speeches of distrust and loathing for the Parliament created by the Reform Bill from which he had once expected so much. The Police Act was inconsistent with religion, sound policy and liberty; it was an attempt 'to engraft one of the most pernicious institutions of continental tyranny on the true English system of popular representation'; it was a product of 'the most corrupt Parliament that ever disgraced this country'; it proved once and for all that 'the present administration had made up their minds both at home and in the colonies, to try to rule the mass of the people, not by moral, but physical, force - not as men, but as brutes'.(55)

This was no passing outburst. Once again Sturge saw himself as a participant in a struggle against deep-dyed evil. Even his friend, Henry Richard, had to admit that he was sometimes capable of 'a dogmatic wilfulness, which made him impatient of other men's opinions', and throughout this episode there was something like an obsessive fury in his attitude both to the new police and to anyone who in any way endorsed the Government's policy. He presided over the Town Council Committee that investigated the events of July (with the help of one-sided testimony from unsworn witnesses, as the Birmingham Journal pointed out), and he was the moving force behind a public meeting in November which protested unsuccessfully against the implementation of the Police Act. Letters from Superintendent Burgess, the commander of the force, teemed with complaints: 'Sturge, Moorsom and others sit daily or nearly so', he told the Home Office, 'secretly at the Public Office in a room there, no doubt for the purpose of concocting measures of annoyance to us'.(56)

Others found it more difficult to maintain their rage. It was not merely, as Sturge put it, that there would always be some men who preferred security to liberty; his opposition was too extreme even for town councillors who had applauded his early statements. Eventually he so far over-reached himself in 'concocting measures of annoyance' that the police were able to humiliate him publicly. Their opportunity arose from one of those incidents that from time to time threw the angularity of Sturge's conduct into high relief: on 11 November 1839 he single-handedly tried to stop a prize fight. It was not difficult to justify his apparent rashness. These bare-knuckle encounters often resulted in deaths, and the Birmingham district had become such a notorious venue for them that the coroner at an inquest in 1831 estimated that in his time there had been a fourfold increase in the number of assize cases arising from this form of manslaughter.(57) Nonetheless it was a quixotic act when Sturge forced his way into a crowd in the Edgbaston Fields, confidently believing, so he subsequently claimed, that if he could reach the pugilists he would be able to dissuade them from their 'inhuman conduct'. Instead, he was hemmed in by pickpockets who ripped his coat and stole his watch. Sturge's embarrassment may be surmised when he was informed two weeks later that the police had made an arrest and requested him to identify his property. With more consistency than wisdom he sent a reply that played into their hands:

> Joseph Sturge is obliged to John Shaw, for sending him the information that a young man is in custody, taken with a watch, supposed to belong to him; but as Joseph Sturge cannot conscientiously accept the aid of the government police for the protection of his person or property, he does not feel at liberty to attend the office to identify the watch.

The magistrates summonsed him, and before a crowded court room obliged him to co-operate with the police. The Birmingham Journal commented unsympathetically that, unwelcome though the new police were, the time had come to concentrate on obtaining some value from them.(58)

Sturge's 'dogmatic wilfulness' came to the fore again that month at the mayoral election in the Town Council when he proposed Captain Moorsom in opposition to P. H. Muntz. It was another demonstration of the division between the 'moral Radical party' and the Political Union radicals, sharpened on this occasion by the knowledge that Muntz had given a donation to a testimonial fund for the Metropolitan Police officers who had served in the town during the riots. The report of the debate suggests that it would have been easy to defeat Muntz, had Moorsom not been an impossible candidate. An Anglican voluntaryist, Moorsom had refused (without resigning) to accept the Town Council seat to which he had been elected in 1838 because he could not conscientiously make the declaration requiring him not to harm the interests of the Established Church. It seemed likely that he would have pursued a similar course as Mayor and left the Town Council leaderless. If the ploy had succeeded, however, Sturge would have achieved two cherished ambitions: he would have excluded Muntz, and he would have precipitated a constitutional conflict over the Church Establishment. Understandably, when he pressed Moorsom's claims 'even to tears', he was rebuked for his headstrong opinions and out-voted.(59)

The Birmingham Journal's comment at this time that Sturge had a 'knack of figuring in minorities' helps to explain his behaviour. For the man of strong moral values political action often amounts to a form of public witness in which pragmatism and compromise (with all their short-term rewards) have no place.(60) As the same newspaper discovered when it attempted to describe Sturge's politics, this stance was not easily defined by the normal labels of the day: 'Chartist he is not, nor Radical, nor even Whig-Radical, though somewhat more than Whig'. The writer would have understood Sturge better, if he had noted that Sturge's attitude to important issues of the day was always defined within his version of Christian philanthropy. He had told the Town Council that he saw Corn Law repeal as a humanitarian and moral policy that transcended party politics. Likewise he 'hoped to see the day, when intelligence and work, and not property, would be the only qualification [for the franchise] that would be required'.(61)

But, if Sturge was no Chartist, it was becoming evident by the end of the year that his anti-police campaign had helped to produce a realignment of radical factions in the town. Whereas in November 1838 an alliance of Political Unionists and Chartists had defeated his first attempt to set up an Anti-Corn Law Association, a year later his anti-police meeting was well supported by a working-class audience which included Chartists. This time it was the turn of P. H. Muntz and R. K. Douglas, prominent members of the now defunct Political Union, to be hissed. It was also at this meeting that Sturge first defined a role that he would assume on various occasions during the next decade. Calling himself the advocate of the religious, civil and political rights of the poor in Britain, he asked his audience to be patient while he summoned up the energies of the 'wise and good of all sects and parties' to assist them.(62) Several of his allusions around this time suggest that this was a direct transference of his anti-slavery experience of pressure group politics and that it was influenced by what he had seen his missionary friends in Jamaica doing for the rights of the black population.

A by-election campaign that took place in Birmingham during January 1840 gave him an opportunity to demonstrate his belief in representative government. Thomas Attwood accepted the Chiltern Hundreds, and Sturge was brought forward to contest the seat against G. F. Muntz, the brother of the new Mayor. Sturge's platform called for Church disestablishment, free trade, the abolition of capital punishment, the repeal of taxation on necessities, shorter parliaments, the ballot and an educational franchise so broadly defined that it would have included any adult male, sound in mind and free from criminal conviction, who had resided in his constituency for twelve months and could present an electoral claim in his own handwriting. Sturge also tried to conduct his campaign in accordance with two principles that would have gone some way towards purifying the notoriously corrupt electoral system of the day. The first was what he called 'the principle of non-interference' by which he undertook to give voters no inducement to vote for him other than a statement of his political principles. The second envisaged something like a primary election at which all men, non-electors as well electors, would have had a part in the choice of the 'Liberal' parliamentary candidate. To this end he unsuccessfully proposed that he and Muntz should submit to the decision of a Town's Meeting.(63)

It was an unrealistically high-minded strategy, but he scarcely wanted to win - even on his own terms. Asking his brother John to withdraw his name if a majority of the inhabitants or electors did not wish him to represent them, Sturge added that a man with his opinions would find the life of an M. P. 'both difficult & irksome consistently to maintain even if supported by the unanimous cordial feeling of the liberal part of the constituency'.(64) When the show of hands went against him on nomination day, he readily withdrew. From the beginning of the campaign it had been evident that he had a weak power base in the Birmingham parliamentary electorate: Joseph Parkes was told privately that there had been 'a yearning desire of many Radicals as well as all the Whigs to cast off Sturge not only as a candidate disagreeable to them but as a fanatic who will not obtain or combine their best Liberal support'. It would seem that those last ditch stands against oratorios (the issue had flared up again in 1837), Sunday trains, public house licences and the new police had been too much for the voters of Birmingham.(65)

In the aftermath of the by-election it must have looked as if Sturge's ventures into elective politics were coming to an end. He asked his supporters never to nominate him for Parliament again, and he stayed on the Town Council only long enough to present his report on the riots. Predictably it found that they had been occasioned by 'the misconduct of the London Police' as well as by the physical force language addressed to the Bull Ring crowds.(66)

NOTES

1.   Report of the Proceedings At Birmingham On the 1st and 2nd of August In Commemoration of the Abolition of Negro Apprenticeship In The British Colonies, [1838], p. 44.
2.   London University Library, Brougham Correspondence, 15431, Joseph Sturge to Lord Brougham, 28 May 1839.
3.   William L. Clements Library, Joseph Sturge Manuscripts, Joseph Sturge to J.G. Birney, 9 May 1840.
4.   British Emancipator, 2 April 1838.
5.   Birmingham Journal, 1 February 1840.
6.   Sturge Papers (P.A.J. Sturge), Joseph Sturge's Account of His Sister Sophia's Last Illness, 1845.
7.   Birmingham Journal, 4 August 1838.
8.   Brougham Correspondence, 10184, Joseph Sturge to Lord Brougham, 12 July 1838.
9.   J.J. Gurney, A Winter In The West Indies, London 1840, p. 182. See also House of Commons, Report from the Select Committee on Negro Apprenticeship in the Colonies, IX (560), 1836, pp. vi, 35.
10. British Emancipator, 2 April 1838; Rhodes House, MSS Brit. Emp. S22 G48, Mr Jos. Sturge's Journal, p. 57.
11. Brit. Lib., Add. MSS. 518719, ff. 88-89, Joseph Sturge to Lord Holland, 28 February 1839; Christian Advocate, 8 October 1838.
12. School of Oriental and African Studies, Methodist Missionary Society, Jamaica, Box 1833-1839, File 1837, Henry Bleby to the General Secretaries, 13 August 1838; British Emancipator, 3 October, 27 December 1838 and 2 October 1839; Brit. Lib., Add. MSS. 51819, ff. 141-46, Sir Charles Metcalfe to Lord Holland, 18 June 1840; Colonial Gazette, 13 July 1844; Hinton, Knibb, pp. 286-321. Joseph Rayner Stephens was a Methodist minister turned popular spokesman on such issues as factory reform, the New Poor Law and Chartism.
13. Rhodes House, E2/6, British and Foreign Anti-Slavery Society Minutes, 27 September 1839.
14. Philanthropist, 19 October 1837; British Emancipator, 27 December 1838; Christian Advocate, 24 September, 1 October 1838 and 25 February 1839.
15. Fenn Collection, E19.Y, Joseph Sturge to John Clark, 27 August, 1 October 1838; Minute Book of The [Birmingham] Ladies Society For The Relief of Negro Slaves, 14 May 1840; Birmingham Journal, 27 July 1839.
16. British Emancipator, 26 June 1839.
17. Fenn Collection E19.Y, Joseph Sturge to John Clark, 1 October 1838.
18. Rhodes House, MSS Brit. Emp. S22.G48, Mr. Jos. Sturge's Journal, p. 42.
19. Birmingham Public Library, Newscuttings Relating to Birmingham (collected by C.D. Sturge), vol. II, West India Land Investment Company, 12 March 1839, and West India Land Investment Company, MS. n.d.; Proceedings Of The General Anti-Slavery Convention Called By The Committee Of The British and Foreign Anti-Slavery Society, And Held In London From Friday, June 12th, To

Tuesday, June 23rd, 1840, p. 371.

20. S.W. Mintz, Caribbean Transformations, Chicago 1974, pp. 158-60; Hinton, Knibb, p. 300; R.G. Walters, American Reformers 1815-1860, New York, 1978, p. 59.

21. A Brief Account Of The Settlements Of The Emancipated Peasantry In The Neighbourhood of Brown's Town, Jamaica; In A Letter From John Clark, Baptist Missionary, To Joseph Sturge Of Birmingham, Birmingham 1852, p. 8.

22. British Emancipator, 16 October, 11 December 1839; Birmingham Journal, 22 June 1839.

23. The monument is in the William Knibb Memorial Baptist Church at Falmouth, Jamaica.

24. Rylands English MSS 741 (114), Sophia Sturge to Mary Anne Rawson, 11 December 1838.

25. Brougham Correspondence, 30,021, Joseph Sturge to Lord Brougham, 29 October 1838; C. Lloyd, The Navy And The Slave Trade: The Suppression of the African Slave Trade in the Nineteenth Century, London 1948, p. 27.

26. British Emancipator, 23 January 1839.

27. Rhodes House, E 2/6, British and Foreign Anti-Slavery Society Minutes, 27 February, 13 March, 17 April, 18 April 1839.

28. Institute of Jamaica, Kingston, MST321d, f. 2, R. Stokes to W. Beldam, 1 January 1839.

29. T.F. Buxton, The African Slave Trade and its Remedy, London 1968 (originally published 1839-40).

30. Buxton, Memoirs, p. 375.

31. Friends House Library, Gurney MSS, I 411, Joseph Sturge to J.J. Gurney, 16 October 1840 and II 434, Samuel Gurney to J.J. Gurney, 25 October 1840. See also J.J. Gurney, A Winter In The West Indies, Described In Familiar Letters to Henry Clay, Of Kentucky, London 1840, vii-viii.

32.Huntingdon Library, Joseph Sturge to Mary Clarkson, n.d.

33. W.R. Ward, Religion And Society In England 1790-1850, London 1972, p. 69; Brit. Lib., Add. MSS. 43722, f. 8, Richard Cobden to Joseph Sturge, 3 January 1854; Temperley, British Anti-Slavery, p. 55; Barclay Fox's Journal, ed. R.L. Brett, London 1979, pp. 197-98.

34. Brougham Correspondence, 15430, 26 April 1839; Rhodes House, MSS Brit. Emp. S18, C11D/95, Joseph Sturge to John Beaumont, 15 April 1842.

35. Birmingham Journal, 6 January, 15 September 1838.

36. Fenn Collection, E19.Y, Joseph Sturge to John Clark, 14 February, 1 August, 14 August 1839.

37. Second Report From The Select Committee Appointed To Inquire Into The State Of Agriculture, 1836, p. 163; Sturge's Annual Corn Circular, 12 January 1831.

38. Richard, Sturge, pp. 270-71; Hansard, House of Commons, 22 May 1838. See also N. McCord, The Anti-Corn Law League 1838-1846, London 1968, p. 40.

39. Anti-Bread Tax Circular, 29 July 1841.

40. Manchester Public Library, J.B. Smith Papers, Corn Laws, vol. 1, no. 234, Joseph Sturge to J.B. Smith, 3 January 1840; Brit. Lib. Add.

MSS. 43659, ff. 210-12, Richard Cobden to Henry Richard, 12 October 1862.

41. J. Hamburger, 'The Whig Conscience' in P. Marsh, ed., The Conscience Of The Victorian State, Hassocks 1979, p. 34.

42. A. Prentice, History of the Anti-Corn Law League, London 1968, vol. I, pp. 155-56.

43. West Sussex Record Office, Cobden Papers 53, Joseph Sturge to Richard Cobden, 6 April 1839; Manchester Public Library, J.B. Smith Papers, Corn Laws vol. I, no. 99, 16 January 1839, Joseph Sturge to J.B. Smith and no. 234, 3 January 1840, Joseph Sturge to J.B. Smith, 3 January 1840. See also the series of letters from Cobden to Sturge, Brit. Lib., Add. MSS. 50131, 26 February 1839 - 3 March 1841, and D. Fraser, 'Birmingham And The Corn Laws', Birmingham Archeological Society Transactions and Proceedings, vol. 82, 1965, p. 8.

44. Birmingham Journal, 1 December 1838.

45. S.G. Checkland, 'The Birmingham Economists, 1815-1850', Economic History Review, 2nd Ser. vol. I, 1948, pp. 1-19.

46. Birmingham Journal, 10 November, 29 December 1838.

47. Ibid., 8 February 1840, 29 December 1838, 26 January 1839.

48. D. Philips, Crime and Authority in Victorian England. The Black Country 1835-1860, London 1977, pp. 53-54.

49. Birmingham Journal, 6 April, 3 August 1839.

50. R.G. Gammage, History Of The Chartist Movement 1837-1854, London 1969, p. 95.

51. Carlos Flick, The Birmingham Political Union and The Movements for Reform in Britain 1830-1839, Hamden 1978, pp. 173-74.

52. Gammage, Chartist Movement, pp. 134-5; Public Record Office, H.O. 40/50 fos ff. 374-76, William Scholefield to Lord John Russell, 19 July 1839.

53. Hansard, House of Lords, 16 July 1839. See also ibid., House of Commons, 23 July 1839; 29 July 1839; 2 August 1839.

54. Birmingham Journal, 10 August, 17 August 1839; Brougham Correspondence 15434, Joseph Sturge to Lord Brougham, 12 August 1839.

55. Birmingham Journal, 10 August, 7 September, 16 November 1839, 1 February 1840.

56. Richard, Sturge, p. 598; Birmingham Journal, 30 November 1839; Public Record Office, HO 65/10, Superintendent Burgess to Home Office, 11 November, 13 November, 19 November, 26 November 1839.

57. Birmingham Journal, 3 September 1831.

58. Ibid., 30 November 1839; Public Record Office, HO 65/10, Superintendent Burgess to Home Office, 26 November, 29 November 1840.

59. Birmingham Journal, 16 November 1839.

60. Ibid., 16 November 1839. See also Parkin, Middle Class Radicalism, pp. 29, 36.

61. Birmingham Journal, 26 January, 28 December 1839.

62. Ibid., 1 December 1838, 30 November 1839.

63. Ibid., 14 December, 21 December, 28 December 1839, 4 January, 11 January, 18 January, 25 January, 1 February 1840.

64. Sturge Papers (M. Sturge), Joseph Sturge to John Sturge, 23

January 1840.
    65. London University, Parkes Papers, Joseph Parkes to E.J. Stanley, 30 November, 19 December 1839.   Sturge denied that he favoured the legal enforcement of teetotalism and sabbatarianism.
    66. Birmingham Journal, 1 February, 9 May 1840; Borough of Birmingham, Report Of The Committee Appointed By The Town Council, September 3rd, 1839, To Investigate The Causes Of The Late Riots, Birmingham 1840, p. 43.

9 The Fellowship of Suffering (1840-41)

Sturge's letter of resignation from the Town Council referred to his objections to the new police system and its adverse effects on local government.(1) He should have added that he had assumed responsibility for an international anti-slavery convention and could spare little time for anything else. As the organiser of three national conventions during the Anti-Apprenticeship campaign in 1837-38 he was something of an expert on this method of promoting reforms, but an international convention was rightly described at the time as 'a novel and bold' venture: there were no precedents to guide him. The idea came from the American Anti-Slavery Society which urged the British and Foreign Anti-Slavery Society to invite abolitionists from Britain, Europe and America to a conference in London where they could devise means of co-operation and take up the task of creating an international anti-slavery public opinion. Sturge responded so enthusiastically that he even considered going to the Americas to work up more support for it, but the demands of the anti-police campaign during the second half of 1839 prevented him from doing more than visiting various parts of Britain to arrange for the election of delegates.(2)

This 'World's Anti-Slavery Convention' disappointed the expectations aroused by its name; it was only in J. G. Whittier's poem that delegates came from 'Lima's Inca-haunted halls' and the 'Land of the dark and mystic Nile'. Large parts of the world were not represented, and individuals (some of them responsible to no one but themselves) spoke for France, Spain, Switzerland, Russia, Canada, Haiti, Sierra Leone, Mauritius and New South Wales. In addition to the United Kingdom which provided most of the 518 delegates, only the United States and the British Caribbean could be said to be well represented.(3) Nonetheless when the Convention opened in the Freemasons' Hall on 12 June 1840 it was a personal triumph for Sturge. Delegates referred to 'Joseph Sturge's parliament', the most imposing gathering to date of those 'men of intelligence and of religion' on whom he had relied during the great campaigns of the 1830s. B.R. Haydon, who had been commissioned by the British and Foreign Anti-Slavery Society to paint a collective portrait of the delegates in session was impressed by their 'awful and unaffected piety'; for this was largely a gathering of Nonconformists with a disproportionately large attendance of Quakers (nearly 100), and the opening ceremony, which provided him with the setting for his painting, was the sort of heart-warming occasion that evangelicals relished. Amidst a reverential silence Sturge assisted Thomas Clarkson, the aged pioneer of the movement, on to the platform and delivered a eulogy of Clarkson's achievements culminating in an emotional prayer that the young Thomas Clarkson, sitting by his grandfather's side, would confer even greater blessings on mankind. While he was speaking, Mary Clarkson heard loud bursts of sobbing from the men around her, and when Clarkson delivered his presidential address 'there was hardly a dry eye in the meeting'.(4)

For the most part during the ten days of the Convention the delegates maintained this high sense of religious dedication as they discussed resolutions and papers on such themes as 'The Essential Sinfulness of Slavery', 'The Moral Influence of Slavery' and developments in the United States, Texas, the European colonies and other parts of the world. One of the most important papers, an exposition of 'the superiority of free labour over slavery', was delivered by John Sturge who seems to have been regarded as an expert on the subject because of the book he had written in 1827. There was obviously a danger that a gathering such as this would have contented itself with declamatory speeches, but the organising committee persuaded the delegates to endorse two courses of action favoured by the British and Foreign Anti-Slavery Society: the denial of church fellowship to slave owners and the exclusion of slave produce from the market by tariffs and other appropriate measures.(5)

Nowadays the Convention is remembered less because of its contribution to the international anti-slavery movement than because it gave rise to one of the most famous controversies of early Victorian history: an 'uproar' over the right of women to participate as delegates.(6) This 'Woman Question' had not been anticipated when invitations were sent out; for the custom was firmly established that respectable women could attend but not address 'promiscuous assemblies' (meetings attended by both sexes). It was not that women were excluded from the public work of benevolent societies; contemporary notions of propriety allowed them an active role only in their own 'auxiliary' associations. This was the accepted model in the United States too, but in 1837 it was successfully challenged by several women who insisted on full rights of participation in all abolitionist meetings. The innovation helped to precipitate a secession from the American Anti-Slavery Society, and when word reached London that some American societies were electing female delegates Sturge's organising committee re-worded the invitation to make it clear that women would be welcome only as visitors. When the women arrived in London to persist with their claims, the dispute dominated the first day's business.(7)

During a confused and angry debate in which both sides attempted to shout each other down (one report refers to ministers brandishing the Bible in the faces of the women and their male champions) Sturge wisely tried to have the dispute treated as a procedural one: that is, the delegates should agree to be bound by the usual practices of public meetings. He eventually had his way, probably the only decision that could have averted the total collapse of the Convention. For a few years the episode had the effect of slowing down the advances that women had been making into this form of public life, and Sturge was often blamed for this, but he was careful to insist that the Convention had not attempted to settle the abstract question of women's rights, and his private opinions may have been quite advanced by contemporary standards. In 1842 he gave Elizabeth Pease to understand that 'under some circumstances' he would be happy to see women voting in parliamentary elections. He did not explain how this could be reconciled with the programme of Complete (i.e. universal male) Suffrage he was then advocating. There was a great deal of confused discussion about women's rights in the 1840s.(8)

What can be said with certainty is that the dispute involved much more than sex distinction: it raised issues of central importance to Sturge's religious convictions. In 1839 Sturge had begun to correspond with a New York merchant called Lewis Tappan, and a close friendship developed that lasted until Sturge's death in 1859. They were almost exactly the counterparts of each other in their respective countries; for Tappan was the leader of a circle of philanthropists who dominated the American benevolent society movement during the thirty years before the Civil War. Like Sturge, he excelled less as a public speaker than as a co-ordinator, shouldering a heavy burden of administration that gave him an unrivalled knowledge of the American philanthropic and reforming movements of his day. Like Sturge too, he could empathize only with evangelicals, and his career was punctuated by disputes with those who did not share his values.(9) One of the most important of these occurred on the eve of the London convention when Tappan, J.G. Birney and other members of their circle seceded from the American Anti-Slavery Society and set up a rival American and Foreign Anti-Slavery Society. The 'Woman Question' was the immediate cause of their decision, but, as Birney pointed out to Sturge's associate, John Scoble, it was associated with 'other questions of still greater magnitude and destructiveness',(10) a reference to the ideas of Lloyd Garrison, the editor of the Boston Liberator, who was fast earning a reputation as an infidel and anarchist. The women anti-slavery delegates who arrived in London were members of Garrison's circle, and British Quakers noted that Lucretia Mott, the best known of them, was a Hicksite minister; in other words, she seemed little better than a deist or Unitarian. Quaker members of the British and Foreign Anti-Slavery Society seem to have gone out of their way to disparage her.(11) Henceforward Garrison and his friends would believe that the 1840 Convention had been the 'fag end' of the Friends Yearly Meeting, and that the British and Foreign Anti-Slavery Society was an instrument of sectarianism.(12)

In the last resort the dispute was about power as Lucretia Mott discovered in the course of a conversation with two of Sturge's associates: 'W. Morgan & Scales informed us "it wasn't designed as a World Convention - that was a mere Poetical license," & that all power would rest with the "London Committee of Arrangements".'(13) This was the general grievance underlying several complaints that the British and Foreign Anti-Slavery Society had allowed 'no real freedom of decision'. Samuel Gurney was 'disappointed at the narrow-mindedness shown by the Convention in refusing to hear F. Buxton on the subject of his [African Civilization] Society', and the promoters of the British India Society discovered that Sturge had even altered the text of Clarkson's address by striking out a favourable reference to their policy of promoting the production and sale of Indian free labour products. These were all examples of what one historian has called the tendency of Victorian reformers to be led on by 'an unyielding, unremitting drive to dominate' rivals regardless of the worth of their 'goals, the cogency of their arguments or the solidity of their facts'.(14)

On this occasion the power struggle was preserved for posterity in B.R. Haydon's painting of the Convention where 'all the heads' were positioned 'according to desert', a procedure that was guided by the secretary of the British and Foreign Anti-Slavery Society. Thus Buxton was relegated to 'a second rate place' in the painting because he had 'behaved so bad to the Society', and Lucretia Mott was reduced to infinitesimal size in the background because of her 'infidel notions'. Clarkson, 'the patriarch of the cause of liberty', was the dominant figure in the painting, and, with a symbolism that must have been missed by few, Haydon placed Sturge beneath his outstretched hand.(15)

Thus the most important result of the Convention was that it deepened the divisions within abolitionism on both sides of the Atlantic, especially when representatives of the two American anti-slavery societies toured the provinces during the following months, leaving a lasting legacy of bitterness within the British movement. It was a squalid episode characterised by what J. A. Collins, Garrison's representative, called 'discord ... falsehood & calumny'. Time after time, as he travelled round the country in the wake of Birney and other opponents, he had to answer the charge that Garrison was identified with 'every infidel fanaticism' - 'no marriage', perfectionism, transcendentalism and opposition to the Sabbath, the Church, the ministry and the Bible. This was notoriously Sturge's opinion: throwing all his influence behind Birney ('a man in whose judgment I have great confidence'), he warned his friends against Garrison. The accusation that he was 'a bigotted Quaker of the Gurneyite School' can be traced to this time.(16)

Another outcome of the Convention was that Sturge decided to visit the United States. He had been thinking for some time of going there on an anti-slavery mission, he told Thomas Clarkson, and on 9 February 1841 he asked J.G. Whittier to be his companion. The two had not met, but obviously Sturge had heard of the American Quaker poet's reputation as a reformer. The principal intentions of their journey, he told Whittier, would be to 'promote an entire unity of action and co-operation between the British and Foreign Anti-Slavery Society and the American and Foreign Anti-Slavery Society, including all that will act upon our principles and not mix up other matters with it'; to try to remove the objections that prevented American Quakers from taking part in anti-slavery societies; to make arrangements with abolitionists for the holding of a second international anti-slavery convention; and to interest Americans in a similar convention 'for the promotion of permanent and universal peace'.(17)

On 10 March Sturge left Portsmouth on the <u>British Queen,</u> one of the new transatlantic paddle steamers. It was no time of the year for such a voyage, and the ship did not reach New York until 3 April after sustaining such severe damage in storms that it had to put into Nova Scotia for repairs. He remained in America until 1 August. Another book (again ghost-written for him by Thomas Harvey) resulted from his journal and letters.(18) It was the document of an obsessive reformer; for, unlike Charles Dickens or even J. J. Gurney, both of whom toured the United States at this time and left accounts of their experiences, Sturge expressed little interest in the passing scene. There were a few excursions, such as a visit to the house of John Woolman, the eighteenth-century Quaker abolitionist, and there was a brief holiday at the Niagara Falls, but he did little sight-seeing. Whittier met him on his arrival, and they travelled out on the new railway and steamboat system to visit Philadelphia, Baltimore, Washington, Boston and several lesser cities. The journey was another example of Sturge overestimating the strength of his friends. Whittier, a younger man whose dashing appearance concealed a weak constitution, had to withdraw and regain his strength at one stage, and Sturge himself most uncharacteristically took a short holiday in Bewdley when he returned home: 'my mind & body have been at a pretty full streach [sic] while in America', he told one of his correspondents.(19)

Of all the overseas missions undertaken by Sturge the visit to the United States was probably the most dangerous. Abolitionists had been attacked by mobs during the 1830s, and three years earlier George Thompson had had to abandon a speaking tour of the United States because of threats to his life. B.R. Haydon's reaction to the announcement of Sturge's journey was understandable: 'I hope that dear Joseph Sturge wont [sic] be murdered in America'. But he was expecting too much when he added that Sturge ought to 'conduct himself with discretion as well as devotion'.(20) Unlike many of his contemporaries who have been described as travelling in the United States with 'their eyes open and their mouths shut', Sturge was not one for moral indignation at home and meekness abroad: wise enough not to address public meetings, he nonetheless took many risks. He visited slave pens and argued with slave traders; he was one of the first to participate in a campaign of 'sit ins' by travelling in a negro carriage on a segregated railway; and he even assisted a couple of escaping slaves. Whittier later noted that they had risked ten years imprisonment by distributing abolitionist tracts in Maryland. Sturge could consider himself fortunate to escape with nothing worse than newspaper attacks and condemnations by members of Congress for his meddling in American politics.(21)

Much of his time was spent visiting the state Yearly Meetings of the Society of Friends to stimulate their members' involvement in the anti-slavery movement. As he knew, contemporary American Quakers were more inward-looking than their eighteenth-century predecessors who had pioneered the anti-slavery movement. Gravely weakened by the Hicksite Schism (in the area of the Baltimore Yearly Meeting Sturge found that 80% of Friends had become Hicksites) the orthodox Society had strongly discouraged any association with interdenominational benevolent societies and seldom allowed its premises to be used for abolitionist meetings. Whittier had been one of the few to stand out for a bold abolitionist policy. Writing to Sturge in 1839, another American Quaker despairingly called for intervention by British Friends: at the very least the London Yearly Meeting would have to send a disapproving Epistle to its American counterparts. But when Sturge attempted to follow up this suggestion at the 1840 Yearly Meeting some of the 'weighty Friends' would only agree to a statement encouraging 'Friends in America to endeavour to press through the difficulties of their position & not to omit any opportunity of forwarding the cause'. They could hardly have gone further. Quakerism was not a hierarchical religion, and American sensitivities would have been ruffled by anything that smacked of British domination. One other possibility remained for bringing British influence to bear on American Quakerism, and that too was suggested by Sturge's correspondent: personal visits to the American Yearly Meetings by 'faithful and fearless advocates of this righteous cause'.(22)

It was a disillusioning experience. Sturge's intervention was so strongly resented that in the end he could only issue an open letter of remonstrance and republish it in his book. The letter, in which he virtually accused the American Quakers of waiting for the 'inner light' as an excuse for avoiding unpopular public duties, is of some interest because it also set out his own robust theological position:(23)

> While I fully believe that the true disciple of Christ will be favoured with immediate guidance of the Holy Spirit whenever it is needful to direct his steps; it appears to me especially important, that, in matters of self-sacrifice and conflicting with our worldly interest or reputation, we should guard against being deluded into a neglect of duty, by waiting for this direct Divine intimation, where the path of duty is obvious and clearly understood, and when testimonies are concerned, which we have long considered it our duty, on all occasions, to support.

Other sections of Sturge's book where he described the divisions of the American anti-slavery movement gave him an opportunity to develop his abolitionist philosophy more fully. He would have nothing to do with one scheme of emancipation that did receive substantial support from American Quakers: the American Colonization Society's attempt to solve the problems of slavery and race relations by promoting negro emigration to Liberia. It was an 'emancipation by removal', he wrote scornfully, a delusive hope born of sinful prejudices. Why not call for the return of the whites to England? There was only one correct response to slavery and that was to enter a 'fellowship of suffering with the enslaved' by working for the day when the whites would 'exercise christian feelings towards the people of colour'. Having been dragged through the streets of Boston on a halter because of his work for emancipation, Lloyd Garrison could claim to know something about the 'fellowship of suffering', but he too stood condemned by Sturge's standards: his anti-sabbatarian and other heterodox statements had exposed the American Anti-Slavery Society to the charge that it was a cover for attacks on 'institutions and opinions justly held in regard throughout the christian world'. Only the founders of the American and Foreign Anti-Slavery Society received Sturge's approval; only they shared his belief that the abolition of slavery was 'intimately connected with the progress of right views among professing Christians'.(24)

Some of Sturge's friends were involved in an important experiment in abolitionist politics when he arrived in America. Disappointed by the failure of their 'pressure from without' on the Whig and Democratic parties, they had decided in 1839 to bring abolitionism into the mainstream of American politics by setting up a third party, the Liberty Party. J. G. Birney had contested the 1840 presidential election as a Liberty candidate while he was in Britain to attend the Anti-Slavery Convention. Sturge attended several of their meetings during his visit, and he was present in New York on 12 May 1841 when the new party was formally launched to enable all Americans 'to unite heartily and fully in the effort to remove all oppressive laws, and to establish equal rights and the impartial administration of justice throughout the land'. Lewis Tappan opposed the new departure, and Sturge found himself acting as a peacemaker in the dispute, using all his influence (backed up by an offer of $1000) to avert a further split in the anti-slavery movement. For several years he retained an interest in the experiment. Like the course pursued by William Knibb in Jamaica, it associated him with a trend towards the widening of abolitionism into a movement for civil liberties.(25)

While he was in America Sturge also met members of the Peace movement and obtained their endorsement of a future international peace convention. He had been a member of peace societies since 1816, but the subject had assumed greater importance for him in recent years because of the British Government's foreign policy and increased expenditure on the armed forces. In 1841 he was particularly concerned by the outbreak of war against China on behalf of British merchants who had been punished for flouting Chinese regulations prohibiting the import of opium. Once again it seemed that the Whigs were dragging the nation into the depths of infamy: 'For let Ministers say what they may', he told Daniel O'Connell, 'the war will be called an Opium War, a war aggressive and therefore wholly unjustifiable'. In March 1840 he had appealed to 'The Christian Public' to condemn the policy of protecting men who sold 'deadly poison' to the Chinese. Silence in the face of such iniquity, he warned, would imprint an indelible stain on British Christianity: Christians must protest to escape guilt and ensure that 'the people of China may hereafter learn that it was not the disciples of Him whose doctrines the Missionaries have preached, who were engaged in their destruction, but a party in power'.(26) At the time Sturge could only call a public meeting to give people an opportunity of voicing their opposition to the war, but from then on he was in search of some means of making Christian public opinion a permanent influence on foreign policy. He knew he could obtain little support from the existing peace movement; in 1832 the London Peace Society had refused to endorse a petition against the British blockade of the Netherlands in case it was accused of meddling in politics. Modestly, but accurately, in 1838 the Society's annual report admitted that its 'labours are not of a nature immediately to captivate by their brilliancy; their movements are tranquil and unobtrusive'.(27)

The Opium War was preying on Sturge's mind while he was in America, and he was greatly moved during a visit to an exhibition where he saw examples of 'the advanced civilisation of the Chinese'.(28) Thus he was in a receptive frame of mind when he was presented with a plan for world peace by William Jay, a lawyer and jurist whom he visited in New York State. Jay had just completed an essay on international arbitration treaties in which he argued that, if two major nations bound themselves to solve their disputes by arbitration, others would follow suit. Eventually there might even be an agreement throughout Christendom (presumably other parts of the world could be left to the missionaries) to establish 'a tribunal for the adjustment of national differences' and a system of 'preventing all forcible resistance to its decrees'. Greatly impressed by this 'beautifully simple' proposal, Sturge agreed to bring it to the attention of the British peace movement. It offered him exactly the sort of agitation in which he was most at ease. The pacifists must learn the lessons of the anti-slavery and temperance movements, Jay wrote: their means must be 'the same by which the commerce in human beings was destroyed, and which are now driving intemperance from the earth - voluntary associations and the press'.(29)

Scattered throughout Sturge's book are comments that suggest his response to the economy, society and government of the United States. He saw what fitted his own point of view, a characteristic he seems to have shared with most of the 230 British visitors who published accounts of their American travels between 1836 and 1860.(30) His reaction to the textile factories in Lowell was a case in point - they reminded him of the stock Anti-Corn Law League theory that British tariffs on corn were forcing the Americans to develop their own industries behind retaliatory barriers.(31)

> It is the restrictive policy of Great Britain that has called into existence Lowell and the manufacturing cities of the United States, producing an immense amount of articles which were once the sole products of British industry and skill. If the same policy is continued, the prosperity of the United States will be impeded, but that of England will be destroyed.

He did not assimilate evidence that upset this simplistic thesis. While he was in Philadelphia he visited some railway workshops that had recently sold locomotives to the Birmingham and Gloucester Railway Company: the cost, he noted, was 'about the same as in England'. As a director of the Company he should also have known that they had out-performed their English rivals in trials on exceptionally steep gradients, and that the sight of the 'Philadelphia', the 'Columbia', the 'Atlantic', the 'England' and six other American locomotives on the line was a daily reminder of a more serious challenge to British industrial pre-eminence than the one described in Anti-Corn Law League tracts.(32)

Other lessons were more heartening as Sturge travelled through the United States behaving, like other travellers of his generation, as if he were visiting a laboratory for experiments in new methods of government and social organisation. He was delighted to see religion, schools and the temperance movement flourishing in a land where Church and State had been separated. He also observed the institutions of democratic government that had brought a vision of hope to British radicals and a spectre of social disorder to conservatives. One of the few visitors to take account of federalism, he carefully differentiated the North from the Federal Government and the South. In the District of Columbia the slave markets that existed within sight of the great national monuments of freedom symbolised for him the stranglehold of the 'slave power' on federal institutions. Even an audience with President Tyler (easily arranged in the days when the presidency had yet to acquire its 'imperial' pretensions) failed to impress him when he was not allowed to present an anti-slavery memorial from Thomas Clarkson. Later, in an address To The Abolitionists of the United States, Who By Their Votes, Contributed To Place A Slaveholder In The Presidential Chair, he would compare Tyler unfavourably with 'Mohammed Ali, the Pasha of Egypt'.(33) Sensibly, Whittier bustled him out of Washington before his outspokenness could provoke a reprisal, and they retreated to the northern states where Sturge was full of admiration for the signs of well-being that he saw all around him. It was there, delighted by 'the republican simplicity and equality of the statutes of Massachusetts' and by 'the absence of the aristocratic element' in the other non-slave states, that he completed his transition to democracy: 'I ... record my conviction, that the great principle of popular control which is carried out almost to its full extent in the free States, is not only beautiful in theory, but that it is found to work well in practice.'(34)

On 13 August 1841 Sturge returned to England after a swift and comfortable voyage on the Caledonia, one of the new Cunard liners. The next sixteen months would be the most controversial of his life, but events could have taken a different course if his anti-slavery and peace society associates had been prepared to follow his advice and hold their international conventions in 1842. Instead they persuaded him to accept a postponement of a year. Disappointed, he attended firstly to an important matter of conscience arising from his Atlantic trip: the Caledonia had departed on a Sunday, providing an 'occasion for the needless profanation of the day by thousands'. The words were those of a petition he had circulated in Boston before his departure, but the Lords of the Admiralty who arranged the sailing times for Cunard were men of a more secular disposition, and they would not be drawn beyond 'the exigencies of the public service'. Sturge could only publish the exchange of correspondence and pass the petition on to Sir Andrew Agnew, the M.P. who had dedicated his life to the defence of the Lord's

Day.(35)   He then turned back to popular politics, prompted by the information that the Anti-Corn Law League had diluted its principles during the General Election which had occurred in his absence.

Sturge was told that the League had agreed to support the outgoing Whig ministers after they had promised, if re-elected, to substitute a moderate tariff for the sliding scale of duties on imported corn. Foreseeing something of the sort, on the eve of his departure for America he had promised that he would raise his contribution from £100 p.a. to £200 p.a. (the League was hard-pressed for funds at the time) if the movement would hold fast to the principle of total and immediate repeal. Now, on 30 September 1841 he published an open letter to Cobden insisting on a pledge of principled behaviour before he would make the promised payments. Cobden's reply provided a classic contrast between 'expressive' and 'instrumental' politics: it would have been a mistake to treat the two main political parties equally, he told Sturge, when the Whigs were advancing some way towards the League's position.   Memories of Buxton's compromises over the Slavery Emancipation Bill in 1833 stirred in Sturge's mind, and he told delegates at a League meeting that the Whigs had tricked them into following a similar course.   He knew he had been nicknamed 'the impracticable Sturge', but he was unrepentant after seeing 'so many attempts to get rid of principle for the sake of expediency in the neighbourhood of St. Stephen's, that he was very jealous of every movement in London'.(36)

Sturge made his payments, and the dispute was patched up, but it was evident that he would be satisfied only with a new reform movement. There was no point in seeking justice for the people from a parliament elected on the existing suffrage, he told Cobden in his open letter; what was needed was 'some association, whose object is by peaceable and Christian means, to secure such a representation of the people as the golden rule of "doing to others as we would they should do unto us" entitles them to claim'.   Any other policy would allow the Government to 'plunge millions into want and misery, if not bring them to a premature grave'.

The reference to 'want and misery' was provoked by the onset in 1841-42 of the gloomiest year of the nineteenth century.   Sturge's statements at this time said little about proposals by some of his contemporaries for reforming the New Poor Law, regulating factory conditions and otherwise actively involving the State in alleviating economic and social problems.   His response to the 'Condition of England Question' was always grounded on the voluntary principle in its widest sense: the Corn Laws would be repealed; cheaper food would be imported; other countries would have less incentive to compete with British industry; commercial interdependence would diminish the need for expensive armed forces; the burdens of aristocratic mismanagement would be removed from the people; and working men would take control of their destiny, assisted by institutions for self-help.   In 1841, for example, he and his brother Edmund were on the Board of the Birmingham Savings Bank when it issued the following appeal to prospective working-class depositors:(37)

> Habits of frugality and economy may be acquired and judiciously practised without any necessary privations, and will almost surely lead to improvement in character, increased industry, and a degree of comfort, independence, and self-respect, incompatible with careless profusion and intemperate indulgence.

But the experiences of the previous ten years showed that this vision would be realised only after parliament was made responsible to the people. By mid-October 1841 (the words were Cobden's) Sturge was 'tending towards Chartism'; by the end of the year he had launched the Complete Suffrage movement.(38)

NOTES

1. Birmingham Journal, 9 May 1840.
2. Proceedings Of The General Anti-Slavery Convention, Called By The Committee Of The British And Foreign Anti-Slavery Society, And Held In London From Tuesday, June 13th, To Tuesday, June 20th 1843, iii; Rhodes House, E 2/6, British And Foreign Anti-Slavery Society Minutes, 31 May, 26 July 1839; Richard, Sturge, p. 210.
3. 'The World's Convention Of The Friends of Emancipation, Held In London In 1840', in The Poetical Works Of John Greenleaf Whittier, London n.d.; Proceedings Of The General Anti-Slavery Convention Called By The Committee Of The British And Foreign Anti-Slavery Society, And Held In London From Friday, June 12th to Tuesday, June 23rd, 1840, London 1841.
4. Rhodes House, MSS Brit. Emp., S18, C110/59, Joseph Sturge to [R.D. Webb?], 10 July 1840; Brit. Lib., Add. MSS. 41267A, ff. 245-47, Description of Haydon's Picture of The Great Meeting of Delegates Held At the Freemason's Tavern, June 1840, For The Abolition of Slavery And The Slave Trade Throughout the World; Accounts of the 1840 Convention by J.H. Webb & Maria Waring in Taylor, British And American Abolitionists. An Episode In Transatlantic Understanding, pp. 94-95; Brit. Lib., Add. MSS. 41267A, ff. 185-86, Mary Clarkson to Mrs Thomas Clarkson, 13 June 1840.
5. Proceedings Of The General Anti-Slavery Convention, 1840, passim.
6. Maria Waring in Taylor, British And American Abolitionists, p. 96.
7. The customary practices are described in my 'Woman's Mission And Pressure Group Politics In Britain (1825-60)', Bulletin of the John Rylands University Library of Manchester, vol. 63, no. 1, Autumn 1980, pp. 194-203. See also Slavery And "The Woman Question", Lucretia Mott's Diary of Her Visit to Great Britain to Attend the World's Anti-Slavery Convention of 1840, ed., F.B. Tolles, London 1952.
8. History of Woman Suffrage, ed., E.C. Stanton, S.B. Anthony & M.J. Gage, New York 1881, p. 62; Joseph Sturge Manuscripts in William L. Clements Library (microfilm), Joseph Sturge to J.G. Birney, 11 June 1840; Elizabeth Pease to Wendell & Ann Phillips, 29 September 1842, in Taylor, British And American Abolitionists, pp. 183-84.
9. B. Wyatt-Brown, Lewis Tappan and the Evangelical War

Against Slavery, Cleveland 1969, passim; L.J. Friedman, Gregarious Saints. Self And Community In American Abolitionism, 1830-1870, Cambridge 1982, pp. 70-74.

10. D.L. Dumond, ed., Letters of James Gillespie Birney 1831-1857, New York 1938, vol. I, pp. 497-98, J.G. Birney to A.A. Phelps, 8 August 1839. See also Proceedings Of The General Anti-Slavery Convention, 1840, p. 41.

11. Garrison's ideas are discussed in Walters, American Reformers, especially pp. 86-90. For Lucretia Mott see O. Cromwell, Lucretia Mott, New York 1968, pp. 77-90; Slavery And "The Woman Question", ed. Tolles, p. 25; E.B. Bronner, The Other Branch, London Yearly Meeting and the I licksites 1027-1912, London 1975, p. 12.

12. James Mott, Three Months In Great Britain, Philadelphia 1841, pp. 43-44.

13. Slavery And "The Woman Question", ed. Tolles, p. 29.

14. Rhodes House, MSS. Brit. Emp. S22, G14, Conferences, Congresses etc., 'Protest By American Delegates Against The Conduct of the Convention', 23 June 1840; Barclay Fox's Journal, p. 203; J.H. Bell, British Folks & British India Fifty Years Ago: Joseph Pease and his Contemporaries, Manchester n.d., pp. 102-104; F.B. Smith, Florence Nightingale. Reputation and Power, London 1982, p. 12.

15. Tyrrell, 'Woman's Mission And Pressure Group Politics in Britain (1825-60)', photograph and pp. 196-97.

16. Taylor, British and American Abolitionists, pp. 134, 272, J.A. Collins to W.L,. Garrison, 27 December 1840, and R.D. Webb to M.W. Chapman, 16 July 1846; Huntingdon Library, Joseph Sturge to Mary Clarkson, n.d.; Rhodes House, MSS Brit. Emp. S18, C110/59, Joseph Sturge to R.D. Webb, 10 July 1840.

17. Huntingdon Library, Joseph Sturge to Thomas Clarkson, 29 January 1841; Richard, Sturge, p. 224.

18. J. Sturge, A Visit To The United States In 1841, London 1842.

19. Rhodes House, MSS Brit. Emp. S18, C110/79, Joseph Sturge to John Beaumont, 16 August 1841.

20. British Library, Add. MSS. 41267A, ff. 232-33, B.R. Haydon to Thomas Clarkson, 19 March 1841.

21. M. Berger, The British Traveller In America, 1836-1860, New York 1943, p. 109; Sturge, A Visit To The United States, pp. 31-35 and 52-53; Sturge Manuscripts in William L. Clements Library, Description of Sturge's Visit to T.D. Weld, 23 October 1841 (microfilm); Rhodes House, MSS Brit. Emp. S18, C110/83, J.G. Whittier to Joseph Sturge, 31 January 1842 and C110/84, Joshua Leavitt to Joseph Sturge, 28 January 1842.

22. Sturge Papers (M. Sturge), manuscript account of Sturge's American journey; Boston Public Library, Arnold Buffum to Joseph Sturge, 9 April 1839; Friends House Library, f.21.40, George Crosfield to Henry Crosfield, 25 May 1840.

23. Sturge, A Visit To The United States, pp. 119-26.

24. Ibid., pp. v, 22-26, cxiii-cxvi.

25. Ibid., pp. 48-50; Library of Congress, The Papers of Lewis Tappan, Journal and Notebooks, 9 June and 12 June 1841; British And Foreign Anti-Slavery Reporter, 14 July 1841.

26. E.M. Spiers, The Army and Society 1815-1914, London 1980, pp. 74-75; University College, Dublin, O'Connell Papers, 68.6, Joseph Sturge to Daniel O'Connell, 29 April 1840; Joseph Sturge, Chinese War. To The Christian Public Of Great 3ritain, Birmingham, 19 March 1840.

27. Richard, Sturge, p. 289; Herald of Peace, October-December 1832 and July 1838.

28. Sturge, A Visit To The United States, pp. 62-70.

29. Ibid., pp. 55-57, Appendix F.

30. Berger, The British Traveller in America, pp. 14, 182.

31. Sturge, A Visit To The United States, p. 155.

32. Ibid., p. 139; C.E. Stratton, The History of the Birmingham and Gloucester Railway, Leeds 1902, p. 6.

33. Sturge, A Visit To The United States, pp. 73-93; Rhodes House, MSS. Brit. Emp. S18, C110/74. The address was toned down for publication in Sturge's book.

34. Sturge, A Visit To The United States, pp. 170-7.

35. Ibid., Appendix N. See also Boston Public Library, Joseph Sturge to ?, 6 July 1841, Lords of the Admiralty to Joseph Sturge, 21 September 1841, Sir Andrew Agnew to Joseph Sturge, 14 October 1841, Joseph Sturge to A.A. Phelps, 18 October 1841.

36. Anti-Corn Law Circular, 11 March 1841; Anti-Bread Tax Circular, 7 October, 21 October 1841; Nonconformist, 19 January 1842.

37. A. Briggs, The Age of Improvement, London 1959, p. 295; Birmingham Journal, 16 January 1841.

38. Manchester Public Library, Wilson Papers, Richard Cobden to George Wilson, 16 October 1841.

10 The Advocate of Freedom (1841-51)

Sturge's adoption of Complete Suffrage puzzled some of his contemporaries, and it has been misunderstood by historians. By his own account there were two reasons. Firstly, America had taught him to reverse his priorities, so that, instead of believing that literacy would lead on to the suffrage, he now saw the suffrage as a means of stimulating the interest of working men in education. Secondly, he had received visits from his 'working friends - the Chartists' with whom he had privately discussed programmes of reform.(1) Other evidence shows that these contacts went back to the time of the anti-police campaign. At the end of 1839 Sturge had sent J. H. Shearman, the former editor of the Philanthropist, to find out from the Chartists what the working people of Birmingham were thinking about the repeal of the corn laws, and when this approach failed he was probably one of the 'gentlemen' on whose behalf Shearman delivered some lectures outlining a scheme for a literacy franchise.(2) This was one of several attempts at that time by middle-class radicals (Samuel Smiles's household suffrage movement is the best-known) to associate Chartists with a new movement for political reform, but they all foundered on the same obstacle: no Chartist, Smiles was told, would depart from 'that only safe conductor of the lightning storm, the People's Charter'.(3)

And yet there was abundant evidence in 1841 that, if they were not obliged to swallow their principles, many Chartists would be prepared to form an alliance with middle-class radicals. All over the country Chartists were refusing to follow the lead of the National Charter Association in which Feargus O'Connor's was the dominant voice and a class-conscious 'Fustian Chartism' was the dominant ideology. Birmingham provided one of the best examples of this trend. Two rival Chartist societies emerged in 1840: the Lawrence Street Chartists (N.C.A. men) and the Newhall Street Christian Chartist Church. The leaders of the latter group, Arthur O'Neill and John Collins, were in touch, not only with other Christian Chartist churches, but also with Henry Vincent's Teetotal Chartists and William Lovett's National Association in London.(4) Chartism, A New Organisation of the People, a book written by Lovett and Collins while they were in prison after the Bull Ring Riots, contained what was probably the most important of the Chartist appeals for middle-class support. They could almost have had Sturge in mind when they promised that, if 'the generous and philanthropic minds with which our country abounds' would help to carry the People's Charter into law, the Chartists, 'animated by such co-operation, would prove the most zealous, temperate, and powerful auxiliaries in banishing intemperance, poverty, and crime, and in raising the intellectual and moral character of the people beyond the expectations of the most sanguine philanthropist.'(5)

Sturge did not know Lovett well at this time, but he established a good relationship with O'Neill and Collins. Easily, almost inevitably, he added the Birmingham Christian Chartist Church to his list of good causes. A summary of their principal preaching topics shows how close they were to his outlook:

The fall and degradation of man by sin, the way of salvation presented in the atonement through Christ, and the carrying out of his sublime precepts and heavenly example in our lives and actions. The necessity of showing our faith by good works, of proving our love to God by love to man. The glorious destinies of man in that immortality, which is brought to light through the Gospel. The full efficiency of Christianity to restore universal happiness, when made the sole standard of government, commerce, education, and every other pursuit of man, and the duty laid upon every Christian not to yield allegiance or assent to a system, that is not in accordance with this universal standard, but by every Christian means to bring about the time, when instead of being the realms of Mammon and Moloch, the kingdoms of this world shall become the kingdoms of our Lord and of his Christ.

The reports of the Christian Chartist Church referred to educational programmes for adults and children, a library, a printing press and a benevolent society for sick and poor members. It is not difficult to see why Charles Sturge could praise O'Neill for doing 'more good than all the parsons in the neighbourhood'.(6)

The co-operation between Sturge and the Christian Chartists is therefore an excellent example of the proposition that middle and working-class radicals of this era could adjust to each other's aspirations without a surrender by either side. It is certainly a mistake to accuse Sturge of a middle-class smugness and condescension that excluded good relations with working men and enfeebled his radicalism.(7) He made no bones about accepting a place in the three class model ('landlords, capitalists and labourers') that John Stuart Mill chided contemporaries for believing in 'as if it were one of God's ordinances', but his speeches and letters often showed him self-consciously standing apart from the middle class on the burning issues of the day. He spoke of placing the rights of the slave and the rights of the working class 'side by side of each other on the same basis of principle', even though he knew that the attempt would cause him to lose 'caste'.(8) There was a strong element of paternalism in this attitude, but it was modified by what he learned from working-class radicals. Sturge's niece, Priscilla Burlingham, remembered 'often' meeting Arthur O'Neill in her Uncle Joseph's house at this time, and doubtless he was one of the 'working friends' whose visits helped to reshape Sturge's political platform between 1839 and 1841. For the Christian Chartists were not working-class toadies like Slyme, the chapel-going teetotaler in Robert Tressell's novel, The Ragged Trousered Philanthropists: they had held to their principles when Samuel Smiles offered them a place in the household suffrage movement.(9) In any case, Sturge's 'moral Radicalism' bore little resemblance to stock notions of Victorian middle-class respectability. As the Christian Advocate had admitted in 1838, there was little to choose between the voluntaryists and Chartists as agitators: 'We that have been so long engaged in agitating for the abolition of Church-rates, ought to be especially cautious how we condemn agitators of any description. Indeed, we have set an example which will bear out any agitation that falls short of an appeal to physical force.'(10)

This was no exaggeration, if we may judge from an episode in Birmingham during September and October 1841. When it was announced that a church rate was to be proposed at a vestry meeting in the Town Hall and that admission would be by ticket, a committee chaired by Charles Sturge sprang into existence to ensure the admission of 'the inhabitants generally'. Any attempt to stop them would probably give rise to a riot, they warned the magistrates. When neither side would back down on polling day, a large crowd forced the organ gallery door and swarmed into the Town Hall, climbing and jumping to obtain places throughout the building. The anti-rate party then carried the election of the chairman and dissolved the meeting amid scenes of chaos. A month later the pro-rate party tried again with similar results. On this occasion spectators were regaled by the sight of Charles Sturge and his committee climbing up to the organ gallery from the floor of the Town Hall to lead the opposition that was carried on for several hours 'with the most determined spirit'. The tone of the proceedings could be gauged from the storm of banter and coarse laughter that greeted the church wardens' estimates for church wine. It was noted that a body of Christian Chartists took an active part in the meeting, and that when Joseph Sturge spoke for the anti-rate case he went out of his way to praise them. The Tory Birmingham Advertiser was appalled by the sight of 'a man of his plain habits, and plain sense on many subjects, attempting wit, and using jeers against the orders of the Church'. It could only lament that members of 'that once unobtrusive sect', the Society of Friends, were now ungrateful for the privilege of being tolerated by the Church of England.(11)

It was not surprising therefore that voluntaryists should join the search for some means of harnessing the energies of the Chartists to a new reform movement in 1840-41. They had always spoken of themselves as champions of civil liberty, and they had claimed to act in the name of the people when they deployed 'the pressure from without' against parliament during the 1830s: why should they not take one step more by endorsing the principle of universal suffrage? This was the theme taken up by the Rev. Andrew Marshall in December 1840 when he addressed the Dissenting ministers of Scotland: they should rally 'the better sort of the people' ('at your back and enforcing your representations' were the words he used to emphasise the respective roles) in a new movement against the traditional hierarchy in church and state. The address was published as a pamphlet and favourably reviewed by Edward Miall, the owner-editor of the Nonconformist newspaper. In October 1841 Miall went on to publish a series of articles entitled 'Reconciliation Between the Middle and Working Classes' in which he coined the term 'Complete Suffrage'.(12)

Miall's move, like Marshall's, was meant to be the trumpet call for a new generation of Dissenters to rally to the good old cause of civil and religious liberty. As a young man in Leicester during the 1830s Miall had been active in a group of Congregational and Baptist ministers who were notorious for their zeal as voluntaryists and reformers. Of their leader, J. P. Mursell, it would later be said that he was so ardent in 'his sympathy with all the advanced movements of the day that he blended their advocacy with almost every fresh effort in connection with his church'. Similar individuals and groups existed all over the country, schooled by the part they had played in anti-slavery and voluntaryist campaigns. Recently several hundred of them had denounced the Corn Laws in ringing tones at an assembly in Manchester;(13) now it remained only to be seen how they would respond to the more overtly political subject of suffrage reform.

Richard Cobden, who met the two brothers in November 1841 was convinced that Charles Sturge was 'even more strongly in favour of a junction with the working class' than Joseph, and it is likely that Charles had a hand in the creation of the Complete Suffrage movement. The brash young man who had spoken of himself as a 'Jacobin' in 1820 had changed remarkably little over the years. In 1837 he had startled that arch pragmatist Daniel O'Connell by offering to support him in an attempt to 'throw expediency to the winds', and later in the same year he had flirted with the revived Birmingham Political Union. He had never assisted the League, he testily wrote to the editor of the Anti-Bread Tax Circular in 1841, nor would he ever do so; 'a small portion of their labour and expenditure of money bestowed in agitating for the Suffrage would probably before this have effected the Corn Laws and many other good measures'.(14) Miall's Nonconformist, on the other hand, struck him as a good investment: it traced the abuses of church establishments to a corrupt political system that could only be reformed by a 'fair and full representation of all'. Charles gave a generous subsidy to the newspaper, and it is likely that he brought his brother and Miall together.(15) Joseph did not yet accept all six points of the People's Charter, but in the Nonconformist he found 'Complete Suffrage' defined as a programme of universal male enfranchisement, leaving other reforms of the electoral system to be decided on in the future. Acting with his characteristic energy, he brought Miall's 'Reconciliation' out as a pamphlet and spoke in support of it at several Anti-Corn Law League meetings during the winter of 1841-42.(16)

From the start Cobden was in two minds about Sturge's new move. He welcomed it as a means of showing that Leaguers were sympathetic to the working class and as an indication to the aristocracy that more radical policies than corn law repeal were being canvassed, but the League was at the lowest point of its fortunes for several months after the 1841 General Election returned the Tories to power, and he feared that it might be superseded by a movement that offered the promise of a shorter and more decisive struggle for victory. 'All sorts of violent remedies are suggested', he told Duncan McLaren in March 1842.(17) To placate Sturge and his supporters on the League Council, Cobden raised no objection when they asked the delegates to stay on for an extra meeting to discuss the suffrage question at the end of a conference in Manchester in November 1841, and he even proposed that Sturge should draw up a Complete Suffrage declaration.   Subsequently, he encouraged Leaguers to sign the declaration as a demonstration of good will to the working class: it was an easy gesture to condemn class legislation and call for 'a fair, full and free exercise of the elective franchise' on the premise that no one should be taxed without his own consent.(18)

But Cobden would not allow the League as a body to be associated with the new movement. Above all, he wanted to have no dealings with Chartists: references in his correspondence show his strong distaste for all who bore that name. Accordingly, he rejected a suggestion from Sturge that he should meet '200 of the peace Chartists in the way of a Conference'. 'Our only plan', he told George Wilson, 'is to leave the two Chartist factions to fight with each other, & raise up a working class party of repealers independent of both'.(19) Thus during the early months of 1842 it became clear that the Complete Suffrage movement would have to proceed independently of the League, and in February Sturge withdrew from the Birmingham Anti-Corn Law Association. Miall's editorials suggested that many others would do the same when the League foundered on the rock of Tory intransigence.(20)

But if Sturge had broken with the League, he was also at pains to make it clear that he would not become a Chartist. At a meeting in Birmingham in March 1842 he and his platform party (including three local Nonconformist ministers and two Radical Town Councillors) offered what they described as a platform for middle and working-class reformers: the enfranchisement of all adult males; repeal of the Corn and Game Laws; withdrawal from the wars currently being waged in China and Afghanistan; and the programme of religious voluntaryism. When a member of the audience intervened and asked the meeting to declare for the People's Charter, Sturge ruled him out of order. He and his friends had come together 'to do the people a little good', he explained, 'and if they could not do any, they would most certainly resign'.   His choice of words shows him remaining true to the paternalism of the early nineteenth-century philanthropic movements which had trained him for public life; his conversion to democratic institutions of government did not carry with it the belief so often expressed by Chartists that the parliamentary reform movement must function democratically itself. Eventually when Sturge denied the leader of the O'Connorite Chartists an opportunity to speak, the meeting was shouted down. There could not have been a clearer augury of the events that were to cripple the new movement nine months later.(21)

In essence, Sturge was offering a modernised version of the 'moral Radicalism' of the 1830s. Then the emphasis had been on negro slavery and the Apprenticeship system; now he spoke of the rights and well-being of the British working class. And it was to the same constituency of support that he instinctively turned. In his introduction to Miall's Reconciliation Sturge commended Complete Suffrage to those 'who wish to be guided, in their political as well as religious conduct by the precepts of the Gospel'. Above all, as he subsequently explained to Francis Place (the veteran London radical did not sympathise) he wanted to get 'that part of the religious and Philanthropic public who do not commonly mix in politics to take the subject up'. He had been encouraged, he added, by the willingness of one hundred Dissenting ministers to sign the Complete Suffrage declaration soon after it was made public.(22) Thus the closest contemporary parallel was not the Anti-Corn Law League or the Chartist movement but the Liberty Party in which his American friends looked to the Bible as a political textbook and used ministers of religion as leading activists. Americans had often commented on the apparent indifference of British abolitionists to the rights of the British working class; now, Whittier told John Quincy Adams they could see in Joseph Sturge 'the advocate of Freedom everywhere'.(23)

During the early months of 1842 sympathisers formed Complete Suffrage Associations in various parts of the country, and Sturge created a Provisional Committee in Birmingham to co-ordinate their activities. The idea of a national conference to set out the terms of an agreement between middle and working-class reformers appeared in one of the Committee's early circulars. Anticipating some sort of opposition from the National Charter Association which had quickly denounced the 'Complete Humbug' as a trap to entice working men into supporting the anti-corn law movement, Sturge carefully stage-managed the conference to prevent any disruption. Only those who had signed the Complete Suffrage Declaration or a Memorial that he had sent out asking for support 'from all classes and regions' were allowed to vote for delegates; Birmingham was chosen as the conference venue in preference to London; and the agenda was drawn up by the Birmingham Committee. Prominent amongst Sturge's assistants was that same William Morgan who in 1840 had read the American female anti-slavery delegates a lesson about the power that a 'Committee of Arrangements' could wield at conferences.(24)

This strategy had the desired effect. Although only 103 delegates accepted Sturge's invitation, those who came seemed to justify the experiment. Common to all of them, middle class no less than working class, was a deep disillusionment with the Reformed Parliament. Some were Chartists (including William Lovett, John Collins, Henry Vincent and James Bronterre O'Brien); some were Leaguers (notably John Bright, T. B. Potter and Archibald Prentice); and others had responded to Sturge's special appeal for support from those who were already 'identified either with the cause of Peace, Temperance, or the Abolition of Slavery'. It was this third group, the 'moral Radicals' of the thirties, that he relied on most of all. Amongst them were some of the keenest voluntaryists in the country: not only J.P. Mursell and Edward Miall, but Dr John Ritchie (the 'Goliath' of the voluntaryists), John Childs (the church rate gaol 'martyr'), James Adam (the editor of the <u>Aberdeen Herald</u>) and Thomas Spencer (one of the most strenuous voluntaryists of the day for all that he was an Anglican clergyman). None of these men was a single issue reformer. The nickname given to the circle of Dublin philanthropists represented at the conference by James Webb would have fitted most of them: they were 'Anti-everythingarians'.(25)

The nickname captured a streak of perverse eccentricity in their public personalities. Wearing his bishop's knee tights, Quaker 'plain' coat, neck-to-waist cravat, 'waggish' hat, gold spectacles and 'immense bunch of watch ornaments', Dr Ritchie struck one of the delegates as 'the most singular specimen of the human race we have ever met or mingled with'. He was one of the very small number of ministers (twelve) who attended the conference; other ministers were prepared to sign Complete Suffrage petitions and to assist the movement in various ways, but they would go no further. And it was very noticeable that only one MP attended the conference - William Sharman Crawford, an Ulster landowner from a family with a distinguished reforming tradition but a feeble orator who had little influence at Westminster. Crawford acted as the parliamentary spokesman for the Complete Suffrage movement throughout its existence. The presence of another Irish representative was scarcely more reassuring for anyone who hoped for a display of strength; Thomas Steele, the 'Head Pacificator of Ireland', had arrived as a proxy for Daniel O'Connell. In 1839 O'Connell had discussed the possibility of co-operating with Sturge in a new radical movement, and Sturge made much of Steele's presence, but the 'Head Pacificator' was no substitute for his leader: he has been described as a 'lovable and grotesque character ... whose brains were more like mice running around than steady grey matter'. Although O'Connell always treated Sturge with respect, the Complete Suffrage movement would receive no help from Ireland.(26)

But, as the Rev. Thomas Swan pointed out in his speech of welcome to the delegates, this was 'Joseph Sturge's parliament'. The proceedings revolved around Sturge: he was 'a first-rate tactitian', one of the delegates noted, and he guided the discussions to a successful conclusion. Under pressure from the Chartists Sturge accepted all the six points of the People's Charter although he had not originally intended to go so far, but for the rest he had his own way. The delegates voted to set up a National Complete Suffrage Union (NCSU), and in practice Sturge was left to manage its business as Provisional President of an executive consisting of three of his Birmingham friends: J. C. Perry, William Morgan and Arthur Albright. The new movement was to draw on the techniques of the 'pressure from without' that he had used so effectively during the 1830s - lectures by agents, petitions, lobbying and intervention in elections, if necessary by offering its own candidates. If all else failed, there was to be an attempt to withhold taxes from the Government. The NCSU was linked to Sturge's existing circle of reforms through a series of conference resolutions appealing for the help of ministers of religion; recommending temperance; and calling on members to oppose 'the horrors of war'. At one stage the discussion centred so much on the evils of liquor and snuff that Mursell chided Sturge for trying to turn the movement into a teetotal society. The conference left one major problem unresolved. It neither accepted nor rejected a proposal by Lovett that the People's Charter should be the foundation document of the NCSU. The very word 'Chartist' aroused middle-class fears, Sturge warned the delegates, and Miall threatened Lovett with 'an entire separation of parties' rather than have it foisted on him. All that could be agreed on was an amendment guaranteeing that a conference would be called in the future to consider 'any documents' which set out the six points.(27)

The next stage, as the <u>Birmingham Journal</u> pointed out, was the testing one for a new movement: its leaders had to be seen 'doing something or projecting something to do'. During the following months Crawford brought on a debate in the House of Commons to identify sympathetic MPs (67 voted in favour), and a team of 'missionaries' consisting of Sturge, the Rev. Henry Solly, Charles Clarke, Henry Vincent, Robert Somers and John Collins visited many parts of Britain to set up branches of the NCSU. By the end of the year there were ninety of them (principally in Scotland, the south-west, Yorkshire and the Midlands in that order of strength), and some of them were large. Paisley had 5000 members, Edinburgh 1200 and Glasgow 1000. 'Everywhere', Sturge reported, 'the best friends of our cause are more or less connected with that of the temperance reformation; and the independent minds of various religious communities are standing forth in behalf of the cause'. Samuel Smiles and the remnants of his household suffrage movement were amongst those who declared for Complete Suffrage at this time.(28)

Almost immediately the movement was presented with an opportunity to test its electoral strength: a few weeks after the Birmingham conference Sturge accepted nomination as a candidate in a by-election at Nottingham which was certain to attract a great deal of publicity. All over the country the previous year's General Election had been an exceptionally corrupt one, and many of the defeated candidates had successfully challenged the results. Aware that neither party could derive much general benefit from these costly legal wrangles, the Tory and Whig managers had drawn together and resolved on a compromise:(29)

> In certain cases, wherein the result of an election might be doubtful or the trial expensive to both sides, one seat of the two was given up; the petition was dropped, and one of the members petitioned against applied for the Chiltern Hundreds, resigning his seat. One of the petitioners was then allowed to stand unopposed.

Nottingham was one of the worst cases of electoral corruption. In 1841 the Whigs had carried both seats in the town, but subsequently under threat of a petition from the Tories they had agreed to allow John Walter, the Tory proprietor of <u>The Times,</u> to stand unopposed.

Outraged by this arrangement, Sturge came forward as the champion of electoral 'purity' despite warnings that he was wasting his time: the Nottingham voters, the Birmingham Journal told him, were 'a mass of unmitigated scoundrelism, who have sold and will sell their souls to the highest bidder, without a moment's inquiry as to his principles'.(30)

Sturge's approach to electioneering would have attracted less attention later in the century when the 'Nonconformist Conscience' was a recognised force in politics, but it was unusual in his own day. He took with him to Nottingham an electoral endorsement from ten Birmingham Nonconformist ministers (three of them even joined his campaign team), and from the moment of his arrival in the town he made it clear that he would do nothing to encourage the carnival atmosphere that usually prevailed during early Victorian elections. Met by a 'mighty multitude', he walked with them from the railway station to the market place where he addressed them on his programme of reforms. 'The procession was most unostentatious', Miall wrote: 'no banners, no flags, no colours, no bands - all was simple and pure, and what was lacking in meretricious adjuncts was well replaced by the deep earnestness and evident consciousness'. Subsquently, one of Sturge's campaign meetings took place in a chapel with a Quaker in the chair, four ministers amongst the speakers, and a rhetoric that made much of such themes as 'civil and religious liberty', 'the moral and intellectual elevation of the people' and 'Truth, Freedom and Religion'. His platform was virtually a summary of the good causes he had taken up during the previous dozen or so years: voluntaryism in religion, free trade, abolition of the death penalty; opposition to war and the maintenance of a standing army; anti-slavery; and the Complete Suffrage programme as defined at the Birmingham Conference.(31)

Briefly, the by-election brought Complete Suffrage to the forefront of radical politics. The Anti-Bread Tax Circular declared for Sturge; one of the Anti-Corn Law League's agents campaigned on his behalf; Vincent and O'Neill spoke at his meetings; and even Feargus O'Connor arrived to support him. Sturge did not welcome O'Connor's participation. The sight of the two men standing side by side on public platforms attracted criticism, and at one stage Sturge narrowly escaped being involved in a pitched battle between O'Connor's Chartists and the mob known as the 'Tory Lambs'. But neither his own virtue nor O'Connor's fists could avert a defeat at the polls: Sturge lost by 1885 votes to 1801.(32) Extracting some value from the defeat, he accused Walter of corruption, kidnapping and impersonation, and with the help of a team of Quakers which met 'night after night and week after week' he had the result annulled.(33) But he did not accept nomination when the seat was re-contested in 1843. Rather surprisingly for one who would go to the polls three times in his lifetime, Sturge had little enthusiasm for becoming a parliamentarian: elections were for expressing principles. During the campaign he had spoken of his right to resign, and he had warned his prospective constituents that he would spend little time in the House. After the election he told a public meeting that 'he had such a feeling about the House of Commons, that if ... he could effect any good to his country by going as many days or hours to Newgate as to that house, he would as soon go there, and he was not quite sure whether he should not find there as many honest men'.(34) In all likelihood the claims of conscience that had made him resign from the Birmingham Street Commissioners and the Town Council would have driven him from Parliament.

It would be easy to over-estimate the importance of this by-election defeat for the NCSU. Lovett's National Association Gazette had been hoping that Sturge would emulate Daniel O'Connell's famous electoral triumph by making Nottingham 'the Clare of England', and Cobden had forecast that, if Sturge won, a large number of Leaguers would 'throw themselves en masse into his ranks & dissolve the League'.(35) But other evidence suggests that Sturge and Miall had alienated their most likely supporters when they accepted the six points of the Charter in April. Miall's sales figures for the Nonconformist said it all: 'Up to the week at which the Birmingham Conference was held, our books show, a regular, uninterrupted weekly increase of circulation. Since that time, until last week, the decrease has been as regular'.(36) Sturge told Elizabeth Pease that most British Quakers were even less sympathetic to complete suffrage than American Quakers were to the abolitionist societies, and that he had been advised to resign from the Society of Friends.(37)

Probably the NCSU never had much chance of success, but it was the deepening of the economic depression and the return of violence that finally ruined its prospects during the grim summer of 1842. In July Sturge was so alarmed by the gathering signs of crisis that he put together information he had received about the condition of the industrial districts and sent it to Lord Brougham - evidence of large scale unemployment, declining wages, emigration by skilled workers, the suspending of payments by sick clubs, shopkeeper bankruptcies, falling property values and empty houses.(38) Even this gloomy picture was an inadequate preparation for what happened a month later when the 'Plug Plot' immobilised much of the textile industry in the North of England, and there were major strikes in the coal, iron and pottery industries of the Midlands. It was one of the few moments in modern British history when a revolution seemed possible: wild rumours swept through Birmingham that thousands of Chartists were marching on the town from the north, and special constables were enrolled, backed up by soldiers and artillery.(39)

The Christian Chartists were active throughout the crisis. Arthur O'Neill attended many meetings of strikers to counsel them against violence and urge them to withhold taxes from the government as the best means of obtaining political reforms. His statements led to his arrest and eventually to his trial and imprisonment in 1843.(40) O'Neill had not attended the April conference, but he had supported Sturge in the Nottingham by-election; now Sturge publicly endorsed his recommendations. A stream of public addresses then went forth in the name of the NCSU: to the Queen, attributing the nation's difficulties to her ministers; to the middle class urging it to make common cause with the working class; to the working class urging it to co-operate with a conference of reformers which would soon be summoned; and to the Irish people asking for their support. Pointing to Quaker precedents of passive disobedience, Sturge called for a great campaign in which the people would throw off their allegiance to the Government until reform was assured: 'they would simply resolve not to obey; they would refuse to be agents of the government, or to serve in the army, or navy, or police; they would withhold all taxes, and abstain from articles of consumption which yield a revenue to the state'. Plans were set in train for a conference to take place in Birmingham on 7 September.(41) It was a dangerous policy, and immediately there were divisons of opinion over it. Resignations were reported from the NCSU Council, and even Miall publicly warned that it was too early to act. Eventually calmer policies prevailed, and the conference was postponed until late in December.(42)

From the first the conference was overshadowed by O'Connor. He had been arrested during the strikes, and in March 1843 he would stand trial for seditious conspiracy, but in the meanwhile he was at liberty and intent on participating in the conference. He urged his followers to attend the pre-conference local meetings and vote for delegates pledged to the Charter 'name and all'.(43) There was little that Sturge could do to stop this after it was announced that a second conference would not be restricted to those who had signed the Complete Suffrage memorial. Instead, the original plan envisaged the election of two sets of delegates chosen separately by electors and non-electors. As on the previous occasion, the organising committee was to have the right to vet delegates' credentials and set out the agenda. One by one these arrangements collapsed. O'Connor and his followers swamped many of the election meetings (with the help of pokers and bludgeons on one spectacular occasion), alienating several Complete Suffragists including J. P. Mursell and Samuel Smiles; Daniel O'Connell held back; and John Bright publicly disowned the Complete Suffrage movement. The situation looked so bleak when Sturge met his closest associates on the eve of the conference that they resolved to secede immediately if the delegates elected O'Connor as chairman.(44)

There was therefore a tense atmosphere when the conference opened in the Birmingham Mechanics Institute on 27 December 1842. Out of the 374 delegates who registered many were unmistakably O'Connor's supporters, and, although the organising committee had resolved to make the attempt, there was never any hope of excluding those who had been irregularly elected. The first hurdle was cleared safely, however, when Sturge was elected chairman without any opposition from O'Connor. The struggle for control then centred on the agenda. O'Connor had boasted that he would make the delegates accept the People's Charter 'name and all' and merge themselves in the National Charter Association: Sturge on the other hand was intent on following the April precedent by ensuring that the NCSU would be allowed to develop as a separate movement. Personalities were important; for William Lovett seems to have been close to the truth when he wrote that Sturge was concerned 'to have no fellowship with Fergus [sic] O'Connor': the case for Complete Suffrage had always been that Chartism was a good cause ruined by bad leaders. And like the dispute over the 'Woman Question' at the anti-slavery convention, the debate over the agenda at this conference was a question of power. The leader whose resolutions were accepted by the delegates would be seen as the custodian of the popular radical programme of parliamentary reform.

To make this position clear the organising committee would not allow the Charter to be taken as the basis for discussion. Instead it offered the delegates a Bill of Rights codifying the six point programme agreed on in April, a document prepared so secretly that William Lovett and other founder-members of the NCSU had not been consulted. There was little to choose between the rival documents as statements of political principle, but at the April conference Lovett had described the Charter as 'the legislative text book of the millions', and he would not abandon it during the heated debate that now broke out. Sturge's friends, on the other hand, saw only that the Charter was the badge of Feargus O'Connor and his violent policies. An exchange between Dr Ritchie and O'Connor summed up much of the debate over the merits of the two documents: 'Not that he [Ritchie] objected to the Charter as a paper, but he disliked it as the symbol of a party. Mr O'CONNOR - Exactly; but that is the reason we support it'. Sturge and his friends would not listen to the compromises offered by some of the uncommitted delegates and they seceded when the supporters of Lovett and O'Connor joined forces to reject the Bill of Rights by 193 votes to 94. The next day they re-assembled in a temperance hotel and accepted the Bill of Rights as the foundation document of the NCSU.(45)

Religious attitudes exerted a strong influence at this stage; for Sturge took with him, not only his middle-class 'moral Radicals', but also Collins, Vincent and O'Neill.(46) Although they have usually been grouped with Lovett, their Christian beliefs were very different from his rationalism, and there had been a parting of the ways earlier in the year when O'Neill refused to promote the sale of Lovett's <u>National Association Gazette</u> on the grounds that it lacked religion, a decision that earned him a stinging rebuke in its columns for 'cant and religious sentimentality'.(47)

Three years later, on her deathbed, Sturge's sister Sophia discussed this episode with him, and his record leaves no doubt as to their deep moral repugnance for O'Connor:(48)

she had no doubt of the soundness of the principle on which I had advocated the rights of the people & was quite satisfied with my having espoused their cause when they were oppressed & trampled upon and when to do so was so unpopular that it was at the sacrifice of my reputation. I had however committed many errors in the proceeding connected with it greatly arising from acting to [sic] precipitately and yielding too much to the opinions of others naming some by whose councils she thought I had been led wrong but that I had in an almost miraculous manner been preserved from difficulties which might have been inextricable & irremediable - She especially mentioned the conference held at Birmingham at the close of 1842 when Fergus O'Connor & those who co-operated with him exerted all the means in their power to identify me with their proceedings. She said it was Thomas Spencer who first informed her of our seperation [sic] from them & it was such an inexpressible source of comfort & relief to her that she was almost ready to ask him to kneel down & return thanks to God.

Sturge attributed his 'preservation' to his sister's prayers: to a more secular mind the whole episode appears as one example amongst many of his inability to participate in public life alongside those who did not share his religious and moral values. He would persevere with the Complete Suffrage movement for another two years, but, as 1843 opened he probably experienced a sense of relief when his attention was drawn back to the task of organising anti-slavery and peace conventions where once again he could mingle with 'The pledged philanthropy of Earth'.(49)

NOTES

1. Gateshead Observer, 1 October 1842; British Statesman, 3 September 1842.
2. Manchester Public Library, Anti-Corn Law League Letter Book (1838-40), vol. 2, 275, J.H. Shearman to Joseph Sturge, 17 October 1839.
3. Leeds Times, 20 March 1841; A. Tyrrell, 'Class Consciousness in Early Victorian Britain: Samuel Smiles, Leeds Politics and the Self-Help Creed', Journal of British Studies, IX, May 1970, pp. 102-14.
4. Birmingham Journal, 9 January, 13 March, 2 October 1841. See also Public Record Office, H065/10, Superintendent Burgess to Home Office, 19 December 1840, 14 January, 19 January, 27 February, 20 March, 23 May 1841.
5. W. Lovett & John Collins, Chartism: A New Organization of the People, Leicester 1969, pp. 5, 18.
6. National Association Gazette, 8 January, 12 February 1842; Sturge Papers (M. Sturge), Charles Sturge to ?, 24 August 1842.
7. M. Hovell, The Chartist Movement, Manchester 1966, p. 265.
8. Perkin, The Origins of Modern English Society, p. 257; Taylor, British And American Abolitionists, p. 83, Elizabeth Pease to Wendell and Ann Phillips, 29 September 1842; Friends Library, Dublin, Portfolio 5B Philanthropy MS, f. 37, Joseph Sturge to Richard Allen, 25 April 1842.
9. Priscilla Burlingham, Reminiscences; R. Tressell, The Ragged Trousered Philanthropists, London 1965, pp. 26-28.
10. Christian Advocate, 1 October 1838.
11. Birmingham Journal, 11 September, 16 October 1841; Birmingham Advertiser, 16 September, 28 October 1841.
12. Voluntary Church Magazine, February 1841; Nonconformist, 4 August, 13 October et seq., 1841.
13. A. Miall, Life of Edward Miall, London 1884, pp. 18-40; A. Mursell, James Phillippo Mursell. His Life and Work, London 1886, pp. 38-58; Anti-Bread Tax Circular, 26 August 1841.
14. Brit. Lib., Add. MSS. 43662, Richard Cobden to Charles Villiers, 19 November 1841; Birmingham Journal, 14 January 1837;

Flick, The Birmingham Political Union, pp. 118-19; Anti-Bread Tax Circular, 2 December 1841.

15. Sturge Papers (M. Sturge), Edward Miall to Charles Sturge, 1 November, 15 November 1841, 15 June 1842.

16. Nonconformist, 24 November 1841, 19 January 1842.

17. West Sussex Record Office, Cobden 71, Richard Cobden to Duncan McLaren, 4 March 1842; Manchester Public Library, Wilson Papers, Richard Cobden to George Wilson, 24 February 1842; Manchester Public Library, Smith Papers, Richard Cobden to George Smith, 4 December 1841.

18. Manchester Public Library, Wilson Papers, Richard Cobden to George Wilson, 16 February 1842; Manchester Public Library, Smith Papers, Richard Cobden to J.B. Smith, 4 December 1841; Brit. Lib. Add. MSS. 43662, ff. 47-48, Richard Cobden to Charles Villiers, 19 November 1841.

19. Brit. Lib. Add. MSS. 50131, ff. 74-75, Richard Cobden to Joseph Sturge, 27 November 1841; Manchester Public Library, Wilson Papers, Richard Cobden to George Wilson, 16 October 1841.

20. Birmingham Journal, 27 November 1841, 15 January, 26 February 1842; Nonconformist, 19 January 1842.

21. Birmingham Journal, 26 March 1842.

22. Miall, Reconciliation, introd; Brit. Lib., Add. MSS 27810, f. 99, Joseph Sturge to Francis Place, 16 February 1842; A. Tyrrell, 'Personality in Politics: The National Complete Suffrage Union and Pressure Group Politics in Early Victorian Britain', Journal of Religious History, XII, December 1983, p. 394.

23. E. Foner, Free Soil, Free Labor, Free Men. The Ideology of the Republican Party before the Civil War, London 1970, p. 78; J.B. Pickard ed., The Life of John Greenleaf Whittier, Cambridge, Mass., 1975, vol. 1, p. 541, J.G. Whittier to J.Q. Adams, 31 January 1842.

24. Brit. Lib., Add. MSS. 27810, ff. 86-88, Birmingham Complete Suffrage Association Circulars 1-3; ibid., ff. 118-19, Birmingham Complete Suffrage Association, Circular 4; Nonconformist, 23 March 1842.

25. 'A Member', Brief Sketches Of The Birmingham Conference, London 1842; Report Of The Proceedings At The Conference Of Delegates Of The Middle And Working Classes, Held At Birmingham, April 5, 1842, And Three Following Days, London 1842; H.M. Wigham, A Christian Philanthropist of Dublin. A Memoir of Richard Allen, London 1886, p. 14.

26. Brief Sketches, p. 13. For Crawford see Illustrated London News, 5 May 1849, p. 285. For O'Connell's willingness to cooperate with Sturge in a movement to rally 'reformers of all Classes' see Friends Historical Library, Swarthmore, Pennsylvania, Daniel O'Connell to Joseph Sturge, 30 December 1839. Steele is described in S. O'Faolain, King of the Beggars, Dublin 1970, p. 286.

27. This description of the April Conference is based on Birmingham Journal, 9 April 1842; Brief Sketches; Report of the Proceedings; Nonconformist, 6 April, 13 April 1842.

28. Birmingham Journal, 16 April 1842; Nonconformist, 27 April 1842 and weekly Complete Suffrage reports for the rest of the year.

29. C. Seymour, Electoral Reform in England and Wales, London 1970, p. 218.

30. Nottingham Mercury, 6 May, 13 May 1842; Birmingham Journal, 14 May 1842.

31. This description of the election campaign is based on Nottingham Review, 20 May, 5 August, 12 August 1842; Nottingham Mercury, 20 May, 5 August, 12 August 1842; Nonconformist, 25 May, 3 August, 10 August 1842; British Statesman, 6 August 1842.

32. Nottingham Review, 5 August, 12 August 1842.

33. Ibid., 31 March, 7 April 1843.

34. Birmingham Journal, 3 September 1842.

35. National Association Gazette, 28 May 1842; Brougham Correspondence, 16942, Richard Cobden to Lord Brougham, n.d.

36. Sturge Papers (M. Sturge), Edward Miall to Charles Sturge, 15 June 1842.

37. Taylor, British And American Abolitionists, p. 183, Elizabeth Pease to Wendell & Ann Phillips, 29 September 1842.

38. Brougham Correspondence, 30953, Joseph Sturge to Lord Brougham, 7 July 1842 and 30035, Sturge to Brougham, 9 July 1842.

39. Birmingham Journal, 27 August 1842.

40. Ibid., 27 August, 3 September 1842.

41. Ibid., 17 September 1842; Nonconformist, 24 August, 31 August 1842.

42. Ibid., 7 September 1842.

43. Northern Star, 21 May, 17 September, 19 November 1842.

44. Nonconformist, 14 September-28 December 1842; Birmingham Public Library, Minute Book of [NCSU] Council Meetings, Containing Cuttings, Reports etc., 26 December 1842.

45. This description of the conference is based on Nonconformist, 28 December, 31 December 1842, 4 January 1843; Birmingham Journal, 31 December 1842; Northern Star, 31 December 1842, 7 January 1843; British Statesman, 31 December 1842; The Times, 21 December 1842; W. Lovett, Life and Struggles of William Lovett, London 1967, pp. 235-37. See also J. Epstein, The Lion Of Freedom: Feargus O'Connor And The Chartist Movement, 1832-1842, London 1982, pp. 290-93.

46. Nonconformist, 18 January 1843 lists Collins, O'Neill and Vincent amongst those who seceded with Sturge. See also Minute Book of [NCSU] Council Meetings, 31 December 1842.

47. National Association Gazette, 18 June 1842. See also my 'Personality in Politics', p. 397.

48. Sturge Papers (P.A.J. Sturge), 'Joseph Sturge's Account of His Sister Sophia's Last Illness, 1845'.

49. The Poetical Works of John Greenleaf Whittier, p. 78.

PART 4

CITIZEN OF THE WORLD

11 A Feast of Fat Things (1843-44)

From the beginning Sturge's ambitions for the 1843 conventions far outran his achievements in 1840: 'This will be a feast of fat things that will I trust tempt thee over', he told Gerritt Smith, the New York philanthropist in September 1841.(1) At that time he had in mind a season of benevolence dedicated to peace, anti-slavery and temperance, the triad of good causes he had discussed with his American friends during his recent visit, but in the course of the next eighteen months he widened the agenda to include Complete Suffrage. The outcome was a programme carefully timed to constitute his circle of friends as something like an interlocking directorate of international philanthropists and reformers. The peace convention (22-24 June) was to follow hard on the heels of the anti-slavery convention (13-20 June), and there was to be a meeting of teetotalers on 27 June followed on the same day by a Complete Suffrage soirée. Sturge shouldered much of the organisational responsibility, and the burden must have been a heavy one, if we may judge from a peace convention report which referred to a flood of circulars, press notices and correspondence.(2) Fortunately, he was assisted as always by Sophia.

The proceedings were carefully staged as an ideal-typical scene of early Victorian earnestness. When the anti-slavery delegates assembled in the Freemasons' Hall, Haydon's painting of the 1840 convention and a portrait of Thomas Clarkson reminded them that they were the inheritors of a distinguished humanitarian tradition, and a painting of a scene on the Slave Coast provided them with an object-lesson on the tasks that lay ahead. The sessions opened with a short period of silent meditation, and ministers of religion were well represented amongst the delegates. Lewis Tappan noted that there were few men of rank: the qualifications for membership seemed to be 'intelligence, piety & moral worth'.(3) The attendance of women visitors added the finishing touch. As he looked beyond the delegates' benches one speaker felt uplifted to see himself 'fenced in' by 'the calm benevolent faces of the ladies'. It would be 'an admirable arrangement for all public assemblies', he added, if ladies were likewise present as 'moral non-conductors, by whom any discordant feelings might instantly be neutralised'. He did not have to labour the point that this was a passive role; the invitations had confined delegate status to men.(4)

A Feast of Fat Things (1843-44)

One predictable result of this restriction was the refusal of Lloyd Garrison to participate in the conventions. 'Of course, the American Anti-Slavery Society and its auxiliaries will not consent to be represented on the occasion, even by "gentlemen",' he told Elizabeth Pease. It was left to Lewis Tappan and members of his circle to attest the closeness between the anti-slavery, peace and teetotal movements on both sides of the Atlantic. Sharing a common evangelicalism, members of this Anglo-American benevolent empire have been described as admiring one another with 'a warmth that is surely rare in the history of international sentiments'.(5) Europe, on the other hand, was a recurrent disappointment. Perhaps nothing demonstrates more clearly the disjunction between British and Continental history at this time than the difficulties faced by Sturge and his friends when they tried to find counterparts across the Channel; as men who were used to the ways of Exeter Hall they were often dismayed to discover that absolute monarchs looked on voluntary societies with suspicion. In 1839 the Birmingham Temperance Society had been obliged to resort to the extraordinary measure of devising an associate membership for several St. Petersburg merchants whom the Czarist authorities had forbidden to form a society of their own, and in March 1842 when Sturge made a special visit to Paris in the hope of establishing contact with French opponents of slavery (they included such well-known liberals as Alphonse de Lamartine and Odillon Barrot), he had been incensed when Louis Philippe's government forbade them to hold a public meeting.(6)

By and large therefore it was an Anglo-American stage army of reformers and philanthropists that enjoyed Sturge's 'feast of fat things'.(7) They were 'citizens of the world', one speaker told them, and as they followed each other from platform to platform they locked their good causes together as a programme for the regeneration of mankind. At the peace convention, for example, resolutions were passed calling for 'the unrestricted interchange of their legitimate productions' between the nations (an indirect condemnation of slave produce as well as a demand for free trade) and describing intemperance as an obstacle to peace.(8) Sturge was 'the life and soul of these gatherings'. He made few contributions as a speaker during the formal sessions, but he was active behind the scenes. An early believer in the adage that much of the best work of a conference is done outside the formal agenda, he rented a house in Bedford Place where, regaled by his 'princely hospitality', select groups could shape·up policies and devise strategies. An entry in Tappan's journal describes four delegates dining there on 14 June to set out anti-slavery policy with reference to the independence of Texas: the entry for the next day shows them descending on the Foreign Office to press their ideas on the Government.(9)

But although the conventions ended on a high note of self-congratulation and a resolve to have similar meetings in the future, this philanthropic season enjoyed only a mixed success if judged by the subsequent history of the four movements it was designed to promote. This was particularly true of anti-slavery; there would be no more international conventions of abolitionists in Sturge's lifetime. The organised movement was now slipping into a long period of decline, broken only by occasional flurries of interest, most notably at the time of Harriet Beecher Stowe's visit to Britain in 1853. By 1845 the British and Foreign Anti-Slavery Society could be dismissed as 'a clique of great unknowns, a squadron of busy-bodies who pursue great objects by small means'.(10) Part of the problem was the disaster that had befallen Buxton's Niger expedition when it reached Africa in mid-1841. The much-vaunted air purification systems failed to keep the ships free from disease, and the model farm became something of a scandal when the outside world learned that the settlers had resorted to the use of forced labour. In January 1843 the African Civilization Society was dissolved, leaving Buxton a broken and discredited man.(11) At a public meeting in Exeter Hall after the anti-slavery convention Sturge had to protest when the Bishop of Norwich implied that they had heard the death knell of the movement:(12)

> We are not responsible for the failure of the benevolent designs of the African Civilization Society; many of us feared and anticipated that result; but because a society, the formation of which was dictated by the most benevolent motives, and which was set on foot under the patronage of royalty in this Hall, has failed, we ought not to give way to despondency and discouragement. (Hear)

Behind his profession of respect the old animosities lingered on. Two years later when news of Buxton's death reached Sophia her instinctive reaction was cruelly frank: 'And so T.F. Buxton is gone - when I opened Josiah Forster's letter first I feared a much more precious life to us, that of his incomparable brother [William Forster], was terminating'. But the damage done to the anti-slavery movement by the Niger Expedition outlived Buxton; in 1853 it would provide Charles Dickens with the inspiration for Borrioboola-Gha, the object of Mrs Jellyby's 'telescopic philanthropy'.(13)

The 1843 convention played a part in this story of decline by reinforcing the rivalries in the movement. Once again members of the British India Society claimed that they had been treated dishonestly: they had been promised time to put their views forward, William Howitt claimed, but the Committee had brought their business on when no one was there to speak for it. Darkly hinting at sordid commercial motives, he accused the organisers of 'an uproarious opposition to free opinions'. The Hibernian Anti-Slavery Society told the British and Foreign Anti-Slavery Society that they would not attend for the same reason: they refused to submit to 'the regulations that all subjects for discussion must first receive the sanction of your Committee, and that none but "gentlemen" shall sit as delegates'.(14) Although some of the other provincial societies did send representatives, during the next few years Edinburgh, Glasgow and Bristol refused to co-operate with what they saw as a dictatorial central body. The disruption of the American Anti-Slavery Society in 1840 now had its parallel in Britain as the 'British Garrisonians' and the 'Sturgeites' brawled their way into the mid-century largely ignored by the British public.

Much more serious in 1843 was a division of opinion over the tariffs that protected British colonial producers of sugar against competition from the slave plantations of Cuba and Brazil. The dispute could be traced to a shift in abolitionist policy for which Sturge was responsible when he founded the British and Foreign Anti-Slavery Society in 1839: its platform called for the exclusion of slave products from the British market by fiscal and other means. This was a departure from James Cropper's doctrine that slavery could not hold its own against free labour on the open market, but Sturge saw no inconsistency in holding both beliefs. It was only in the long run that free labour was more economical than slavery, he argued; in the short run free trade would encourage slave owners to open up new territories and drive their slaves mercilessly in a bid to dominate markets. Therefore he saw no inconsistency when the 1840 convention published his brother John's paper on the superiority of free produce as well as passing a resolution endorsing discriminatory tariffs.(15) But others were less willing to square the circle, and there was a series of public disagreements. The first occurred in 1841 during Sturge's visit to America when the Birmingham Anti-Slavery Society voted to drop its support of the sugar tariff policy. This was soon put right. On his return Sturge simply called the members together again, instilled sound doctrine into them, and had them reverse the decision.(16) The problem was not so easily resolved: unwavering in his conviction that free trade was the panacea for the problems of mankind, in 1839, 1840 and 1841 Cobden unavailingly called on Sturge to drop the fiscal approach to anti-slavery, and in 1843, he arrived to press his case from the floor of the convention. After a heated exchange the best that Sturge could do was to put the previous question.(17)

The debate raged on, reaching its climax in 1844 when the two sides vied with each other in attempts to pack the anniversary meeting of the British and Foreign Anti-Slavery Society. One of Sturge's letters shows him drumming up support from Dissenting ministers: 'I should not be at all surprised if the free trade party got a majority into Exeter Hall if this is not done'. He was unsuccessful, and George Thompson, who had taken service with the Anti-Corn Law League as a lecturer, carried an amendment against the Society's fiscal policy. It made little difference. Sturge and his committee promptly called a special general meeting of the Society (at too short notice for their opponents to rally support) and re-instated the previous policy. The decision, the Anti-Slavery Reporter firmly concluded, would 'have the effect (as we trust) of preventing any further interference with the proceedings of the Committee by those who hold a different opinion'.(18) But if this was a victory, it was a Pyrrhic one. A year later an official of the Society privately admitted that the committee were so fearful of further opposition that they had decided to retreat from Exeter Hall and hold the annual meeting in the obscurity of the Hall of Commerce. Over the next few years it was evident that Sturge had been fighting a hopeless battle: sugar, no more than corn, could withstand the triumph of free trade in mid-nineteenth century Britain. Between 1846 and 1854 the protective tariffs were whittled away.

The dispute made one point abundantly clear: Sturge's

abolitionism was more important to him than economic theory. In the words of Mary Darby Sturge, it was Cobden and his followers who were selling their souls for free trade, and they attacked Sturge with great bitterness.(19) He was indulging a scruple, John Bright told him.(20)

> Hitherto no result but injury to our own people has followed your policy - you are in effect leagued with those who abet the worst crime ever perpetrated against a people - the supporters of Monopoly & you range yourself against the truth of free trade by assuming that to be the truth which is admitted on all hands to be utterly and palpably impossible.

Sturge was certainly keeping strange company at this time. He was in touch with Sir Robert Peel and even with his old enemy, W.E. Gladstone, sending them information calculated to stiffen the existing sugar tariff policy. It was not that he agreed with other Tory policies, he told them frankly, but he wanted them to uphold one simple moral proposition: slave produce was stolen property which no honest man or government could admit as a legitimate item of commerce.(21)

This was a difficult case to argue. Early Victorians did not live by sugar alone, and Sturge's arguments logically extended to all slave products. Mercilessly, Cobden made him the butt of a satirical sketch in which Lord Ripon, the President of the Board of Trade, appears as the defender of the sugar tariff policy against the Brazilian ambassador who argues that the British are hypocrites for dealing in other commodities produced by slaves. Ripon is replying that he has been influenced by Sturge's representations when there is an interruption: 'The door opens, and enter Joseph Sturge, with a cotton cravat; his hat lined with calico; his coat, etc. sewn with cotton thread, and his cotton pockets well lined with slave-wrought gold and silver. The Brazilian ambassador and Lord Ripon burst into laughter.'(22)

It was a shrewd hit, but an unfair one. The scrupulous conscience that made Sturge refuse to have commercial dealings with the drink trade at this time had already troubled him so much over the cotton trade that he had revived his earlier boycott strategy and resumed Cropper's attempt to bring free labour products on to the British market. It is not possible to say when he began the practice of excluding all slave produce from his own household - Harriet Beecher Stowe was told that he had done so for 'many years' when she visited him in 1853 - but in July 1839 Sturge told Gerritt Smith that he was giving a great deal of thought to the manufacture of free labour cotton: unfortunately, however, he had not been able to find a plan that excluded deception. This was a real problem to judge from the later complaint of a Manchester manufacturer that his competitors were falsely labelling their goods as free produce, but by the end of 1844 Sturge thought he had succeeded.(23) With the help of a group of sympathetic Quakers he raised a fund to purchase a supply of free labour cotton for reliable manufacturers, and by 1 January 1846 the scheme had matured sufficiently for a committee consisting of Sturge, J.J. Gurney, George Thomas, Joseph Eaton and G.W. Alexander to inform the anti-slavery public that free labour merchandise with a distinguishing label would soon be sold on a non-profit basis.(24) Over the next few years retail depots were set up, and Sturge spent a great deal of time and money on the venture.

The search for alternatives to slave produce was world-wide. Taking over the policy of the now defunct British India Society, Sturge turned to the East Indies as a source of supplies: the Americans, he told Thomas Clarkson in November 1845, 'know if the power of free labour in the cultivation of Cotton & Sugar were fully developed in British India it must destroy the value of the produce of their Slave Labour all over the world'. A year later he was said to be on the point of establishing a commercial house in New Orleans to buy American free labour corn, cotton, sugar and rice. Raw cotton was obtained from the American Free Produce Association, particularly after Sturge provided $500 in 1847 to finance a trip to the South by one of their agents, and the search went on elsewhere. Ralph Clarence, one of Sturge's Quaker admirers, went to Natal and recruited Methodist immigrants in 1848 to assist with a scheme designed to provide Lancashire with much of its cotton, and there was talk of obtaining supplies from Queensland.(25) None of this came to much. The free produce movement failed to provide a focal point for British abolitionism, and it became little more than another Quaker 'peculiarity'. Thus after 1843 the anti-slavery movement lost much of its importance in Sturge's circle of reforms. Month after month he attended the Society's committee meetings in London, but this was very much a matter of routine, and a tour of the provinces that he made towards the end of 1845 failed to revive public interest. Over the years the Government courteously received representations from the Society - there must be no pretext for a surge of 'English public opinion (1833 & 1838)', the then Lord Stanley wrote in 1858 - but behind the scenes the Colonial Office was less respectful about the abolitionists: according to the Earl of Carnarvon they had 'lived too long for their own credit'.(26)

The anti-slavery movement was also weakened during these years by signs that 'the great experiment' of emancipation had failed in the British plantation colonies. In 1847 Sturge wrote to the Rev. John Clark that Mauritius was on the verge of bankruptcy, and by then he knew too that Jamaica had resumed its long economic decline, dispelling the euphoric hopes of the abolitionists.(27) Droughts, cholera and other natural disasters contributed to the scenes of despair that appeared in the letters sent home at this time by the Baptist missionaries. Much of the population moved away from the plantations served by the missions, and the religious zeal of the freedmen fell off so sharply that the missionaries, far from achieving their Jamaican millennium, spoke of the mission 'breaking up fast, very fast'.(28) In an ironic reversal of fortune the high level of contributions made by the slaves to the missionaries sharply declined within a few years of freedom. In 1841 William Knibb and his fellow pastors were described as rolling around the island in 'phaetons drawn by expensive horses'; in 1842, the Baptist Missionary Society's jubilee year, the Jamaican Baptists undertook to support themselves without assistance from England; in 1843 they sent teachers to a new Baptist mission in West

Africa; but in 1844, they had to send desperate appeals to their benefactors overseas.(29)

Their situation was depressed still further by evidence that cast doubt on all their earlier achievements. The belief of the missionaries that paganism would soon be dispelled by their teaching was shattered in 1842 by the appearance of a syncretic cult known as Myallism in which traditional African religious beliefs and practices were mingled with Christianity. Proclaiming that Christ was coming to end the world, 'angel people' danced in a ritual frenzy 'pulling' obeahs (harmful spirits) and catching shadows from the cotton trees. When some of them were taken before the magistrates, a report described them as swaying rhythmically and crying 'It is the Lord Jesus Christ; We no mad; Who say we mad? We da dig out all dem badness; uush! uush! uush!' Similar outbreaks occurred several times during the 1840s, and before the decade was over 'angel people' had danced through the streets of Sturge Town. For a time Jamaica was the despair of the missionary world.(30)

The peace movement, the second of the four good causes that Sturge tried to promote through the 1843 convention season, showed more promise during the next few years. Judge Jay's international arbitration plan was accepted - proposed by the Marquis de Rochefoucauld Liancourt, seconded by Sturge - and became the policy of the peace movement during the 1840s and 1850s.(31) Meanwhile, much as he had done in the anti-slavery movement ten years earlier, Sturge had already started to experiment with more radical forms of the 'pressure from without' than those favoured so far. It is likely that he was one of the critics of the Peace Society referred to in April 1842 by the Christian Examiner:

> There are other eyes beside [sic] mine watching their movements; and even some of their constituents are beginning to inquire for what do we subscribe money? Is it to pay the rent of a snug office? to pay salaries to officers? to maintain a periodical which scarcely ever extends its circulation beyond the circle where its principles are known and cherished? Assuredly not: we want to see work done - we must have the country aroused.

In an obvious reference to the usual rivalry between London and the provinces the headline read: 'Metropolitan Inactivity - the Peace Society'.(32)

A month later - it was one of several demonstrations of his closeness to the Christian Chartists at the time he was launching the Complete Suffrage movement - Sturge collaborated with Arthur O'Neill to sabotage the army's recruiting efforts in Birmingham. Annually at the time of the fair a recruiting team complete with horses, bright uniforms and musical instruments paraded through the streets in the hope of winning over some of the town's youth, and the circumstances would probably have been favourable in 1842, a year of massive unemployment, had not O'Neill and Sturge arranged for the recruiting sergeant to be followed by distributors of tracts with titles such as A Few Hints about the Army and Rhymes for the People about Battle,

Glory and Murder. It was in vain that The Times condemned 'an organised conspiracy amongst the Chartists, assisted by certain "Friends"': apparently the strategy was successful, and it was followed on subsequent occasions in Birmingham and other parts of the country.(33)

The outcome was a very noticeable radicalisation of the peace movement during the 1840s. 'Moral Radicals' in many parts of Britain joined forces to press for international arbitration and to oppose government policies designed to increase the naval estimates and revive the militia. The report of a large meeting in the Birmingham Town Hall during March 1845 shows what was happening. The platform party consisted of Dissenting clergymen, radical town councillors and 'most of our fellow-townsmen who are known to take a leading part in all questions which affect the public weal': facing them was a large working-class audience. Sturge was unanimously elected chairman, and the meeting then heard him excoriate British foreign policy in a speech which ranged freely over the uselessness of the anti-slavery naval squadron, the inhumanity of British policy towards China and India, and the iniquity of a government which imposed an armed police on Birmingham.(34) Obviously, O'Connell's aphorism that the reformer must be 'always beginning' told only one part of the truth about Sturge's career: there was always an unmistakable continuity between the movements in his circle of reforms.

The national Peace Society was reformed at this time to canalise the 'pressure from without', and in 1844-45 its report referred to 270 public meetings as evidence that it had made greater progress than at any previous time in its history. Ominously, however, when the Society sent one of its agents, Stephen Rigaud, to the Continent in 1844 he found that La Société de la Morale Chrétienne, the only similar movement in France, had been weakened by secessions and that he could arouse little interest in Switzerland (the country was drifting into civil war), Germany and the Netherlands. The best that the Society could say for his efforts was that he had displayed 'much Christian meekness and wisdom, under circumstances peculiarly trying'. The small amount of support that the movement received from Ireland could be traced to equally 'trying' circumstances as Rigaud had discovered earlier. When he arrived in Kilkenny to give a peace lecture, the Catholics greeted him with cries of 'No swaddler' (the nickname for a Protestant), and he was locked in a back room for his own safety while the partisans of the rival religions settled their differences regardless of his cries that a peace meeting was no place for a brawl.(35)

The temperance movement fared less well than the peace movement from Sturge's 'feast of fat things'. There was no lack of good will. Circulating amongst the delegates during the anti-slavery and peace conventions, Lewis Tappan noted how many of them were teetotalers, and they easily agreed that there should be a full scale temperance convention in London within a year or two. Then, as soon as the convention season was over, Sturge and Tappan travelled to Liverpool where they helped to launch Father Mathew, the Irish Capuchin friar, on a great temperance crusade which took him to many parts of England. They spoke from his platform and saw him administer the temperance pledge in Irish and English to a large working-class crowd.(36) A few months later when Mathew arrived in Birmingham Sturge made the most of the occasion by organising a great procession through the town followed by a public meeting at which 1500 people took the pledge.(37)

By this stage, however, the temperance movement was entering a new phase of its history as the early millennial hopes of sudden triumph gave way to the recognition that long-term planning would be necessary. Sturge became one of the principal promoters of the National Temperance Society in an attempt to provide the movement with a national framework, and he worked hard to win working-class supporters: a report of a meeting in Exeter Hall in May 1846 shows him addressing a working-class audience including a row of coal-heavers.(38) But there was a sense of stagnation in the movement. These were years when realists turned their eyes to the next generation, and the idea was emerging that led the Rev. Jabez Tunnicliff to set up the first Band of Hope for juveniles. Sturge attempted to graft teetotalism on to the Sunday School movement, and in 1845 he began the practice of paying for railway excursions to take Sunday School children out of Birmingham and away from the traditional scenes of heavy drinking on public holidays.(39)

Sturge also tried at this time to persuade the Society of Friends that it should take the same stand for temperance that it had taken for anti-slavery. Later in the century one of his cousins would write that Friends who were involved in the drink trades were 'looked upon as delinquents, and admonished, if not disowned', but it was very different at this time. Quakers owned several well-known breweries, and at the 1838 Yearly Meeting it was noted that the principal temptation of which Friends accused themselves was 'frequenting taverns & drunkenness'.(40) Aware of the opposition to their ideas, Sturge, Samuel Bowly, Robert Charlton, Cyrus Eaton and G.W. Alexander started to hold conferences that were carefully timed to act as a 'pressure from without' on the Yearly Meeting. It was a slow but winning process if we may judge from the diaries of William Lucas: in 1839 he dismissively noted that some Friends were dropping hints that he should give up his business as a brewer, but by 1843 he was regretting his connection with the trade and hoping that his sons would not follow him in it.(41)

Complete Suffrage, the fourth of the movements that Sturge made part of his 1843 convention season, seems out of place at first sight - a British political movement roughly tacked on to international crusades for humanitarian and moral reform. This was not how it seemed to the American delegates who attended the NCSU soirée and a subsequent business meeting: they brought with them a negro minister who indicated his sympathy for the disfranchised white slaves of Britain, and they urged Complete Suffragists to take the Liberty Party as a model of Christian politics. Their advice matched Sturge's sentiments.(42) He told J.P. Mursell in May 1843 that, although he had been 'mixed up with many movements of a philanthropic and political nature, none had ever given so much satisfaction', and two years later he was still describing Complete Suffrage as the first step towards the abolition of 'the monstrous evils of war, the punishment of death for crime, and many other things to which Christianity stood opposed'.(43)

Thus, far from destroying the NCSU, the clash with the Chartists in December 1842 was followed by two years of strenuous efforts to breathe new life into the movement. In 1843 and 1844 Sturge and a team of spokesmen - Henry Vincent, Thomas Spencer, Thomas Beggs and others - travelled round the country delivering lectures, setting up Complete Suffrage associations, and arranging for the distribution of tracts.(44) For a time the movement even had its own Birmingham newspaper, the Pilot. Sturge always denied that he was the owner, and in a technical sense this was true, but Herbert Spencer who was sub-editor for a few weeks (until he revealed his rationalist opinions and was transferred to a part of Sturge's business empire where he could influence fewer hearts and minds) found that effective control was in the hands of Joseph and Edmund Sturge. 'I have no interest in the paper in the common acceptation of the term', Sturge told him, 'and it has no connexion with the Complete Suffrage Union, but I am one of the contributors to a fund for starting it, with the understanding that it advocates certain principles'.(45)

In a further attempt to revive the NCSU during 1843 and 1844 Sturge and Sharman Crawford devised a more extreme version of the tactics that had been deployed against the negro Apprenticeship in 1838. While Sturge brought the 'battering ram' of public opinion to the doors of Parliament, Crawford and other sympathetic MPs were to exploit the forms of parliamentary procedure and delay the passing of the budget by moving amendments on every motion; a political crisis would ensue; and eventually the Complete Suffrage Bill of Rights would be carried. It is a measure of Sturge's contempt for the Reformed Parliament that he was prepared to disrupt its business, even if this 'Supply Movement' received the support of no more than twenty MPs.(46) He had found what seemed to be an encouraging precedent in the seventeenth century - the actions of Pym and Hampden in Charles I's parliaments - and in the 1880s Parnell's Irish Party would demonstrate how effective this weapon could be, but, as Cobden had pointed out, only 'a corps of desperadoes' could carry out a coup of this sort, and no one would ever have applied such a term to Sharman Crawford. Nor was public opinion much exercised when the experiment was attempted: there was no repetition of the mass petitioning and the determined lobbying by hundreds of delegates which had made the Colonial Secretary and MPs quake in 1838. The Government easily brushed the manoeuvre aside.(47)

To be fair to the Complete Suffragists it must be said that they had not intended to succeed on their own: in the hope of obtaining help from other radicals they now called themselves 'the friends of civil, religious and commercial freedom, of justice to Ireland and of universal peace'.(48) This was another pipe dream. Cobden was more interested in defeating Sturge over the sugar duties than in co-operating with him; O'Connor disrupted a Complete Suffrage meeting on the eve of one of Crawford's supply motions; and other reformers held aloof.(49) Events fully justified the Birmingham Journal's sceptical prophecy that the experiment would fail because of the 'general rule of hobby-horsicalness' that had divided radicals in the past, and there was good political sense in the same newspaper's warning that the Complete Suffragists had fashioned a rod for their own backs by using tactics which could be turned against them by those who wished to repeal Catholic Emancipation or to reinstate the negro Apprenticeship.(50)

But, and it was an indication of how far he was willing to go at this time, Sturge was prepared to succeed with Irish help, even if the other English radicals would not support him. 1843 was the Repeal Year when Daniel O'Connell held a series of 'monster meetings' to force the Tory Government to restore the Irish Parliament. The intention was to repeat the strategy of 1828-29 when Peel and Wellington had been obliged to concede Catholic Emancipation, but this time Peel held out by banning a 'monster meeting' at Clontarf and imprisoning O'Connell. Greatly concerned by this use of force to suppress public opinion, Sturge visited Dublin in November 1843 to see if he could reach agreement with the Irish Repealers on a definition of 'justice for Ireland'. It was the opening of an exchange of ideas that continued for several months culminating in March 1844 at a great meeting at the Birmingham Town Hall attended by O'Connell.(51)

Sturge's policy was similar to the one offered by Liberals later in the century. Clearly uneasy about the prospect of an Irish Parliament with unrestricted legislative powers, Sturge proposed what would later be called 'Home Rule all round': a form of federation in which England, Scotland and Ireland would have subordinate parliaments for local business, leaving matters of common concern to be settled by an Imperial Parliament elected by Complete Suffrage. It was a new policy which opened up opportunities for dealing with an old grievance, he told a public meeting; federalism would begin the process of cutting back the excessive power which London wielded over the provinces.(52) But never was O'Connell more difficult to pin down than at this time when his influence was waning. He chopped and changed in every public statement, moving from federalism to Repeal, and from household suffrage to universal suffrage.

O'Connell's hesitation probably owed something to a well-founded scepticism about the value of an alliance with English radicals. He would co-operate with the Complete Suffragists, he told Sturge, if enough English reformers came forward to make the sacrifice of Repeal worth while.(53)   But this did not happen; for after the economic depression lifted in 1843 there was great difficulty in arousing English public opinion on political issues. Admittedly, the Dissenters were active, but they too were following 'the general rule of hobby-horsicalness'. In 1843 when Sir James Graham, the Tory Home Secretary, brought in an Education Bill that offered advantages to the Church of England, Dissenters all over the country overwhelmed it by a great campaign of public meetings, petitions and lobbying. In the following April Edward Miall seized the opportunity to revive voluntaryism by organising a conference at which over 700 delegates (mostly 'unknown men' from the provinces) launched the Anti-State Church Society to press for the separation of Church and State.(54)

Sturge attended the conference and joined the executive

committee of the Society. He was worried not only by Graham's scheme - 'so monstrous in its leading features', he told Miall - but by a threat nearer home. In July 1843 the Church party carried a rate in the Edgbaston vestry with a ruthlessness that ought to have wrung a grudging admiration from their voluntaryist opponents. They kept the arrangements for the vestry meeting so secret that the voluntaryists only found out by scaling the church wall to consult a belatedly posted notice; they sent carriages to bring supporters from Birmingham; and for one day they even set up their 2d. church rate as a higher law than the contemporary belief that women would be unsexed by voting. According to the Birmingham Journal, 'nearly one-fourth of those who voted for the rate were women, who are usually only called in when the contest becomes severe'. Sturge consoled himself with the hope that the renewed militancy of the Church of England would prove to 'the most supine of the middle classes that the nation is at the mercy of an oligarchy determined to trample upon our civil, political, social and religious liberty', but most Dissenters did not define the issue in this way, and neither the NCSU nor the Supply Movement gained much from the revival of voluntaryism.(55)

The failure of the Complete Suffrage movement to provide a rallying point for radicals during 1844 was confirmed by a decisive demonstration of its weakness as an electoral force. NCSU policy was to contest all elections where local supporters could field a candidate, and Sturge came forward in July when a by-election was caused by the death of Joshua Scholefield, one of Birmingham's two MPs. The old BPU radicals selected Scholefield's son as the Liberal candidate, but Sturge refused to stand down even when the Tories mounted a strong challenge. John Bright thought he had been 'struck with something like madness' to divide the anti-Tory vote in this way, but the differences between the two Liberal programmes were so significant that Sturge found himself in the perennial dilemma of a left wing faction leader in a two party system: he could sacrifice strict principle to the overriding necessity of keeping the Tories out or he could stand for principle regardless of the result. Sturge chose the latter course, and until the end of a bitter campaign he kept up an attack on what he called 'undefined liberalism'. His platform showed the continuing evolution of his political thought: Complete Suffrage, ecclesiastical disestablishment, free trade in legitimate items of commerce, opposition to military and naval establishments, home rule for Ireland, the transfer of taxation from necessities to property, and a reform of the Poor Law to ensure that honest poverty was given a more suitable form of relief. For the rest, he went out of his way to emphasise that he was the candidate favoured by the non-electors of the town.(56)

The result (Spooner 2095; Scholefield 1735; and Sturge 346) inevitably brought a tirade of abuse down on Sturge for handing the seat over to the Tories, and he was disappointed by his share of the votes. He blamed the intrigues of the Whigs and the drink interest. Instinctively, Lewis Tappan knew how to console him: 'What difference to a Free [sic] Suffrage man whether a whig or a tory is returned to Parliament! ... They should vote to bear their testimony'.(57) Before the year was out Tappan was given an opportunity to follow his own advice: during the American presidential election J. G. Birney ran again as the Liberty candidate despite what turned out to be well-founded claims that he was taking votes away from the Whigs and allowing the pro-slavery Democrats to win. It was another 'triumph' of principle over party, Sturge told a Complete Suffrage meeting after the election results arrived from the United States.(58) Such were the rewards of Sturge's 'expressive politics' between 1839 and 1844.

NOTES

1. Arents Research Library, Syracuse University, Joseph Sturge to Gerritt Smith, 18 September 1841.

2. Peace Society, Meetings of Committee of London Peace Society, 1 November 1842; Herald of Peace, August 1843, 'Proceedings Of The First General Peace Convention', pp. 366-68. All the manuscript records of the Peace Society cited in this book are in the possession of the Society. I was allowed to scan them very briefly.

3. Proceedings Of The General Anti-Slavery Convention, Called By The Committee Of The British And Foreign Anti-Slavery Society, 1843; Library of Congress, Papers of Lewis Tappan, 1843 Journal, 20 June 1843.

4. Proceedings Of The General Anti-Slavery Convention, 1843, p. 326.

5. Taylor, British And American Abolitionists, p. 189, W.L. Garrison to Elizabeth Pease, 28 February 1843; Wyatt-Brown, Lewis Tappan and the Evangelical War Against Slavery, p. 253.

6. British Temperance Advocate and Journal, 15 April 1839; British and Foreign Anti-Slavery Reporter, 30 November 1842; Boston Public Library, Joseph Sturge to A. Phelps, 18 June 1842; Richard, Sturge, pp. 342-46.

7. Apart from Britain and the United States only France, the Netherlands, Jamaica, Haiti and Canada were represented at the Anti-Slavery Convention; the story was little different at the Peace Convention.

8. Thistlethwaite, The Anglo-American Connection, p. 92; Proceedings Of The General Anti-Slavery Convention, 1843, p. 8; Herald of Peace, 'Proceedings Of The First General Peace Convention', p. 397.

9. Library of Congress, Papers of Lewis Tappan, newscutting from Evening Post, 9 June 1859 and 1843 Journal, 14 June, 15 June, 23 June 1843.

10. The Atlas quoted by Birmingham Journal, 31 May 1845.

11. Temperley, British Antislavery, pp. 57-61.

12. British And Foreign Anti-Slavery Reporter, 28 June 1843.

13. Sturge Papers (P.A.J. Sturge), 'Joseph Sturge's Account of His Sister Sophia's Last Illness, 1845'; Charles Dickens, Bleak House, pp. 34-36. See also Charles Dickens, 'The Niger Expedition' in The Works of Charles Dickens, London n.d.

14. W. Howitt, A Serious Address To The Members Of The Anti-Slavery Society, On Its Present Position And Prospects, London 1843, pp. 10-15; Rhodes House, MSS Brit. Emp., S18, C12/94, Richard Allen &

James Haughton to the Committee of the British and Foreign Anti-Slavery Society, 24 April 1843.

15. Manchester Public Library, Smith Papers, Joseph Sturge to J.B. Smith, 13 December 1844; Proceedings Of The General Anti-Slavery Convention, 1843, pp. 334, 440; Brit. Lib., Add. MSS. 40541, ff. 164-66, Joseph Sturge to Sir Robert Peel, 12 March 1844; ibid., f. 168, Joseph Sturge to Anti-Slavery Reporter, 13 December 1841; C.D. Rice, 'Humanity Sold For Sugar! The British Abolitionist Response to Free Trade in Slave Grown Sugar', Historical Journal, XII, 1970, pp. 402-18.

16. Birmingham Public Library, Birmingham Anti-Slavery Society Minute Book, 12 November, 24 November 1841.

17. Brit. Lib., Add. MSS. 50131, ff. 15-16, Richard Cobden to Joseph Sturge, 15 May 1839; ibid., ff. 24-25, Cobden to Sturge, 31 October 1840; ibid., ff. 40-41, Cobden to Sturge, 26 February 1841; Proceedings Of The General Anti-Slavery Convention, 1843, pp. 144-62.

18. Rhodes House, MSS Brit. Emp. S18, C111/95, Joseph Sturge to ?, 18 April 1844; British and Foreign Anti-Slavery Reporter, 29 May, 12 June 1844.

19. Sturge Papers (M. Sturge), Mary Darby Sturge to ?, n.d.

20. Brit. Lib., Add. MSS. 43845, ff. 12-15, John Bright to Joseph Sturge, 1 September 1843.

21. Ibid., f. 16, Sir Robert Peel to Joseph Sturge, 13 March 1844; ibid., f. 20, W.E. Gladstone to Joseph Sturge, 27 March 1844; ibid., Add. MSS 40541, ff. 164-66, Joseph Sturge to Sir Robert Peel, 12 March 1844; ibid., Add. MSS. 40562, f. 68, Sturge to Peel, 7 March 1845; ibid., Add. MSS. 40569, f. 328, Sturge to Peel, 26 June 1845; ibid., Add. MSS. 40591, f. 363, Sturge to Peel, 12 May 1846.

22. Brit. Lib., Add. MSS. 50131, ff. 55-56, Richard Cobden to Sophia Sturge, 16 October 1841. Williams quotes the dialogue in his Capitalism & Slavery, p. 161.

23. Stowe, Sunny Memories Of Foreign Lands, pp. 183-84; Arents Research Library, Syracuse University, Joseph Sturge to Gerritt Smith, 31 July 1839; Friends House Library, MS Box 8.4, J.F. Browne, To The Members of Anti-Slavery Societies, And All Friends Of The Slave, n.d.

24. British And Foreign Anti-Slavery Society Reporter, 12 November 1845, 1 January, 2 March 1846; Richard, Sturge, pp. 384-89.

25. Huntingdon Library, Joseph Sturge to Thomas Clarkson, 4 November 1845; New Britain Institute, Elihu Burritt's Journals, Journal 6, 6 October 1846; R.K. Nuermberger, The Free Produce Movement. A Quaker Protest Against Slavery, Durham N.C. 1942, p. 71; L. Billington, 'British Humanitarians and American Cotton, 1840-1860', American Studies, XI, 1977, pp. 313-34; A.F. Hattersley, The British Settlement Of Natal. A Study In Imperial Migration, Cambridge 1950, pp. 90, 227-31; Rhodes House, E2/6, British and Foreign Anti-Slavery Society Minutes, 1 October 1847.

26. I am indebted to Bruce Knox of Monash University for these references to Stanley and Carnarvon.

27. Fenn Collection, E19Y, Joseph Sturge to John Clark, 30 November 1847.

28. Institute of Jamaica MS 378, f.242, Walter Dendy to Rev. J. Angus, 19 July 1846.

29. School of Oriental & African Studies, Archives of the Council for World Mission, LMS West Indies - Jamaica, Incoming Letters, Box 3, John Vine to Rev. A. Tidman, 7 September 1841; Hinton, Knibb, pp. 404, 463-64, 373-78.

30. Scottish Missionary Register, January 1843; Mintz, Caribbean Transformations, p. 168.

31. Herald of Peace, August 1843, 'Proceedings Of The First General Peace Convention', pp. 378-82.

32. Christian Examiner, April 1842.

33. Public Record Office, H.O. 45 OS/260, ff. 35, 67; H.O. 45/261, ff. 17, 39, 45, 47, 48; H.O. 65/10 Police Letter Book (Birmingham) 20 May, 23 May 1842; The Times, 23 May 1842.

34. Pilot, 1 March 1845.

35. Herald of Peace, October 1844, June 1845, October 1841.

36. Library of Congress, The Papers of Lewis Tappan, 1843 Journal, 'Lewis Tappan's Address'; Nonconformist, 28 June 1843.

37. Birmingham Journal, 16 September 1843.

38. London Teetotaler Or General Temperance Intelligencer, 30 May 1846.

39. Pilot, 3 January 1846.

40. William Sturge, Some Recollections Of A Long Life, pp. 43-48; Barclay Fox's Journal, p. 126.

41. A Quaker Journal, vol. I, p. 160 & vol. II, p. 306.

42. Nonconformist, 21 June, 28 June 1843.

43. Ibid., 10 May 1843; Pilot, 16 August 1845.

44. Birmingham Public Library, Minute Book of [NCSU] Council Meetings etc., 7 August 1843, and NCSU Minute Book of Committee for General Purposes, 11 September, 27 November 1843, 15 January 1844.

45. Herbert Spencer, An Autobiography, London 1904, vol. I, pp. 248-59; D. Duncan, The Life And Letters Of Herbert Spencer, London 1908, p. 47.

46. Nonconformist, 28 June, 30 August 1843.

47. Ibid., 7 February 1844; West Sussex Record Office, Cobden 30, Richard Cobden to Henry Ashworth, 7 April 1842; Nonconformist, 13 March 1844.

48. Nonconformist, 7 February 1844.

49. Brit. Lib., Add MSS. 50131, ff. 108-109, Richard Cobden to Joseph Sturge, 18 January 1844; Nonconformist, 7 February 1844.

50. Birmingham Journal, 25 November, 9 December 1843.

51. Taylor, British And American Abolitionists, p. 208, H.C. Wright to M.W. Chapman, 28 November 1843; Birmingham Journal, 9 March 1844.

52. Friends Historical Library, Swarthmore Penns., Daniel O'Connell to Joseph Sturge, 25 February 1844; Birmingham Journal, 9 March 1844; Nonconformist, 18 October, 13 December 1843, 19 June, 13 November, 11 December 1844.

53. Nonconformist, 17 January, 20 March 1844.

54. Ibid., 1 May 1844.

55. Birmingham Journal, 29 July, 1843.

56. Nonconformist, 10 July 1844; Birmingham Journal, 6 July, 13

July, 20 July, 10 August 1844; Manchester Public Library, Wilson Papers, John Bright to George Wilson, 13 July 1844.

57. Rhodes House, MSS Brit. Emp., S 18, C111/111 Joseph Sturge to ?, 16 July 1844; Nonconformist, 11 December 1844; Library of Congress, The Papers of Lewis Tappan, Lewis Tappan to Joseph Sturge, 11 October 1844.

58. Library of Congress, The Papers of Lewis Tappan, Lewis Tappan to Joseph Sturge, 11 October 1844, 28 February 1845; Nonconformist, 11 December 1844.

12 Entr'acte (1845-46)

To the end of his days Sturge never threw off the trait that had brought him into public life as the advocate of freedom: his first instinct (the criticism was T.F. Buxton's) was always to take a stand on 'abstract justice' regardless of the consequences. Thus he never disavowed the Complete Suffrage Bill of Rights, and he did not dissolve the NCSU even when it became moribund in 1845.(1) Throughout the 1840s he insisted that working men must have a say in the national and local institutions that claimed to represent them. In May 1844 he called for the enfranchisement of non-ratepayers in Poor Law elections; a year later he opposed the amalgamation of the local authorities in Birmingham on the grounds that the reform did not give the vote to the working class; in 1845 he took the lead in setting up a Birmingham Working Men's Registration Committee to get as many working men as possible on to the existing voters' rolls; and when a committee was set up to provide public baths and walks in the town he pressed for working-class representation.(2) Nonetheless it is evident that the mid-1840s were something of a watershed in his career. Since 1830 he had made Parliament the focal point of his agitations, using the 'battering ram' of public opinion against the politicians who opposed his 'moral Radical' policies on slavery, on religious voluntaryism, on the Corn Laws and on Complete Suffrage. But his success in overthrowing the Apprenticeship had been his only triumph, and his strategy had culminated in the abject failure of the Supply Movement to force reforms on Parliament. Implicitly recognising that he had reached a dead end, over the next few years he moved towards a strategy with a different emphasis, one that looked less to Parliament and more to policies that could be implemented by individuals and voluntary societies.

The shift of emphasis in Sturge's pursuit of reform mirrored national developments. The economic depression which had settled over the industrial districts during the late 1830s lifted in 1843, and radicals were driven to despair by the lack of interest shown by working men in political reform. But when bad times returned in 1847-48 there was only a brief revival of political radicalism; for British society was already falling under the influence of the mid-century mood of consensus and stability. 'One is struck', a historian has written about the social relations of these years, 'by the tendency of all classes to invoke shared ideals on every conceivable occasion, and by the extent to which a common outlook was embedded in recurring patterns of activity'.(3)

Birmingham was one of the best examples of a city where this cohesive culture flourished (the good relationship between masters and men in its small workshops is one of the clichés of nineteenth-century British history); and Sturge was one of its principal exponents. The values of brotherhood must displace those of class, he told a meeting in November 1844. As a writer in the Democrat and Labour Advocate pointed out, this aspiration was open to the obvious objection that it was inappropriate in a laissez-faire capitalist society: why should 'the working classes so tamely submit to be ... mocked and plundered' by 'sham philanthropists' drawn from the ranks of 'gamblers, who traffic in our food ... Landlords, money-mongers, and white slave drivers'?(4) But the Pilot's report of one of Sturge's peace meetings shows him proceeding unhindered by hostile sentiments of this sort.(5)

Being the first town's meeting ever called by the Mayor for the evening, it was truly gratifying to see such a splendid sight; and notwithstanding our mayors have hitherto refused to call evening meetings, on the ground that they would, in all likelihood, become turbulent and noisy, not a single jarring word or movement was heard or seen during the whole time of the meeting. All were pleased to think that the hall had been opened at an hour when the tradesman as well as his employer could conveniently attend; and the most grateful feeling was evinced towards the Mayor when it was announced that he had cheerfully complied with the request of the requisitionists to call the meeting at seven o'clock.

The improvement of Birmingham for the benefit of the working class became one of the most prominent themes in Sturge's public life during the 1840s and 1850s. He supported a move to provide public baths and walks; he gave a library to a Polytechnic Society which was set up to provide members with a wide variety of facilities ranging from advanced adult education classes to baths and showers; and he became one of the patrons of the Birmingham Association for the Abridgement of the Hours of Labour, a society which exerted pressure on shopkeepers to curtail the hours worked by their employees. His ideals of brotherhood led him into public criticism of selfish individuals and vested interests in the upper classes: wealthy men who supported the Government's militia schemes in the knowledge that they could buy exemptions; profiteers who made fortunes from the 'war system' (a provocative criticism in a town where armaments production was a major industry); and employers who would not shorten the hours of their workpeople. Surprisingly - it is another example of one of his reforms acquiring a momentum of its own - Sturge even argued that ultimately the State might have to legislate against these employers.(6)

But probably the best example of the way his mind was setting in the mid-1840s was the Friends First Day School Association, one of the most successful forms of working-class adult education during the nineteenth century. Sturge found the model for this experiment in 1842 when he was standing as the Complete Suffrage parliamentary candidate for Nottingham and was taken to see a Sunday school conducted by his fellow Quaker, Samuel Fox. Three years later he transplanted the idea to Birmingham by persuading some of the young Quakers of the Bull Street Meeting to combine and offer a programme of reading, writing and Scripture study for the working-class youths and young men of the town. The scheme survived the harassment of a Church of England clergyman who objected to the teaching of writing in his parish on Sundays, but it was not an immediate success. Those who enrolled from an unmanageably wide age group were often unclean, disorderly and disrespectful to the Scriptures; and the young volunteer teachers were unreliable. Not surprisingly the attendance fell from 78 to 28 in 1846. During the next ten years, however, the experiment was consolidated and expanded. The school started to meet between 7.30 a.m. and 9.30 a.m. instead of during the evening (a test of dedication for all concerned); it concentrated on the over-fourteen age group; women's classes were introduced in 1848; peace and temperance themes were interwoven with the teaching; and thrift was encouraged through a savings fund which offered unusually advantageous rates of interest. Sturge did not teach in the school, but he recruited the teachers and presided over its development. Each Sunday he provided breakfast for the teachers at 7 a.m. and started the classes by reading from Scripture. He was in the chair in December 1847 when a national Friends First Day School Association was launched to co-ordinate the work of schools which had been set up on the Birmingham plan in several towns.(7)

The address that Sturge sent out on behalf of the new Association was couched in the usual early Victorian language of benevolence and social control. Moral habits were to be encouraged, together with obedience, punctuality and orderly behaviour. 'The peculiar importance of some of these habits to the labouring classes of the community is too obvious to need insisting upon', he firmly concluded. But, and here Sturge was reinforcing the shift away from the more abrasive social attitudes of the early nineteenth century, the address also emphasised the role the schools were to play as agents of social harmony within the class structure:(8)

> They [the schools] bring into personal and immediate contact different ranks of Society, in a manner in which they are seldom brought together on other occasions. The intercourse between them which takes place in the ordinary business of life, is, for the most part, devoid of that freedom and absence of interested motives without which the souls of men cannot easily be brought into union. In a First-day School they meet together on a subject of common interest, and in some measure on common ground; the one to receive, the other to impart, knowledge equally necessary to both. We therefore view such schools as important links in that social chain, which in its perfect state, would unite into one harmonious whole the universal family of man.

Sturge also saw the experiment as a means of rekindling the religious zeal of the Quakers by giving them a more modern sense of mission, and in this respect he was remarkably successful. There was no intention of proselytising: in 1859 Sturge's nephew described it as an advantage that working-class people did not see the Friends' schools 'as so many nets to catch church members', and the numbers of those who became Quakers by convincement because of them was never large. But the schools imparted a sense of earnestness to the large number of young Friends who taught in them, and Sturge would doubtless have been delighted by a late-nineteenth century survey which gave them the credit for 'an accession [of new members of the Society of Friends] ... from the thoughtful section of the working classes'.(9)

The impression that the mid-1840s were a watershed in Sturge's career was strengthened by important changes in his private life. One of them, Sophia's death, even made him consider withdrawing from public life. At the end of 1844 she was stricken by an illness for which contemporary medicine had no cure. Her doctors disagreed over a diagnosis of lung disease (a post-mortem confirmed it), and by the time of her death on 6 June 1845 she had endured a range of remedies that included blister applications and the water cure. As her condition declined Joseph cancelled most of his public commitments, and for several months he seldom left home. Seeking comfort from his religious faith, he carefully treasured her words as those of a dying saint and hoped that at the end he would see her enjoying a vision of the next life. The narrative record that he compiled of her experiences at this time amounts to thirty-eight pages. 'I was earnestly desirous', he wrote, 'that I might have witnessed the deeply instructive spectacle of a mind so rarely endowed by nature & grace & so inexpressibly dear to me passing in brightness from time into eternity'. Thus he was deeply disappointed when she spent her last hours in delirium. His record shows how heavy a burden these expectations could impose on a dying person; at one stage Sophia even had to reprimand an inquisitively pious neighbour.(10)

> She declined to give him a full and distinct answer and spoke strongly against trusting to such statements from persons in great bodily & mental weakness and while fully admitting that through the mercy of God in Christ Jesus a death bed repentance was often accepted she wished to convey her strong opinion of the danger of trusting to it & also her belief that many who in health had made the greatest advances in the christian life had little to announce on their death bed.

By this time death had dealt harshly with this generation of the Sturge family: in May 1846 when Sturge's sister Rebecca looked down on Bewdley from the heights above the town she reflected that four of the brothers and sisters who had once formed part of the family circle in Netherton were now no more. Priscilla had died in 1835; John had succumbed to typhus in 1840 (a deathbed of spiritual triumph); and Henry, a man of deep religious aspirations, had died in 1842. Mary, a sister who had married during her parents' lifetime, also died in 1842 after an unhappy life with a husband who had shocked the Sturges by failing in 'the steady industry and rectitude necessary to meet the necessities of a large family'.(11)   The brothers and sisters had been warmly supportive of each other, but none of them had been as close as Joseph and Sophia.   There had been an element of idolatry in her affection for Joseph, Sophia admitted, and she had entered heart and soul into his career.   How heavily he had relied on her was shown shortly before her death when he asked her if he should retire from public life, because, as he put it, 'I should no longer have her to watch over me & warn me of danger'.   It was at this time that they discussed his 'preservation' from Feargus O'Connor in December 1842.   She did not encourage his diffidence: in future he should be more cautious, but she had no doubt as to the soundness of his principles when he 'advocated the rights of the people'.(12)   Whittier echoed her sentiments in his poem To My Friend On The Death Of His Sister:(13)

Up then, my brother! Lo, the fields
        of harvest
Lie white to view!
She lives and loves thee, and the God
though servest
To both is true

Thrust in thy sickle! - England's toil-
worn peasants
Thy call abide;
And she thou mourn'st, a pure and holy
presence,
Shall glean beside!

During the second half of 1845 Sturge returned to public life.(14)   The revival of his 'elasticity' (Lewis Tappan's term) was confirmed by another important change in his family circumstances: he re-married, taking as his bride Hannah, the daughter of Barnard Dickinson, a Coalbrookdale Quaker ironmaster.   The two must have known each other well; for Charles Sturge had married her sister Mary in 1831, and there was a close friendship between the two families. Sturge proposed to Hannah while they were in London at some time in 1846, and they were married in the Coalbrookdale Meeting House on 14 October.   She was twenty-nine on her wedding day, and he was fifty-three.   Hannah is described in a family genealogy as a tall, fine woman with high colouring and brown hair, but the same source also calls her 'eccentric, morbid, warm-hearted, affectionate, very nervous', and there seems to have been some tension in the marriage.   In 1857 Charles complained to his wife about her, adding that Joseph had 'more than once admitted when I talked [to] him about her doings that she is beyond his control'.   But philanthropy was one of her favourite pursuits, and there was no denying that this was an advantageous match in another respect: in 1851 money inherited from Barnard Dickinson helped to keep the J. & C. Sturge business partnership solvent.   Most important of all, Hannah bore Sturge five children.(15)

Sturge was delighted to have children, and he took his responsibilities to them seriously. His son, the seventh and last in the line of Joseph Sturges that stretched back to the sixteenth century, was born in 1847 and over the next seven years four daughters followed: Sophia (1849), Priscilla (1850), Eliza (1852) and Hannah (1854). They were brought up in a household where religious earnestness was balanced by love and a concern for their happiness. The American authoresses Grace Greenwood and Harriet Beecher Stowe who saw Sturge with 'his young wife and his happy group of children' described the joy the whole family took in the extensive gardens and pet animals at Southfield, the family home.(16) The children were given ponies when they were old enough, and Sturge went riding with them every morning. He prayed with them every evening. Their upbringing showed the mellower aspects of evangelical domesticity.

Another indication that he had recovered from the blow of Sophia's death was the part Sturge played in the controversies surrounding two international conventions in mid-1846: the world's temperance convention and the inaugural meeting of the Evangelical Alliance. As Sturge knew from personal experience, these international philanthropic and religious gatherings usually attracted trouble-makers; reluctantly, he now found that he had to play this role. His actions were dictated by his interlocking commitments. If slaveholders attended their convention, he told his fellow teetotalers, he would walk out rather than extend the hand of fellowship, and in a crude display of wealth he even offered £50 as a douceur to the National Temperance Society if it would take the same stand.(17) The strength of his feelings on this subject owed something to the decision of the newly founded Free Church of Scotland to accept financial assistance from churches in the American South, which sanctioned slave-holding: Sturge and other abolitionists had taken up the cry 'send the money back'.(18)

Many prominent teetotalers shared Sturge's range of interests - a list of their good causes includes anti-slavery, corn law repeal, peace, and church disestablishment - but there was strong opposition to the imposition of an anti-slavery test on the temperance convention delegates. Ironically, the argument Sturge had used against the champions of women's rights at the 1840 anti-slavery convention was now turned against him: he was mixing issues which were better kept apart. He did not have his way and had to content himself with the knowledge that no slave-owners were present. Having cleared his conscience by reminding the delegates that 'the slave-holder should be placed on the same footing in our social and public intercourse as the pirate and murderer', he allowed them to proceed with the discussion of a series of topics arising from the proposition that 'alcohol, the intoxicating principle, is a subtle poison, at war with the physical, intellectual, social and religious interests of men'. Later in the proceedings he made an important contribution to the development of the movement by urging that high priority should be given to the task of persuading young people 'to attach their names to the pledge'. The Convention passed a resolution in favour of juvenile temperance associations, adding to the momentum that resulted in the foundation of the first Band of Hope a year later.(19)

The Evangelical Alliance was even less amenable to his influence; for, to his great indignation, Sturge discovered that he was ineligible for membership. Writing publicly to J.A. James, he condemned the decision of a preliminary meeting in Liverpool to exclude those who did not accept the 'divine institution of the Christian ministry, and the authority and perpetuity of the ordinances of Baptism and the Lord's Supper'. In other words, Quakers could not attend, and the inference could be drawn that they were not evangelicals.(20) The rebuff threw him back on the distinctive Quaker beliefs he had kept in the background during the years when he had worked alongside James and other Nonconformist ministers in the name of a broadly defined evangelicalism. He had expected them to use their influence over their congregations, but he had never accepted the Christian ministry as a 'divine institution'. In 1844 he had told an Anti-State Church meeting in Birmingham that he could not see why some congregations of Dissenters remained in bondage to their ministers when there was no need for a regularly educated and ordained ministry. A later report would show him speaking of the cloth with a blunt disrespect that seemed eccentric to a Victorian audience: though he had a high regard for many ministers, 'yet he believed it would be better for them and for Christianity if they followed some calling for their own support rather than be supported by others (cheers and laughter)'.(21)

James answered Sturge's letter by pointing out, reasonably enough, that the vocal prayer and hymn singing at Evangelical Alliance meetings would have been enough to keep Quakers away, but the debate ranged widely in the press, and the Alliance came in for considerable criticism on several scores. The knowledge that delegates from churches in the American South were eligible to attend the convention provoked the comment that it was a strange form of Christianity that excluded Quakers but offered fellowship to slave-owners, and an anonymous correspondent who disagreed with James's letter to Sturge went on to condemn the Alliance as a new sect based on 'an organized opposition to popery'. This was fair comment: a prominent member admitted that the movement could be traced to feelings 'sprung chiefly from the Maynooth affair', the uproar provoked by Sir Robert Peel's decision to increase the Government's grant to the principal Irish Catholic seminary in 1845.(22)

Maynooth had divided the nonconformists: some were happy to join members of the Church of England in an old fashioned 'No Popery' outcry, whereas others took their stand on the full voluntary principle. The distinction had been sharply set forth in Birmingham where a meeting was held on 17 April 1845 to let J.A. James and other speakers express 'the opinions of the members of the Established Church and various other religious denominations'. On that occasion a 'most respectable audience' loudly approved the chairman's opening statement about a religion 'that was not in accordance with the word of God', and then settled down for an evening of ranting about Latimer, Cranmer, Ridley, the Inquisition and the ruin of Spain. Nearly three weeks later another meeting was held in the Town Hall. Sturge was not present (it was shortly before Sophia's death), but the speakers were members of his circle - Thomas Morgan, J.H. Wilson, Arthur O'Neill and Arthur Albright - and the audience was 'principally composed of the working classes'. They opposed the Maynooth grant, but they also opposed all forms of state intervention in religious matters. 'Why did he object to that grant?', Morgan asked: 'Was it merely because it was to [be] given to his Roman Catholic fellow-subjects? By no means. If the sum was proposed to be given to any other religious denomination he should equally protest against it'.(23)

For the moment, however, the 'No Popery' cry was less important than other events of that year which seemed to prove that more pacific influences would soon triumph. Faced with the news of famine in Ireland, Peel had announced his conversion to corn law repeal in December 1845 and thrown the forces of Conservatism into disarray. Once again the prospects of progress seemed to be limitless. Addressing a meeting in the Birmingham Town Hall soon after Peel's decision Sturge 'rejoiced in the belief, that if the Corn Law should be abolished, that it would be the harbinger of that delightful period when there would be a free intercourse with all nations, and men would learn war no more, and when there would be no rivalry but rivalry in acts of kindness and benevolence'.(24) Eight months later, when the parliamentary battle for the repeal of the corn laws had been won, he became the patron of a new movement with a title that summed up his aspirations during the late 1840s - The League of Universal Brotherhood.

NOTES

1. The Papers of Sir Thomas Fowell Buxton, T.F. Buxton to Priscilla Johnston, 24 November 1837. The last entry in the NCSU Committee's Minute Book is dated 16 January 1847.

2. Birmingham Journal, 18 May, 19 October 1844, 31 May 1845; Pilot, 7 June 1845.

3. Leeds Times, 5 October 1844; Tholfsen, Working Class Radicalism in Mid-Victorian England, p. 159.

4. Birmingham Journal, 23 November 1844; Democrat And Labour Advocate, 3 November 1855.

5. Pilot, 1 March 1845.

6. This paragraph is based on reports in the Pilot and the Birmingham Journal during the mid-1840s.

7. W. White, Our Jubilee Year, 1895, London 1895, pp. 12-13; Bull Street Meeting House, Severn Street First Day School, First Minute Book, 12/8/45-12/11/52; Pilot, 29 November 1845; Richard, Sturge, pp. 550-54.

8. Friends House Library, London, Friends' First Day School Association Reports, 1847-49, report of meeting on 25-27 December 1847.

9. Report Of The Proceedings Of A Conference Of Teachers In Friends' First Day Schools, Held In Liverpool, On The 24th, 25th and 26th of First Month, 1859, With An Appendix Containing Papers Read At The Conference, London 1859, p. 47; Woodbrooke College Library,

Birmingham, newscutting from the Christian Citizen, n.d.

10. Sturge Papers (P.A.J. Sturge), 'Joseph Sturge's Account of His Sister Sophia's Last Illness, 1845'.

11. Sturge Papers (M. Sturge), Rebecca Sturge to Mary Darby Sturge, 29 May 1846; Priscilla Burlingham, Reminiscences.

12. 'Joseph Sturge's Account of His Sister Sophia's Last Illness, 1845'.

13. The Poetical Works Of John Greenleaf Whittier, p. 170.

14. D.L. Dumond, ed., Letters of James Gillespie Birney 1831-1857, New York 1938, vol. 2, p. 1012, Lewis Tappan to J.G. Birney, 29 April 1846.

15. Sturge Papers (P.A.J. Sturge), Wedding Certificate for Joseph and Hannah Sturge, 14 October 1846; Sturge Papers (Lewin), Record Of Family Faculties; Sturge Papers (M. Sturge), Charles Sturge to Mary Darby Sturge, 23 September 1857; Sturge Papers (Lewin), Joseph & Charles Sturge.

16. 'Grace Greenwood', Haps and Mishaps Of A Tour in Europe, p. 10; H.B. Stowe, Sunny Memories Of Foreign Lands, pp. 141-42.

17. National Temperance Chronicle And Temperance Recorder, June 1846; Teetotal Times or Monthly Temperance Messenger, June 1846.

18. British And Foreign Anti-Slavery Reporter, 1 June 1846; The Proceedings of the World's Temperance Convention Held In London, August 4th And Four Following Days, London 1846, p. 2.

19. Harrison, Drink And The Victorians, p. 174; The Proceedings Of The World's Temperance Convention, Held in London, August 4th, And Four Following Days, With The Papers Laid Before The Convention, Letters Read, Statistics And General Information Presented, etc. etc., London 1846, pp. 2, 19, 25, 32-33; National Temperance Magazine, July 1846.

20. Pilot, 11 April 1846.

21. Birmingham Journal, 20 April 1844, 13 April 1850.

22. Pilot, 11 April 1846; Christian Examiner, May 1846; Eclectic Review, July-December 1846; C. Binfield, George Williams and the Y.M.C.A. A study in Victorian social attitudes, London 1973, p. 160.

23. Birmingham Journal, 19 April, 10 May 1845.

24. Ibid., 20 December 1845.

13 People Diplomacy (1846-51)

Let Cobden cipher, and let Vincent rant,
Let Sturge preach peace to democratic throngs,
And Burritt, stammering through his hundred tongues,
Repeat, in all, his ghostly lessons o'er,
Timed to the pauses of the battery's roar.
    J.G. Whittier (The Peace Convention At Brussels)(1)

Despite their reputation for austerity the evangelicals of Sturge's generation were romantics; there was always a cherished place at their public meetings for the speaker who could satisfy their craving for the exotic. The League of Universal Brotherhood was the pet scheme of one of these platform celebrities, Elihu Burritt, 'the learned blacksmith' from Connecticut. Burritt's hands still showed 'the dents of the hammer upon them', but there was nothing rough about his public performances: he was a self-help cult figure who claimed that he had taught himself to read fifty languages (the number varied from report to report) and had abandoned his trade to take up lecturing, journalism and the advocacy of reforms. Dressed like a country clergyman, he travelled the American lecture circuit during the early 1840s delivering 'poetical and dreamlike' addresses about the transformation that would be wrought upon mankind if evangelical principles were applied to social problems.(2) Lewis Tappan, who befriended him, saw Burritt as 'a whole souled philanthropist' because of his work for the Liberty Party, teetotalism and peace. More realistically, Richard Cobden described him as a 'child in the worlds [sic] affairs', but Burritt had no difficulty in obtaining acceptance as a member of the interlocking directorate that framed the policies of the peace and anti-slavery movements on both sides of the Atlantic.(3)

No one believed more strongly in the importance of a special relationship between Britain and the United States; for Burritt came very close to saying that God was an Anglo-Saxon. The two nations had been united in the 'bonds of brotherhood', he told J.A. James in 1843, not only by 'Anglo-Saxon genius & blood', but by 'the blood of the Lamb'; it was their peculiar duty to lead the rest of the world into the millennium of peace, prosperity and righteousness foreshadowed by the

Scriptures. In 1845-46, however, a dispute which threatened to plunge Britain and the United States into war placed all Burritt's hopes in jeopardy: it would be 'the greatest curse that has visited this world since the fall of man!', he wrote.(4) Fortunately, he consoled himself, in the great crises of human history God had always raised up instruments to do His will, and in this instance peace movements stood ready to act on both sides of the Atlantic. All that they required was the correct strategy to concert their efforts, and by the end of the war crisis Burritt was convinced that he had discovered it.

At the beginning of 1846 when the crisis was at its height four Manchester Quakers - Joseph Crosfield, George Bradshaw (of Bradshaw's Monthly Railway Guide), W.P. Cunningham and Peter Allen - sought Burritt's help for a scheme whereby British and American towns would exchange 'International and Friendly Addresses'. Burritt, who had already started to send 'Olive Leaves' (short articles on peace) for publication in foreign newspapers, took up the idea enthusiastically, and before the crisis was over several messages of good will were exchanged between towns in both countries.(5) Nothing like this had ever been attempted. To use Burritt's term, it was 'people diplomacy', a new means of conducting international affairs by ordinary citizens who wanted to establish friendly relations with each other regardless of the wishes of their feuding governments.(6) Thus when Parliament moved towards the repeal of the Corn Laws that year Burritt was just as excited as his Manchester friends. By throwing open her ports to all comers, he told them, Britain would send forth 'the Commercial Harbinger of the Millennium' to 'fuse the nations into one peaceful and happy brotherhood'. The 'learned blacksmith' never had any difficulty in harmonising what he called 'the religion of the Ledger' with more ethereal arguments for peace.(7)

Sturge's name was on the list of those who sympathised with the objects of the first Friendly Addresses, and Burritt soon approached him for support. Prompted by a letter he had received from 'an American blacksmith ... who, as he understood, was master of thirty languages', Sturge moved a resolution at a public meeting in January 1846 which looked forward to the time when all nations would be united in 'the bonds of brotherhood'.(8) Soon afterwards he sent money to bring Burritt over to Britain. The 'learned blacksmith's' earliest thoughts about the purpose of the visit were characteristically dreamy:(9)

> On our arrival, we propose to take a private hickory staff, and travel on, like Bunyan's pilgrim, through the country, at the rate of about ten miles a day ... We propose to avoid the lions of the country, and confine our walks to the low lands of common life; and to have our conversation and communion chiefly with the labouring classes. Perhaps we might get together a knot of them some moonshiny night and talk to them a little on temperance, peace and universal brotherhood.

And this was how the League of Universal Brotherhood originated. In July 1846 at a meeting in Pershore attended by some twenty labourers

Burritt obtained the first signatures for the League's membership pledge. They undertook to give no support to any war; to promote friendly intercourse between the nations; and to work for the 'abolition of all institutions which do not recognize and respect the image of God and a human brother in every man, of whatever clime, colour, or condition of humanity'.(10)

'Joseph Sturge enters into all my views with the liveliest sympathy', Burritt wrote in October 1846. He was fortunate in his patron; for with Sturge's support he could loosen Quaker purse-strings and rally some of the most active philanthropists and reformers in Britain to his side. Not surprisingly, reports show that the League was the 'moral Radical party' under yet another name: 'The men who took part were long tried labourers in those arduous fields of philanthropic effort, Peace, Temperance, Anti-Slavery, and other departments of moral reform'. Lawrence Heyworth, Edward Miall, George Thompson, Richard Allen, Arthur O'Neill, Henry Vincent and Thomas Spencer were amongst those who had often supported Sturge in the past. But there was one important change: the League was the first fully-fledged transatlantic reform society, and by the end of 1846 Burritt was claiming a membership of '10,000 on both sides of the water'. The Bond of Brotherhood, the monthly magazine that Burritt launched in August that year (with a regular subsidy from Sturge), was published in Worcester Massachusetts, as well as in London and Birmingham. Burritt proudly called it 'the first international periodical ever issued'.(11)

The League of Universal Brotherhood was always meant to be much more than a peace society. Burritt spoke of a movement that would be to 'Slavery, War, Intemperance, Ignorance, Political & Social Inequalities what the Anti-Corn League [sic] was to Monopoly'. During the closing months of 1846 he travelled throughout Britain hoping to win the support of 'hundreds of philanthropic capitalists' for a plan to establish a network of 'factories and shops for the manufacture & sale of Free Labor Cotton'.(12) Then, in February 1847, he went over to 'poor Ireland to fathom its misery & to find a remedy' for the Famine which had gripped that country since the autumn of 1845. Burritt had already drawn up a plan whereby each English region would assume responsibility for an Irish district; now he hoped to produce a report that would excite American compassion. It was a tragic venture. Burritt was so unnerved by the suffering in the West of Ireland - 'I have seen as much as my flesh and blood can bear', he told Richard Allen - that he remained only a few days.(13) A pamphlet entitled A Journal Of A Visit Of Three Days to Skibbereen, And Its Neighbourhood summarised his impressions of the visit. Sturge wrote an introduction and once again foreshadowed the Irish policies of later Liberals. He envisaged legal changes to abolish primogeniture and entail; to offer tenants security for their outlay of labour and expenditure; and to give the poor the right to be relieved by the landowners. In places such as Skibbereen, he wrote, philanthropy and emergency relief schemes could not even guarantee the poor a decent burial.(14) Once again it was evident that a deeply-held humanitarian conviction could drive Sturge towards forms of state intervention that would otherwise have been anathema to a man of his voluntaryist convictions.

Increasingly, however, most of the League's resources went into the promotion of 'people diplomacy'. In 1846-47, when Britain and France were on the brink of war, its supporters in Birmingham, Manchester, Liverpool and other British cities arranged for Friendly Addresses to be sent across the Channel, and in March 1848 after Louis Philippe was deposed Sturge led a deputation to present another of these addresses to the Provisional Government of the Republic.(15) The idea of holding international peace congresses was revived in these circumstances. According to Burritt, it was first discussed (probably on 23 February 1848) while he and George Bradshaw were travelling from Manchester to attend a meeting in Bolton, and it rapidly took shape during the brief period between February and June when Paris looked like a suitable venue under its new liberal government. The violence of 'the June Days' when hundreds perished on the barricades upset these hopes, but the congress was transferred to Brussels where it opened on 20 September. At first Sturge was reluctant to be involved, but it would have been uncharacteristic of him to stand aside, and he shouldered much of the burden of organising the series of peace congresses which met in Brussels, Paris, Frankfurt, London, Manchester and Edinburgh between 1848 and 1853: he was the 'animating spirit' of this movement.(16)

Inevitably some members of the London Peace Society saw the League of Universal Brotherhood as a rival, and on 13 July 1847, when the League held a meeting to set up a national organisation, the Secretary of the Peace Society arrived to pour cold water on the idea. His intervention provoked Sturge into a kneejerk defence of the new venture as a counterbalance to the 'strong leaning to centralism in London', but surprisingly soon the two societies learned to co-operate.(17) In January 1848 they set up a joint committee to agitate against a rearmament programme which the Government had proposed, and they shared the responsibility for organising the Brussels congress.(18) When John Scoble, the abrasive secretary of the British and Foreign Anti-Slavery Society, persisted with attempts to undermine Burritt's position, Sturge brought him to order by threatening to withdraw from both of the peace societies unless they would work together.(19) The outcome was a 'Conference of the Friends of Peace' which Sturge chaired on 31 October 1848, when it was agreed that there should be a programme of joint operations leading up to a peace congress in Paris the following year. A Peace Congress Committee was set up on this occasion, and the London and Manchester sections of its Finance Committee divided the country between them to raise a fund of £5000. Sturge was not a member of the Peace Congress Committee, but, as in the case of the British and Foreign Anti-Slavery Society, he held an associate status and chaired many of its meetings. The appointment of a new secretary of the Peace Society, Henry Richard, greatly strengthened these arrangements.(20)

Thus, without any of the schisms they had precipitated within the anti-slavery and temperance movements during the 1830s, Sturge and the 'moral Radicals' continued with the radicalisation of the peace movement during the late 1840s. James Stubbins, the secretary of the Birmingham Peace Society, saw the older leaders being ousted by men 'who watched more narrowly the progress of the public opinion, and were better able to enlist public sympathy. This tended to an enlargement of their views, and while the old members shrunk back even from their own success, the new saw in these signs but the dawn of hope, and the realisation of their schemes'.(21) Once again it was all too much for Samuel Gurney. By June 1849 the 'City King' was angrily threatening to leave the Peace Society because his membership was associating his name with radicals such as Joseph Sturge, Samuel Bowly, Henry Vincent, Elihu Burritt and George Thompson. He had been appalled, he continued, by Bowly's insulting references to the aristocracy: he 'did not go to a meeting of the Peace Society to hear attacks made on that class'. Impenitently, the Committee replied that liberals and radicals were their best supporters.(22)

It would have been difficult to give any other answer when it was well known that prominent peace men had been actively involved in radical politics during 1847 and 1848. Shortly before the general election of 1847 Sturge had been so angered by Lord John Russell's decision to spend £100,000 on public education that he attended a conference in London where he spoke out against what he saw as an attempt by the Government to obtain a corrupt influence over the people.(23) The conference led to the setting up of a Parliamentary Committee to help Dissenters contest elections in their own right instead of relying on the Whigs to represent their interests, and soon afterwards Edward Baines, the proprietor of the Leeds Mercury, suggested that Sturge should stand for one of the Leeds seats during the general election. The invitation made it clear that voluntary education would be the central issue, but Baines agreed that Sturge should campaign on a much wider platform acceptable to non-electors as well as electors. The town was subsequently placarded with slogans such as 'Complete Suffrage', 'Sturge and Equal Rights for All', 'Sturge and Freedom of Education', 'Sturge and Religious Liberty', 'Sturge the Friend of the Negro', 'Down with Monopoly' and 'Sturge and peace'. Voluntaryism was a divisive issue - influential Unitarians in the town favoured state aid for education - and J.G. Marshall, the owner of the famous Holbeck flax mills, also stood as a liberal. Each elector in a two-member constituency such as Leeds had two votes, but it was highly unlikely that both of the liberal candidates would defeat the sitting Tory member, William Beckett, and the poll book suggests that Marshall and Beckett controlled the situation by directing their supporters' second vote to each other. Many of Sturge's supporters retaliated by 'plumping' (casting only one of their two votes), but it was not enough to save the day, and once again he ended up at the foot of the poll.(24)

This was Sturge's last attempt to enter Parliament, but it was not the end of his interest in radical political reform. Burritt's journal shows that the French Revolution in February 1848 brought the expectations of the League of Brotherhood to a white heat: when the news of Louis Philippe's abdication reached them during one of their meetings in Liverpool it fell 'like a clap of thunder upon the audience, and caused a tremendous explosion of joy and enthusiasm'. A few days later the deputies at a League conference in London were still so excited by the news that they discussed 'the adoption of some measure which would unite the Chartists, Complete Suffragists and other societies in an effort to enfranchise the people'. Sturge was in the chair on that occasion, and it was this meeting that sent him to Paris as the bearer of a Friendly Address to the new Government.(25) Then, returning to Birmingham he went straightaway to a large meeting of working men in the Town Hall where he urged his listeners to press peacefully for the programme of the People's Charter. If they retained the House of Lords, another speaker commented, it should consist of men such as 'Mr Sturge Duke of Edgbaston'.(26)

The parliamentary reform movement quickly faded away, but in one of those shifts of emphasis that have been seen as a characteristic of middle-class pressure groups through to our own day 'peace' was taken up as a rallying cry by many of those who had participated in earlier reform movements. The government's militia schemes and the army's recruiting campaigns were condemned at peace meetings in 1848, not only because they were preparations for war, but because Sturge and his friends saw them as a threat to the whole process of moral and social reform which had been transforming the nation since the end of the Napoleonic Wars: 'our Literary and Scientific Societies, our Mechanics' Institutes, our Young Men's Associations for mutual improvement, and numerous similar organizations and arrangements'. According to this analysis only the aristocracy and the vested interests which battened on 'Old Corruption' stood to gain from the existing military and foreign policies. Peace meetings often looked like Complete Suffrage reunions.(27)

They could also resemble Anti-Corn Law League meetings, for in 1848 Sturge came to an agreement with Richard Cobden that did more than anything else to make the peace movement into a major radical crusade. The grounds for their co-operation had long existed: Cobden had always described free trade as a means of promoting international co-operation. When the Corn Laws were being repealed he had even told Sturge that the 'best effect of all will be that the whole civilized world will become <u>quakers</u> in the practice of peace & mutual forbearance'.(28) Thus, although Cobden did not go as far as the full pacifist principle of the Peace Society and the League of Universal Brotherhood, a close relationship developed between the two men in 1848. 'I feel that I have the animus within me to battle successfully with the war-spirit if I can be supported out of doors', Cobden wrote to Sturge on 6 September, and he suggested that they should work together to press for arbitration treaties and international disarmament. Sturge's 'Conference of the Friends of Peace' accepted the offer on 31 October, and the Peace Congress Committee was required as its first task to work up a public agitation in support of an arbitration motion that Cobden was to introduce in Parliament during 1849.(29)

Some Quakers and members of the Peace Society condemned the agreement with Cobden on the grounds that it was a form of compromise, a criticism that pointed to the opening of a new stage in

Sturge's political education. He would never retract his pacifist principles, Sturge told the critics, but he did not see why he should refuse to work with anyone who only went part of the way with him. Who amongst them, he asked, would 'be deterred by any difference of opinion or even by defects in moral conduct, from intercourse with others for pecuniary gain in commerce and trade?'(30) Evidently the exponent of 'total and immediate' policies of reform was being converted to pragmatism, a conclusion supported by the long run of letters from 1848-1859 which shows Cobden coaxing Sturge along like a slow learner who had yet to acquire the 'wisdom of the serpent'. The letters also show Cobden's reliance on Sturge to provide 'the pressure from without' which would strengthen the claims of a policy that would be unpopular in Parliament.(31) For his part Sturge was remarkably deferential to Cobden: it was 'no small privilege', he would write in July 1852, 'to hand if it be but as the "cup of cold water" to those who are much more able labourers than myself'.(32)

They were a formidable combination, and between them Sturge and Cobden imparted a spirit of purpose to the Peace Congress Committee when it set to work in the closing days of 1848. Memories of all the movements in which Sturge had been involved since the early 1830s must have stirred as he and a team of spokesmen including Samuel Bowly, Arthur O'Neill, Henry Vincent, Elihu Burritt and Henry Richard toured the country in a six months campaign of public meetings and petitioning that reached its climax in a great meeting at Exeter Hall on the eve of Cobden's arbitration motion. Burritt, who had never seen the 'pressure from without' in operation, was fascinated by the power it generated: using the new Penny Post, the organisers sent out 50,000 letters to create 'a constituency of earnest minds in almost every town in the kingdom which sent a representative to Parliament'; 'hundreds of thousands of printed leaves' were scattered amongst the people; night after night public meetings were held all over the country to send in petitions 'from John O'Groat's to Land's End'; 'the one idea' was taken up by the press and 'echoed and re-echoed among the populations far and near'; and finally one thousand platform tickets were sent out 'to nearly 400 ministers of the gospel, to the editors and literati, and other men of influence and standing in London and vicinity' urging them to attend the great meeting in Exeter Hall. The display of public opinion reinforced Burritt's belief in the special relationship between Britain and the United States: nowhere else were Governments brought under such a salutary influence.(33)

Cobden's motion was defeated in Parliament by 97 votes on 12 June 1849, but it was so successful in winning press and public attention that the peace movement could be said to have satisfied the 'three conditions' that he later set down 'for the success of any great project of reform, - namely a good cause, persevering advocates, and the hostility of the Times'.(34) These credentials seemed less convincing on the other side of the Channel. Many European liberals and nationalists saw no alternative to using force against their despotic rulers, and they sometimes criticised the peace congress movement for advocating policies of non-resistance that would have denied the peoples of Europe any prospect of reform. This was certainly not the intention; for Sturge wished to see a Europe of nation states and institutions of self-government. He had little sympathy for Julius Haynau, the Austrian general who was attacked by the Barclay and Perkins draymen during a visit to London in 1850 after he had repressed risings in Italy and Hungary: 'had they stopped at bespattering him with dirt and not struck him it w^d I think have had in it very little that the most peaceful could blame'. Condemning the part played by Russian armies in the destruction of Hungarian independence and the oppression of the Jews, Sturge called on the British government to recognise Hungary as an independent state.(35)

Unlike many British radicals of his day, Sturge did not adopt a double standard when his own countrymen adopted policies of repression; in 1850 he was also calling for a mass movement of protest against the massacres of the Dyaks by James Brooke ('Rajah Brooke') in Borneo. But he always added that the correct response by oppressed peoples was passive resistance, and when Louis Kossuth, the exiled Hungarian leader, was given a hero's welcome in Britain in 1851 Sturge and Henry Richard issued an address to members of the Peace Society advising them against doing anything to endorse wars of liberation: freedom would prevail when the policies of disarmament favoured by the peace congress movement left monarchs with no resources to rule by force.(36) In a spectacular misreading of the future Cobden urged Charles Sturge to pray for peace if he wished to see liberalism triumph in Russia: 'twenty years of peace will revolutionise Russia - 20 years of war would leave the serfs of that country where they are'.(37) Inevitably sentiments of this sort sounded hollow when the peace congress met in Paris in 1849 shortly after the defeat of the Hungarians and the suppression of the Roman and Venetian Republics. The French caricaturist Honoré Daumier cruelly lampooned scenes at the congress, and the newspaper La République referred to 'la naiveté quaker'. There was even a suggestion that, for all their high moral protestations, the delegates from perfidious Albion were promoting their own commercial interests by calling for free trade and disarmament.(38)

It was certainly true that the religious and worldly beliefs of peace men were so intermingled that they could scarcely be separated. When they referred to prophetical Scripture and spoke of a millennium of peace, they were not fleeing from reality; they were exulting in the progress of their age. In 1849 Sturge wrote that he rejoiced in 'the bright indications of the approach of that day "when nation shall not lift up sword against nation" '. Success had fed upon success he told his audiences at meetings that year: reforms that once seemed utopian - he mentioned the abolition of slavery, the Corn Laws and duelling - had been achieved in his lifetime, and he entertained 'sanguine hopes' of peace. 'Living as they did, in these railway and electric telegraph times, he would appeal to every philanthropic heart to say whether humanity should stand still while science was progressing'.(39) The peace movement's proposals must be related to this context, for there is no substance in the claim that Cobden provided practical policies while the peace societies mouthed empty words of pacifism.(40) They had devised the techniques of 'people

169

diplomacy', and they provided most of the policies debated at the peace congresses - not only proposals for international arbitration, a world court and an assembly of nations, but also schemes for universal postal and measurements systems which would facilitate international communication.

Thus the Peace Congress movement was very much an Anglo-Saxon Protestant businessman's version of internationalism: Sturge and his associates were living contradictions of their claims that the nations were abandoning their differences. Wearing their 'great moral hats', the Quakers retained their status as a people apart when they attended the congresses, and together with the other evangelical delegates they were distressed by much of what they saw in Brussels, Paris and Frankfurt. Appalled by the continental Sunday, they would only accept a special invitation to view the waters of Versailles when the date was changed from the Sabbath. Everywhere they saw signs of Catholic 'superstition', and when a party of British delegates stumbled across the gambling rooms of Wiesbaden during an excursion, they recoiled 'with befitting horror'.(41) Sturge had to be warned not to be too fastidious in his dealings with Victor Hugo who presided at the Paris Peace Congress (a prime example of 'the modern Satanic school' of literature, in Whittier's words), and when he pressed the French organising committee to open the congress sessions with a short period of silent prayer he was grieved by their unshakable objection that such behaviour would provoke an outburst of laughter in Paris. Even Richard Cobden, 'the international man', approached the French in the belief that their public men were dishonest.(42) Nor did Elihu Burritt's linguistic skills contribute anything to the cause of international understanding; Henry Richard noticed 'Mr Burritt's extreme and somewhat mysterious antipathy to asking the way' when they were in Paris, and it eventually transpired that 'the learned blacksmith' could not speak French.(43)

But any misgivings were swept aside by the signs of success. Descriptions of the congresses by the British and American delegates conveyed a thrilling sense of pioneering a movement that would soon triumph in Europe and other parts of the world. Despite the haste with which it had been chosen as a substitute for strife-torn France, Belgium provided an excellent venue for the first of the congresses in 1848. When the 130 British delegates and visitors reached Ostend they found the vessels in the harbour had been decorated in their honour and that a special train was awaiting them on the orders of the Belgian Government. With the help of the Minister of Mines, Auguste Visschers, they obtained the use of the Salle de la Societé de la Grande Harmonie in Brussels, where they were joined by delegates from Belgium, the Netherlands, France, Italy and the United States. Even the Governor of Liberia put in an appearance. With the exception of a sceptical Spaniard who was eventually voted out of order and a Catholic priest who vindicated the concept of defensive wars, the delegates easily agreed on a peace programme consisting of international arbitration treaties, an international court, a Congress of Nations, an international code of law and general disarmament.(44)

By the time the next congress met a year later motions calling for arbitration and disarmament had been introduced in the national legislatures of France, Britain and the United States. This time the Congress met in Paris - a triumph in itself - and the presence of one hundred French delegates seemed to suggest that at last a viable French peace movement was emerging. They were further heartened by a powerful speech from their chairman, Victor Hugo, in which he looked forward to the time when the world would be united by a eurocentric ideal of technological progress: 'There would be nowhere barren plains, nor moors, nor marshes. Cities would be found where there are now only deserts. Ports would be sunk where there are now only rocks. Asia would be rescued to civilization; Africa would be rescued to man'.(45) In 1850 there was another congress: this time in St Paul's Church, the chamber in Frankfurt where the ill-fated German assembly had sat during the revolutions of 1848. Sturge and his friends knew that units of the Austrian, Bavarian and Prussian armies were nearby, but even the arrival of General Haynau to view the proceedings did not daunt them.(46)

Sturge said little during the public sessions of the congresses; his role was organisational, and his influence was exerted behind the scenes to focus the delegates' attention on arbitration as their policy and to prevent them from endorsing any measure that conflicted with Quaker peace principles. But the Frankfurt congress gave rise to one of the most famous incidents in his career - the peace mission to Denmark and the Duchies of Schleswig and Holstein in September 1850. By then the German monarchs were fast recovering their authority after the revolutions of 1848, but national sentiment was still being aroused by the attempts of the predominantly German-speaking Duchies to assert their independence from the Danish Crown by force. The rules forbade references to current events, but on the last day of the congress a member of the Prussian constitutional party, threw the session into turmoil by calling on the delegates to send a commission of inquiry to the scene of hostilities.(47) Although the organising committee ruled that the request was out of order, Sturge decided to intervene in the dispute on his own initiative. In Quakerly language he told Burritt that he had 'a concern' to go to the Duchies and 'bear a testimony in favour of arbitration'. 'I feel little expectation of any benefit from it', he wrote to his brother Charles before setting out, 'except a conviction that we have done what we can to prevent the continuance of the war & I hope we shall do no harm'. Accompanied by Elihu Burritt and Frederick Wheeler, a Quaker, he set out for Berlin where he received some help from the Prussian Government before travelling on to Hamburg, Kiel, Rendsburg and Copenhagen.(48)

The Times and other critics found it easy to mock the idea of three simple-minded enthusiasts throwing themselves between the armies of Denmark and the Duchies, but Sturge, Burritt and Wheeler were received with courtesy everywhere they went. In Rendsburg where the Schleswig army was encamped they passed 'through ranks of soldiers with shotted muskets, and cannons loaded for the battle' to meet the Stadtholder, cabinet ministers and the Duke of Augustenburg; in Copenhagen they were received by the Danish Prime Minister and Foreign Secretary. At no stage did they enjoy official status, and they had no policy to resolve the dispute, but they obtained copies of the relevant treaties, and, encouraged by references to an arbitration procedure, they acted as a medium through which the Duchies' Government tried to bring the Danes to the negotiating table.(49) Cobden saw the episode as a striking example of 'people diplomacy': 'You have done good service', he told Sturge, 'by breaking through the flimsy veil with which the diplomatists of the world try to conceal their shallow craft & penetrating into their mysterious domain by your startling expedition to Rendsburgh & Copenhagen.'(50)

The Danish and British governments viewed the mission very differently; for, despite Burritt's claim that the three 'ambassadors of Christ' had no interest in the political aspects of the Schleswig-Holstein question, they were unmistakably pro-German in sympathy. Sturge told his brother Charles that he saw 'no prospect of Denmark listening to any proposition coming through us yet from what I can learn the Dutchies [sic] will be quite ready to offer a fair and impartial arbitration which will help to put them right in the sight of England in opposition to Lord Palmerston's later protocol with Russia and Austria which appears to have created general indignation in Germany'. Burritt's journals show Sturge behaving, as ever, like a Christian philanthropist who saw his task as one of encouraging righteousness and appealing to the hearts of the unregenerate. At Rendsburg where he was well received by the Duchies' Government 'Good Joseph Sturge walked in with his broad brim on, and his face like the new moon in spring, beaming upon them'. But a few days later when he met the Danish Prime Minister Sturge's 'voice began to break with emotion, until he almost sobbed aloud, while the tears coursed down his benevolent face'. As Burritt innocently noted after a second occasion of this sort, the Danish Foreign Minister 'evidently felt that the presence of such a man was a privilege which is rare to diplomacy'.(51)

Less 'rare to diplomacy' were the threats of coercion that the mission directed against the Danes; for in the last resort there was nothing divinely child-like about these peacemakers. When the Danish Government did not comply with their appeal, Sturge and his friends despatched a 'plainly written' letter threatening 'to publish to the world the object and result of their mission', and Sturge returned to England with the intention of creating an agitation on the model of the one that had brought the West Indian planters to heel in 1838.(52) He would publish a full report of his journey, including all the letters he had received from both sides; he would bring the full resources of 'the pressure from without' to bear on Lord Palmerston; British policy would be dramatically reversed; and the Danes would have to negotiate. Soon after his return Sturge began this process by drawing Palmerston's attention to the arbitration provisions of the treaties (a peevish marginal comment in the Foreign Office Papers suggests that the information was not gratefully received by that self-styled authority on the Schleswig-Holstein problem), and he sent a warning to the Danes that, if they alienated British public opinion, they might be deprived of their right to collect dues from vessels navigating the Sound at the entrance to the Baltic. Meanwhile he went ahead with plans for a public meeting in London.(53)

172

At this stage, however, Cobden hurriedly intervened to counsel Sturge against taking sides or requesting intervention by the British Government. The mere idea of sending Palmerston out to preach arbitration to the Danes would reek of hypocrisy so soon after the Don Pacifico affair when the Royal Navy had blockaded Athens over 'a scoundrelly claim upon the Greek government': Sturge's policy should be to withdraw gracefully, respecting the confidentiality of the documents he had received, and leaving the way open for a similar mission on some future occasion. It is a measure of Sturge's deference to Cobden at this stage of his career that on the whole he followed this advice and eventually recalled Burritt to England when that simple soul sent a letter to The Times which attracted another mocking editorial. By then the Danish Government had announced in unmistakable terms that it preferred to negotiate through 'proper authorities and responsible men of business'.(54)

The peace congress which opened a few months later produced none of these awkward encounters with reality. Revolutions, wars, official suspicions of their intentions and the perennial difficulty of obtaining halls vanished when London was the venue. 1851 was the year of the Great Exhibition, and the nations of the world were gathering in the Crystal Palace to celebrate what Prince Albert called 'a period of most wonderful transition, which tends rapidly to accomplish that great end, to which indeed all history points; "the realisation of the Unity of mankind" '.(55) Restored to their true element in Exeter Hall, all that Sturge and his friends had to do was to proclaim the impending triumph of their principles. One thousand delegates, more than ever before, attended the congress sessions that year including representatives of municipal and religious bodies, magistrates, Members of Parliament, college professors, scientists, theologians and writers. Germany, France, Italy, Spain, Belgium, the Netherlands, Austria, Sweden and the United States (with the largest foreign contingent of delegates) were amongst the countries represented. Urged on by opening speeches from the Revs J.A. James and William Brock who hailed the approach of the millennium, the congress euphorically passed a series of resolutions in favour of stipulated arbitration, non-intervention in other countries' affairs, disarmament, a code of international law and non-aggression towards 'aboriginal and weaker tribes'.(56)

Sturge spent much of that summer in London promoting another season of meetings for his circle of good causes, and for several weeks he rented a town house in St James's Place where he could provide his fellow philanthropists with a forum for an informal exchange of views. On the first evening of the peace congress, he invited a hundred guests to a discussion of slavery and the free produce movement. Two evenings later he provided a reception for the foreign delegates at which the possibility was raised of holding the next congress at Amsterdam or Turin. Several days later it was the turn of the League of Universal Brotherhood to gather under his roof for an evening of 'short addresses, conversation-circles and all kinds of social enjoyment'. Then there was a temperance soirée where Sturge brought together a hundred prominent teetotalers to discuss 'the juvenile movement and the literature of the cause'. It was a relentless pace, but even when he received news that his business had been robbed of £6000 Sturge did not falter as the 'serene' host. Probably there was no time when his vision of a reformed world seemed closer to success.(57)

NOTES

1. The Poetical Works of John Greenleaf Whittier, pp. 203-5.
2. P. Tolis, Elihu Burritt: Crusader for Brotherhood, Hamden Conn. 1968, pp. 1-122; C. Northend ed., Elihu Burritt; A Memorial, New York 1879, p. 478; Birmingham Journal, 4 November 1848.
3. The Papers of Lewis Tappan, Lewis Tappan to Joseph Soul, 10 June 1846; Brit. Lib., Add. MSS. 50131, ff. 252-54, Richard Cobden to Joseph Sturge, 12 December 1850.
4. Tolis, Elihu Burritt, p. 97; E. Burritt, Sparks From The Anvil, London n.d., p. 42.
5. Advocate of Peace and Universal Brotherhood, March 1846, letters to Burritt from George Bradshaw, Joseph Crosfield and Peter B. Allen, from Crosfield, Allen & W.P. Cunningham to Burritt, from Crosfield, Allen & Cunningham to Burritt, and from Burritt to Crosfield, Allen and Cunningham.
6. Friend, November 1852.
7. Advocate of Peace and Universal Brotherhood, March 1846; Friend, November 1846.
8. Birmingham Journal, 24 January 1846.
9. Tolis, Elihu Burritt, p. 144; The Papers of Lewis Tappan, Elihu Burritt to Lewis Tappan, 1 May 1846; London Teetotaler Or General Temperance Intelligencer, 6 June 1846.
10. E. Burritt, Olive Leaves For The People, Worcester Mass. 1850, pp. 31-34. In two previous articles I have mistakenly referred to this society by the name of its official periodical, The Bond of Brotherhood: 'Personality in Politics: The National Complete Suffrage Union and Pressure Group Politics in Early Victorian Britain', Journal of Religious History, XII, December 1983, p. 388 and 'Woman's Mission And Pressure Group Politics In Britain (1825-60)', Bulletin of the John Rylands University Library of Manchester, 63, Autumn 1980, p. 218.
11. New Britain Institute, Elihu Burritt Journals, Journal 6, 6 October and 28 December 1846; Bond of Brotherhood, July 1848; Central Connecticut State College, Elihu Burritt Papers, E. Burritt to ?, 5 September 1846.
12. Tolis, Elihu Burritt, p. 148; Burritt, Journals, Journal 6, 3 October, 6 October 1846.
13. Central Connecticut State College, Burritt Papers, E. Burritt to ?, 4 February 1847; Burritt, Journals, Journal 7, 21 December 1846; Friends Library, Dublin, Room 4, Shelf T1, 2(a), E. Burritt to Richard Allen, 25 February 1847.
14. E. Burritt, A Journal Of A Visit Of Three Days To Skibbereen, And Its Neighbourhood, London 1847.
15. Herald of Peace, December 1846; Tolis, Elihu Burritt, p. 165; Bond of Brotherhood, April 1848.
16. Burritt, Journals, Journal 10, 23 February 1848, Journal 18, 16

September 1853, Journal 11, 29 July 1848; Bond of Brotherhood, July 1859; Richard, Sturge, p. 428.

17. Burritt, Journals, Journal 8, 13 July 1847.

18. Ibid., Journal 10, 13 January 1840; Reports Of The Peace Congresses At Brussels, Paris, Frankfort, London, and Edinburgh, In The Years 1848, 1849, 1850, 1851 and 1853, London 1861, Brussels Congress, p. 1.

19. Burritt, Journals, Journal 12, 7 September, 30 October, 7 November 1848; Rhodes House, MSS Brit. Emp. S18, C112/13, Joseph Sturge to John Scoble, 14 October 1848.

20. Herald of Peace, December 1848; Peace Society, Peace Conference Committee Minutes (1848-55), 31 October 1848.

21. Birmingham Journal, 4 November 1848.

22. Peace Society, Minute Book of the General Committee, 13 June 1849.

23. Birmingham Journal, 10 April, 17 April 1847; Eclectic Review, July-December 1847.

24. Brit. Lib., Add. MSS. 43845, ff. 33-34, Edward Baines jun. to Joseph Sturge, 22 May 1847; Leeds Mercury, 22 May, 5 June, 12 June, 26 June, 31 July 1847; The Poll Book Of The Leeds Borough Election, July 1847, Leeds 1847.

25. Burritt, Journals, Journal 10, 25 February, 28 February, 1 March, 3 March, 4 March 1848.

26. Birmingham Journal, 18 March 1848.

27. Parkin, Middle Class Radicalism, pp. 38-39; Herald of Peace, February 1848; Bond of Brotherhood, December 1848.

28. Brit. Lib., Add. MSS. 43656, ff. 13-14, Richard Cobden to Joseph Sturge, 26 March 1846.

29. Ibid., ff. 43-44, Richard Cobden to Joseph Sturge, 6 September 1848; Herald of Peace, December 1848, January 1849.

30. Herald of Peace, October 1849.

31. Brit. Lib., Add. MSS. 43656, ff. 359-64, Richard Cobden to Joseph Sturge, 30 September 1855. See also West Sussex Record Office, Cobden Papers 63, Richard Cobden to Joseph Sturge, 13 November 1848.

32. Brit. Lib., Add. MSS. 50131, ff. 275-76, Joseph Sturge to Richard Cobden, 27 July 1852.

33. Herald of Peace, July 1849; Burritt, Journals, Journal 13, 11 June 1849.

34. Mr Cobden And The Times, Manchester 1864, p. 9.

35. Sturge Papers (M. Sturge) Joseph Sturge to Charles Sturge, 17 September 1850; Birmingham Journal, 18 August 1849.

36. Standard of Freedom, 1 December 1849; Brit. Lib., Add. MSS. 50131, ff. 153-54, Richard Cobden to Joseph Sturge, 29 January 1850; Herald of Peace, March 1850, December 1851.

37. Sturge Papers (Lewin), Richard Cobden to Charles Sturge, 29 December 1849.

38. G. Bourgin & M. Tarrier, 1848, Editions Tel 1948, nos 208-9; La République, 3 August, 22 August, 7 September 1849.

39. Tyrrell, 'Making the Millennium', pp. 79-83; Birmingham Journal, 3 March 1849.

40. A.J.P. Taylor, The Trouble-makers. Dissent over foreign policy 1792-1939, London 1969, pp. 47, 49.

41. Central Connecticut State College, Burritt Papers, 'The Frankfort Congress'; Reports Of The Peace Congresses, Paris Congress, p. 56; Friend, 1 July, 1 August 1849; Herald of Peace, October 1850.

42. Brit. Lib., Add. MSS. 50131, ff. 133-35, Richard Cobden to Joseph Sturge, 9 October 1849; Letters of J.G. Whittier, ed. Pickard, vol. II, p. 89, J.G. Whittier to Thomas Tracy, 6 May 1847; Burritt, Journals, Journal 14, 22 August 1849; Brit. Lib., Add. MSS. 43656, ff. 150-51, Richard Cobden to Joseph Sturge, 9 August 1849.

43. National Library of Wales, MS 10200A, Henry Richard's Journal of Tours in France 1849 and 1856.

44. Reports of the Peace Congresses, Brussels Congress.

45. Ibid., Paris Congress.

46. Ibid., Frankfort Congress.

47. Ibid., pp. 43-50.

48. Burritt, Journals, Journal 14, 26 August 1850; Sturge Papers (M. Sturge), Joseph Sturge to Charles Sturge, n.d.

49. The mission to the Duchies and Denmark is described in successive entries of Burritt's Journals, 14 & 15, 24 August 1850 - 11 December 1850, and Public Record Office, FO22, 187, f. 204, Denmark And The Duchies: To The Members of the Late Peace Congress at Frankfort. See also Richard, Sturge, chap. XXI.

50. Brit. Lib., Add. MSS. 50131, ff. 207-10, Richard Cobden to Joseph Sturge, 9 October 1850.

51. Sturge Papers (M. Sturge), Joseph Sturge to Charles Sturge, 30 August 1850; Burritt, Journals, Journal 14, 4 September 1850, 12 September 1850; ibid., Journal 15, 14 September 1850.

52. Burritt, Journals, Journal 15, 13 September 1850.

53. Public Record Office, FO 22.187, f. 200, Joseph Sturge to Lord Palmerston, 28 September 1850; Burritt, Journals, Journal 15, 19 October 1850.

54. Brit. Lib., Add. MSS. 50131, ff. 221-22, Richard Cobden to Joseph Sturge, 25 October 1850; ibid., ff. 230-32, Richard Cobden to Joseph Sturge, 31 October 1850; ibid., ff. 239-40, Richard Cobden to Joseph Sturge, 6 November 1850; ibid., ff. 241-42, Richard Cobden to Joseph Sturge, 8 November 1850; Burritt, Journals, Journal 15, letter from Danish Foreign Minister to Elihu Burritt, 29 October 1850.

55. The Society of Arts, Addresses delivered on public occasions by his royal highness the Prince Albert, president of the society for the encouragement of arts, manufactures, and commerce (London 1857), pp. 60-61.

56. Reports Of The Peace Congresses, London Congress.

57. Burritt, Journals, Journal 16, 11 July, 22 July, 24 July, 1 August 1851; Friends House Library, Elihu Burritt MS vol. S101, ff. 70-72, Elihu Burritt to A.M. Southall, 8 August 1851; British Temperance Advocate, 1 July 1851.

PART 5

THE WORLD OF THE CHRISTIAN PHILANTHROPIST

14 Life in Earnest

In 1851 two decades of almost full-time commitment to reform stretched behind Sturge; ahead of him lay his last few years when he would see his plans swept aside by a wave of war hysteria that he was powerless to stem. Thus the early 1850s offer a good vantage point at which to interrupt the narrative of his career and survey the characteristic features of his life as a philanthropist and reformer. Sturge never seems to have set out a statement of his aspirations; as Richard Cobden pointed out, he was 'a doer and not a talker or writer, & he left few records of himself to illustrate the depth or intensity of his feelings, or the lofty motives which impelled him to a life of incessant labor in the cause of humanity'.(1) To understand what he was trying to achieve Sturge's biographer must show him in action, a task that involves following him across a benevolent empire which radiated out from his household and family-circle to Birmingham, London and the rest of the world.

It was often remarked that Sturge's personality matched his role as a 'Christian philanthropist': he looked 'benevolent' and 'good'. Until late in life Sturge sustained this appearance at the cost of an inner struggle that Henry Richard found 'quite a study to watch';(2) for there was a strong disposition towards combative self-righteousness in his behaviour that sometimes called to mind the harsher stereotype of the seventeenth-century Puritan. If Sturge had lived in Cromwell's day, one observer wrote, 'sword and bible would have been well used by him'.(3) In the course of the 1840s, however, a gentler presentation of self was becoming the dominant expression of Sturge's personality, providing him with an immediately recognisable social identity - one that aroused the veneration of those who appreciated the theatre of evangelical public life. At the opening of the Anti-Slavery Convention in 1840 the diarist William Lucas was so impressed by Sturge's emotional introduction of Thomas Clarkson that he believed George Thompson, one of the most eloquent men of the day, lost by comparison. Thompson's demeanour was not appropriate to such an occasion: 'How different from the honest, humble, benevolent face of Jos. Sturge'. Several years later Henry Richard observed the delegates at the peace congresses instinctively gathering around Sturge, 'just as the swarm clusters around the queen bee'.(4) During the early 1850s there was a sudden onset of ageing, but this enhanced his appearance of benevolence. Grace Greenwood, an American authoress who visited Sturge in 1852, saw him as a patriarchal figure: 'How distinctly rises before me now the pleasant, kindly face of the beloved old man - the clear blue eyes beaming with a welcoming smile, the smooth white forehead, the soft brown hair, silver-touched with only an added beauty, the ruddy cheeks, the sweet tremulous mouth'.(5)

There was more to being a 'Christian philanthropist' than looking the part: in Sturge's case it was a way of life constructed around an obsession with the correct use of time and money. Thus, although a list drawn up for a family record later in the century referred to 'natural history; riding; amelioration of human suffering' as Sturge's favourite pursuits, he seems to have spent little time on the first of these after his early years and the second amounted to no more than an early morning ride. The third was the all consuming interest of his life. He was spurred on by one of the most basic truths of his evangelical faith: to stand inactive was to bring down on oneself the condemnation fit for a sinner 'who knoweth to do good, and doeth it not'.(6) Voluntary societies in his day could not have functioned without people of this sort; for the impressive lists of patrons, committee members and subscribers were facades, and the tendency was for a small number of men to provide the active leadership.(7)

Although Sturge's diaries have not survived, and there is no way of re-creating a calendar of his activities, the outline is clear enough. As Cobden recognised when he paid a debt in postage stamps because he knew Sturge had plenty of use for them, a 'citizen of the world' had to spend much of his time writing letters.(8) Then there was the round of committee and public meetings through which Sturge transacted much of the work and canvassed support for his good causes. At certain times of the year, especially in May when the Friends Yearly Meeting and the anniversaries of the religious and benevolent societies took place in London, Sturge passed days on end in this way. And, probably most strenuous of all, there were the recurrent occasions when he travelled extensively in Britain or overseas to promote reform.

The titles of two books he recommended for purchase by the Birmingham Friends Book Society - The Art of Improving Time and Life in Earnest - support the impression that he had no time for relaxation. In 1843, the year in which he made most recommendations to the Society, his choices were Pfizer's Life of Luther; Philippo's History of Jamaica; The Narrative of a Mission of Enquiry to the Jews by the Scotch Church; Isenberg and Krapf's Abyssinia; The Life of Dr Hope and Baird's History of Religion in the United States of America. This was 'useful information' according to the early Victorian definition: 'A beneficent Creator', Sturge wrote on one occasion, 'has implanted within us a thirst for information about other scenes and people'.(9) Fiction had no place in his reading. It was always difficult for evangelicals to see novels as anything other than worthless and immoral incitements to an undisciplined imagination. Only once did Sturge request the purchase of a novel, and that was Harriet Beecher Stowe's Uncle Tom's Cabin, a special case, as he explained to John Clark:(10)

It is certainly a wonderful production & required in the author a combination of qualifications very rarely united - an intimate knowledge of facts and a wonderful power of conveying them with trajic [sic] effect to the judgment & feelings of mankind - and above all a Christian attainment which alone could qualify for drawing such characters & such death bed scenes as those of Eva and Uncle Tom.

Business continued to claim some of his time even after Charles had set him free from the responsibilities of day-to-day management in 1831. To have withdrawn altogether from the partnership, as Sturge sometimes threatened to do when he had lost patience with Charles's reckless over-trading, would have struck at the source of the wealth which had earned him a reputation for his benefactions. In 1844 he calculated that he was worth £7000 to £8000, and shortly before his death he told his nephew that over the years his income from business had averaged less than £1000 per annum. This did not constitute great wealth, and there were some signs that his gifts had to be carefully planned.(11)

Henry Richard was told by 'one who had the best means of knowing' that up to the time when his family increased Sturge devoted 'more than half his entire income to charitable purposes, afterwards about one third', but this is not a very informative guide to Sturge's actual expenditure for public purposes during the 1850s when he was using capital as well as interest to promote some very expensive good causes.(12)   In any case the distinction between household and philanthropic expenditure is untenable; Sturge's personal life was interwoven with his philanthropic pursuits. To understand the scale of his commitment to philanthropy and reform it is necessary to realise that his household was a benevolent empire in its own right, a privately owned landscape of reform on which he carried out social experiments and from which his influence was diffused into Birmingham and beyond.

NOTES

1.   National Library of Wales, Henry Richard Letters, MS 14021 D, f. 113, Richard Cobden to Henry Richard, 25 May 1864.

2.   Herald of Peace, July 1859.

3.   Morning Star, 17 May 1859.

4.   A Quaker Journal, vol. 1, p. 201; Richard, Sturge, p. 430. See also D.M. Rosman, Evangelicals and Culture, London 1984, p. 80. On the 'presentation of self 'and 'social identity' see E. Goffman, The Presentation Of Self In Everyday Life, Harmondsworth 1971, chap. 1 and Stigma. Notes on the Management of the Spoiled Identity, Harmondsworth. 1968, chap. 1.

5.   British and Foreign Anti-Slavery Reporter, 1 February 1860.

6.   Sturge Papers (Lewin), Record Of Family Faculties; Miall, Reconciliation Between the Middle and Labouring Classes, introd. Sturge.

7.   See, for example, Rhodes House, MSS Brit. Emp. E2/6, British

and Foreign Anti-Slavery Society Minutes, 22 April, 5 August, 2 September, 5 October, 20 October 1853.

8.   Brit. Lib., Add. MSS. 43722, ff. 202-203, Richard Cobden to Joseph Sturge, 16 January 1857.

9.   Friends Book Society, Birmingham, Minutes; Sturge, A Visit To The United States In 1841, p. 67.

10. Fenn Collection, E19Y, Joseph Sturge to John Clark, 1 December 1852.

11. Sturge Papers (M. Sturge), Joseph Sturge to Charles Sturge, 2 August 1844; Sturge Papers (P.A.J. Sturge), Joseph Sturge to Wilson Sturge, 13 May 1859; W.D. Rubinstein, ed., Wealth and The Wealthy in the Modern World, London 1980, p. 53.

12. Richard, Sturge, p. 590.

15 The Great Philanthropist of Our Town

Sturge did not live as an ascetic. Harriet Beecher Stowe who visited him in 1853 was delighted by Southfield his home at 64 Wheeley's Road, Edgbaston: there was 'an abundance and variety of all that is comfortable and desirable', and the gardens with their carefully planned spinneys, shrubberies and rockwork were perfect examples of the English skill in re-creating the 'wildness of nature'. For all that, the household was an object lesson in evangelical earnestness. When Sturge spoke to her about the free produce movement, she was affected by the 'very great force' of his arguments, 'the more so from the consistency of his example' in refusing to allow any slave produce across his threshold. Important discussions, including a meeting of nearly one hundred people, took place during her visit, and it was evident that Sturge saw his home as part of the circuit of hospitable meeting places that provided philanthropists and radicals with an equivalent of the country seats where the leading parliamentarians of this age carried on much of their politicking.(1) After the 1830s when Birmingham was at the centre of the national railway network visits were easily arranged, and the house was often full of guests, including some very well known reformers from both sides of the Atlantic: Daniel O'Connell, Richard Cobden, John Bright, William Lovett, Henry Vincent, Lewis Tappan, J.B. Gough, J.G. Birney and many others.

By 1850 this form of hospitality was so much a part of Sturge's daily life that in his own grounds he even erected a small version of Exeter Hall, the London meeting place of the evangelical societies. Sometimes referred to as 'the play-room' because it was used for this purpose by his children, it could seat 200 people. J.A. James called it a 'place of convocation for the sons and daughters of mercy to meet, and concert and execute their schemes of benevolence'. Meetings of Sunday School teachers and children took place there, and, as John Bright discovered in 1850, it was a good venue for informal, conversational gatherings. At a time when reformers were so deeply divided over their education policies that they could not have had a constructive public meeting, he and Cobden joined a large company there to participate in a discussion of German education led by a professor from Hamburg.(2)

Walking through Sturge's extensive gardens, Harriet Beecher

Stowe discovered another outpost of this domestic benevolent empire: 'On one side of the grounds was an old-fashioned cottage, which ... Mr Sturge formerly kept fitted up as a water-cure hospital, for those whose means did not allow them to go to larger establishments'.(3) She was referring to a fashionable therapy which had originated during the 1820s in Austrian Silesia where Vincenz Priessnitz, a farmer's son, claimed to have healed himself by applying cold wet compresses and drinking large quantities of water after his ribs had been crushed in an accident. By the late 1830s Priessnitz had won such a reputation for curing others by using variants of this simple treatment that his home village of Graefenberg became a major international healing centre, and establishments for the new science of 'hydropathy' were set up in many countries including Britain.(4)

Hydropathic establishments bore little resemblance to older mineral spas like Bath. Any kind of pure water would provide a cure because of its supposed ability to dissolve 'morbific matters' in the body and bring impurities to the surface of the skin. Copious quantities were applied internally as a drink, externally as a bath or douche, and by wet sheets wrapped around the patient to induce the heavy perspiration which expelled supposedly harmful substances from the body. Just as important, and here the contrast with Bath and other spas was especially striking, patients had to submit to a strict regimen of regular hours, diet and exercise. Many hydropathic doctors insisted on total abstinence from alcoholic drinks; simplicity in clothing to expose the body to the air; avoidance of undue stimulation of the nervous system such as occurred at balls or theatres; and withdrawal from all sources of anxiety. Disease was caused by 'artificial habits', Dr Edward Johnson, one of the earliest advocates of hydropathy, wrote, and the patient should be brought back to the simple God-given laws of nature.(5)

Sturge was probably introduced to hydropathy through that other cult of cold water, the temperance movement. Total abstinence pledges had been weakened by escape clauses which allowed the use of wines and spirits for medical purposes, and teetotalers were delighted to make common cause with a form of medicine which had no place for intoxicants. But it was Sophia's last illness that brought the 'water cure' into his household. She believed, almost certainly with justification, that the drugs she had received as a child had undermined her health, and for a time she refused to see anyone who would prescribe medicines. She did consent to be treated by Edward Johnson, and, although she was not cured, Sturge must have been impressed.(6) One aspect of hydropathy worried him, however: water cure establishments were for the wealthy. This was a time when Sturge commonly described himself as the advocate of the working classes - for several years after the Complete Suffrage venture he spoke of nearly all the reforms he supported as working men's causes - and he took up hydropathy in the same spirit. In 1850, after Edward Johnson and his son Walter had settled at Umberslade Hall near Birmingham (Florence Nightingale and Tennyson were amongst their patients), he transformed the cottage in his grounds into a 'Self-Supporting Hydropathic Institution' and arranged for the younger Johnson to administer out-patient treatment there for a small fee. The venture seems to have been abandoned early in 1853 when the Johnsons left Umberslade Hall and followed the well-beaten track to Malvern, 'the capital of the water cure'.(7)

As one experiment ended another began. In 1853 Sturge extended his benevolent empire by purchasing 'a small estate' of 75 acres at Stoke Prior in Worcestershire about 16 miles south-west of Birmingham as the setting for one of the most remarkable episodes in his career: he established his own reformatory as a farm school for delinquent boys.(8) Sturge did not invent the juvenile reformatory; originality was not one of his characteristics as a reformer. His contribution was always the strength of his commitment to what he had learned from others. In this case he was responding to a major social problem that was attracting considerable attention in Birmingham - the plight of neglected children. In 1845 a newspaper report described the town as probably worse in this respect than other places of comparable size: each day a large class of 'juvenile outcasts' was 'brought before the Magistrates by the police, and charged with sleeping in the open air on door steps, or perhaps in out-offices attached to dwelling houses, with intent or on suspicion of committing a felony'.(9)

Sturge's solution seems to have been suggested to him by his mentor, James Cropper, who had set up a farm colony on his lands at Fearnhead in Lancashire to educate children of this sort, and as early as 1839 the two men had corresponded about a plan Sturge had devised for sending boys there. Two years later Sturge briefly turned aside from his anti-slavery and peace activities in the United States to visit 'The Refuge' in Philadelphia where he was impressed by its attempt to carry out 'the just and benevolent principle that offences against society, committed by very young persons, should be disciplined by training and education, rather than by punishment'. Likewise when he was in Hamburg during the Schleswig-Holstein crisis in 1850 he visited the Rauhe Haus, a land settlement for juvenile criminals where the children lived in family-sized houses under the supervision of a house-father and were trained in agriculture or crafts.(10) Experiments such as these were arousing some interest in Britain where the old penal system was in transition, and the promoters of domestic missions, temperance societies and ragged schools spoke of being overwhelmed by the alarming social problems in large towns. The very title of Mary Carpenter's famous book, Reformatory Schools for the Children of the Perishing and Dangerous Classes and for Juvenile Offenders, gives some insight into contemporary fears.

Sturge attended a conference which Carpenter organised in Birmingham in 1851, and a year later he opened his own reformatory in three cottages at Ryland Road under the care of John Ellis, a London ragged school teacher who had acquired a reputation for his successful work with delinquent children. 'Now I want some of the very worst boys you have in Birmingham', Sturge told Police Superintendent Stephens, and in due course eleven of them arrived from Birmingham Gaol. C.B. Adderley, a prominent local landowner and paternalistic Tory, was impressed by this small scale experiment, and in 1853 he and Sturge set up two larger institutions to take its place. With some help from a committee on which Sturge served for a time Adderley built a reformatory at Saltley, and Sturge moved out to Stoke Prior.(11)

No mean judge in such matters, Adderley told a public meeting at this time that Sturge's 'munificence had reached an extent which, if mentioned, would startle them'. When Stoke Prior opened in March 1853 it had accommodation for about fifty boys in a farmhouse which had been enlarged and fitted up with dormitories, a school-room and workshops. The staff consisted of a superintendent, a schoolmaster, a labourer and a female housekeeper.(12) It was one of the first seven reformatories to receive certification under the terms of the Act of 1854, a typical piece of mid-century legislation which married the voluntary principle to a cautious but active view of state involvement: privately funded and managed, the reformatories had to be officially certified and inspected. Living conditions were to be plain, and the children were to work at manual tasks. Some of its promoters seem to have been drawn to the system because it lent itself to primitive 'short, sharp shock' views of penology, but the dominant model was one in which small groups of children would be supervised by substitute parents.

Stoke Prior was at the merciful end of the spectrum. An inspector who was satisfied with its cleanliness, good order and spirit of industry thought its discipline and dietary were 'too indulgent' and the boys 'too rough and independent'.(13) This was a deliberate policy on Sturge's part. He spoke of his charges as victims of their social circumstances, especially parental drunkenness, and he would not allow the use of disciplinary cells or flogging. No human being had a right to punish another, he believed; penology should concern itself with the reformation of the offender.(14)

Events in Birmingham confirmed his opinion at the time he was setting up his reformatory. In 1853 news leaked out that brutal practices had been sanctioned by the Governor of the local gaol, and an official inquiry subsequently showed that prisoners, including some of the boys who were eventually sent on to Ryland Road, had been punished by being strapped to the walls in strait-jackets and collars. Several suicides had occurred as a consequence. The brutality was the more evident because the previous Governor, Captain Alexander Maconochie, had been dismissed to appease some vocal critics of his attempts to modify the 'separate system' (solitary confinement with labour on machines called 'cranks') which was supposed to be applied to all prisoners in the Birmingham Gaol. In his place the magistrates had appointed the Deputy Governor, Lieutenant William Austin, who promptly instituted what was later described as 'almost a uniform system ... of pain and terror'. The episode had all the ingredients of a classic mid-Victorian scandal, and Charles Reade took it as the plot for his novel It Is Never Too Late To Mend. Like Maconochie and Reade, Sturge opposed the 'separate system'. In 1841 he had seen it in action in Philadelphia, and he had recoiled from its 'tremendous and undiscriminating severity'; now he seized the opportunity to expose its abuses, and he was one of those who demanded the official inquiry.(15)

In the meanwhile Sturge set out to show that a humane regime could be instituted for young offenders. John Ellis's duties at Ryland

Road were as follows: 'He had first to act as a father and feed and clothe them; next he had to feel for them like a mother, and then he became their employer, schoolmaster, moral teacher, counsellor, judge and doctor. All was done by means of the affections.' Stoke Prior was run on similar lines. The staff ate with the boys and took responsibility for all aspects of their welfare. Sturge organised treats such as railway excursions, and, more importantly, he spent time with them, often staying overnight in an attempt to bring his influence to bear more strongly.(16) The evidence suggests that this experiment showed the best side of the tradition of voluntary public service which has been so important in modern British history: it should be contrasted with Mary Carpenter's reformatory regime which has been condemned for its 'sadism, deceit and self-righteousness'.(17)

The sight of the benevolent empire that was spreading across Sturge's lands during the early 1850s did not always arouse admiration. In 1855 some of his Edgbaston neighbours sent him a letter of protest when they learned that he intended to use eight acres he had leased in nearby Wheeley's Lane for another philanthropic project. Known as 'Sturge's Field', this was to be a recreation area for the use of working-class children. The objections were understandable: Sturge's neighbours anticipated annoyance and deterioration of property; beer shops, stalls and booths might be attracted to the area; and there might be a 'congregating of characters of the worst description'.(18) But, as they knew, no one could deny the need for parks. The town's green belt of 'guinea gardens' had been swallowed up by an urban sprawl of such unrelieved bleakness that there was not one freely accessible open space for the recreation of its poorer inhabitants. In February 1848 the Birmingham Journal printed a letter of complaint from a working man who had even been denied permission to walk in a cemetery because he was wearing fustian, the coarse cloth of the poor.(19)

Concerned by the lack of public recreation facilities in Birmingham, over the years Sturge had supported several unsuccessful schemes for providing parks: one of the most imaginative would have linked Birmingham by rail with a miniature Crystal Palace at Sutton Coldfield.(20) During the second half of 1853 he brought the matter forward more urgently. In collaboration with a committee of working men he approached local landowners for support, and at a public meeting he pressed the Town Council to accept several offers of land, including the Wheeley's Lane acres, for public parks. His action was simple justice, he argued: landowners had seen their property values rise because of their proximity to the growing town whereas the generality of the inhabitants who once had access to '5000 little gardens on the outskirts of the town' had been reduced to a situation where 'in most instances a child had not even a back yard to go to'. Convinced though he was that land-owners had rights, he saw land as 'a kind of property that peculiarly involved duties too'. Only when the Town Council refused to act did Sturge brave the displeasure of his neighbours, and go ahead on his own. 'Sturge's Field' continued to be used for games and sports for several years after his death.(21)

Sturge was fortunate that his family did not share the objections of his neighbours to living in an environment where the requirements of benevolence over-rode the distinction between private and public life; they were still the closely-knit circle they had been at Netherton in Bewdley. Harriet Beecher Stowe discovered a particularly striking instance of the family's continuing intimacy during her stay. 'The grounds of Mr Sturge are very near to those of his brother [Edmund] - only a narrow road interposing between them. They have contrived to make them one by building under this road a subterranean passage, so that the two families can pass and repass into each other's grounds in perfect privacy.'(22) If she had gone a little further, she would have discovered Charles's house in nearby Frederick Road (John had owned the adjoining house in the 1830s) and if she had arrived a year later she could have found their unmarried sister Rebecca living in Wheeley's Lane. They had their own ideas and favourite good causes - John, for example, was a keen phrenologist; Edmund took up homoeopathy and gymnastics; and Charles remained on the Town Council after Joseph's resignation - but reform was something of a family business for the Sturges, and, as if through a series of interlocking directorships, they all contributed to Joseph's over-arching ideal of social change.(23)

Thus, although Sturge's forays into local government were short-lived and controversial, they did little to harm his standing and opportunities as a local reformer: in the words of H.H. Horton, an observer of mid-century Birmingham, Sturge was 'the great philanthropist of our town'.(24) This was a role of considerable importance at a time when the town badly needed to be given a vision of itself as a place of purposeful endeavour for the general well-being. Local government powers were consolidated in the Town Council, but laissez-faire opinions held sway, and control of municipal affairs passed into the hands of a 'cheap government' faction led by Joseph Allday. In the 1850s the Town Hall, once Birmingham's pride and joy, symbolised the public squalor that was the other face of the 'Victorian virtues' of self-help: one of the <u>Birmingham Journal's</u> correspondents complained that as a consequence of the Town Council's 'Cheap and Nasty Government' the northern end of the building had been allowed to become 'a huge urinal'.(25)

Sturge was unhappy about the state of local government in Birmingham: he wanted to see the people being enfranchised, and he spoke of the day when they would elect professing Christians to take responsibility for the temporal welfare of all classes.(26) But, like many of his contemporaries, Sturge was heartened by the number of working-class people who were already surmounting their bleak surroundings by striving for self-improvement and respectability. In 1858 he told a temperance meeting that he had seen a wonderful change in the habits of those with whom he associated: bull baits, prize fights and duels had all been 'put down by public opinion within his recollection'.(27) For nearly forty years he stimulated the positive aspects of this public opinion through his patronage of the plethora of local societies which tried to introduce model lodging and dwelling houses; shorter working hours and Saturday half-days; as well as baths, parks, recreational facilities, and educational ventures of various sorts. None of this penetrated to the structural problems of contemporary urban life, but it placed Sturge in the forefront of an important shift in middle-class attitudes during the mid-century. While Allday's faction held to a strict interpretation of the principles of Political Economy, Sturge was offering an alternative and more mellow version of middle-class liberalism which would bring the working-class desire for self-improvement into an alliance with middle-class paternalism and schemes for urban reform.(28)

NOTES

1. Stowe, Sunny Memories, letter XII.
2. J.A. James, Christian Philanthropy: As Exemplified In The Life and Character of the Late Joseph Sturge, Esq. A Sermon Delivered in Carr's Lane Chapel on Sunday Morning, May 22 1859, London 1859, p. 23; T. Pumphrey, 'Joseph Sturge', C. & J. Clark Archive, Street, John Bright's diaries, 25 November 1850.
3. Stowe, Sunny Memories, p. 186.
4. R. Metcalfe, Life of Vincent Priessnitz, Founder of Hydropathy, Richmond Hill 1898.
5. Edward Johnson, Hydropathy. The Theory, Principles, And Practice Of The Water Cure Shewn To Be In Accordance With Medical Science And The Teachings Of Common Sense; Illustrated with many Important Cases, London 1843.
6. Sturge Papers (P.A.J. Sturge), 'Joseph Sturge's Account of His Sister Sophia's Last Illness, 1845'. Lewis Tappan also praised the water cure. See The Papers of Lewis Tappan, Lewis Tappan to Joseph Sturge, 17 September 1849.
7. The Truth Tester Temperance Advocate And Manx Healthian Journal, 20 August 1846; National Temperance Chronicle, October 1852; Birmingham Journal, 23 February 1850.
8. Birmingham Journal, 25 December 1852.
9. Ibid., 7 June 1845.
10. Cropper Papers, James Cropper to Joseph Sturge, 29 July 1839; Sturge, A Visit To The United States, pp. 70-71; Sturge Papers (M. Sturge), Joseph Sturge to Charles Sturge, 22 September 1850; J. De Liefde, The Romance of Charity, London 1867, pp. 3-42.
11. Report Of The Conference on Reformatory Schools in Birmingham, 1851; See also Report of Proceedings At A Public Meeting For Establishing The Birmingham Reformatory Institution With List of Officers and Subscriptions, Birmingham 1853; Birmingham Journal, 25 December 1852; Report of the Proceedings of the Second Conference On The Subject of Juvenile Delinquency And Preventive and Reformatory Schools, Held at Birmingham, December 20, 1853, London 1854, pp. 7-8.
12. Birmingham Journal, 29 January 1853; Parliamentary Papers, First Report Of The Inspector Appointed Under The Provisions Of The Act 5 & 6 Will. IV, c38, To Visit The Different Reformatory Schools Of Great Britain, vol. XXIX, 811, 1858, pp. 34-35.
13. Parliamentary Papers, First Report etc.
14. The Authorized Report Of The First Provincial Meeting Of The National Reformatory Union, Held At Bristol, August 20th, 21st, and 22nd, 1856, London 1856, pp. 105-107; Transactions Of The

National Association For The Promotion Of Social Science, 1857, Inaugural Addresses And Select Papers, London 1858, pp. 331-32; Birmingham Journal, 25 October 1851.

15. Birmingham Journal, 10 September, 8 October 1853; J.V. Barry, Alexander Maconochie of Norfolk Island. A Study Of A Pioneer In Penal Reform, Melbourne 1958, pp. 197-204; Sturge, A Visit To The United States, p. 72. Sturge had unsuccessfully attempted to prevent Maconochie's dismissal.

16. Birmingham Journal, 25 December 1852; Parliamentary Papers. First Report Of The Inspector etc., pp. 34-35; Richard, Sturge, pp. 555-61.

17. Smith, Florence Nightingale, p. 151.

18. Brit. Lib., Add. MSS. 43845, ff. 48-49, letter to Joseph Sturge from several inhabitants and property owners near Wheeley's Lane and Carpenter's Road, 3 April 1855.

19. Birmingham Journal, 12 February 1848.

20. Ibid., 30 July 1853.

21. Ibid., 3 December, 24 December 1853; Richard, Sturge, pp. 541-45.

22. Stowe, Sunny Memories of Foreign Lands, p. 185.

23. Priscilla Burlingham, Reminiscences; Journal of Health, September 1854.

24. H.H. Horton, Birmingham. A Poem, Birmingham 1853, p. 284.

25. Birmingham Journal, 1 December 1855. This era is described by E.P. Hennock, Fit and Proper Persons. Ideal and Reality in Nineteenth-Urban Government, London 1973, chap. 1.

26. Friends Historical Library, Swarthmore Penns., Joseph Sturge to Henry Richard, 25 August 1856.

27. Birmingham Journal, 16 October 1858.

28. Tholfsen, Working Class Radicalism in Mid-Victorian England, chap. 4.

16 A Provincial in London

One of the most noticeable characteristics of provincial radicals in Sturge's lifetime, one that he shared to the full, was their hostility for London. Members of Sturge's circle saw the capital as the centre of aristocratic and Anglican misgovernment: even to go there was to run the grave risk of losing one's principles. 'All advise me to keep myself clear from London society', Edward Miall wrote when he was raising funds to launch the <u>Nonconformist</u> in 1840; 'all regard that as the greatest peril I shall have to encounter'.(1) But Miall did settle in London, and his newspaper was the more influential as a consequence. For, although the anti-Apprenticeship campaign had demonstrated that occasional raids from the provinces could influence national policy-making, this was not enough. Some of the changes desired by provincial reformers could only be achieved through persistent pressure on Parliament, and they were ineluctably drawn to Westminster on a more permanent basis. This was particularly evident in the case of the British and Foreign Anti-Slavery Society which relied so heavily on lobbying the Colonial Office that it took rooms in the City and set up a paid bureaucracy consisting of a secretary and two assistants to deal with the flow of business.

During the 1830s Sturge joined the drift to London, especially after 1838 when the London and Birmingham railway line was completed, and the connection between the two cities rapidly improved. A journey which took six to six and a half hours in 1839 was cut to two hours and forty minutes by an express train in 1845.(2) Birmingham continued to be his home and his base, but he could now pay frequent short visits to the capital. He could even stay for long spells in surprisingly congenial surroundings. Between 1839 and the early 1850s several of the societies he supported opened offices within a short distance of each other in the City: the British and Foreign Anti-Slavery Society at 27 New Broad Street; the Peace Society at 19 New Broad Street; the Voluntary School Society (Sturge was making large donations to it in the late 1840s and 1850s) at 26 New Broad Street; and the League of Universal Brotherhood and the Free Labour Depot at 35 and 22 Broad Street Buildings respectively. Above the office of the Anti-Slavery Society Sturge had his own pied-a-terre, 'a large, well-furnished apartment' where he could stay overnight.(3)

Although London would always be an alien city for him, here at least he was on an enclave of friendly territory.

A few minutes walk from New Broad Street took Sturge to another important building in his London landscape, Devonshire House at Bishopsgate where the Friends Yearly Meeting was held. There his influence sharply diminished. He was an active participant in the Society's business, but his proposals were usually blocked by the 'weighty Friends' who dominated the meetings and issued the public documents. In their own way they were as well-intentioned and interested in reform as he was, and they did useful work in schools, prisons, asylums for the insane and even in Robert Owen's New Lanark, but the Quakers had risen in the world since Elizabeth Stirredge had confronted Charles II with his sins, and some of the 'weighty Friends' were on remarkably intimate terms with men of the highest rank. William Allen, the Duke of Kent's business advisor, was expressing a commonly held opinion when he wrote in 1817 that it was important 'to be known to those in the higher ranks of society' if he was to be 'more extensively useful'.(4) Sturge's radical ideas threatened the world in which the 'weighty Friends' had found this honoured niche. Even the relentless orthodoxy of his condemnation of luxurious living must have been deeply disturbing to some of them; for all observers were agreed that the Quakers of this era were a 'comfort loving people'. Wealthy Quakers wore 'plain clothing', but, as R.S. Surtees pointed out, their 'beautiful brown Saxony coats with little inside velvet collars and fancy silk buttons' could have set a standard for 'dandified simplicity'. Samuel Gurney and other 'weighty Friends' lavishly entertained their guests in splendid mansions staffed by liveried servants.(5)

Repeatedly during the 1840s Sturge failed to have his way at the London Yearly Meeting. An informal record in 1840 shows him three times bringing on heated discussions which were terminated by Samuel Gurney, William Forster, William Allen and Samuel Tuke who would not consent to his proposals that the American Friends should be spurred on to greater activity against slavery and that the British Government should be condemned for the Opium War with China; it was enough that 'several weighty friends ... expressed that they could not see it right to do so'. He was in trouble again in 1842 after some harsh comments were received from the Philadelphia Yearly Meeting arising from his American visit.(6) A year later, obviously disturbed by the opposition of many Quakers to his Complete Suffrage campaign, he precipitated the worst clash of all. Barnard Dickinson described it in a letter to Sturge's sister-in-law:

> In the meeting last evening thy dear Brother was allowed fully to express his feelings he considering that his public acts have prejudiced him amongst his friends. I am sorry to say that what he communicated with I doubt not the best intentions altho under greatly excited feelings were [sic] far from being satisfactory to the Meeting, which was <u>clearly</u> & <u>publicly</u> stated ... I thought what Sam Tuke said in reply to thy dear Brother was very <u>correct</u> but expressed in rather too harsh language.

The Epistle issued by the Yearly Meeting soon afterwards contained an unmistakable reprimand: 'we desire ever to be found of those who are quiet in the land'. The twentieth-century opinion that Sturge was 'the consummate flower of Quakerism in the nineteenth century' would have surprised most of his contemporaries.(7)

If Tuke and the 'weighty Friends' hoped to silence him, they were disappointed. Two years later, on the eve of another Yearly Meeting, he published a letter he had sent to the Meeting for Sufferings, the executive committee of the Society, strongly objecting to their condemnation of some Quakers in Indiana who had seceded and reconstituted as a separate Society of Anti-Slavery Friends. Sturge insisted that the matter should be re-opened at the Yearly Meeting and that mediators should be sent to Indiana. He succeeded on this occasion, but when the mediation was fruitless an alliance of 'weighty Friends' defeated his attempts to have the seceders recognised.(8) He was deeply disillusioned during these years. Writing what was virtually an open letter in December 1844, he described the Yearly Meeting and 'some leading and valued Friends' as an obstacle to progress: they had objected at first to the immediate emancipation of the slaves in the British Empire; they had opposed teetotalism; and now they were hostile to 'the advocacy for an equal participation of civil rights'. Seven years later he wrote that 'the usefulness of our Society in its corporate capacity in the World at large is very much come to an end'.(9)

Despite Lewis Tappan's suggestion, he did not join another church.(10) He fought on and was never isolated; for one of the features of Quakerism during the 1840s and 1850s was the existence of a faction that Samuel Bowly called 'the liberal party in the Yearly Meeting': men who shared Sturge's views about the Society and were themselves dedicated to 'usefulness ... in the World at large'. Bowly was one of the best examples. He and Sturge worked together for thirty years in the anti-slavery movement, corn law repeal, voluntaryism, education schemes and the peace movement. 'All their sympathies were in unison', Bowly's daughter wrote, 'and they took counsel together on all the leading questions of the day'.(11) Thus at all times, even in 1843 when the public reprimand from the 'weighty Friends' was fresh in everyone's memory, many Quakers attended Sturge's reform meetings.

They were joined by 'moral Radicals' from other churches. Lewis Tappan noted the large number of Baptists at the international conventions in 1843, and Henry Richard estimated that most of the Anglo-Saxon delegates who attended the Paris Peace Congress in 1849 were evangelical Dissenters: the corollary as Horace Greeley noted in 1851, was the absence of members of the social and ecclesiastical 'Establishment'.(12) The ministers among them were the very type of the 'political Dissenter', turning easily from the pulpit to the public platform as the stage for oratorical performances that could soar to the highest pitch of moral indignation and plunge close to the joky irreverence of the music hall. Thus another important building in Sturge's London landscape was Exeter Hall, the gathering ground of British evangelicals. J.E. Ritchie, who often saw Sturge there in the mid-nineteenth century, described it as their parliament and the instrument through which they dreamt of regenerating society.(13)

Parliament itself was almost completely closed to them. In the course of the 1840s and 1850s several of Sturge's friends contested elections, and a few of them were successful, but for the most part they had to rely on sympathetic MPs to act as their spokesmen. In the words of the assistant secretary of the British and Foreign Anti-Slavery Society, they needed help from a politician such as Lord Brougham who 'does things other dont [sic] care to'.(14) Daniel O'Connell and Sharman Crawford were politicians of this type. So was Richard Cobden, although the relationship would have been much closer if Sturge had had his way. The two disagreed on too much: on anti-slavery, temperance (a fear of 'singularity of habits in social life' kept Cobden from the pledge), voluntary education, franchise reform and even on peace because of the care with which Cobden distinguished between Quaker pacifism and his own more limited support for arbitration and disarmament.(15)

From London Sturge's benevolent empire stretched out to encompass the world: to China because of his condemnation of a war that had been fought to protect the opium trade; to the Dyaks of Borneo, whose misfortunes at the hands of 'Rajah' Brooke he brought to public attention; to New Zealand where he sent some of his reformatory boys; to India and Natal where he tried to obtain free labour cotton; to Cuba and Brazil whose slave produce he attempted to exclude from the British market; and to Europe where three of the international peace congresses were held. His closest ties were always with the British West Indies where he continued to help the Baptist missionaries in their work for the former slaves, and, most important of all, with the United States. Communications improved between both sides of the Atlantic during the 1830s and 1840s. The mail service was excellent, Sturge wrote in 1846, and he had never lost a letter. In 1841 his own journey from Nova Scotia to Liverpool only took nine days.(16) It was very much a two-way traffic. Sturge travelled to America to promote the anti-slavery and peace movements: in return his own work as a reformer was powerfully influenced by American ideas and experience.

Reports pointed to one important by-product of these international contacts - a stream of foreign missionaries, American teetotalers, Africans, Red Indians and escaped slaves who brought their tales of suffering and triumph to Sturge's meetings in London and Birmingham. Thus a typical vignette of Sturge as a 'citizen of the world' would show him at a meeting such as the one he chaired in January 1848 when the platform party included not only those tried and trusted draw-cards, J.A. James and Henry Vincent, but also a Jamaican missionary, and an Ojibway chief and his son. Dressed in their native costume, the two Red Indians had come to bring greetings to the Birmingham 'chief (Mr Sturge)'.(17) Displays such as this were too 'Cooper-ish' for some observers, and there were cases of imposture, but the mixture of eager faith and histrionic romanticism that produced a craving for these performances was an irremovable feature of the world of the Christian philanthropist.(18)

NOTES

1. Miall, Life of Edward Miall, p. 45.
2. Birmingham Journal, 12 January 1839, 10 May 1845.
3. Burritt, Journals, Journal 6, 8 October 1846. The addresses are taken from a variety of publications put out by these societies.
4. Life of William Allen With Selections From His Correspondence, London 1846, vol. I, p. 303.
5. The Papers of Lewis Tappan, 1843 Journal, 18 June, 4 July 1843; R.S. Surtees, Mr Sponge's Sporting Tour, Oxford 1982, p. 3.
6. Friends House Library, Portfolio 21.40, George Crosfield to Henry Croofield, 25 May 1040; Friends Library, Dublin, Grubb Collection, SGC, f. 45, Benjamin Grubb to Anne Grubb, 23 May 1842.
7. Coalbrookdale Letters, ff. 261-62, Barnard Dickinson to M.D. Sturge, 1 June 1843; Epistles From The Yearly Meeting Of Friends, vol. II, p. 324; R.M. Jones, The Later Periods of Quakerism, London 1921, vol. II, p. 803.
8. British Friend, 30 April, 31 May 1845; Friends House Library, BH2/1, Notes by Jacob H. Cotterell of Bath, Yearly Meetings, 1845-46.
9. British Friend, 31 December 1844; Betty Fladeland, Men And Brothers. Anglo-American Antislavery Cooperation, Urbana 1972, pp. 291-92.
10. Tappan suggested that he should 'break off from the Quakers & go to Mr James's meeting', The Papers of Lewis Tappan, Lewis Tappan to Sophia Sturge, 11 September 1843.
11. M. Taylor, Memorials of Samuel Bowly, Gloucester 1884, pp. 18, 35-36.
12. The Papers of Lewis Tappan, Lewis Tappan's Address, 1843; National Library of Wales, MS 10200A, Henry Richard's Journal of Tours in France 1849 and 1856; H. Greeley, Glances At Europe, New York 1851, pp. 279-80.
13. J.E. Ritchie, Here And There In London, London 1859, p. 84 and Christopher Crayon's Recollections: The Life And Times Of The Late James Ewing Ritchie, As Told By Himself, London 1898, pp. 213-14.
14. St John's College, Cambridge, Clarkson Papers, Slavery Box 1, Folder 2, Joseph Soul to Thomas Clarkson, 21 March 1844.
15. West Sussex Record Office, Cobden 30, Richard Cobden to Joseph Livesey, 10 October 1849. Cobden referred to his followers as a distinct 'party' from Sturge's, 'seeking for a reduction of our fighting establishment'. Brit. Lib. Add. MSS. 43656, ff. 73-76, Richard Cobden to Joseph Sturge, 13 November 1848.
16. Huntingdon Library, Joseph Sturge to Mrs Clarkson, 16 April 1846; Sturge, A Visit To The United States, p. 165.
17. Temperance Gazette, February 1848.
18. The Times, 27 August, 28 August 1850.

17 Joseph Sturge's Millennium

As Christians, we will never yield to Socialists in the purest, and highest, and most enthusiastic philanthropy .... Yes we do expect a new moral world, when a marvellous transformation shall be produced; - when there shall be a change effected on animated nature.

(Lindfield Reporter, or Philanthropic Magazine, November 1839)

When a writer in the National Temperance Chronicle surveyed the reform movements supported by Sturge and his associates in 1851, he was struck by the extent to which they were bound together by overlapping memberships and shared ideals: they constituted a 'circle of moral and philanthropic movements' connected by 'great truths' around which 'the same leading men' had rallied again and again to promote the welfare of mankind.(1) The remark was more penetrating than he could have realised; for it helps to identify Sturge as an early example of a recurrent type figure in modern British history - the middle-class radical who takes up reform movements as 'capsule statements' for a wide-ranging ideology of moral values and concerns himself with general social issues and the problems of the underprivileged rather than the narrow politics of class-interest. This form of political action, which can be seen in the peace, ecological and other public interest groups of our own day, has attracted support from a minority of Christians who wish to see the Church 'nail its colours to the mast of radical moral protest'.(2) Sturge was one of a similar minority of Christians during the early Victorian era. Thus the journalist who jocularly referred to them as the 'Anti-everythingarians' was missing one of their most important characteristics; Sturge's 'moral Radicals' opposed important features of British political and social life, not because of some simple-minded wish to be different, but because their 'great truths' provided them with a bold and broad vision of a better society.(3)

Sturge and his circle of friends were products of the early nineteenth-century evangelical revival: men of 'the age of societies', fascinated by the religious and benevolent network which had suddenly opened up the possibility of converting the world and overcoming the

196

material problems of human existence. By comparison, conventional religion seemed conservative, limited and lax. Setting aside the eighteenth-century quietist model of the Dissenter as a man of religion withdrawn from worldly strife, Sturge, Miall, Mursell, Thomas Spencer, Dr Ritchie and others were like the adherents of the present-day 'liberation theology'; they were reformers who chafed at the restraints imposed by their denominational leaders. In Elihu Burritt's words, those who joined peace, temperance, anti-slavery and other societies saw themselves as offering 'an apology for the short-comings of the Christian Church; a kind of extraneous supplement to her integrity; a kind of half excommunicated faculties [sic] which should have been as dear to her as the apple of her eye; faculties which she should have wielded, with unanimous purpose, to the glory of God and the good of mankind'.(4) This was not, as is sometimes suggested, a form of secularisation: the interdenominational society was to some extent taking the place of the sect, but the aim was still the conversion of the world. Playing a role rather like newly founded religious orders in the Catholic tradition, Sturge's societies at one and the same time enabled their members to voice a sense of dissatisfaction with the Protestant churches and to breathe new life into them.

Societies were ideal instruments for another reason. Sturge and his friends needed a means of collective action that would not violate the voluntary principle, a term they defined very widely: seen from their perspective those who assumed arbitrary authority over another person, even for a good purpose, were denying him the opportunity of making the free choices which were the essence of Christian behaviour. Taking up where the 'telescopic philanthropists' of his day left off, Sturge stretched this principle to oppose forms of 'slavery' imposed on the British people by an unrepresentative government - in commerce, religion and political rights. The Anti-Corn Law League, the NCSU and the voluntaryist societies were to push back these encroachments on freedom while the temperance movement, schools and societies for social reform prepared the people for the future by teaching them how to make the most of the liberties they already possessed. Looking out over a world full of philanthropic and political associations in 1833, the Temperance Magazine and Review saw the age as a watershed: formerly 'no extensive project of benevolence could be brought to bear upon the people except by means of the government. The people now are becoming their own friends; and they have adopted a plan of making their friends love them, according to the proverb, by helping themselves'.(5)

There was nothing unusual about the doctrines of free choice and self-help in early Victorian Britain. Sturge's ideal type, the self-made Christian, could look like an exponent of the 'Gospel of Work' - a businessman like himself who had eaten bread and cheese while he got on in the world or a working man such as those who made use of evening classes, savings banks or building societies. But this was no workaday notion of what could be achieved by the power of a penny; the 'moral Radicals' were inspired by a vision of human perfection and the millennium. Swept up by the 'rage of prophecy' that Thomas Carlyle saw as a feature of British life at this time, they were to be found somewhere along the spectrum that stretched from 'the Millennarians ... on the right hand [to] the Millites on the left', the former prophesying the Second Coming and the latter a 'heaven of earth' to be created by Bentham's principles.(6)

Sturge's millennium had elements of both extremes. It was biblical in inspiration, but its eschatology placed the Second Coming after the 1000 years of peace and happiness; it was a 'heaven of earth' which would be brought in by a programme of practical activities. Pari passu, Christians would sanctify themselves, leaven the rest of mankind and fulfil the prophecies without any direct supernatural intervention. It would be a triumph of the voluntary principle, a world in which representative governments would, for the most part, leave the individual free to perfect himself and to associate with others in collective plans for progress. The work was expected to proceed rapidly, and hopes were high in the 1840s when everything seemed to point to the breaking up of the old systems. Similar beliefs flourished in the heady atmosphere produced by the great religious revivals in the United States, helping to create the unity of purpose that was evident in the relations between Sturge, Tappan and other members of their circle. To use the image favoured by Thomas C. Upham, an American Professor whose Manual of Peace was circulated extensively on both sides of the Atlantic, teetotalers, abolitionists, pacifists and other Christian reformers were all engaged in the same work; they were labouring to raise their principles one by one like so many pillars in the 'millennial temple'.(7)

Coupled with this brisk and businesslike view of the millennium was a similar doctrine of universal sanctification which Joseph and Sophia Sturge found most compellingly expressed in another of Upham's books, The Principles of the Interior Or Hidden Life. Upham's 'evangelical or gospel holiness' was based on the premise that all men 'ought to be, and may be, holy'; his ideal required no extravagant feats of religious zeal. The seven evidences of sanctification were: rationality of behaviour; a quickly operative and effective conscience; a well regulated state of natural sensibilities; decency, propriety and courtesy; union with the divine providences; conduct in harmony with Scripture; and a dedication to the promotion of God's glory in the world. There was a three class model in Upham's scheme of things, and it was from the third and highest class of Christians, those who lived the 'LIFE OF FAITH' and had experienced a 'crucifixion of self', that a new type of public man was to come. Sturge was always diffident about his own spiritual attainment, but this was the book he and Sophia instinctively turned to for inspiration.(8)

Although Upham was careful to separate his theory of sanctification from the idea of physical perfection, the connection was easily made. Just as man had a duty to cultivate holiness and to work for the millennium, so should he care for and develop his bodily health. What at first sight looks like a series of minor fads in Sturge's family circle - John's phrenology, Edmund's homoeopathy and gymnastics, and Sturge's own interest in hydropathy - was in fact a manifestation of the widely held belief that a new era in health was beginning when simple, self-help forms of preventive and curative medicine would set people free from the harmful treatments and mysteries of the doctor's craft. Sturge had a brief experience of 'Grahamism', the best known of the American physiological reform systems, when he visited the United States in 1841. It was 'a Roman simplicity of living', he wrote, which excluded meat, butter, coffee, tea and intoxicants. 'Grahamism' was too extreme for most people, but in the 1840s everyone seemed to be learning lessons of personal cleanliness, exercise, sobriety and diet. Before them was a heartening prospect. Restored to a simple and pure way of life, mankind would enjoy good health as a matter of course; people would live the full natural span; and death would occur in most cases only because the body had worn out. In short, physical well-being would be a matter of choice for the individual: to use the term that was coined by one writer, it was all achievable by 'physical puritanism'.(9)

Thus by the end of the 1840s Sturge had become the universal reformer, not only in the geographical spread of his concern but in his refusal to accept the permanency of any part of the existing social and political system: as he told the Friends Yearly Meeting in 1854, he had 'small reverence for precedents'.(10) All around him he saw vested interests blocking progress - in the churches, philanthropy, politics, international relations, penology and medicine - and he spared none of them. Even the conventional alphabet was not sacrosanct: 'It is remarkable', he told the guests at the Birmingham Phonetic Festival in 1849, 'that while we have progressed so far in railways, commerce, and the arts of life, we should take for granted that the alphabet which we have been using for centuries is the best possible mode of conveying instruction to mankind'.(11) This was no throw-away remark; during the late 1840s he had become a patron of 'the Reading and Writing Reform' which Isaac Pitman had devised as the way to 'Progress in all things'. Setting mankind free from the drudgery of conventional writing and spelling, Pitman's 'phonetic' system was intended to achieve prodigious levels of literacy; to provide a basis for a world language thereby dispelling one of the principal causes of international misunderstanding; and to bring the 'golden dream of a happy Millennium' to fulfilment. For Sturge it was 'one of the greatest blessings to mankind ever thought of': for his biographer it provides a particularly revealing insight into a mentality that bore little resemblance to the crude stereotype of the Victorian middle-class reformer.(12)

Thus when contemporaries called Sturge an extremist or fanatic they were closer to the truth than historians who have described him as respectable and moderate. By the end of the 1840s, after the Complete Suffrage movement had failed to take Westminster by frontal assault, he was behaving as if he could simply by-pass the politicians. He saw his circle of societies as something like a voluntaryist forum for canvassing a wide range of policies through which he and his friends could lead the world into a new era of peace and perfectibility. It was an exhilarating thought, and as he surveyed the state of public opinion in 1851 Sturge was understandably optimistic about the future: it was 'highly encouraging', he told his cousin Joseph Clark, 'to see that the newspapers of all parties seem to treat the

Great Exhibition as a great step on the side of Permanent & Universal Peace'.(13)

NOTES

1. National Temperance Chronicle, September 1851.
2. Parkin, Middle-Class Radicalism, pp. 2-3, 38, 41, 45, 60-77.
3. Wigham, A Christian Philanthropist Of Dublin, p. 14; Parkin, Middle Class Radicalism, pp. 27-31.
4. Bond of Brotherhood, June 1849.
5. Temperance Magazine and Review, April 1833.
6. T. Carlyle, 'Signs of the Times' in Thomas Carlyle: Selected Writings, ed., A. Shelston, Harmondsworth 1971, p. 63.
7. T.C. Upham, The Manual Of Peace, New York 1836, p. 145. See also my 'Making The Millennium: The Mid-Nineteenth Century Peace Movement', passim.
8. T.C. Upham, Principles of the Interior Or Hidden Life Designed Particularly For The Consideration Of Those Who Are Seeking Assurance Of Faith And Perfect Love, London 1874, pp. xiv, 12, 346-51, 415-16; West Sussex Record Office, Joseph Sturge to Richard Cobden, 6 May 1856. According to Lewis Tappan Sturge had a daguerrotype of Upham, The Papers of Lewis Tappan, Lewis Tappan to Joseph Sturge, 17 February 1856.
9. Sturge, A Visit To The United States, p. 107; [Samuel Brown], 'Physical Puritanism', Westminster And Foreign Quarterly Review, 1 April 1852, pp. 405-40.
10. Friends House Library, MS. Vol. S366, John Stephenson Rowntree's Account of Yearly Meeting, 1854.
11. Fonotipic Jurnal, 1849.
12. A. Baker, The Life of Sir Isaac Pitman (Inventor Of Phonography), London 1908, pp. 86-87; Phonetic Journal, 3 January 1852; Birmingham Journal, 16 December 1848; The Reading Reform, Bath, n.d.
13. C. & J. Clark Archive, Street, Box 386 Whitenight's (Sturge Papers), Joseph Sturge to Joseph Clark, 17 May 1851.

PART 6

DOWN THE HILL
OF LIFE

18 The Ravages of War (1851-55)

In 1851 eight strenuous years lay ahead of Sturge, the closing years of his life when he recognised that success would finally elude him. His hopes had hinged on the peace movement since the mid-1840s, and he had been optimistic as to its success, but in July 1852 he confessed to Cobden that he had 'little expectation of seeing any thing like the triumph of the Peace Cause' in his lifetime. Two years later he told his Baptist missionary correspondent, John Clark, that he foresaw 'all that is good' being thrown back for half a century as a divine judgment on the aggressive policies pursued by the British Government in the Near and Far East.(1) By then it was evident that the Great Exhibition had been an ambiguous indicator of public opinion, an interlude of international co-operation in an era that Cobden would call the time of 'The Three Panics', when public opinion displayed itself most typically in volatile swings from invasion hysteria to jingoistic bloodlusts.(2)

During the winter of 1850-51 Sturge had found himself in the midst of a remarkable outburst of xenophobic feeling after Pope Pius IX instituted the first Catholic diocesan hierarchy in England since the Reformation. The decision affected no one outside the Catholic Church, but it was provocatively announced and easily translated into the language of Protestant nationalism as 'The Papal Aggression', an attempt by a foreign power to exercise jurisdiction over England. It was the anti-Maynooth agitation over again. In Birmingham the 'pulpit drum ecclesiastic' was well beaten, virulently anti-Catholic graffiti appeared on the walls, and excited public meetings took place. This was one of the occasions when Sturge diverged most sharply from J.A. James; for the demon of Popery had lost none of its fascination in Carr's Lane. James urged his fellow Congregationalists to rally round the Church of England in opposition to the Pope, and at a town's meeting he endorsed an address to the Crown calling for action against 'one of the most foul, daring, and dangerous aggressions of modern times'. At every turn, however, James and his Anglican associates were opposed by a group describing itself as 'The Friends of Civil and Religious Liberty'. Sturge wrote to the press condemning the Church of England for causing the outburst, and at the town's meeting he led a succession of speakers who offered an amendment defending the liberties of Catholics. With fine impartiality the audience of 10,000 voted against both the address to the Crown and Sturge's amendment, but in the circumstances this was seen as a check to the 'No Popery' faction.(3) Congratulating Sturge for his 'stand against the plague of bigotry', Cobden commented favourably on the progress of the public mind in Birmingham since the 'Church and King' riots of 1791.(4)

It was a temporary victory. In 1852 there was another outburst of hysteria after Louis Napoleon carried out a coup d'etat as the first step to declaring himself 'Emperor of the French'. Britain, it was said, would soon be invaded by an army eager to avenge the defeat at Waterloo. For several years the possibility of an invasion had been used to justify proposals for national rearmament, and there was a growing literature, much of it written by army officers, pointing to the supposed weakness of Britain in comparison with the growing power of France. The quality of what could pass for an analysis of defence and foreign policy at this time may be seen in Sir Francis Bond Head's book, The Defenceless State of Great Britain. After setting out the belief that the French had secured an advantage in the technology of steam-powered warships, the book builds up to a climax where Head describes the likely course of events after a sudden invasion across the Channel by 200,000 troops. Marching under standards inscribed with the words 'BOOTY, BEAUTY, AND REVENGE' the French easily occupy London where they commandeer the best houses for themselves and stable their horses in the churches. Plunder and heavy war indemnities reduce the country to anarchy, allowing 'the enemy within' (to use a modern term) to exploit its long-awaited opportunity: 'English republicans'; demagogues inciting the poor to 'plunder and rapine'; and bodies of men swarming 'out of the shafts of our collieries and of our mines, from our manufactories and from our fields'.(5) Head was a fanatic, but his book provides an excellent case study in the pathology of the English upper class mentality; for ideas such as these were well received in some surprising quarters. George Grote and Sir Joshua Walmsley, Radicals though they were, wrote to Cobden recanting the support they had given to his disarmament proposals: the mere thought of French soldiers marching on London was enough to make anyone shudder, Grote confessed.(6)

Cobden's letters to Sturge registered a sense of despair about his fellow countrymen during these years. Such was Britain's reputation for belligerence, he wrote on 3 January 1852, that he had read about rumours circulating in the fastnesses of Tibet to the effect that 'the English were a species of sea-monster, with red hair vomited out of the ocean upon the coast of China'. He did not agree with Sturge's belief that a wide franchise would provide a remedy by making the Government responsive to the wishes of the people, but they both agreed that a sinister vested interest was benefiting from the war scares - 'Old Corruption' in its modern form of Clubland where peers and MPs schemed and plotted to provide military careers for their dependents.(7) Time after time Sturge and Cobden summoned up the resources of the peace movement to resist the recurrent outbreaks of war fever. In 1852 a Militia Bill provided them with a focus for their agitation, and on 6 February the Peace Congress Committee was reconstituted to organise a campaign of public meetings across the country. 'Myriads' of tracts and posters were sent out to every place where a sympathiser could be found to distribute them, and 1400 petitions with a quarter of a million signatures were sent to Parliament. 'If a dozen men in the Kingdom would work as you do', Cobden told Sturge at this time, 'we should never hear again of a militia'.(8)

Sturge and Cobden worked well together, but there was a major difference between their approaches. Cobden's opposition to the Militia Bill was conducted through Parliament, public meetings and the press: when the Bill was passed he was content to wait for its bad effects to justify repeal.(9) Sturge, on the other hand, was prepared to use any means short of violence to stop the implementation of a scheme that would destroy all the social progress achieved since the Napoleonic Wars. At a young man's anti-militia meeting in Finsbury Chapel on 26 May 1852 he and other members of the platform party roundly described the militia as an unbearable outrage which would take 'intelligent, virtuous and religious young men' from work, family and education to expose them to flogging and billeting in gin shops.(10) When the Militia Bill was enacted in June the Peace Society quickly unleashed a vigorous campaign to sabotage the new system by flooding the country with illustrated placards entitled Flogging in the New Militia and Don't Enlist in the New Militia. Alexander Somerville, whose brutal experiences in the Scots Greys twenty years earlier provided the inspiration for the placards, saw them 'posted on the pillars of gateways, on the stumps of wayside trees, on the bridge, on the stile, down the meadow, up the hill, on the corner house of the village'. Spencer Walpole, the Home Secretary, hotly challenged the peace movement's right to act in this way, and there were reports of country magistrates, policemen and clergymen destroying the posters and instituting prosecutions. One clergyman even fired a shot through a window shutter where a placard was displayed. It was all too much for the more timid and respectable members of the Peace Society, men such as the 'weighty Friend' Josiah Forster who had opposed this sort of campaign from the first. Henry Richard publicly likened them to 'sentimental ladies', but the campaign was called off.(11)

Sturge would not concede victory to the Government as easily as this. On 3 December 1852, he and his brothers Charles and Edmund joined sixty members of the Peace Society in sending a declaration to the Home Secretary where they took full responsibility for the anti-militia posters and insisted that any prosecutions should be directed 'not against printers and bill-stickers, but against ourselves'. Cobden and Bright simultaneously threatened a back-bench revolt, and Lord Palmerston, the new Home Secretary, wisely allowed the matter to drop. The episode was an interesting demonstration of the importance of the 'pressure from without' in nineteenth-century Britain. The peace movement had lost the contest over the militia, but it had widened the issue into one where civil rights were involved and had consolidated the area of personal liberty. Nonetheless, there was certainly something to be said for Palmerston's reference at this time to a group of 'well-intentioned fanatics': all too easily Sturge's crusades could degenerate into eccentric posturing.(12) In September 1852 when the Duke of

Wellington died and was honoured by a magnificent state funeral, Sturge's supporters divided the Birmingham Town Council over a proposal that the shops should close on that day, and subsequently he and his friends had handbills posted all over the town objecting on Christian principle to the use of death as a triumphant spectacle of militarism.   On the day of the funeral the lonely figure of Charles Sturge was to be seen bearing silent testimony as he stood at his usual place in the Corn Exchange.(13)   It was all to no avail: private consciences could be satisfied in this way, but public opinion was unmoved.

Throughout 1852 Sturge and his friends resisted the invasion scare on two fronts. While they opposed the Militia Bill in Britain they were trying to strengthen relations with the French people in the hope of stopping the two Governments from drifting into war.   This was another exercise in 'people diplomacy'.   The League of Universal Brotherhood had virtually been absorbed into the Peace Congress movement by this time, but Burritt, always something of a 'ladies' man' according to Sturge, had launched a women's 'Olive Leaf Mission' in 1850 to create an international public opinion favourable to ideas of peace. In the early 1850s there were 150 local Olive Leaf Circles with a combined membership of 3000, and they were paying for the insertion of Olive Leaf peace messages in European newspapers 'from the Sicilies to Iceland, and from the Straits of Gibraltar to the White Sea'. During the French war scare they obtained signatures from nearly fifty large towns in Britain for 'friendly international addresses' which Burritt delivered to similar towns in France.(14)

But the day for demonstrations of this sort was passing. Cobden's argument was unanswerable; the greatest threat to peace was at home. Throughout 1852 and 1853 he held Sturge to 'a practical line', cautioning him against any idea of making direct overtures to Napoleon III or doing anything to create the impression that this was a movement of 'Sturge & Co. against the world'.(15)   The international peace convention planned to take place in Amsterdam during 1852 was cancelled, and with the help of Charles Gilpin (his nephew) and Henry Richard, Sturge organised a national conference in Manchester on 27-28 January 1853 to withstand the invasion hysteria. Such was the state of public opinion that Richard was fearful of failure until the last minute, but Sturge would listen to no doubts 'as to the wisdom & sure success of the Conference', so intent was he on making this the most important mobilisation of the movement yet held.(16) It was certainly the most practical and purposeful. There were none of the Red Indians and escaped slaves who had titillated audiences at the earlier peace congresses; this time reports referred to over 500 'gentlemen of status and character' from all over Britain, including 17 MPs, the chief magistrates of several large towns, over seventy ministers and a large contingent of merchants, manufacturers and professional men. George Wilson, the former President of the Anti-Corn Law League, was in the chair, and there was a deliberate attempt to revive the rhetoric and strategy that had forced The Times to accept the League as 'a great fact' ten years previously.   In its most important decision the conference set up £10,000 fund to pay for a team of lecturers and a massive distribution of tracts to hold the country back from the brink of war.(17)

Never did the peace movement look more impressive than at this time. The conference set up a Home Conference Committee which divided the task of agitating the country between the Peace Congress Committees of London and Manchester. £8000 were raised; and in nine months 160 public meetings were held in England and Wales and half a million pamphlets were distributed.(18) Sturge did not address many public meetings, but he was 'overwhelmed with engagements in trying to stop this war cry'. At the Manchester Conference he and Thomas Thomasson, a wealthy Lancashire manufacturer, pledged £500 if eight others would do the same, and subsequently he was the principal fund-raiser of the movement. He served on the Agency Committee which was set up after the Conference, bringing with him as lecturers many old friends from the reform movements of the previous ten years: Henry Vincent, Arthur O'Neill, Thomas Beggs, Samuel Bowly and Robert Charlton.(19) One of his most important services was to act as a link between the Quaker-dominated Peace Society and the free traders whom Cobden had attracted into the new movement: at a time when fears were sometimes voiced that the pacifist principle was being eroded by the more limited policies of arbitration and disarmament, Sturge stood guarantor that nothing would be done to violate the beliefs of the Quakers who were making a disproportionate contribution to the movement's work and funds. 'I hope that nothing was said or done ... to weaken the Quaker zeal in our movement', Cobden told Henry Richard in October 1853. 'If so, Sturge ... & the more orthodox of the leaders must set to work to solder the crevices. - We are nothing without the "Friends".'(20)

Briefly the movement seemed to be successful: by June 1853 Henry Richard was able to report that the peace lecturers were obtaining a hearing 'beyond their most sanguine expectations' and that they need only persevere to convince 'the enlightened communities'.(21) Sturge felt free to turn aside and concentrate on another of his good causes, the languishing anti-slavery movement. He was encouraged to do so by the remarkable success of Harriet Beecher Stowe's novel, Uncle Tom's Cabin, which appeared in forty editions within a year of its publication in Britain in 1852, exciting public opinion about the horrors of slavery for the first time in a decade. The news that Mrs Stowe was to visit Britain in 1853 must have looked like a heaven-sent opportunity to bring the British anti-slavery movement back to life. It mattered very little that she was undistinguished in appearance: 'a little body', Henry Richard called her, 'with a countenance plain enough, but not wanting in intellect, slovenly in her dress and shambling in her gait, leaning with her elbows on the table in a manner that would not be deemed very lady-like in this country'.(22) Her name was what counted, and by inviting her to Birmingham for a private visit at the beginning of May 1853 Sturge persuaded her to endorse the free produce movement, the one flickering sign of life in British abolitionism.

The use Sturge made of Harriet Beecher Stowe was a good example of the separate sphere allocated to women in public life.

Because of its connection with household management the free produce movement was often described as a suitable philanthropy for women, and the possibility that a 'female pen' would be 'the instrument of overthrowing the monster slavery' in America raised 'interesting and glorious' prospects for Sturge when he invited Mrs Stowe to Birmingham.(23)   According to her own account, Sturge set her womanly mission before her with all his 'unflinching perseverence and energy of purpose'. At 64 Wheeley's Road she was shown the range of comforts that a free produce household could provide; she heard of Sophia's work for the sugar boycott in the 1820s; and she was told that Elizabeth Heyrick's pamphlet, Immediate Not Gradual Abolition, was the foundation document of British abolitionism. Even when she went sightseeing to Stratford-on-Avon there was no respite: as they rode along Sturge kept up 'a brisk conversation on the peace question, on the abolition of slavery, on the possibility of ignoring slave-grown produce, on Mr. Cobden and Mr. Bright, and, in fact, on all the most wide-awake topics of the present day'. The Women's Olive Leaf Circles were associated with the anti-slavery movement, and Sturge brought Elihu Burritt to Birmingham to present Mrs Stowe with a declaration which emphasised the importance of 'a full and strong testimony to the disuse of slave grown produce'. Eventually, at a gathering of 150 people in his house, he received his reward when Professor and Mrs Stowe endorsed the free produce movement.(24)

The next move had been prepared by the time of the Stowes' arrival. With Hannah Sturge taking a prominent part, the Birmingham Ladies Negro Friend Society had assumed responsibility for raising an 'Uncle Tom Penny Offering' to stimulate public interest and give Mrs Stowe £2000 to spend on abolitionist good causes of her choice. A group of prominent philanthropists consisting of the Earl of Shaftesbury, the Earl of Carlisle, Sir E.N. Buxton, Samuel Gurney, George W. Alexander and Sturge agreed to act as trustees. But, although contributions were raised from four hundred places, it was all rather disappointing. Only £1800 were raised (helped out by some large donations), and any favourable impact on public opinion was quickly swept aside by the worsening international situation during the second half of 1853.(25) On 2 June, exactly a month after Mrs Stowe's visit to Birmingham, the British Cabinet despatched a fleet to Besika Bay near the Dardanelles to strengthen the position of the Turkish Government which had rejected a series of Russian demands for protectorate rights over the Sultan's Christian subjects. Undeterred, on 2 July a Russian army invaded the Turkish province of Moldavia. In a series of moves and counter-moves which a later age would have called 'brinkmanship' Britain and Russia drifted towards a war that was desired by neither government.

Henry Richard's optimistic belief that the anti-French hysteria would soon vanish was vindicated, but not in the way he anticipated. Napoleon III, who had his own quarrel with the Czar, sent a fleet to co-operate with the Royal Navy at Besika Bay and by a sudden bouleversement of public opinion the French were hailed as allies against the threat from the East. 'What strangely inconsistent beings professing Christians are', Sturge told Tappan on 8 July:(26)

A few months ago Louis Napoleon was held up as a monster in human shape, and we were put to great expense to prepare against the pretended danger, that he and his people would turn pirates, and suddenly come over to murder and rob us. Now we are uniting our fleet with that of this very monster to fight with the Turks against a professedly Christian country, whose Emperor tells us that he has no object of conquest in view, but solely the protection of his fellow-Christians from the persecutions of those Turks.

Sturge's comment missed the most important point: Russophobia was so endemic in Britain during the nineteenth century that, with the possible exception of the Irish, no nation had a less flattering stereotype in British eyes than the Russians. They were savage tribes only awaiting the emergence of a latter-day Attila to send them surging across the civilised world; they were a nation of serfs ruled by the most autocratic monarchy in Europe; and they were a threat to British imperial interests in the Mediterranean and Asia. Many liberals and radicals remembered the Russians as the conquerors of the Poles in 1831 and the Hungarians in 1849, and there was a general tendency to endow any enemy of the Russians with the most remarkable of virtues. No nation benefited more from this blinkered vision than the Turks: after centuries of execration as the scourge of Christendom they were suddenly transformed during the mid-Victorian era into a free-trading, tolerant and reforming people led by Sultans who could be ranked with 'the Alfreds and Edwards' of English history. There was an onrush of indiscriminate enthusiasm for things Turkish, and David Urquhart, who introduced the Turkish bath to Britain at this time, founded Foreign Affairs Committees in many parts of the country to whip up anti-Russian sentiment. Joseph Constantine marvelled to see former Chartists and Owenites rallying to a 'strange mixture of a creed of faith - Free Trade, Foreign Affairs, and Turkish Baths - Politico - Medico - Sanitary'.(27) It was to no avail that Cobden and other peace spokesmen urged their compatriots to do nothing to support the Turks 'with their polygamy, slave-trade, plague & indolence'; they could not shake the dominant stereotypes.(28) Nor could they dispel what they saw as the naiveté of democrats who had condemned the 'rotten House of Commons' for twenty years and now wanted its members to stand forth as the champions of liberty.

Even before the Russian crisis deepened Sturge and his friends had been making arrangements to hold a Peace conference in Edinburgh at which they could develop their organisation and strategy. Now they turned it into a demonstration of opposition to the preparations for war with Russia, and with the help of the United Presbyterian and Scottish Baptist Churches they prepared the ground well by the time the conference opened on 12 October. 200,000 pamphlets were distributed in Scottish towns and care was taken to ensure a large attendance. In the circumstances the conference was something of a triumph. Not only did the delegates condemn any war with Russia, but they set out their programme at length to vindicate themselves against the charge that they had no positive policy proposals. They called for arbitration of disputes, arms reductions, non-intervention in the affairs of other nations, and the reform of colonial government to avoid threats of war. To unite the peoples of the world they proposed international free trade, an international mercantile law, cheap international postage and the introduction of common weights, measures and coinage.(29)

But the conference was immediately overtaken by events. A few days earlier the Turks had declared war on the Russians, and public pressure on the British Government to intervene welled up after 30 November when the Russians destroyed a Turkish flotilla off Sinope in the Black Sea. This 'massacre' produced such a frenzy that the Government was swept along by what Lord Aberdeen called the bullying tone of the newspapers, and embarked on a gradual escalation of preparations for war. Sturge despaired to see the number of defectors from the peace movement at this time. On 17 December 1853 he told John Clark that there was little likelihood of averting Britain's involvement in a 'mad war', so strong was the prevalent Russophobia 'especially amongst those who sympathise with Kossuth & the Hungarians'. 'I am sorry to say', he added, 'that amongst these are some even of the Dissenting ministers. I may name one of your Body Mursell of Leicester'.(30)

The peace movement did not even dare to hold public meetings at this time. A tract entitled Ought England To Go To War with Russia was widely distributed, and in a last demonstration of their efficiency as agitators the Peace Society and the Peace Congress Committees of London and Manchester sent a packet of tracts to every elector in Liverpool, Leeds, Carlisle, Bradford, York, Leicester, Hull, Halifax, Lancaster, Oldham, Bury, Doncaster, Knaresborough, Wigan, Clitheroe, Pontefract and Beverley. In Manchester, Sheffield and in several other places they sent tracts to every house.(31) But by the beginning of 1854 Sturge had lost faith in this strategy; he could see no alternative to one last desperate expedient - a direct appeal to the Czar. His decision illustrates the perennial difficulty of peace movements during the last one hundred and fifty years: unlike the liberal West, the eastern autocracies have not allowed appeals to public opinion. In this case there could be no exchange of 'friendly international addresses' between British and Russian towns, no 'people diplomacy' involving private citizens in the Czarist state. But by a swift change of argument this was now portrayed as an advantage: in Russia there was only one person to win over.(32)

Horrified by the proposal, Cobden wrote several letters to Sturge condemning an 'irrational step' which could only weaken the peace movement at home, and Sturge himself was frankly pessimistic about the prospects. He told his brother Charles that he scarcely expected even to reach St Petersburg, but that he had been strongly urged to go and did not believe he could refuse.(33) Robert Charlton and Henry Pease agreed to act with him, and they persuaded the Society of Friends to accredit them as a religious mission. Sturge was entrusted with an address which did not 'presume to offer any opinion upon the question now at issue' but only asked Nicholas I to follow peaceful policies which would 'exhibit to the nations... the efficacy of the Gospel of Christ'. The appeal was less forlorn than it looked. Quakers had enjoyed a special relationship with members of the Russian royal family since the reign of the pietistic Alexander I, and they could count on a favourable reception at the Imperial court.(34)

On 20 January the deputation set out on its difficult and dangerous mission. At the age of sixty Sturge was embarking on a journey through Russia by road in the depth of winter knowing that at any moment he might be caught up in the outbreak of war. He was not afraid, he told Charles, but realistically he left instructions about the arrangements which were to be made in the event of his death. They provide an interesting revelation of the thoughts that came instinctively to his mind. One third of his capital was to be disposed of for charitable and benevolent objects before his children came of age, so that they would not be corrupted by inherited wealth; he wished to have a sailors' home opened in Gloucester complete with newspapers and non-intoxicating drinks; and measures were to be taken to break up the afternoon public house market in the same town. For the rest he strictly charged Charles to avoid business risks and not to give excessive credit.(35)

The first part of the journey across the Continent was accomplished swiftly and comfortably by rail as far as Koenigsberg in East Prussia, but there were few railways in backward Russia, and from there Sturge and his friends had to proceed by road in an enclosed carriage. At Riga the wheels were removed, and the carriage was placed on a sledge to avoid the extreme conditions of the road to St Petersburg. Apart from 'an occasional great shake' and one minor mishap near the frozen shores of Lake Peipus when their driver ran the vehicle off the road they travelled safely, and Sturge found the climate invigorating. Following the precedents of his earlier missions to the West Indies and the Duchies, he had refused to act through official British representatives, and he was furious when he heard from Charles that someone had told the Cabinet about the mission. A brief encounter was enough to convince Sturge that the British ambassador in St Petersburg was unfit for his post, and 'of course' he declined an invitation to dine. Instead he directly appealed to Count Nesselrode, the Imperial Chancellor, who granted an interview and arranged for the deputation to see the Czar on 10 February. In the meanwhile Russian officials treated them cordially, even throwing open the great art collections of the Hermitage in the belief that this would afford the three Quakers some pleasure. Sturge, who had 'very much outlived' his curiosity for such spectacles, went along only to avoid giving offence and was much more gratified a day later when he was taken to see a school.

The interview with the Czar passed off well. Sturge was allowed to read the address from the Society of Friends, and a general discussion took place which gave him an opportunity to air his views on arbitration. Robert Charlton thought that Nesselrode and the Czar were impressed by Sturge's 'frank and open manner, his obvious sincerity and transparency of character, and the great simplicity and depth of feeling with which he advocated the cause of peace'. In his reply the Czar stood by his determination to protect the Orthodox

Christians in the Turkish Empire and uphold the honour of his country, but briefly Sturge's hopes soared when he was given to understand that he might be entrusted with an official message to take back to Britain. This came to nothing after reports reached St Petersburg that further demonstrations of Russophobia had occurred in the House of Commons, and on a second visit to the Court the deputation was treated with cold formality by members of the Royal Family. Fearing the worst, they returned home, arriving in London on 23 February 1854.(36) Although Lord Aberdeen granted Sturge an interview, the Cabinet had already despatched the fleet into the Black Sea, and on 27 February Britain and France sent an ultimatum demanding the withdrawal of Russian forces from Turkish territory. On 31 March they declared war.

Sturge was never inactive for long, but the outbreak of the Crimean War threatened to paralyze even his energies: 'We have little right to admonish other nations on slavery or anything else', he told Louis Tappan in December 1854, 'while we are sending our people to commit wholesale murder on the territories of another sovereign'.(37) Therefore it was only with reluctance that he allowed himself to be involved in an attempt to revive the anti-slavery movement at the end of 1854. After twelve years of bitter feuding with Garrison's followers, John Scoble had resigned as secretary of the British and Foreign Anti-Slavery Society in 1852, and his place had been taken by Louis Alexis Chamerovzow, a tolerant and witty man who even succeeded in wringing from the earnest Henry Richard the concession that laughter had a 'medicinal' value. Seeing himself as a peacemaker, Chamerovzow made overtures to the British Garrisonians and obtained their support for a conference of reconciliation which met in London on 29 and 30 December 1854. For a time it looked as if he would succeed. George Thompson, the best known of the British Garrisonians, was prepared to accept Sturge's insistence that only the most anodyne of references should be made to the rival American anti-slavery societies, and Sturge accepted the presence of women delegates. But the conference broke down when Parker Pilsbury, an American visitor, truculently vindicated Garrison's actions. Chamerovzow and Thompson covered up the failure of the conference as best they could, but the lingering decline of the movement was resumed.(38)

The peace movement declined more rapidly at this time. The movements of the British and French navies in the Baltic and Black Seas, the landing of the expeditionary force in the Crimea, and the early battles gave the war an irresistible momentum for several months. The rise of a popular press during the previous two decades meant that this was the first major war ever to be extensively reported, and an overwrought public opinion was buoyed up by hopes of a victory which would enable Britain to re-draw the map of Europe and the Near East. Speakers at public meetings - 'our fighting democrats' Cobden called them - looked forward to the independence of Poland, Hungary and Italy as the fruits of war.(39) Probably the greatest disappointment for Sturge was the return to Birmingham of the military recruiting parties which he and Arthur O'Neill had ousted during the previous decade. With its drums, fifes and ribbons, the first to be seen in the town for many years attracted large crowds, and soon there were ten of them at work. The steady trickle of defectors from the peace movement now became a flood. Mouthpieces of Dissent such as the Patriot and the Leeds Mercury called for a vigorous war effort, and eventually they were joined by Edward Miall's Nonconformist. Opponents of the war were branded as traitors; John Bright was burned in effigy; and Anthony Trollope digressed from his plot in The Warden (published in 1855) to sneer at Cobden and the Quakers for the aid they were giving the Czar. Sturge, Pease and Charlton were blamed for the war because of the impression they were supposed to have given of Britain's weakness.(40)

Sturge never made any attempt to hide his conviction that Britain was responsible for an unjust war: public opinion must take the blame, he told the Peace Society's annual meeting in mid-1854.(41) More boldly still, towards the end of the year he and George Wilson organised a poster campaign in Birmingham, Manchester and other cities to challenge the prevailing cult of military glory. One of the posters which was entitled 'War and Dear Bread' plunged him into a highly embarrassing controversy; as Sturge ought to have known, Quaker corn dealers had been blamed for bread shortages and high prices on many occasions during the previous hundred years, and in a predictable riposte he was accused of war profiteering. Harriet Martineau, the celebrated authoress of the Illustrations of Political Economy, gave her support to the case against him, and a former employee accused J. & C. Sturge of 'selfishness, hypocrisy and cunning'. Sturge defended himself in a pamphlet, The Russian War. To My Fellow Townsmen of the Working Classes, but the damage had been done.(42) Conspiracy theories were more attractive than the obvious truth that high bread prices were inevitable when warfare affected the Black Sea ports from which Britain at that time obtained much of her grain supply.

The charge of war profiteering re-emerged in mid-1855 after the Royal Navy devastated the Russian port of Kertch at the entrance to the Sea of Azov: it was said J. & C. Sturge had lost large amounts of grain from stocks they had been using to trade with the Russian Government. Much of this was wishful (and spiteful) thinking, but the reports were not as fanciful as Sturge's Corn Circular made out when it denied that the firm had been holding grain at Kertch. What the Circular did not say was that J & C Sturge had bought up 10,000 quarters of wheat in other Sea of Azov ports when prices had dropped to one third of their normal value because of the Allied blockade. All through the war the Sturges must have followed reports of fleet movements with considerable anxiety. They were lucky; only a small amount of their stock was destroyed, and when the ports were re-opened the partnership made a profit of £11,400.(43)

Sturge was undeterred by the personal attacks. By the beginning of 1855 he was convinced that the war fever was abating and that the time had come to revive the peace movement. In January he chaired a meeting in London which launched a placard campaign throughout the boroughs of England, and he personally assumed responsibility for overseeing this work in ten counties. Later in the month he went to Manchester to arrange further action. Back in London, at a meeting on

213

13 February he offered to organise a lecture campaign, and during the next few months he sent out a team of speakers. George Thompson toured the northern towns; Arthur O'Neill went through the Midlands; and Samuel Bowly, Robert Charlton and Henry Richard took to the platform in other parts of the country. The news of Nicholas I's death in March (this 'wonderful providence' Sturge called it) and the signs that Napoleon III was becoming war weary raised hopes of peace, and in April Sturge spoke of pressing the combatants to accept American mediation. The suggestion brought down on him the obvious rejoinder from Cobden that recent history scarcely qualified the United States for the role of peacemaker. Elihu Burritt had independently reached the same pessimistic conclusion. Returning to America he had received the chilling reply from President Pierce that, although American foreign policy could accommodate arbitration as a general principle, no action would be taken to imply that the American Government would allow third parties to restrict its own right to expand 'in any legitimate direction' such as Cuba.(44)

Throughout 1855 Sturge and his friends persevered with the campaign of pamphlet distribution and lecturing. Some of their meetings were interrupted by patriotic crowds, but there was remarkably little violence on the whole, and by the end of the year their efforts were being reinforced by a very active 'Stop the War' movement in which George Thompson, L.A. Chamerovzow, Bronterre O'Brien and other public speakers went out to give lectures to working-class audiences.(45) Eventually, however, the burden of organisation and fund-raising proved too much even for Sturge's strength. In August 1855 Elihu Burritt wrote that he had never seen Sturge looking so feeble. He suffered from severe attacks of lumbago and walked with difficulty, but he would not relent until at the beginning of December a heart-attack almost killed him. Only then did he agree to go for a month's recuperation to Torquay, but all too soon he was assuring his correspondents that he was 'nicely recovered' and taking up his burdens again. Lewis Tappan's advice did nothing to slow him down: 'These illnesses are warnings, very kindly meant to prepare us for our removal, which must take place ere long'. During the four years that remained to him Sturge was spurred on by the belief that he would soon die.(46)

NOTES

1. Brit. Lib. Add. MSS. 50131, ff. 275-76, Joseph Sturge to Richard Cobden, 27 July 1852; The Fenn Collection, E19Y, Joseph Sturge to John Clark, 1 April 1854.

2. Richard Cobden, 'The Three Panics. An Historical Episode' in The Political Writings Of Richard Cobden With An Introductory Essay By Sir Louis Mallet, C.B., London 1878, pp. 301-94.

3. Birmingham Journal, 7 December, 14 December 1850.

4. Brit. Lib. Add. MSS. 50131, ff. 252-54, Richard Cobden to Joseph Sturge, 12 December 1850.

5. Spiers, The Army and Society 1815-1914, pp. 91-92; Sir Francis Bond Head, The Defenceless State Of Great Britain, London 1850.

6. Brit. Lib. Add. MSS. 43668, ff. 148-51, George Grote to Richard Cobden, 26 December 1851; West Sussex Record Office, Cobden 62, Richard Cobden to Joseph Sturge, 12 October 1852.

7. Brit. Lib. Add. MSS. 43656, ff. 237-38, Richard Cobden to Joseph Sturge, 3 January 1852; ibid., ff. 227-8, Richard Cobden to Joseph Sturge, 6 October 1851; West Sussex Record Office, Cobden 62, Richard Cobden to Joseph Sturge, 16 October 1852.

8. Herald of Peace, June 1852; West Sussex Record Office, Cobden 64, Richard Cobden to Joseph Sturge, 11 April 1852.

9. Brit. Lib. Add. MSS. 43656, ff. 311-12, Richard Cobden to Joseph Sturge, 19 October 1852.

10. Herald of Peace, June 1852.

11. Minute Book of the Transactions Of The Peace Society, 13 July, 11 August, 6 September, 13 September, 27 September, 6 October 1852. On 11 November the committee made a payment to Somerville in response to a begging letter complaining about their use of his name. See also A. Somerville, Conservative Science Of Nations, (Preliminary Instalment,) Being The First Complete Narrative Of Somerville's Diligent Life In The Service Of Public Safety In Britain Montreal 1860, pp. 296-99; Herald of Peace, September, October and November 1852.

12. Herald of Peace, March, June 1853; National Library of Wales, MS 10199B, Henry Richard's Diary, 26 February 1853.

13. Woodbrooke College, Bevan-Naish Collection, vol. 2, 3002, collection of handbills dealing with Birmingham's response to the arrangements for Wellington's funeral.

14. The Olive Leaf Circles, Their Constitution And Operations, London n.d.; Friend, 1 October, 1 November 1852. The reference to Burritt as a 'ladies man' is in Rhodes House, MSS Brit. Emp. C111/19, Joseph Sturge to L.A. Chamerovzow, 17 November 1854.

15. Brit. Lib., Add. MSS. 43657, f. 180, Richard Cobden to Henry Richard, 18 January 1853; West Sussex Record Office, Cobden 64, Richard Cobden to Joseph Sturge, 30 January 1852.

16. Manchester Public Library, Wilson Papers, Henry Richard to George Wilson, 1 October 1852, Joseph Sturge to George Wilson, 2 October, 7 December, 9 December 1852; Minute Book of the Transactions Of The Peace Society, 6 October 1852; National Library of Wales, MS 10199B, Henry Richard's Diary, 7 January 1853.

17. Herald of Peace, February, April, June 1853.

18. Peace Conference Committee Minutes (1845-55), 14 February 1853; Reports Of The Peace Congresses At Brussels, Paris, Frankfort, London, and Edinburgh, In The Years 1848, 1849, 1850, 1851 and 1853, London 1861, Edinburgh Congress, pp. 4-5.

19. National Library of Wales, MS 10199B, Henry Richard's Diary, 24 January-26 February 1853; Manchester Public Library, Wilson Papers, Joseph Sturge to George Wilson, 10 February, 28 February, 11 April 1853; Herald of Peace, April, May, June 1853.

20. Brit. Lib., Add. MSS. 43657, ff. 217-18, Richard Cobden to Henry Richard, 17 October 1853.

21. Manchester Public Library, Wilson Papers, Henry Richard to George Wilson, June 1853.

22. National Library of Wales, MS 10199B, Henry Richard's Diary, May/June 1853.

23. The Slave; His Wrongs, And Their Remedy, January 1851; Richard, Sturge, p. 390.

24. H.B. Stowe, Sunny Memories Of Foreign Lands, Letters X, XII; Elihu Burritt, Journals, Journal 18, 2 May 1853; Friend, June 1853; British and Foreign Anti-Slavery Society Reporter, June 1853; Rhodes House, MSS Brit. Emp. S18, C111/4, Joseph Sturge to L.A. Chamerovzow, 2 May 1853; Friends Library, Elihu Burritt, MS Vol. S101, Elihu Burritt to A.M. Southall, 3 May 1853; Birmingham Journal, 7 May 1853.

25. Birmingham Ladies Negro Friend Society, Reports (1845-1889), Reports for 1853 and 1854; British and Foreign Anti-Slavery Society Reporter, June, July 1853 and May 1854.

26. Richard, Sturge, p. 461.

27. J.H. Gleason, The Genesis of Russophobia in Great Britain; a study in the interaction of policy and opinion, Cambridge, USA 1950; Kingsley Martin, The Triumph of Lord Palmerston, London 1963, especially chap. VI; Taylor, The Troublemakers, chap. II; J. Constantine, Fifty Years Of The Water Cure With Autobiographical Notes, London 1892, pp. 34-35.

28. Sturge Papers (Lewin), Richard Cobden to Charles Sturge, 11 August 1853.

29. Reports Of The Peace Congresses At Brussels, Paris, Frankfort, London, and Edinburgh, In The Years 1848, 1849, 1850, 1851 and 1853, Edinburgh Congress; Herald of Peace, November 1853.

30. Fenn Collection, E19Y, Joseph Sturge to John Clark, 17 December 1853.

31. Herald of Peace, June 1854; Minute Book of the Transactions Of The Peace Society, 18 January 1854.

32. Richard, Sturge, p. 463.

33. Brit. Lib., Add. MSS. 43722, f. 8, Richard Cobden to Joseph Sturge, 3 January 1854; ibid., ff. 10-11, Richard Cobden to Joseph Sturge, 15 January 1854; ibid., Add. MSS. 50131, ff. 278-80, Richard Cobden to Joseph Sturge, 10 January 1854; Sturge Papers (M. Sturge), Joseph Sturge to Charles Sturge, 19 January 1854.

34. Herald of Peace, March 1854; Richard, Sturge, pp. 463-65.

35. Sturge Papers, (M. Sturge), Joseph Sturge to Charles Sturge, 18 January 1854.

36. The Russian mission is described in J. Sturge, R. Charleton, H. Pease, Some Account of a Deputation from the Religious Society of Friends to The Emperor of Russia, London 1854; Sturge Papers (M. Sturge), letters from Joseph Sturge to Charles Sturge, 18 January, 20 January, 29 January, 2 February, 4 February, 7 February 1854; A.F. Fox, Memoir of Robert Charleton. Compiled Chiefly From His Letters, London 1873, chap. V; Richard, Sturge, pp. 465-86.

37. Richard, Sturge, pp. 488-89.

38. Empire, 2 December, 9 December 1854, 20 January, 27 January 1855; British and Foreign Anti-Slavery Society Reporter, 1 January 1855; Dr Williams's Library, Estlin Collection, 24.120, Bristol and Clifton Auxiliary Ladies Anti-Slavery Society Minute Book, 16

November, 24 November, 7 December 1854; Rhodes House, MSS Brit. Emp. S18, C111/18, Joseph Sturge to L.A. Chamerovzow, 16 November 1854.

39. Brit. Lib., Add. MSS. 43722, ff. 38-39, Richard Cobden to Joseph Sturge, 11 January 1855.

40. Birmingham Journal, 29 April 1854; Brit. Lib., Add. MSS 43845, f. 47, Edward Baines to Joseph Sturge, 19 January 1855; Miall, Life of Edward Miall, p. 190; A. Peel, Three Hundred Years: A History Of The Congregational Union of England And Wales, 1831-1931, London 1931, p. 201; H. Ausubel, John Bright. Victorian Reformer, New York 1966, pp. 70-71; A. Trollope, The Warden, Oxford 1980, p. 131.

41. Herald of Peace, June 1854.

42. John Rylands University Library of Manchester, Raymond English Collection, F.W. Chesson Diaries, 21 October, 5 November, 9 November, 14 November, 18 November 1854; Birmingham Journal, 25 November, 9 December, 16 December, 30 December 1854, 3 February, 10 February 1855; Joseph Sturge, The Russian War. To My Fellow Townsmen Of The Working Classes, 2 December 1854.

43. Brit. Lib., Add. MSS. 43722, ff. 72-73, Richard Cobden to Joseph Sturge, 6 July 1855; J. & C. Sturge Corn Circular, 4 July 1855; Sturge Papers (Lewin), Joseph & Charles Sturge, 'Note On War With Russia'.

44. Manchester Public Library, Wilson Papers, Joseph Sturge to George Wilson, 3 January, 6 January, 3 March, 23 March, 14 April, 26 May, 8 June 1855; Minute Book of the Transactions Of The Peace Society, 14 May 1855; Peace Conference Committee Minutes (1848-55), 13 February, 23 May 1855; Herald of Peace, April, May, June 1855; Brit. Lib., Add. MSS. 43722, ff. 64-65, Richard Cobden to Joseph Sturge, 17 May 1855; Elihu Burritt, Journals, Journal 19, 24 March 1854.

45. Empire, 10 November 1855.

46. Burritt, Journals, Journal 20, 4 August 1855, 1 January 1856; West Sussex Record Office, Cobden 53, Joseph Sturge to Richard Cobden, 29 December 1855; Manchester Public Library, Wilson Papers, Joseph Sturge to George Wilson, 3 January 1856; The Papers of Lewis Tappan, Lewis Tappan to Joseph Sturge, 17 February 1856.

19 Faithful unto Death (1856-59)

Sturge's recovery in January 1856 coincided with the last phase of the Crimean War. Sebastopol had been stormed on 8 September 1855, and, although plans were made for extending the operations in the Black Sea and the Baltic, the winter was given over for the most part to the diplomatic manoeuvres which led to the opening of peace negotiations in Paris on 15 February 1856. The onset of peace brought little rejoicing in Britain: although war casualties had been high, as Cobden told Sturge on 21 January, this was 'one of the most resultless wars ever known'.(1)

> Everything for which everybody thought he was fighting will be unattained. The Turk will be a dying man, the Poles worse off by the hundreds of thousands dragged into the Russian army & half of them killed - the Circassians & Hungarians just where they were, & Austria more firmly fastened on the back of the Italians than ever.

Sturge was more single-minded; for him the ending of hostilities was a virtue in its own right, and the task was to transform it into a lasting peace. He had scarcely recovered from his heart attack before he was raising the possibility of launching an agitation for an arbitration treaty between the European Powers. Early in February 1856 the Peace Society got up a petitioning campaign to this end, and on 14 March Sturge was one of a large deputation from the Peace Committees of London and Manchester which pressed the idea on Lord Palmerston, the Prime Minister. They received a predictably chilly reception, but Sturge, Henry Richard and Charles Hindley proceeded to Paris a few days later with a memorial from the peace movement asking the assembled diplomats and their sovereigns to submit any disputes arising from the peace treaty to arbitration. Before they left, Cobden gave them his usual lecture on the mistake of sending 'missions to crowned heads and despotic governments': it was the equivalent of a Catholic pilgrimage to the shrine at Loretto, he told Sturge, 'a loss of labor & money' in both cases.(2)

It seemed at first that Cobden was right; Sturge's letters referred to the humiliating and unsuccessful experience of seeking an audience with Napoleon III.   Sturge was also embarrassed by a request from the British and Foreign Anti-Slavery Society that he should present the plenipotentiaries with an address condemning slavery in the Turkish Empire. Eventually he decided not to do so for fear of damaging the peace mission, a good indication of his altered priorities since the 1830s.   Then there was the difficulty of deciding what to do when Charles wrote and told him of the Russian government's procrastination in opening the ports on the Sea of Azov where J. & C. Sturge's speculative grain purchases were stored: the temptation to raise the matter with the Russian diplomatic mission in Paris was one he resisted with some difficulty. But his self-sacrifices seemed to be fruitless. By 30 March, when he saw Paris illuminated in honour of the peace, Sturge had failed to make any official contacts.(3)

As always he suspected that the Foreign Office and the Diplomatic Corps were intriguing against him, and he considered returning home, but suddenly he started to make progress. On 9 April he wrote that he had seen Lord Clarendon, the Foreign Secretary, who had agreed to press the other diplomats to insert an arbitration provision in the peace settlement. Possibly Clarendon had already decided to do this, for later there was some dispute over the extent to which he had been influenced by the Peace Society, but for whatever reason the Foreign Secretary kept his word. Writing to Palmerston a few days after the interview with Sturge he reported that he and Lord Cowley, the ambassador to Paris, had persuaded the Congress to issue a declaration in favour of mediating future disputes. With the proviso that they were not restricting their governments' freedom of action the plenipotentiaries had made this the twenty-third protocol of the peace treaty.(4)

On hearing the news Cobden handsomely recanted his opposition to the mission, congratulating Sturge on a great personal 'triumph' which had made arbitration a practical proposition for future diplomats. Sturge too was delighted, although the protocol fell short of the binding commitment he would have preferred: 'I think it would be difficult too highly to estimate the great moral effect which the Protocol No 23 will have through the world,' he wrote, 'adopted as it was unanimously by all the plenipotentiaries'.(5) It was time for a celebration, and he organised one in typical style. On 19 May, led by two bands of music, flags and banners, 4,000 children marched through the streets of Birmingham to Bingley Hall where he and Hannah presented them with books and a special peace medal, regaled them with milk and buns, and led most of them back to Sturge's Field for a session of sports and games.(6)

There was another reason for self-congratulation at this time. Thanks to Sturge's efforts, in March 1856 a London penny daily newspaper had been launched to support the peace movement. This was the outcome of the perennial grievance of Radicals that their ideas were under-represented and misrepresented by the press, especially by The Times, the opinion-maker of the political nation. Sturge and his friends saw The Times as the leader of the 'incendiaries' who had created the war hysteria of the 1850s, and when they learned that newspaper sales had increased during the Crimean War they concluded that most of the British press had acquired a vested interest in Palmerston's adventurous foreign policy.(7)

The solution favoured by many Radicals during the early 1850s was the repeal of the taxes which artificially increased the price of newspapers, for, naive though it now seems, they believed that a cheap press would place control of public opinion in their hands. The law had to be changed G.J. Holyoake (one of its victims) wrote, so that a newspaper proprietor would no longer be obliged to provide his products with official stamps if he wished to avoid having 'all his presses broken up, all his stock confiscated, himself and all persons in his house, imprisoned'.(8) Between 1851 and 1855 an Association for the Promotion of the Repeal of the Taxes on Knowledge carried on a spirited campaign to reform these obstructive laws. The movement caught up a wide variety of Radical and reforming opinion, but, as Cobden pointed out to C.D. Collet, its leading activist, it relied most heavily on the support of those who had been schooled in the ways of the 'moral Radical' movements of the previous two decades: 'cast your eye over the subscription list of the 'Association,' and you will see how exclusively, almost, we comprise steady, sober middle-class reformers - free trade, temperance, education, peace advocates - who will stand by you from year to year, and gather about them an increasing moral power'.(9) Sturge was an early supporter. As its Vice President, he told the annual meeting of the Birmingham Association for the Abolition of Taxes on Knowledge in January 1851 that these taxes were the worst parts of the evil of indirect taxation, and he attributed the higher educational standards of America to its cheaper literature and newspapers. Welcoming Sturge's interest, Cobden looked forward to the day when there would be a penny press.(10)

Sturge and Cobden returned to the idea early in 1855, encouraged by their belief that the Russian War had been created by the press. They must have a daily newspaper in London, Cobden told Sturge on 16 February, 'one representing the humanities - peace, temperance, antislavery etc. - in fact a New York Tribune, but avoiding its many errors & with some views on free trade which that paper has not - & it should go for free trade in land'. Taking up one of Sturge's suggestions, he went on to sketch out the scheme which ultimately gave rise to the Morning Star: a reliable publisher should be found to bring out the newspaper; capital should be raised from sympathisers throughout the country; and Bright, Wilson and Cobden should have the final say on policy.(11) The proposal was given momentum by the repeal of the newspaper stamp duty on 5 June 1853, and further discussions took place to which Horace Greeley of the New York Tribune provided advice and encouragement. It was agreed that a capital of £5000 would be needed to launch the newspaper of which roughly £3000 would have to be raised from members of the peace movement to give them a preponderating influence. The scheme was accepted at a meeting which Sturge attended in August, and policies were laid down for the new penny daily: parliamentary reform, religious equality, economical government and moderate taxation, opposition to the Russian War, non-intervention in foreign countries' affairs, smaller armed forces, and a decentralised form of public education which interfered with no one's religious rights.(12)   At the end of August Sturge set out on what he called 'a begging trip' that took him to Bristol, London and the towns of the North - Darlington, Sunderland, Newcastle, Carlisle and Kendal amongst others - where he brought his persuasive powers to bear on the Peases, Backhouses and other liberal Quakers.   He was so successful that by 15 September Cobden could congratulate him on his 'never-tiring energy in collecting so much money'. In all he seems eventually to have raised *2700.(13)

On 17 March 1856 the Morning Star and its companion, the Evening Star, appeared for the first time. 'You ought to be proud of your work', Cobden wrote to Sturge two days later: 'It is the most successful effort in the cause of peace & intelligent progress which even you have ever made'.(14)   But the venture was dogged with difficulties. It was typical of Cobden and Sturge that they should see the Morning Star as a provincial invader of the territory occupied by the 'Cockney press', and an impossible situation resulted when George Wilson and Henry Rawson (the owner of the Manchester Examiner) who had agreed to become the newspaper's proprietors, would not spend time in London, although the first editor, W.T. Haly, was unsatisfactory and his stop-gap replacement, John Hamilton, was unreliable and uninformed.(15)   The letters of Sturge, Richard, Bright and Cobden bristle with indignation about such mistakes as the transposition of marriages to the deaths column and vice versa; Hamilton's references to 'Aragonese' as the name of a Spanish general; the inaccurate publication of the corn market news which Charles Sturge had obtained; and the typographical errors which made the newspaper difficult to read.(16)   Then there was the problem of outside interference with reporting and editorial policy. It was all very well for Sturge to tell Wilson that 'the best plan to get it [the Star] as near perfection as possible is for its best friends to look out with an Eagle eye for its remaining faults and pointing them out for correction': he harassed   the editorial staff with his corrections.   The Star was intended to be a 'great moral engine', he wrote, but he had been disappointed by its line on peace. Nor had he expected to find theatre reports and sporting news designed to provide 'the blacklegs with gambling intelligence'.(17)

Gradually a routine emerged which satisfied Sturge on the whole, and together with Cobden and Bright he even discussed the idea of launching a weekly and a string of similar provincial dailies.(18) But nothing came of these plans, and the Star itself was never a success: in an era of exuberant nationalism it acquired such a reputation as 'a thoroughly anti-British paper' that it never had a high circulation. Although Sturge complained that he had not only spent two years' income but also made inroads into 'a limited capital' to launch the paper at a time when there were 'numerous other claims' on him, he had to go begging again in 1857. As late as May 1859, the month of his death, he received a further request for financial assistance. Before it was eventually swallowed up by the Daily News in 1869 the Morning Star is said to have lost £80,000.(19)

One of the reasons why the Star was so attractive to Sturge and his associates in 1856 was that it presented them with a means of profiting from the lessons of the previous two years; for the fear expressed by the Quaker diarist William Lucas was now becoming the conventional wisdom - there had been too much of 'a flash' about the peace movement before the war.(20) But, there was still some talk of taking up where the movement had left off in 1854, and when relations between Britain and the United States sharply deteriorated in 1856 a campaign was organised to send friendly international addresses from British churches and towns to their American counterparts. The League of Universal Brotherhood directed this 'people diplomacy', and Burritt, as ever, was soon pressing for the resumption of the series of peace congresses in Europe.(21) Sturge too was still attracted to the old ways, and for a time he tried to return to the model provided by the pre-war meetings at Manchester and Edinburgh: on behalf of the 'Peace Friends' he wrote to Cobden on 18 June 1856 urging him to attend a conference with them that summer or autumn. But Cobden would have no part of this 'doing something' policy. The 'old plan of agitation totally failed', he told Sturge, and never again would he waste his time exchanging 'the same generalities with the same people'.(22)

As Sturge's letter had confessed that the 'Peace Friends' would not proceed without Cobden's support, this reply destroyed any idea of further agitation in the near future, but soon Sturge was back again asking Cobden for advice on a very different sort of scheme: 'I am going on an expedition which thou wilt probably say has something of Romance in it although at 63 our day of Romance ought to be over'. The reference was to his imminent departure for Finland, where the coastal population had suffered from the blockade and raids carried out by the Royal Navy during Britain's war against their Grand Duke, the Czar of Russia. Sturge was convinced, he told Cobden, that restitution must be made for the wanton destruction of private property in the Baltic and the Sea of Azov. He would even have liked to see Parliament assuming a responsibility for relieving the sufferings inflicted by British forces on the Czar's civilian subjects, but not surprisingly he had been unable to think of an MP who would bring forward this unusual proposal that the victor should pay war reparations to the vanquished: he had decided therefore to proceed with a plan for a private subscription. Charles had promised full support, and the two brothers were ready to assume responsibility for raising a fund of £3000. This money would go to the poor: 'Merchants like ourselves of course must take care of themselves'. Warning him against the difficulties of the task, Cobden advised Sturge to concentrate on bringing back 'striking facts' to arouse public sympathy in Britain and under no circumstances to have any dealings with the Russian Government, unless he wished to repeat his experience in 1854 when he had been accused of being flattered and cajoled into acting as its tool.(23)

Thomas Harvey, Sturge's companion during the earlier trip to the West Indies, agreed to accompany him again, and on 8 September they set out, intending in the first instance to travel to the scenes of hostilities in Finland and then, in Sturge's case, to continue across European Russia as far as the war-ravaged shores of the Sea of Azov. In autumn weather they travelled with greater comfort and pleasure than Sturge had experienced on his previous visit to the Czar's empire. A swift railway journey took them to Lubeck, and after a more leisurely voyage by steamer they reached Helsinki on 15 September, observing the signs of bombardment on the outlying fortress of Sweaborg as their vessel, 'freighted with peace and goodwill', entered the picturesque island-strewn harbour.(24)

Sturge and Harvey reacted favourably to Finland: in 35 pages their report portrayed scenery and people more vividly than the large books that Sturge had published about his travels in the West Indies and the United States.(25) This was probably a necessary task if they were to win sympathy for these relatively unknown subjects of the Czar in the immediate aftermath of a bitter war. Admittedly, much of the farming was 'slovenly'; intemperance was the 'national vice'; and a section of the peasantry lived in conditions that caused an estimated 50 per cent infant mortality rate, but the general impression was a favourable one as Sturge and Harvey travelled through a lakeland of great natural beauty interspersed with peasant houses, quaint churches and the mansions of the nobility. The Finns were a nation of literate Protestants, they wrote, in which every family had a bible. The report even gave the merchants and middle classes of the coastal towns the supreme accolade by describing them as 'so much like our own countrymen (language excepted), of the same condition, that in England they would scarcely be taken for foreigners'. All in all, the Grand Duchy appeared 'rather like a country occupied by Russia for naval and military purposes, than an incorporated portion of the Russian empire'.

They had no difficulty in finding their counterparts in such a country. Leaving Helsinki within a day, Sturge and Harvey travelled by road to Tammerfors (Tampere) where they had arranged to meet Ferdinand Uhden, a cotton master and 'Christian philanthropist' of a reassuringly English type. Provided with advice and an interpreter they journeyed on to the coastal town of Abo (Turku) where they met Erik Julin, another 'influential and public-spirited' man, who assisted them with their interviews in the coastal areas of Nystad (Uusikaupunki) and Raumo (Rauma). As always Sturge's inquiry was designed to find evidence for a belief that had been unshakably formed in advance. One woman he interviewed said

> her husband was some years ago inspector of weights and measures in Raumo, for which, in lieu of salary, he had the occupation of the small island Korkian-Karri, five or seven versts off shore, and belonging to the town.... His boat was destroyed in Raumo harbour when the shipping was destroyed, and the English boats also destroyed all his property on the island; buildings, nets, sails and furniture, viz. on the 25th of July, 1855. They are now living without means, dependent on friends in the town; she estimates their loss at about seventy silver roubles.

It was all very predictable, and less 'striking' than one would expect from an episode that has been commemorated in Finnish folk song.(26) Some of the casual asides in the report would even have given English readers the impression that the Royal Navy's prowess in time of war was closely rivalled by the talent of the Finns for burning down their wood-built towns in peacetime.

By the end of the visit Julin, Uhden and several other merchants had agreed to form a 'Committee of Relief' to carry out a detailed investigation of cases of hardship and to expend the fund which Sturge intended to raise in Britain. On 20 September Sturge wrote to his brother Charles that he intended to make himself 'personally responsible' for sending 30,000 silver roubles (slightly less than £5000) even if the public appeal failed to raise this amount. The scheme took no account of Russian sensitivities. In his letter Sturge was confident that the Russians would raise no difficulties, but he was mistaken, possibly for a reason that he had unknowingly provided when he told Charles that the Czar had sent 6000 roubles for war relief from his private purse. In comparison with Sturge's benevolence this gesture of paternalism from 'the little Father of all the Russias' might have appeared parsimonious in the eyes of the Finns. Count Berg, the Governor-General, would not allow Sturge to proceed: the dignity of his country would not even permit him to transmit such an offer to the Czar. After several months of negotiation Berg was overruled, but there were further difficulties, and it was noticeable that when the scheme was eventually put into practice government officials were associated with it. Once again that great political and cultural divide, the English Channel, had been in evidence: the ways of Exeter Hall were not those of the absolute monarchies of Europe.(27)

Largely because of Berg's opposition Sturge cancelled his plans for proceeding to the Sea of Azov. Instead he and Harvey continued only as far as St Petersburg where they made further representations on behalf of the relief scheme. They did not seek an interview with Alexander II, but at a time when the capital was seething with news of the new Czar's plans for reform Sturge took the opportunity to submit an address to the Russian government offering advice and encouragement on three matters of policy: arbitration as a means of resolving international disputes; 'the elevation of the labouring class from the condition of Serfs into that of free agents'; and the need for a free circulation of the Scriptures if there was to be an 'emancipation of the mind' as well as the body. Having disburdened themselves of this 'piece of quiet impertinence' as Cobden described it, Sturge and Harvey then travelled home by steamer and rail, reaching London on 17 October 1856.(28)

Although difficulties continued to plague the Finnish Relief Scheme, it was eventually a success. Members of the Society of Friends responded generously to Sturge's appeal, and his case was strengthened when the Finnish harvest failed in 1856, giving rise to comparisons with the plight of Ireland ten years previously when Friends had administered an extensive programme of famine relief. Joseph and Charles Sturge contributed £500 each, and outside the Society of Friends some large sums were raised from such wealthy donors as the Baring and Rothschild companies. In all nearly £9000 were raised by the time the final report was issued in 1859. Most of the money was spent on meal, seed corn, potatoes and clothing.(29)

Sturge's energy at this late stage when he often complained that he was 'rapidly going down the hill of life' was still impressive. Within a day of returning from Finland he was writing to Cobden wanting to know if 'nothing can be done for the good cause'. Cobden, who was full of admiration for Sturge's efforts on behalf of the Finns - the report of the journey was like a 'chapter of the "Acts of the Apostles" ' - could not restrain him. 'Our good & great friend Sturge has been here', he told Wilson two weeks later, and 'he has been anxious for some movement in the peace cause. - He has no idea of progress excepting it be signalised by action, & in fact he has such a wonderful energy that it can only be kept in equilibrium by a constant succession of tasks'. Under very strong pressure, Cobden added, he had agreed that Sturge should canvass the idea of holding a conference in Manchester where the delegates would be asked to find a substitute for the existing system of secret diplomacy which constituted a threat to international peace.(30)

Nothing came of the proposal, and 1857 turned out to be one of the worst years yet for the peace movement. It was a sign of weakness when the League of Universal Brotherhood suggested a merger with the Peace Society in February that year: there were still, it was explained, about one hundred Olive Leaf Circles, and the Bond of Brotherhood had attained a self-supporting circulation of 4000 monthly, but they had lost most of their sources of income and had had to scale down their operations. On 18 May 1857 the Peace Society agreed to the union. Elihu Burritt, who had returned to the United States, was disheartened when he was told: 'All the enterprizes which I have launched before this have broken down. The League of Brotherhood is dead. I gave to it ten of the best years of my life, but it could not live, while I was absent from England. The Christian Citizen [Burritt's newspaper] died because of my absence from America. The Ocean Penny Postage movement is suspended. The Free Labor undertaking has miscarried'.(31) A year later the Peace Congress Committee was also swallowed up by the Peace Society, bringing to an end the millennial hopes of the late 1840s.(32)

Throughout 1856 and 1857 the difficulties of the peace movement were compounded by the personal and political problems which beset Cobden and Bright. In April 1856 the Cobdens' fifteen year old son died, reducing Mrs Cobden to a state of depression which aroused great concern for the rest of the year, and Cobden told Sturge in June he would rather resign as an MP than be away from her at such a juncture.(33) Bright's political effectiveness was also destroyed at this time. He had contributed little to the peace movement before the Crimean War, and he remained sceptical about it: 'I have never advocated the extreme peace principle, the non-resistance principle in public, or in private', he told Sturge in September 1857. But Bright's opposition to the Crimean War had associated his name with peace, and any weakening of his influence was seen as a threat to the movement. Early in 1856 his health broke down, and for over a year he spent little time in Westminster or his constituency. When Palmerston called a general election in March 1857 Bright paid a heavy price for his inability to defend his unpopular ideas. Although Cobden campaigned for both of them, they lost their seats.(34)

Sturge was hissed at public meetings in Birmingham during the election campaign, and he was distressed by the unpopularity of the peace party. He could hardly sleep for two nights after hearing the result, he told Cobden on 6 April, and a week later he was still so overwrought that he drew a comparison between the ingratitude of the British people to Cobden and the demands of the Jews for Christ's crucifixion.(35) The election disaster was the more disturbing to him because it seemed to confirm a worsening in the conduct of British foreign policy. Palmerston had dissolved Parliament after Cobden successfully introduced a censure motion condemning Sir John Bowring, the British Governor of Hong Kong (a former member of the Peace Society), for ordering the bombardment of Canton after the Chinese authorities had detained the Arrow, a vessel which was plying an active trade of piracy shielded by its dubious right to fly the Union Jack. The resultant war revived Sturge's interest in China. Greatly concerned about the opium trade, in 1857 he joined the Society for Suppressing Opium Smuggling; in 1858 he became one of the most active members of the Anti-Opium Association; and he pressed unsuccessfully for a parliamentary inquiry which would expose the full effects of this lethal traffic.(36) As he told a public meeting in Birmingham during the election, he was also concerned about the effect of the war on a missionary scheme which was exciting the Christian world at this time, the attempt to send one million copies of the New Testament to China. Reports had reached Britain that the Taipings, a movement which incorporated Christian beliefs and practices, had conquered a large part of China. The rebels retained many 'grievous and grotesque errors' from native Chinese beliefs, but Sturge's friend, J.A. James, had seen 'the finger of God' in their successes and issued an appeal on behalf of the Chinese missions. Sturge had given £100, and now he regretted to see the venture placed in jeopardy by Bowring's belligerence.(37)

Neither Sturge's public meetings nor the special fund which the Peace Society set up to assist sympathetic MPs during the general election had much effect; it was evident that Palmerston was a better judge of public opinion. The diary of John O'Neil, a Lancashire weaver of Liberal opinions, makes interesting reading during these years with its laconic entries about the widespread destruction inflicted by the Royal Navy on the Chinese as a punishment for their 'insolent' behaviour and 'horrible atrocities'. When news arrived that Cobden and Gibson, the mover and seconder of the censure motion on Bowring, had lost their parliamentary seats, O'Neil and his Clitheroe workmates were 'very well pleased that they are both kicked out of Parliament and a great many more that voted with them'.(38) The mortification of Sturge and his friends was the worse because of the trimming policy pursued by Charles Hindley at this time. 'MR HINDLEY', the Herald of Peace reported:

explained the reason for his not voting at all on Mr Cobden's motion. He could not vote against it; and seeing plainly that the Tories were making it a party question, he could not vote for it. He was not surprised that a number of peace candidates had lost their seats at the late election, so strong did the war spirit prevail in the country. Indeed, he was convinced he should himself have lost his seat if he had spoken out very boldly upon the subject.

Hindley was the President of the Peace Society.(39)
It was some consolation that Sturge soon carried through a successful counter-stroke; in August 1857 he was instrumental in having John Bright returned as one of the MPs for Birmingham after the death of George F. Muntz. Discussions between the Liberal factions in the town revealed that Bright would have an excellent chance of being returned unopposed, and when his name was brought forward at a Town's Meeting early in August it received overwhelming support. Bright had not been consulted, and his illness made it unlikely that he would accept the call, but Sturge, seizing his chance to gain 'a great moral advantage', immediately set off for Rochdale to discuss the proposal with Bright's wife and brother. Then, travelling on to Edinburgh, he met Bright at the home of Duncan McLaren, Bright's brother-in-law. On the understanding that Bright would re-enter public life only when he felt fit, Sturge was allowed to take back a letter of acceptance to the Birmingham Liberal Election Committee. The arrangement was confirmed at a meeting in Tamworth at which Bright, McLaren, Sturge and some of the Birmingham Liberals produced an address to the constituency.(40)
Everything happened as Sturge forecast in a letter to Cobden on 8 August: the other candidates withdrew, and Bright walked the course in absentia. Ever a pessimistic source of advice at this stage of his career, Cobden had warned Sturge against pursuing any such plan: 'The times are not favourable to earnest politicians', he commented sourly. But the result delighted him. The Birmingham men, he congratulated Bright, had 'kicked the posteriors' of the 'political snobs & fops in Manchester'.(41) Although Bright was not all that Sturge would have wished of an MP - the two men differed over the conduct of international relations, suffrage reform, public education and teetotalism - on the whole Sturge had every reason to be pleased by the change in Birmingham's parliamentary representation. He had brought to the town the MP who best exemplified the rhetorical power of moral earnestness as an engine of political reform, and, although it seems to have passed unnoticed, he had also won the campaign he had opened in the 1830s: the official Liberal candidate had been chosen at a Town's Meeting, i.e. by non-electors as well as electors.(42)
For the rest, however, 1857 was a dismal year. 'It would appear', Sturge told John Clark on 15 September, 'as though the interpretation of our Plymouth Brethern [sic] was right and that before the Reign of the Messiah upon Earth, the power of the Devil was to [become] Universal'. This apocalyptic vision which contrasted so sharply with his earlier optimistic millennialism had been suggested to him, he added, by the 'spirit of vengeance ... towards the poor East Indians' during the Indian Mutiny which broke out that year.(43) The harsher racist attitudes which were becoming a feature of the British mentality during the mid-Victorian years were given full vent by the British press, and the reporting was hysterical. Members of the peace

movement noted the increasing resort to terms such as 'nigger' and 'the supremacy of the Anglo-Saxon race'. No description of Sepoy brutishness was too far-fetched for belief; no degree of severity on the part of the British army was reprehensible. By the time of the Fair in 1858 toy Sepoys complete with wire nooses around their necks were on sale to the children of Birmingham.(44)

Sturge and his Peace Society friends were never more isolated than at this time. T.B. Macaulay, who despised the religiosity of Exeter Hall, saw them as a spent force: the 'effeminate mawkish philanthropy of the Ewarts and Sturges ... will lose all its influence', he wrote, and 'that is a very good thing'. Britain was 'in conflict with the Eastern world', The Times reported with evident satisfaction on 3 August 1857: 'From Aden to Hongkong the British flag has been unfurled, and at various spots throughout this great section of the globe the inhabitants of these little islands are actually engaged in hostilities with well nigh one-half of the human race'.(45) Sturge was grieved to see the bloodlust affecting 'not only professed Xtian men but Xtian ministers'. Lord Shaftesbury, C.H. Spurgeon and Edward Miall were three amongst the many who rallied to the flag in the belief that India must be held by force and converted to Christianity. For a time even Cobden lost his customary rationality: 'the murderous rebels', he told Sturge on 1 July, must be shot like 'so many tigers'.(46)

Cobden soon recovered from his slip into what he called the 'tomahawk style' of The Times, but he held fast to the opinion he expressed to Sturge on 5 July that only the long term lessons of free trade would teach the British how unwise it was to possess colonies; in the meanwhile force would be needed to maintain order in India.(47) Bright's statements were very similar. He was keeping quiet about India, he answered on 24 September 1857 after Sturge had tried to bring him forward as a critic of official policy, and two weeks later he made no attempt to conceal his impatience when Sturge returned to the subject. Where Cobden was usually careful to coach Sturge in 'the wisdom of the serpent', Bright roundly denounced the Peace Society and the peace congress movement. Hardly anyone accepted the Peace Society's pacifist principle, he chided Sturge; and other 'arguments of humanity, or of finance, or of common justice' were rejected because they had been associated with it. 'I admire thy steadfast labors in the cause of Peace', he concluded, 'but I grieve to see them so unproductive'. It was a letter, Bright's wife commented, that would have discouraged anyone but Joseph Sturge.(48)

Margaret Bright was correct; Sturge was not to be put off in this way. He had so often referred to the misgovernment of India and to the likelihood that it would bring down a divine retribution on Britain that he felt obliged to speak out. 'England', he told the annual meeting of the Peace Society in 1858, 'had no more to do in India than the Indians had in England. Many of these poor creatures were defending their own and their country's rights'.(49) In circumstances that bore some resemblance to the Jamaican slave rising in 1831 he returned to the only form of agitation in which he ever felt completely at ease: he summoned up 'the pressure from without' to rally the conscience of the nation against government policy. In September 1857 he and Arthur

O'Neill launched the movement in Birmingham by bringing out a placard and newspaper advertisement entitled 'Vengeance in India', which was subsequently distributed in many parts of England and Ireland. Sturge and his friends then arranged a meeting in Manchester on 13 October, and, undeterred by an attendance of only 27, Sturge presided over a discussion which gave rise to two decisions: firstly, through tracts and lectures the British people were to be instructed on their duty to give India a government founded on justice; and secondly there was to be an appeal on behalf of India to parliamentarians, ministers of religion and the Christian people of England. From three centres (London, Birmingham and Manchester) the movement sent out speakers who delivered 200 lectures in most of the principal English towns over the next eight months, and the ladies' Olive Leaf Circles and auxiliary peace societies broke new ground in womanly behaviour at this time by placarding several cities with anti-vengeance material.(50)

Once again Sturge's mind turned to the idea of sending a mission to the scene of hostilities to bring back first-hand information. He offered a large sum to any competent person who would go to India for this purpose, and when no one volunteered he suggested that he and Henry Richard should go. The programme he drew up for the mission shows not only that he hoped to repeat the strategy that had led to success in the West Indies between 1836 and 1838 but that he intended to promote other reforms that overlapped with the problem of ensuring good government in India. He wanted to give the Indians an opportunity of communicating their grievances; to find out from them and from sympathetic Europeans how Britain could promote their welfare and 'secure their attachment to this country'; to examine the circumstances of the cultivation and trade in opium; to see how Indian sugar could be brought into competition on the world market with slave-produced sugar from the Americas; to establish 'a permanent association in India to report to friends of India in England'; and to 'bring home one or more natives' to set the point of view of the Indians before the British people. Yet again Cobden warned him not to look overseas for solutions to problems that originated at home. He could imagine no two people less likely to succeed, he told Richard: 'It would be a foregone conclusion, & afford all but the members of the Old Peace Society the pretence for pronouncing your report whatever it might be a mere party document'. Wisely, considering the dangerous conditions prevailing in India, Sturge allowed himself to be talked out of the idea.(51)

Thus, at the beginning of 1858 peace was still Sturge's highest priority, and after Charles Hindley died he agreed to become the President of the Peace Society. But he kept up and even extended his range of interests in philanthropy and reform during his last years. For instance, he never retracted what some of his friends saw as his dangerously radical views on Complete Suffrage. Although he had been sympathetic to the Freehold Land movement since the late 1840s, he disagreed with Cobden's belief that this attempt to create a class of respectable artisans with houses (and therefore voting qualifications) offered a satisfactory answer to the demands for parliamentary reform.(52) Thus in April 1857 when Washington Wilks, the former sub-editor of the Nonconformist, asked him to help revive the franchise movement in the aftermath of the humiliating general election he responded cordially: although he was too old to take a prominent part he would support a movement which concentrated on manhood suffrage and accepted some sort of compromise on the other points of the People's Charter. This was very close to the position he had taken at the end of 1841 when he and Edward Miall had first declared for Complete Suffrage, and, as on that occasion, he saw political reform and moral reform as two sides of the same coin. By giving all men the vote he hoped to destroy the power which public houses and beer shops wielded over a small electorate. Of course, he did not see political reform as a panacea, he explained to an unsympathetic Cobden at this time, but they must not 'condemn the people until they have been fairly tried'. Cobden would not budge. 'Don't be drawn into any dogmatic theory about "Complete Suffrage" ', he told Henry Richard at the Morning Star on 13 April 1857: 'It is our Friend Sturges [sic] bantling & he has an overwhelming love for it'. Once again Sturge had to proceed according to his own lights. On 20 April he attended a meeting of parliamentary reformers in London and spoke 'very plainly' to them about the importance of manhood suffrage; in November he was still in touch with John Hamilton of the Morning Star offering to help the universal suffrage movement 'in a quiet way'.(53)

He was heartened to find that on returning to public life in 1858 Bright was eager to propose a new Reform Bill as a private member. He organised a meeting in his conference room in October to acquaint Bright with the views of local Radicals, and a few days later at Bright's first Town's Meeting in Birmingham he emphasised his continued 'interest in the full, fair and free representation of the people'. In November he and his brother Charles joined the Committee of the Birmingham Reform Association to support Bright's Bill when it was made public. Their intention, Sturge told W.S. Crawford (another former Complete Suffragist) was to have the Bill based on the principle of manhood suffrage at the age of 25.(54) He was disappointed therefore when Bright's proposals stopped short at a ratepayers' franchise supplemented by the secret ballot and some electoral redistribution. There was no breach between the two men, and Sturge helped to pay Bright's expenses during the general election in April 1859, but he spoke freely of the difference of opinion to Handel Cossham shortly before his death: 'Well, Mr Bright does not go far enough for me; I still hold to the right of every man to a vote, apart from all property qualification'.(55)

Anti-slavery was another long-standing commitment that Sturge kept up after the Crimean War. He was still the acknowledged 'heart and soul' of the movement, but, truth to tell, there was very little life left in it. In 1856 the British and Foreign Anti-Slavery Society even had to cancel its annual meeting because its funds were depleted, a plight which was almost certainly the consequence of a serious quarrel at the previous year's meeting when Samuel Gurney stormed from the chair after some of the speakers attacked Lord Shaftesbury and the supporters of the [American] Western Turkish Mission Aid Society for

associating with slave owners.(56)   The free produce movement was
likewise in decline despite the efforts that had been made to provide
supplies of textiles through a chain of recommended depots and shops.
Thomas D. Crewdson, a Manchester manufacturer, told the Birmingham
Ladies Negro Friend Society in November 1858 that the demand, never
large, had diminished so much in recent years that no realistic
businessman could cater for it.(57)

Everywhere, the British anti-slavery movement seemed to be on
the defensive. Far from vindicating James Cropper's theory that free
labour would lead to an economic resurgence and make the British West
Indies a show-case for cheap and efficient production, emancipation
seemed finally to have destroyed their ability to compete against the
slave-produced sugar of Brazil and Cuba.   Jamaica, which always
provided the bench-mark for the British Caribbean, provided a story of
continuous decline: the former slaves would not work dependably for
wages; the island was ravaged by drought and cholera; and the
population, it was said, was fast sinking into barbarism.   Thomas
Carlyle's notorious summary of 'the Nigger Question' ('beautiful Blacks
sitting there up to the ears in pumpkins') was not very different from
some missionary reports. 'The Jamaican planter', wrote J.H. Buchner
the historian of the Moravian Mission, 'labours at present under great
difficulties, which would try the utmost patience of any man; he sees
his work neglected, his property going to ruin, and is at the mercy and
caprice of his labourers who do just as much or as little as they
please'.(58)

Sturge was still the patron of missionary and educational work in
the West Indies. In the mid-1850s, for example, he gave £100 to help
Lewis Tappan and the American Missionary Association purchase a
Jamaican estate where young American men and women ('all anti-
slavery, temperance, peace & tobacco abstaining people') could instruct
the local population in religion, general education and the mechanic
arts. He also organised a West Indies Cholera Fund in 1854 to alleviate
the sufferings of widows and orphans.(59) But, above all, his attention
was repeatedly drawn back to the Caribbean by what he saw as an
attempt to revive the slave trade through schemes devised by the
colonial legislatures to introduce a more tractable labour force of
Asian coolies.   Sturge's letters to John Clark and Lord Brougham
between 1857 and 1859 show him acting as the intermediary by
soliciting information from Jamaica and lobbying Brougham to use his
influence in Parliament against the immigration schemes. Thanks to
their efforts, the British Government had disallowed a Jamaican
Immigration Act, he told Clark in April 1858.   A year later he
congratulated Brougham on a speech against another 'Jamaica Slavery
reenactment bill': all the evidence he had received showed that
immigration was 'nothing less than the Slave Trade with all its former
horrors'. In any case, as he told a Birmingham meeting, there must be
no question of introducing 'hordes of Pagans and idolators among the
half-civilised and Christian races of Jamaica'.(60)

More than anything else, Sturge came to believe that he must
find a decisive argument to refute the charge that the West Indian
black population was indolent. In 1852 he asked Clark to compile a

statement of facts about 'the present state of the negro population in our West India colonies, and especially the social advancement of the emancipated classes in Jamaica'. But, although Clark produced a survey of the free villages in the neighbourhood of his mission station and concluded that 'probably ... no people on the face of the earth ever made greater progress in the same space of time', the accusations did not die away, and in January 1857 Sturge again had to write to him for information which would enable the British and Foreign Anti-Slavery Society to answer the claims that religion and morality were declining in Jamaica.(61) A much bolder counter-stroke seemed to be needed, and in the same year Sturge decided what it would be: he became a West Indian planter.

His intention was to sustain a case he had often made: the West Indian economy was declining, not because of the sloth of the former slaves, but because of the incompetence of absentee landlords. Salvation, Sturge told a Birmingham meeting in February 1859, would have to come from 'a body of enterprising capitalists who would speedily make terms with the indigenous labourers'; therefore to set an example he had purchased a sugar estate of 1100 acres in 1857 (he named it Elberton after his birthplace) on the island of Montserrat. His strategy, and there was nothing shame-faced about it, was to make money and demonstrate the benefits of a humanely managed capitalism. The venture provided another example of the interlocking commercial and philanthropic interests of the Sturge family. In the same year Edmund commenced an even more promising experiment on an estate on the island, a plantation (named Olveston after the village where the family had lived at the beginning of the century) which was to produce raw materials for the manufacture of citric acid in his Birmingham chemical works. In due course lime orchards were planted, giving rise to an important lime juice industry.(62) Thus, Sturge's public statements on West Indian matters during the last two years of his life could open with the words 'Speaking as a proprietor', enabling him to cite his own experience as proof that there was no need to recruit coolie labour. 'He had expressly purchased an estate in Montserrat under great disadvantages', he told Sir Edward Bulwer-Lytton, the Colonial Secretary, in January 1859, 'for the purpose of testing the question, and the result of his own experience was, that there was no difficulty in finding sufficient labour, if the resident labouring population were judiciously and kindly treated'.(63)

Thus, far from sacrificing the West Indies to the vested interests of a capitalist system that had no place for them (as he has been accused of doing) Sturge was attempting to summon capitalism to the assistance of the colonial population for reasons that were fundamentally moral. The experiment was still in its early days when he died, but shortly before his death he told a friend that it had been 'entirely successful'. He was therefore spared the disillusionment which Thomas Harvey, his assistant in 1836-37, experienced during a visit to Jamaica a few years later in the aftermath of the 1865 rising. Although he believed that on balance emancipation had benefited the population, Harvey admitted the possibility that the 'British anti-slavery christians' had underrated the difficulties of raising the population 'to the dignity of a free, christian manhood'.(64)

During his last years Sturge was also drawn back to his earlier quest for the reform of the Society of Friends. Here too there was unmistakable evidence of decline. It was small comfort when the Annual Monitor correctly pointed out that the Society's influence could not be measured by the small numbers of those who were joining it by convincement; the Quakers showed every sign of dying out as a denomination. Their numbers were steadily falling - from 16,425 in 1840 to 15,492 in 1847 - and it was anxiously noted that young Friends were less inclined to obey the rules enjoining plainness and forbidding marrying out of the Society.(65)

The Quaker 'Liberal party' was very active at this time, helped along by sympathetic reporting in the Friend which was edited until 1857 by Charles Gilpin, Sturge's nephew. Throughout the 1830s and 1840s the 'weighty Friends' had refused to allow anyone to publish the discussions at the Yearly Meeting - Sturge clashed with them over this in 1847(66) - but Gilpin ignored their protests during the 1850s, and they often found themselves reduced to the same position as a beleaguered government whose shortcomings were mercilessly exposed in Hansard. By wasting so much time discussing lay impropriate taxes they were straining at a gnat and swallowing a camel, Sturge told them in 1853; by insisting on minor testimonies they were retarding the progress of the Society, Bright added. In 1856 Sturge opened up a heated debate on the condition of the Society by delivering a strong attack on the 'plain clothing' regulations and suggesting that attention would be better directed to intemperance amongst Friends. During the same meeting other sources show that he spoke strongly against the marrying out rules, warning the members that 'those who enacted unchristian laws were sowing the seeds of their own destruction'. He returned to the attack in 1857 by condemning the plainness testimonies as 'a mark unsanctioned by Xtianity' which was 'doing more injury to the Society than any other single thing'. At another stage in the proceedings that year he was described as making 'one of his rough & vigorous onslaughts upon the existing [marriage] arrangements'. Why, Sturge asked his listeners repeatedly during these years, would they not face up to real problems such as the correct use of their wealth? Why would they not admit the need for 'a cheerful self-denial of the use [of] intoxicating liquors as a beverage & also for those engaged in its manufacture & sale to be advised against so continuing?'(67)

In 1858 he and Samuel Bowly carried the day: under their pressure the Yearly Meeting referred the plainness testimonies to a special conference consisting of the Meeting for Sufferings and other Friends. In December this conference recommended that 'plainness of speech, behaviour and apparel' should no longer be matters of discipline. The first major changes were made in 1860.(68) By then the signs that teetotalism was triumphing in the Society were no less evident. In 1857 Sturge and Bowly successfully proposed that the General Epistle of the Yearly Meeting should contain a paragraph recommending teetotalism to Friends and expressing sympathy with those who were active in the temperance movement. 'The decanter and the wine glass are rapidly disappearing from the tables of Friends',

Charles Gilpin noted with satisfaction.(69)

This was only one of Sturge's services to the temperance movement during the 1850s. He was President of the Birmingham Temperance Society, by this time an impressive empire with auxiliary societies for women, children, youths and reclaimed drunkards. In January 1858 the Society honoured his services when he took part in the ceremonial laying of the foundation stone of a splendid new temperance hall: sealed beneath the stone (he was the only person to be commemorated in this way) was 'a neatly executed photograph of Mr Sturge'. But he was not fully in sympathy with the prohibitionist policy espoused by the recently formed United Kingdom Alliance. It was not that he was totally opposed to the idea of using legislation against the drink trade; he was one of the Vice-Presidents of the Alliance between 1855 and 1857, and the National Temperance League of which he was also a Vice-President advocated a gradualist policy of legislative action. But he preferred to act with the support of public opinion, and he was sure that 'this could not be done in any better way than by beginning early with the young'.(70) During his last years therefore he worked so closely with the emerging Band of Hope, that he was called the 'father' of the local movement: in 1853 he became the President of the newly formed Birmingham Band of Hope Union. The experience seems to have widened his tolerance of public leisure pursuits. At a time when most Quakers would not give their patronage to any form of public festivity Sturge often presided over Band of Hope gatherings where brass bands and choirs took a prominent part.(71)

As 1859 opened therefore Sturge was still fully extended in a wide range of good causes and reform movements. In mid-1858 he had been ill again: the consequence, so Cobden told him, of 'doing the work of a dozen young men' and forgetting that he was more than sixty years old.(72) The signs of severe illness returned later that year, and Hannah noticed an uncharacteristic 'languour' setting in during November. He had difficulty in walking and in giving speeches even to small gatherings. His sister Rebecca had died in 1857, and he thought about the recent deaths of members of his own generation who had shared in his life's work.(73) The thought was a call to greater efforts. In the early months of 1859 he travelled to many parts of England trying to reorganise the peace movement and stimulate the interest of young people in its work. During the crisis that preceded the outbreak of war between France and Austria in May 1859 he and Henry Richard sent a memorial to Napoleon III urging him to submit the dispute to arbitration.(74) The problem of Rajah Brooke surfaced again at this time too; shortly after suppressing a Chinese revolt with great brutality Brooke had returned to Britain at the end of 1857 hoping to regularise the status of his regime and interest British businessmen in the economic development of Sarawak. During the previous ten years Sturge had followed Brooke's career of conquest with fascinated horror, and now he published a pamphlet entitled The Sarawak Question to warn the Birmingham Chamber of Commerce against a scheme of 'Fillibusterism and piracy' reminiscent of Pizarro's activities in Peru. When his advice was ignored and the Chamber petitioned Parliament in favour of granting protectorate status to

Sarawak, he was obliged to end his public life in Birmingham as he had begun it - with a publicised resignation.(75)

No public matter seemed to be too large or too small to merit his attention at this time; the day before his death he approached John Cadbury to see if a horse trough could be installed on the boundary between Birmingham and Edgbaston.(76) Sturge's last day was a busy one, Hannah remembered. The May Meeting season had started, and he was planning to spend two weeks in London attending the Quaker Yearly Meeting and the gatherings of other societies. With the reform of the Society of Friends reaching a crucial stage and the international situation worsening, he had many preparations to make, but he found time to write to his nephew, Wilson Sturge, about the family business. It was the letter of a dying man. Worried in case Wilson followed Charles's exuberant business practices, Sturge emphasised that his own life was increasingly uncertain and urged his nephew to exert a sound influence on his acquaintances by carefully attending to his commercial and household affairs. There was no greater threat to 'vital Xtianity' in the Society of Friends, he warned, than the lavish hospitality of many of its members. That night he prayed for peace at his son's bedside. One of his daughters never forgot how the next day, 14 May 1859, began; she couldn't understand why her nurse was so long in coming to help her dress for the usual ride with her father on that beautiful morning. Sturge had risen early, but he was pierced by a sudden pain and driven to his knees in agony. Such medical treatment as was ready to hand had no effect, and he died almost immediately. There was no parting word or look, but it was a great consolation to the pious Hannah that 'there was a heaven lit expression' on his face.(77)

The funeral six days later, it was said, had no parallel in Birmingham's history. Three hundred gentlemen headed by the mayor and followed by sixty carriages processed through the town, escorting the cortege through lined streets and past closed shops to the Quaker burial ground. Aldermen, councillors, clergymen, Dissenting ministers, deputations from many of the societies Sturge had supported in the town - the United Kingdom Alliance, the Anti-Slavery Society, the Peace Society, the Band of Hope Union, the Baptist Missionary Society, the Friends' First Day School: 'every class and body in the town was well represented'. The editorial in the Friend a few days later spoke of the loss of 'one who was ever ready to raise his voice in support of the principles of sound Christian liberality'.(78)

NOTES

1.   Brit. Lib., Add. MSS. 43722, ff. 102-103, Richard Cobden to Joseph Sturge, 21 January 1856.

2.   Herald of Peace, April, May, June 1856; Brit. Lib. Add. MSS. 43722, ff. 109-10, Richard Cobden to Joseph Sturge, 17 March 1856.

3.   Sturge Papers (M. Sturge), Joseph Sturge to Charles Sturge, 23 March, 26 March, 27 March, 29 March 1856.

4.   Ibid., 4 April, 10 April, 12 April 1856; West Sussex Record Office, Joseph Sturge to Richard Cobden, 9 April 1856; Herald of Peace, June 1856; Public Record Office, FO27 1169, Lord Clarendon to

Lord Palmerston, 15 April 1856.

5. Brit. Lib., Add. MSS. 43722, f. 116, Richard Cobden to Joseph Sturge, 21 May 1856; Manchester Public Library, Wilson Papers, Joseph Sturge to George Wilson, 20 May 1856.

6. Birmingham Journal, 21 May 1856.

7. Herald of Peace, March 1850; Brit. Lib. Add. MSS. 43650, ff. 166-67, Richard Cobden to John Bright, 4 January 1856; ibid., Add. MSS. 43722, ff. 19-21, Richard Cobden to Joseph Sturge, 18 April 1854.

8. C.D. Collet, History Of The Taxes On Knowledge, London 1933, introd. p. xii.

9. Ibid., p. 113.

10. Birmingham Journal, 25 January 1851; Brit. Lib., Add. MSS. 43656, ff. 181-82, Richard Cobden to Joseph Sturge, 15 January 1851.

11. Brit. Lib., Add. MSS. 43722, f. 49, Richard Cobden to Joseph Sturge, 16 February 1855.

12. Ibid., ff. 74-75, Richard Cobden to Joseph Sturge, 28 July 1855; ibid., Add. MSS. 43723, ff. 41-44, John Bright to Joseph Sturge, 23 August 1855.

13. Manchester Public Library, Wilson Papers, 1 September, 6 September, 10 September, 17 September 1855; Sturge Papers (M. Sturge), account of Sturge's journey to collect financial contributions to the Star; Brit. Lib., Add. MSS. 43722, ff. 79-80, Richard Cobden to Joseph Sturge, 15 September 1855; Ibid., Add. MSS. 43723, ff. 65-66, John Bright to Joseph Sturge, 28 December 1855.

14. Brit. Lib., Add. MSS. 43722, ff. 111-12, Richard Cobden to Joseph Sturge, 19 March 1856.

15. Ibid., ff. 77-78, Richard Cobden to Joseph Sturge, 15 September 1855; ibid., ff. 135-36, Richard Cobden to Joseph Sturge, 5 July 1856.

16. See, for example, ibid., Add. MSS. 43658, ff. 26-27, 18 March 1856.

17. Manchester Public Library, Wilson Papers, Joseph Sturge to George Wilson, 3 June, 14 July, 19 July 1856.

18. Brit. Lib. Add. MSS. 43664, ff. 54-5, Richard Cobden to Joseph Parkes, 3 November 1856.

19. S. Koss, The Rise and Fall of the Political Press in Britain. The Nineteenth Century, Chapel Hill 1981, pp. 123-27; West Sussex Record Office, Cobden 53, Joseph Sturge to Richard Cobden, 5 May 1857; Manchester Public Library, Wilson Papers, Joseph Sturge to George Wilson, 8 September 1856; Brit. Lib., Add. MSS. 43723, ff. 136-37, John Bright to Joseph Sturge, 12 May 1859.

20. A Quaker Journal, II, pp. 433-34.

21. Herald of Peace, June 1856.

22. Brit. Lib., Add. MSS. 43722, ff. 129-30, Joseph Sturge to Richard Cobden, 18 June 1856; ibid., ff. 147-48, Richard Cobden to Joseph Sturge, 27 July 1856; Manchester Public Library, Wilson Papers, Richard Cobden to George Wilson, 17 November 1856.

23. West Sussex Record Office, Cobden 4, Joseph Sturge to Richard Cobden, 3 September 1856; Brit. Lib. Add. MSS. 43722, ff. 157-60, Richard Cobden to Joseph Sturge, 4 September 1856.

24. Joseph Sturge & Thomas Harvey, Report Of A Visit To

Finland, In The Autumn Of 1856, Birmingham 1856, pp. 3-6.

25. The following description of the Sturge-Harvey mission to Finland is based on Sturge & Harvey, Report Of A Visit To Finland; Sturge Papers (M. Sturge), two letters sent by Joseph Sturge to Charles Sturge from Abo, 20 September and 23 September 1856; and Richard, Sturge, chap. XXV.

26. W.R. Mead, Finland, London 1968, p. 141.

27. Sturge Papers (M. Sturge), Joseph Sturge to Charles Sturge, 20 September, 23 September 1856; Brit. Lib., Add. MSS. 43650, f. 242, translation of letter from Count Berg, Governor General of Finland, 2/14 November 1856; ibid., Add. MSS. 43664, ff. 67-68, Richard Cobden to Joseph Parkes, 28 December 1856; Fenn Collection E19Y, Joseph Sturge to John Clark, 16 January 1857.

28. Sturge and Harvey, Report Of A Visit To Finland, pp. 32-35; Brit. Lib., Add. MSS. 43664, ff. 54-55, Richard Cobden to Joseph Parkes, 3 November 1856; ibid., Add. MSS. 43722, ff. 167-68, Richard Cobden to Joseph Sturge, 3 November 1856.

29. Friend, March, April, May 1857, February 1858, May 1859; S.G. Harvey, Memorials of Thomas Harvey, Compiled From A Short Autobiography, and from His Own Writings and Letters, n.p. 1886, p. 24.

30. Birmingham Journal, 30 October 1858; Brit. Lib. Add. MSS. 43664, ff. 54-55, Richard Cobden to Joseph Parkes, 3 November 1856; Manchester Public Library, Wilson Papers, Richard Cobden to George Wilson, 17 November 1856.

31. Minute Book of the Transactions Of The Peace Society, 24 February, 4 May, 18 May 1857; Burritt, Journals, Journal 21, 1 July, 18 July, 23 July 1857.

32. Minute Book of the Transactions Of The Peace Society, 9 August 1858.

33. John Morley, The Life Of Richard Cobden, London 1906, pp. 644-48; Brit. Lib. Add. MSS. 43722, ff. 127-28, Richard Cobden to Joseph Sturge, 10 June 1856.

34. Brit. Lib., Add. MSS. 43723, ff. 85-86, John Bright to Joseph Sturge, 24 September 1857; K. Robbins, John Bright, London 1979, pp. 115-26.

35. Birmingham Journal, 28 March 1857; West Sussex Record Office, Cobden 53, Joseph Sturge to Richard Cobden, 6 April, 12 April 1857.

36. West Sussex Record Office, Cobden 53, Joseph Sturge to Richard Cobden, 6 June 1857, Bond of Brotherhood, January 1859; Herald of Peace, December 1858, March 1859; The Colonial Intelligencer; Or, Aborigines Friend, February-September 1858.

37. Birmingham Journal, 21 January 1857; R.W. Dale, The Life And Letters Of John Angell James: Including An Unfinished Autobiography, London 1861, pp. 427-28; M. Broomhall, The Bible in China, London 1934, pp. 74-77.

38. 'The Journals Of A Lancashire Weaver 1856-60, 1860-64, 1872-75', ed. M. Brigg, Record Society Of Lancashire And Cheshire, CXXII 1982, pp. 31, 35, 37.

39. Herald of Peace, June 1857. See also the half-hearted

obituary notice for Hindley in ibid., February 1858.

40.   This account of Bright's adoption as MP for Birmingham is based on West Sussex Record Office, Cobden 53, Joseph Sturge to Richard Cobden, 8 August 1857; Brit. Lib. Add. MSS. 43384, ff. 104-106, John Bright to Richard Cobden, 15 August 1857; Sturge Papers (Lewin), Jacob Bright to Charles Sturge, 31 July 1857.

41.   Brit. Lib., Add. MSS. 43656, ff. 379-80, Richard Cobden to Joseph Sturge, 15 June 1857; ibid., Add. MSS 43650, ff. 256-57, Richard Cobden to John Bright, 11 August 1857.

42.   Birmingham Journal, 5 August 1857.

43.   Fenn Collection, E19Y, Joseph Sturge to John Clark, 15 September 1857.

44.   James Bryne, 'British Opinion And The Indian Revolt' in P.C. Joshi ed., Rebellion 1857, a symposium, New Delhi 1957, pp. 291-311; Herald of Peace, November 1857, May 1859; Birmingham Journal, 2 October 1858.

45.   J. Hamburger, 'The Whig Conscience' in P. Marsh ed., The Conscience Of The Victorian State, Hassocks 1979, p. 26; J. Cell, 'The Imperial Conscience' in ibid., pp. 201-203.

46.   Fenn Collection, E19Y, Joseph Sturge to John Clark, 15 September 1857; Brit. Lib., Add. MSS. 43722, ff. 249-50, Richard Cobden to Joseph Sturge, 1 July 1857.

47.   Brit. Lib., Add. MSS. 43658, ff. 382-83, Richard Cobden to Henry Richard, 14 August 1857; ibid., Add. MSS. 43722, ff. 251-54, Richard Cobden to Joseph Sturge, 5 July 1857.

48.   Ibid., Add. MSS. 43723, ff. 85-86, John Bright to Joseph Sturge, 24 September 1857; ibid., Add. MSS. 43845, ff. 50-53, John Bright to Joseph Sturge, 11 October 1857; ibid., ff. 54-57, John Bright to Joseph Sturge, 19 October 1857.

49.   Herald of Peace, June 1858.

50.   Minute Book of the Transactions Of The Peace Society, 5 October 1857; Herald of Peace, November 1857, June 1858.

51.   T. Pumphrey, 'Joseph Sturge, The Christian Citizen. A Biographical Sketch'; Richard, Sturge, pp. 526-28; Brit. Lib. Add. MSS. 43658, ff. 390-91, Richard Cobden to Henry Richard, 8 November 1857.

52.   West Sussex Record Office, Cobden 53, Joseph Sturge to Richard Cobden, 12 April 1857.

53.   Ibid., Joseph Sturge to Richard Cobden, 6 April, 12 April, 20 April, 25 April 1857; Brit. Lib. Add. MSS. 43658, ff. 303-7, Richard Cobden to Henry Richard, 13 April 1857; Friends House Library, Temp. Box 28/4, Joseph Sturge to J. Hamilton, 25 November, 27 November 1857, 11 January 1858.

54.   Birmingham Journal, 30 October, 13 November 1858; Belfast Public Record Office, D856/D/138, Joseph Sturge to William Sharman Crawford, 15 November 1858.

55.   Sturge Papers (M. Sturge), 'Death of Mr Charles Sturge', Daily Post, 2 May 1888 (newscutting); Cossham, Lecture On The Life, Labours, & Character Of The Late Joseph Sturge, Of Birmingham, p. 15.

56.   British and Foreign Anti-Slavery Reporter, June 1855, June 1856.

57. Friend, January 1859.

58. 'The Nigger Question', in T. Carlyle, Selected Essays, London 1972, p. 306; J.H. Buchner, The Moravians In Jamaica, History Of The Mission Of The United Brethren's Church To The Negroes In The Island Of Jamaica, From the Year 1754 To 1854, London 1854, p. 169.

59. The Papers of Lewis Tappan, Lewis Tappan to Joseph Sturge, 27 November 1854, 3 January, 3 April 1855; British and Foreign Anti-Slavery Reporter, September 1854.

60. Fenn Collection, E19Y, Joseph Sturge to John Clark, 16 April 1858; London University, Brougham Correspondence, 10187, Joseph Sturge to Lord Brougham, 6 February 1859; British and Foreign Anti-Slavery Reporter, May 1859.

61. A Brief Account Of The Settlements Of The Emancipated Peasantry In The Neighbourhood Of Brown's Town, Jamaica; In A Letter, From John Clark, Baptist Missionary, To Joseph Sturge, Of Birmingham; Fenn Collection, E19Y, Joseph Sturge to John Clark, 16 January 1857.

62. British and Foreign Anti-Slavery Reporter, May 1859; Sturge Papers (Lewin) Joseph & Charles Sturge; Sturge Papers (M. Sturge), Argus, 29 June 1893 (newsclipping).

63. British and Foreign Anti-Slavery Reporter, February 1859.

64. Pumphrey, 'Joseph Sturge, The Christian Citizen. A Biographical Sketch'. cf. Richard, Sturge p. 533. See also Thomas Harvey & William Brewin, Jamaica in 1866. A Narrative Of A Tour Through The Island, With Remarks On Its Social, Educational and Industrial Condition, London 1867, pp. 68, 71, 74-75.

65. Annual Monitor, 1855; Friend, May 1852; J.P. Sturge, Observations On The State Of The Society of Friends, Bristol 1860.

66. Friends Library, MS Vol. S111, S. Alexander's Yearly Meeting Notes, 1847, 1852.

67. This description of the Yearly Meetings during the 1850s is based on Friend, June 1853, June 1856, June 1857; Friends House Library, MS Vol. S367, J.S. Rowntree's diary of the 1856 Yearly Meetings; ibid., MS Vol. S127, J.S. Rowntree's diary of the 1857 Yearly Meeting.

68. Friend, June, December 1858; Friends House Library, MS Vol. S128, J.S. Rowntree's diary of the 1858 Yearly Meeting; Taylor, Memorials of Samuel Bowly, pp. 35-37; A Quaker Journal, vol. II, p. 517; Isichei, Victorian Quakers, pp. 158-59.

69. Friend, June, July 1857.

70. Birmingham Journal, 16 January 1858. See also National Temperance League, report for 1856, pp. 3, 18-19; United Kingdom Alliance. The Alliance Reports, 1853-67, Third & Fifth Reports.

71. Jubilee Souvenir (1847-97) of the Birmingham Band of Hope Union, n.p. 1897, pp. 10-11; National Temperance Chronicle, June 1856.

72. Brit. Lib., Add. MSS. 43722, ff. 298-99, Richard Cobden to Joseph Sturge, 18 June 1858.

73. West Sussex Record Office, Hannah Sturge to Catherine Cobden, 29 July 1859; Fenn Collection, E19Y, Joseph Sturge to John Clark, 16 August 1858.

74. Herald of Peace, June 1859.

75. Joseph Sturge, The Sarawak Question, n.p. 1859; Richard, Sturge, p. 532.

76. Sturge Papers (M. Sturge), 'Birmingham Reminiscences. Joseph Sturge, Philanthropist' (newscutting).

77. West Sussex Record Office, Hannah Sturge to Catherine Cobden, 29 July 1859; Sturge Papers (P.A.J. Sturge), Joseph Sturge to Wilson Sturge, 13 May 1859; Lily Sturge, A Short Life of Joseph Sturge, n.p. 1907, pp. 39-40.

78. Alliance Weekly News, 28 May 1859; Friend, June 1859.

CONCLUSION

20 The Genealogy of Reform

Joseph Sturge is still part of the passing scene in the 1980s; his statue stands at Five Ways on the boundary between Birmingham and Edgbaston. Dressed in the lapel-less coat of the 'plain Quaker', hand on Bible he commends to passers-by the message of 'Charity', 'Peace' and 'Temperance' (carved in letters of gold on the pedestal) that he did so much to promote in his lifetime.(1) The statue, J.A. James explained in 1859, was to be 'a kind of open air preacher', and when it was unveiled three years later John Bright hoped that it would 'raise up other men who in their generation' would pursue justice and mercy as Sturge had done.(2) The sentiment was one that Sturge himself had often voiced towards the end of his life: his work must be carried on by those who survived him and by their children. And something very like this did happen during the next sixty or so years; for just as Sturge had followed and developed the example of the previous generation of Quaker philanthropists and evangelical reformers, so did others in his circle carry on from where he had left off. They were all part of the genealogy of reform, 'the vertical linkages between reforming movements over time'.(3) The Birmingham Daily Gazette noticed this when local abolitionists revived the anti-slavery movement in 1865 by setting up a National Freedmen's Aid Committee to assist the newly emancipated slaves in the United States: it was only fitting that the venture should 'be inaugurated in the town which is adorned by the statue, and which has charge of the character and memory, of Joseph Sturge'.(4)

Only one of Sturge's societies, the Birmingham Anti-Slavery Society, seems to have died with him, and this was of little importance: for many years the work of the movement in the district had been carried on by the Ladies Negro Friend Society, and members of the Sturge family kept it going until late in the century. Everything else continued for many years much as he had intended: his reformatory, the Montserrat plantation experiment, the Friends First-day School Association, his temperance work and even the peace movement, despite the severe trial it passed through during the early 1860s when members on both sides of the Atlantic, including Charles Sturge and Lewis Tappan, broke ranks and declared their support for the Union armies during the American Civil War.(5) The Quaker

'Liberal party' of which Sturge had been one of the most active members - 'his sweet spirit' was invoked to support the case for reform even after his death - continued its efforts to breathe new life into the Society of Friends. After more than 150 years of continuous decline membership statistics bottomed in 1864 and then began to rise, a revival that was often attributed to the religious earnestness which young Friends acquired from their work on behalf of Sturge's First-day School Association. Less than ten years after Sturge's death it was estimated that 1000 out of the Society of Friends' total membership of 15,000 were teaching there.(6)

Henry Vincent's claim that he knew many men who were Sturge's 'political children' and followed Sturge's example by putting 'Christian principle into political action' sheds further light on this genealogy of reform. Vincent could have been describing his own career;after coming under Sturge's influence in the NCSU he went on to spend 'the best years of his life' (the words are those of a historian of the Free Churches) 'indoctrinating his countrymen in all parts of the land with Puritan principles and elevated social and political ideas'.(7) Arthur O'Neill was another of Sturge's Chartist friends who followed this course and developed into the very type of the 'political Dissenter'. Peace, temperance, parliamentary reform, trade unions, Irish Home Rule and anti-slavery all received his support during a career that lasted almost until the end of the century.(8) Arthur Albright, the Quaker businessman turned full-time philanthropist and reformer, resembled Sturge even more closely. Having served his apprenticeship in public life as one of Sturge's assistants in the anti-slavery, peace, temperance and Complete Suffrage movements, Albright pursued similar interests to the end of his very long life. Two of the reforms he took up - the campaign against the Contagious Diseases Acts and the movement for women's suffrage - exemplify a tendency on the part of some members of Sturge's circle to widen their notions of liberty during the third quarter of the century. Just as Sturge had championed the voteless 'white slaves' of Britain after helping to emancipate the black slaves in the colonies, so now the old arguments for freedom were extended to include the rights of women.(9)

Albright was related to Sturge by marriage, a reminder that kinship networks were some of the most important of 'the vertical linkages between reforming movements over time'. Very much the benevolent widow, Hannah took a personal interest in several of Joseph's philanthropies for many years, and when Duncan McLaren visited her in 1865 he was delighted to find that an 'atmosphere of benevolent thought and action' still prevailed at 64 Wheeley's Road.(10) Sturge's brothers, Charles and Edmund, who outlived him by thirty years also sustained his good causes. In Charles's case, however, the continuity was impaired by attitudes that Joseph would have found repugnant. He acquired an unenviable reputation on the magistrates' bench for meting out 'stern justice to petty offenders', and, not content with supporting the 'cheap government' faction on the Town Council, he took a stand against what he saw as indiscriminate charity in a town where 'everything needful was provided for the poor in the workhouse'.(11) Edmund's attitudes were very different. In 1853

Harriet Beecher Stowe had noticed that he prominently displayed a life-size engraving of Joseph in his house, and for much of his life he seems to have taken his famous brother as a model. For a time during the 1860s he lived on Montserrat to direct the affairs of the Montserrat Lime Juice Company, and he was active in a large number of good causes at home. But he was dissatisfied with part-time philanthropy, and he resigned from his chemical business to settle in London where he became the Secretary of the British and Foreign Anti-Slavery Society and a prominent member of the Peace Society, the Aborigines' Protection Society, the Howard Association and the Society for the Suppression of the Opium Trade. Describing him as a man devoted to philanthropy and an assiduous lobbyist in Whitehall, Vanity Fair nominated him as the 'Man of the Day' on 20 November 1886.(12)

The next generation of the family carried Sturge's influence well into the twentieth century. It was almost inevitable that Quaker children, growing up in what was still a sheltered atmosphere of piety and benevolence during the early Victorian era, should enter the world of philanthropy and reform. 'I remember in those times', the daughter of another Quaker reformer wrote, 'we children playing with our dolls, and saying "Now thee's going to a slavery meeting; now thee's going to a temperance meeting" '.(13) The memoir of a niece, Priscilla (née Southall) Burlingham, shows that in Sturge's family circle the children likewise followed his example as a matter of course.

> My uncle Joseph was I think our ideal of a perfect man and his house during our early days seemed very like a second home. While in every way thoughtful for our comfort and advantage, his large interests in public and philanthropic affairs could not fail to give a direction to our energies, and widen our look out on life. He owed much to the sympathy and wise advice of our Aunt Sophia who kept his house and loved him with devoted affection.

In her memoir she describes the 'Spartan Society' that she and her cousins set up in the late 1830s to express 'a queer mixture' of ideas derived from their study of Greek history and their experience of the Society of Friends. Guided by a system of Quakerlike Queries and Advices, members were 'to discard self-indulgence' and become 'strong men and women fitted for every good word and work'.(14)

Not surprisingly this generation of Sturges was noted for its commitment to reform. A family record refers to the teaching of basket weaving to Irish peasants, the peace movement, war relief, prison work, adult schools, refugee relief schemes, Esperanto, work for deprived children, the Women's Voluntary Service, temperance and the Workers' Educational Association.(15) The list is too modest; Sturge's nephew, Charles Gilpin, was active in several radical movements before becoming M.P. for Northamptonshire between 1857 and 1874, and Sturge's niece, Eliza Mary Sturge, made a name for herself as a powerful public speaker on that rising public issue of the 1870s, women's rights. The report of a public speech she gave in the Birmingham Town Hall on 6 December 1872 shows her sweeping aside the notion that women should not work or take a share in the political life of the nation: it was 'idleness, political or otherwise', that degraded a woman. She made the most of her opportunities by becoming the first woman to be elected to the newly established Birmingham School Board in the 1870s.(16)

Sturge had been delighted when Hannah bore him 'a Jos and Sophia Sturge of another generation', and to some extent the relationship that developed between his son and daughter resembled his own relationship with his sister. Together with another sister Eliza (Lily) they set up house together, finding in their father's work 'a great heritage and an inspiration'.(17) The seventh and last of the unbroken line of Joseph Sturges that stretched back to the sixteenth century, Joseph entered the family business and was active in many of his father's philanthropies, especially the Montserrat Company which he served as managing director from 1875 to 1922.(18) It was an eminently worthy but dutifully predictable career, lacking the restless drive that had taken his father through an ever-widening circle of reform movements with a reckless disregard for the status quo and his own reputation. In these respects the mantle fell on the daughter, whose long life was described by her biographer as the pursuit of 'one personal enterprise after another with a compelling energy and enthusiasm': peace, temperance, women's franchise, unemployment and land settlement schemes, Indian reform, and the work of the Women's Liberal Social Council. She became an authority on handcraft industries as a result of her attempts to set up basket-making and toy-making ventures in Ireland as a form of reparation for what she saw as the destruction of the Irish economy by the historic injustices of English rule.

By the early twentieth century she was increasingly concerned by the threat of war. She became a pro-Boer and attended a new round of peace and arbitration conferences including one in Boston where her host was William Lloyd Garrison jun. Always she seems to have been mindful of her father's example. She spoke of his visit to Russia in one of her conference speeches, and with other members of the family she persuaded the sympathetic Stephen Hobhouse to start writing a new biography of her father. Therefore it was very much as her father's daughter that she watched the mounting crisis in July 1914. She became a member of the Neutrality League and went to London where she helped to raise a fund to put down 'the war madness'. Like her father, she was undaunted by failure,and she spent the rest of her life working for a 'constructive internationalism' through the Union of Democratic Control and the League of Nations: to the last (she died in 1936) she was an advocate of unilateral disarmament by Britain. Unworldly wise in an increasingly mad world, she never faltered in the quest that was summarised by the motto on the seal she had inherited from her father: 'We follow better things'.(19)

NOTES

1. In 1925 the statue was removed from the middle of the crossing at Five Ways to an adjacent area. A plate was added with the following inscription: 'He laboured to bring freedom to the negro

slaves, the vote to British workmen and the promise of peace to a war-worn world'.

2. Richard, Sturge, pp. 579, 584. See also G.B. Smith, The Life and Speeches of the Right Hon. John Bright, M.P., London 1881, vol. II, p. 131.

3. B. Harrison, 'A Genealogy Of Reform In Modern Britain' in C. Bolt & S. Drescher eds, Anti-Slavery, Religion, And Reform: Essays in Memory of Roger Anstey, Hamden, Conn. 1980, p. 119.

4. Quoted by C. Bolt, The Anti-Slavery Movement And Reconstruction. A Study in Anglo-American Co-operation 1833-67, London 1969, p. 101.

5. Sturge Papers (M. Sturge), Henry Richard to Charles Sturge, 18 December 1862.

6. Isichei, Victorian Quakers, p. 159, and chap. IX; Currie, Gilbert & Horsley, Churches And Churchgoers. Patterns Of Church Growth In The British Isles Since 1700, p. 156; W. Tallack, George Fox, The Friends, And The Early Baptists, London 1868, p. 12; Mrs G. Cadbury, 'Adult Schools' in J.H. Muirhead, ed., Birmingham Institutions, Birmingham 1911, pp. 200-18.

7. Richard, Sturge, pp. 329-30; H.S. Skeats & C.S. Miall, History of the Free Churches Of England, 1688-1891, London 1891, p. 659. Charles Vince (a Chartist turned Baptist minister) and T.B. Smithies (the publisher of the British Workman) were others who expressed a filial respect for Sturge. See Richard, Sturge, pp. 328-29; R.K. Dent, Old And New Birmingham: A History Of The Town And Its People, Wakefield 1973, vol. III, p. 580; Friend, June 1859.

8. 'The Rev. Arthur O'Neill', Birmingham Faces And Places, 1 February 1890, pp. 152-55.

9. Sturge Papers (M. Sturge), 'Death of Mr Arthur Albright. An Interesting Career' (newscutting n.d.)

10. J.B. Mackie, The Life And Work Of Duncan McLaren, Edinburgh 1898, vol. 2, p. 270. The importance of the kinship networks is discussed by D. Gorham, 'Victorian Reform As a Family Business' in A.S. Wohl, ed., The Victorian Family, London 1978.

11. Sturge Papers (M. Sturge), 'Death of Mr Charles Sturge', Daily Post, 2 May 1888 (newscutting); ibid., Morning News 1875 (newscutting); ibid., 'Dinner To The Ex-Mayor' (newscutting n.d.).

12. H.B. Stowe, Sunny Memories Of Foreign Lands, p. 186; Sturge Papers (M. Sturge), 'Man Of The Day. Mr E. Sturge', Vanity Fair, 20 November 1886; ibid., 'The Late Mr Edmund Sturge', Anti-Slavery Reporter, July & August 1893 (newscutting).

13. Wigham, A Christian Philanthropist of Dublin. A Memoir of Richard Allen, p. 14.

14. Burlingham, Reminiscences.

15. Sturge Papers (Lewin), The Sturge Family (typescript).

16. M. Stenton, Who's Who of British Members of Parliament, 1832-1885, Hassocks 1976, vol. I, entry for Charles Gilpin; E.M. Sturge, Miss E.M. Sturge On Women's Suffrage, Birmingham 1872.

17. Fenn Collection, E19Y, Joseph Sturge to John Clark, 15 February 1849; W.R. Hughes, Sophia Sturge. A Memoir, London 1940, p. 15.

18. Sturge Papers (Lewin), <u>Birmingham Post</u> 1934, obituary notice of Joseph Sturge; Sturge Papers (M. Sturge), <u>Joseph Sturge. Died June 27, 1934, aged 86 years.</u>

19. The preceding account of Sophia Sturge is based on Hughes, <u>Sophia Sturge. A Memoir.</u> See also S. Hobhouse, <u>Forty Years and An Epilogue: An Autobiography (1881-1951)</u>, London 1951, pp. 139, 143-44, 173-76.

Bibliographical Note

The sources which have been consulted are indicated at the end of each chapter. References have been made to the private papers of the Sturge family as follows:

Sturge Letters (Marshall). The Marshall Papers XVII/1/1 Sturge Letters./ 1 Olveston (1786-1819), Oxfordshire County Record Office. Part of the series of letters in Sturge Papers (M. Sturge)

Sturge Papers (Lewin). An extensive collection of letters by and to members of the Sturge family; also miscellaneous publications, materials relating to the J & C Sturge firm and short family biographical sketches. In the possession of Mrs Sylvia Lewin

Sturge Papers (Maud Sturge). Several letters by and to Joseph and Eliza Sturge. In the possession of the late Mrs Maud Sturge

Sturge Papers (M. Sturge). An extensive collection of letters by and to members of the family dating from the late eighteenth century until the late nineteenth century; also miscellaneous materials relating to family history. In the possession of Miss Monica Sturge

Sturge Papers (P.A.J. Sturge). A small collection of miscellaneous family manuscript materials, including 'Joseph Sturge's Account of His Sister Sophia's Last Illness, 1845'. In the possession of Mr Philip Sturge

Cropper Papers (including letters exchanged by Joseph Sturge and James Cropper). These show the omissions and alterations made in the lithographed collection, Extracts from Letters of the Late James Cropper, Transcribed For His Grandchildren, By Their Very Affectionate Mother and Aunt, Anne Cropper. In the possession of Mr James Cropper

Coalbrookdale Letters relating to the Dickinson Family. In the possession of Mr Michael Darby

Priscilla Burlingham, Reminiscences (typescript). In the possession of Mrs Kathleen Wormleighton

Index